THE WORLD TODAY SERIES

East, Southe~~~ and the Wester~~~

STEVEN A. LEIBO, Ph.D.

30TH EDITION

STRYKER–POST
PUBLICATIONS
HARPERS FERRY
WEST VIRGINIA

ANNUALLY UPDATED

NEXT EDITION—AUGUST 1998

Steven A. Leibo . . .

A former Fulbright Scholar, he is Director of the International Studies Program at Russell Sage College, Troy, New York, and lecturer in Asian and world history at the State University of New York (SUNY) in Albany. Receiving his doctorate from Washington State University, he is the author/editor of many books and articles, including *Transferring Technology to China: Prosper Giquel and the Self–strengthening Movement, Journal of the Chinese Civil War, 1864,* and *International Conflict in the 20th Century.* He has taught at many institutions of higher learning, including the University of Cincinnati, Skidmore, Union and Blackburn colleges. Widely experienced with the electronic media, he has served as a international political analyst for television and as a commentator for regional radio stations. Within the Internet, Professor Leibo is known as the co–founder/co–editor of H–ASIA, a forum for Asian study professionals that includes over 1400 academics from more than 30 countries. The author travels extensively throughout Asia.

Photographs used to illustrate *The World Today Series* come from many sources, a great number from friends who travel worldwide. If you have taken any which you believe would enhance the visual impact and attractiveness of our books, do let us hear from you.

First appearing as a book entitled
The Far East and Southwest Pacific 1968,
revised annually and published in succeeding years by

Stryker–Post Publications
P.O. Drawer 1200
Harpers Ferry, WV. 25425
Telephones: 1–800–995–1400
    From outside U.S.A.: 1–304–535–2593
    Fax: 1–304–535–6513
    VISA–MASTERCARD

International Standard Book Number: 1–887985–05–0

International Standard Serial Number: 1043–2140

Library of Congress Catalog Number 67–11540

Cover design by Susan Bodde

Chief Bibliographer: Robert V. Gross
Associate Bibliographer: Edward Jones

Cartographer: William L. Nelson

Printed in the United States of America
by Braun–Brumfield, Inc., Ann Arbor, Michigan

Typography by Stryker–Post Publications
and Braun–Brumfield, Inc.

Table of Contents

Gold dragon on the roof of the Happiness and Long Life Temple at the Chinese Emperor's summer palace

UNIFORMS . . . lifesize clay warriors, 4000 strong, somberly guard a Chinese emperor's tomb near Xian (roughly, She-yan), while Japanese baseball ("Yah-kyu") players thrill their fans in Tokyo.

East, Southeast Asia, and the Western Pacific Today

A card party on an old street in Beijing, China

Photo by Miller B. Spangler

The year 1997 marks an important and dramatic year for not only Asia, but for users of *East, Southeast Asia, and the Western Pacific*. For Asia, of course, this last summer marked not only the long awaited return of Hong Kong to the People's Republic—the dramatic and very real end of more than a century of Western Colonialism in China—but the death of long–time leader Deng Xiaoping, who had done so much to transform the entire region.

For users of *East, Southeast Asia and the Western Pacific*, which has admirably served its readers for more than a quarter of a century, 1997 marks the year that this text will begin to integrate the newer resources that have become available through the Internet with the strong introductory material long available in this volume. In previous years, the annual revisions of the volume allowed for it to be far more up to date than its other sources. With the arrival though of the Internet and its plethora of on–line newspapers and other daily news sources, materials never before available have become so at the click of a computer mouse. It is today extraordinarily easy to "keep up."

Unfortunately, the availability of materials on the day to day developments in Indonesian politics, for instance, is meaningless without the broader context necessary to understand those events. The goal of *East, Southeast Asia, and the Western Pacific* is to offer the historical, political, social and economic background necessary to follow contemporary events.

The new author/editor would like to thank the volume's previous authors, the late Harold Hinton and Patrick M. Mayerchak for their insights which still enrich large parts of the work. Moreover, several others have helped the present author/editor make the 1997 volume much better than it might otherwise have been. They are Marilyn Levine, John Tribble and Robert Drake. Sara Zaidspinner–Leibo was especially involved at every stage in editing and proofreading. Her help was of enormous consequence. Lastly, special thanks to Philip Stryker and Pierre Dostert for asking me to take on this exciting project.

The author/editor would also like to enthusiastically request that future readers, teachers and students alike, contact the author with suggestions on how the book can better serve their needs.

Steven A. Leibo. Leibos@sage.edu

Albany, NY, June 1997

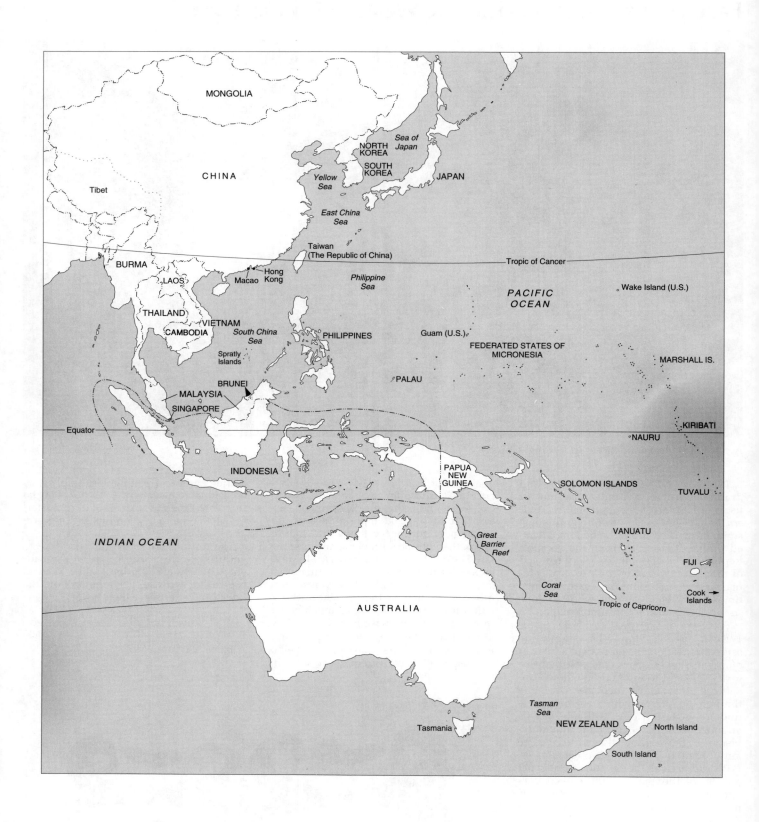

A Diversity of People

The region covered by this volume, *East, Southeast Asia, and the Western Pacific*, covers an enormous range of different ethnic and linguistic groups—from the Mongoloid communities of East Asia and the Caucasian immigrant communities of Australia and New Zealand to the heavily pigmented peoples of Micronesia who most closely resemble the aborigines of Australia. With the exception of a few countries like North Korea, almost every nation in the area includes many different ethnic and linguistic groups. While East Asians, Chinese, Japanese and Korean are largely made up of people from the "Mongolian" racial community, they are sharply divided by their linguistic heritage.

Chinese, for example, is part of a Sino–Tibetan language group which, although it bears a vague similarity in its written appearance, is totally different from the languages spoken in Japan and Korea. Southeast Asia is even more diverse and has at times been called an "anthropologist's delight" in recognition of the extraordinary diversity of ethnic communities found there. Although most nations in Southeast Asia have a "dominant majority" ethnic community almost all of them include both indigenous minority communities like the Montagnards of Vietnam and more recent ethnic communities, often made up of Chinese and South Asians, who immigrated to places other than their origin during the colonial era. The Island communities of the Western Pacific themselves include a wide variety of communities most notably divided into three groups, Polynesia, Melanesia and Micronesia. More than a thousand different languages are spoken there.

Although not often discussed in the West, many of these communities from East Asia to the Western Pacific, have experienced considerable tensions between the majority and minority communities. In some parts of the region, people of Indian origin are regularly treated as second class citizens and the Chinese in places like Vietnam have had similar experiences. In Burma, the efforts by the Burman majority to dominate the political life of the nation have led to decades of tensions and struggle with non–Burman peoples.

Historical Background

Religious Beliefs

Confucianism

The original Confucianism of early Chinese civilization was more a social philosophy than a religion, perhaps more like the Hellenic thoughts of Aristotle and Plato than the divine musings of the Hebrews across the Mediterranean. In fact, Confucius himself was not particularly interested in issues of the supernatural. For Confucius and his followers, what mattered was the world of humans and how best they could govern themselves.

Originating from a feudal elite society of blood nobility, Confucius nevertheless developed a new theory of nobility based on merit, rather than birth. And how was that merit defined? By a single–minded commitment to nurturing the truly noble of the heart.

The core emphasis was based on the ideas of family and hierarchy with true stability gained from that society in which all understood the appropriate relations between people. And how was that stability to be maintained? By an extraordinary emphasis on the ability of education to elevate the soul of humanity.

Later Confucian thinkers, especially people like Mencius, further emphasized the necessity of the development of "virtue" specifically through the study of various writings from antiquity known eventually as the Five Classics. Over time, mastery of the material came to be the key to a successful career through the developing Chinese Civil Service Examinations that dominated the selection of elites during the last 1000 years of traditional China's existence. (See the China section). As time went on however, Confucianism was challenged by other more spiritual philosophical and religious traditions—like Daoism and Buddhism, it began to assimilate aspects of their more metaphysical orientation. Thus was born the Neo–Confucianism of later traditional history.

Although it has been generations since millions of Chinese males spent their lives preparing to pass the Confucian civil service exams from whom future bureaucrats were chosen, its influence as a social philosophy remains tremendously strong.

Confucianism, both as a religious and intellectual tradition and as an ongoing theory of social behavior continues to be very influential throughout most of the region covered by this volume. From China to Korea, from Taiwan to Japan, Confucianism continues to be influential not only among the millions of ethnic Chinese who live in the People's Republic, Singapore and Taiwan, but among those millions of others who live as Chinese minorities from the Philippines to Malaysia and Indonesia. Moreover, it remains important among many other societies whose people, if not ethnically Chinese, were nevertheless fundamentally influenced by Confucianism even as they developed their own unique cultures. These include not only the Vietnamese and Koreans but other more distant neighbors, like the Japanese, who did not share a common border with China.

Obvious examples of Confucian influence are easy to note. Despite the assaults on Confucianism under Mao Zedong, the Confucian priority given to education and the family remain strong in East Asia. Moreover, the strong sense of the group over the needs of the individual, while perhaps lessening somewhat at the end of the 20th century, still figures prominently as a clear contrast to the Western preoccupation with the individual.

Buddhism

Buddhism remains one of the strongest religious traditions throughout East and Southeast Asia. From Thailand to Vietnam, from Burma to Beijing, Buddhism is present if not in the lives of everyone in the region, then as part of their cultural and architectural heritage. Even within the People's Republic, which saw so much energy directed against traditions like Buddhism in the 1960s, a revival has been going on. Paired about the same time that Confucius lived, Buddhism was founded in Nepal by Gautama. (See Russell, *The Middle East and South Asia*). It eventually became an extraordinarily influential tradition through much of Eastern Asia.

Not surprisingly, it often required considerable modification of the originally rather pessimistic Buddhist message to assimilate into the generally optimistic Chinese environment. It actually was, in some ways, a protest against the teachings of Brahmanism, or Hinduism, which was then dominant in India. The Buddha, as Gautama is called, preached the message that beings moved through a series of lives in this world which was largely an experience of pain and suffering. Within Buddhism there is a deep belief that fate can be influenced by human efforts—through the force of "Karma," so that a good person moves upward through successive existence to an ultimate reward. The greatest reward possible, according to this belief, was the attainment of Nirvana—a philosophically complicated concept which essentially postulated that a person who had attained "Nirvana" reached a state of individual nonexistence, often compared to the snuffing out of a flame which as a "practical" matter ended the process of constantly being reborn into a series of burdensome lives.

These teachings, which urged withdrawal from the world for meditation, created monastic communities in the ensuring centuries. The stress on personal and universal religious experience made this much more of a missionary religion than Hinduism and was thus more similar to Islam and Christianity in its core belief in the universality of its message.

The form in which Buddhism migrated to Southeast Asia is known as Hinayana ("the Lesser Vehicle"), Theravada ("the Way of the Teachers") or simply, the Southern School of Buddhism. This school, which is closest to original Buddhism of its early years, had its major home on the island of Sri Lanka (Ceylon) which was converted to Buddhism in the 3rd century B.C.

Hinayana countries in Southeast Asia—Vietnam, Laos, Cambodia, Thailand and Burma—all have large communities of monks devoted to the daily practice of Buddhism. In recent times, these communities have been influential and increasingly active in national and political affairs. Although the Hinayana Buddhists share the same central beliefs, there is no over arching system of central authority comparable to Vatican Catholicism which attempts to regulate the entire community. Almost every country has its own Buddhist individual sects.

Buddhism also spread north and northeast from India in the first centuries of the Christian era in the form known as Mahayana ("Greater Vehicle"), which entered Tibet, China, Korea and Japan. This form of the religion places less emphasis on good works and monastic withdrawal for contemplation, and greater weight on elaborate scriptures and faith. The canon (authorized texts) was printed in China in the 10th and 11th centuries, using some 130,000 wooden blocks on which characters had been carved. It was widely followed in central Asia until almost eliminated by the growing influence of Islam.

Mahayana Buddhism became widespread in China in the first centuries of the modern era, during a period of considerable social disruption associated with the collapse of the Han (206–222 BC) and con-

Inside the Liu Rong Buddhist temple (479 A.D.) in Guangzhou, China   Photo by Miller B. Spangler

Historical Background

tinued to grow in influence until it reached its height under the Tang Dynasty (618–907). Thereafter, its official influence began to wane, although it continued to be profoundly influential in the lives of ordinary Chinese.

A form of Buddhism developed in Tibet known as Tantrism, which was heavily influenced by a type of Hinduism that engaged in demon worship and varieties of magical practices. It still exists today, particularly in eastern Tibet, but has been largely replaced by another form known as Lamaism, or "The Yellow Sect" to distinguish it from Tantrism. This is a combination of a purer form of Buddhism similar to Mahayana with an elaborate monastic organization common to Hinayana, but actually even more highly formalized. Lamaism, of which the Dalai Lama is the leading figure, spread to Inner and Outer Mongolia in the 16th century.

The teachings of Buddhism have changed over the centuries, and have been modified by many varied external influences. It does not contain a formal universal hierarchy similar to practice in Catholicism and is in general more administratively decentralized in the fashion of traditions such as Protestantism, Judaism, Hinduism and Islam.

Naturalism

Long before the formal development of the major schools of Chinese thought, Confucianism, Taoism and Buddhism, the Chinese had already developed an elaborate intellectual system. It covered ideas of governance (see Mandate of Heaven in the China section) to metaphysical ideas associated with the stability of the entire cosmic order—from the universe to each person's physical body. Chief among those ideas were the concepts of *Yin* and *Yang,* and the entity known as *Qi.*

Yin and *Yang* are often difficult for Westerners to understand because they superficially resemble aspects of the Western idea of duality, of the idea of "good" and "evil." The resemblance though is purely superficial. In the West, this ancient idea, originally derived from the Persian religion of Zoroastrianism, involves a duality of forces in the universe, one evil, one good, that struggle over the fate of the universe and humanity.

Yin and *Yang* are quite different. This Eastern version of duality is one of complementary opposites which both need each other. Some things are associated with *Yin* more than *Yang* but both are always present and vital for cosmic and personal stability. This distinction may appear minor but in fact it has had dramatic differences in its impact on how the two societies have viewed the world around

Buddhist statue, Japan

them. An understanding of *Yin* and *Yang* are critical to an understanding of things Chinese, from philosophy to medicine. In the same vein, *Qi* is another important aspect of this naturalist world view.

According to Chinese tradition, every living thing possesses a sort of "vital element" that, in the case of humans, is drawn both from our parents and our environment. This *Qi,* which is said to flow through the body is considered absolutely vital to good health. It is the flow of *Qi* that Chinese traditional physicians still attempt to manipulate with techniques like acupuncture and acupressure to heal patients. Thus, an understanding of naturalist thought, issues like *Yin* and *Yang* and *Qi,* from the earliest history of China, remain today a vital part of the tools necessary to understand that enormous civilization which has so influenced most of the rest of East Asia.

Daoism (Taoism)

Daoism (Taoism) is in many ways a complementary parallel to China's long Confucian tradition. Daoism, which was formalized at about the same time as Confucianism, and is often portrayed as a

clear contrast to Confucianism's obsession with how human beings in society should behave. Daoism is less social in its orientation and more interested in the individual's relationship with the natural and metaphysical world. A flavor of this tone is captured in the famous Daoist dictum for government that what was really important was keeping people's heads empty and their stomachs full. Overall Daoism is more personal and self–consciously contemplative than the social activism of Confucian practice. Daoism varies enormously from an association with a popular religion of magic and spirits to a very philosophical discussion of the relationship of beings to the universe. On a practical level, the early Daoist's interest in the search for elixirs of life brought to Chinese civilization an acute interest in nature which continues to have a strong influence on contemporary Chinese food and medicine.

Christianity

Although Christian missionaries have been active in Asia for centuries, few people in the region have been influenced by any of its various sects. In China, for ex-

4

ample, Christianity was often seen simply as part of Western imperialism and rejected out of hand. Today, although Christianity is a vigorous tradition within the People's Republic, the actual numbers, given China's enormous size, are relatively insignificant. On the other hand, some of the countries covered by *East, Southeast Asia, and the Western Pacific* have been terrifically influenced. The Philippines and Vietnam both developed large Catholic communities during the colonial eras. The Philippines today is almost exclusively Christian with the exception of the southernmost island of Mindanao where Islam remains influential.

Among the East Asian nations, Korea is the most influenced by Christianity due to a curious irony of history. During the nineteenth century Christian missionaries in Korea often sided with the Koreans against the colonizing Japanese thus linking Christianity to the emerging Korean nationalism. Not surprisingly in today's Korea Christianity is a very influential tradition with millions of followers.

The Pacific Islands people are largely committed to the various Christian traditions. Christians are found widely throughout the region among those whose families were originally converted by the earliest Protestant and Catholic missionaries and, more recently, to new denominations ranging from Jehovah's Witnesses in Tahiti–Polynesia, Fiji and New Caledonia and the Solomon Islands, to Mormons in Tonga and Western Samoa. The Anglo communities of New Zealand and Australia, made up as they are largely of immigrant communities from England are, of course, largely Christian as well.

Shinto

Shinto emerged in the earliest period of Japanese history and originally was an animistic religion which gave human form to the various gods that rule the forces of nature. Although indigenous to the Japanese home islands, this religious tradition is in many ways similar to the animistic beliefs found in Southeast Asia, Africa and among many traditional native American beliefs—in that a strong sense a divinity exists among many natural objects in nature from beautiful trees to waterfalls. Shinto, a tradition that refers to the "Way of the Kami," puts its emphasis on what might be called entities of "awe", the Kami which include myriad objects from ancestors to legendary heroic figures and natural phenomena. Especially important within the tradition is the belief that the Sun Goddess, Amaterasu, sent her descendants to Earth to create the Japanese home islands. It was the association of the Yamata clan line with

that tradition that became the basis of its claim to imperial power.

Unlike traditions such as Buddhism and Christianity which developed very elaborate traditions of religious ritual and sacred texts, Shinto tended to be very much more loosely organized and was not surprisingly overshadowed in Japan by the arrival of Buddhism in the 6th century. As Mahayana Buddhism entered the islands, the two beliefs tended to influence each other. Thus, it was possible to profess the ideologies of both without feeling inconsistent.

Buddhism in Japan eventually split into numerous sects, and for several centuries Shinto beliefs were somewhat dormant, although not forgotten. In the late nineteenth and early twentieth century, the Shinto heritage became the state religion; it was reemphasized that the emperor was a descendant of the sun goddess and possessed her divine powers. Although the imperial house had long been respected in traditional Japan, the late nineteenth century development of a cult–like imagery around the imperial house was not a

product of Japanese tradition, but rather part of the modernizing effort. It was believed by nineteenth century thinkers that Japan needed a "unifying element" to fully join together the nation. Enhancing the symbolism of the emperor was thought the most appropriate way to do so. Thus, the imperial house was far more celebrated in the late nineteenth and early 20th century than it had been for centuries. In many ways it is helpful to think of this revival of Shinto as "State Shinto" in contrast to the more decentralized tradition of Japan's earlier history.

This revival corresponded with a rise of militarism in Japan, culminating with World War II. After defeat by the allies, Japan renounced the idea of the "divinity" of the Emperor; Shinto lost its official status. Ironically the supposed "imperial divinity" which Westerners found offensive about the Japanese system was only remarkable when viewed from the outside by Westerners bred in the traditions of monotheism. In the Japanese context the spiritual aspects of the Japanese emperor had operated in a very different context.

A Shinto shrine in Japan

Islam

Although most Americans tend to associate Islam with the Arab communities of the Middle East, the reality is that the largest communities of Muslims in the world are found in Asia and among a very wide variety of ethnic groups. Especially large communities of Muslims are found in South Asia (see Russell, *The Middle East*

and South Asia) but they are also a very important religious community in East and Southeast Asia as well. From western China to the southern Philippines, from Malaysia to Indonesia (itself the largest Muslim nation in the world) Islam is very important to this region.

Islam itself, which emerged in the 7th century, is part of the enormously rich Middle Eastern monotheistic religion

Historical Background

which had earlier seen the development of Judaism and Christianity. Muhammad, a poor merchant from the Arabian peninsula, developed the religion after experiencing what he called a revelation from the angel Gabriel regarding the Unity of God. As a tradition, Islam is a militantly monotheistic creed that requires giving charity to the poor and a life of regular daily prayer including, if at all possible, a pilgrimage at some point to the holy places at Mecca in today's Saudi Arabia.

Though Islam is a growing movement within the United States, few Americans know much about it and would probably be surprised at how much of its theology it shares with both Christianity and Judaism. The tradition includes the idea of a heaven and resurrection and a system of predestination. Seeing itself as a clear continuation of the line of revelation which had begun with the Patriarch Abraham, Muhammad, revealed himself to be the "final prophet" in a long tradition which extended back through both the traditions of the Old and New Testament. Basically, Muhammad taught that the Judeo–Christian biblical texts are not complete. Thus, the Islamic movement embraced a new document, said to have been dictated by God. That text is known as the Qur'an (Koran). Nevertheless this new sacred document, which makes reference to biblical texts, is distinctly influenced by the Judeo–Christian traditions which had preceded it.

Sometimes stories are derived from the bible texts and modified with startling results. For example, the story of the fall from Eden is also found in the Qu'ran yet in the Islamic version, the female, Eve, is not blamed for the transgression against God! A very thought–provoking modification, especially for those who think Islam can be easily categorized on issues of gender. The text of the Qur'an itself includes 114 chapters which Muslims believe confirms and clarifies the revelation received earlier by the Christians and Jews.

Like many religions, Islam was spread through a complicated series of developments that ranged from militant conquest to merchant activities and mystical religious missionaries. Today it is found widely in parts of Southeast Asia and western China.

The resurgence of militant Islam in the Middle East and northern Africa has had its effect in such Southeast Asian countries as Indonesia and Malaysia. Here, it has taken the form of increased wearing of the traditional dress, stricter dietary rules, and the establishment of Muslim banking operations. Though Islam is more strictly adhered to in Malaysia, religious resurgence in that country or in any other part of Southeast Asia does not approach the fervor which is found today in the Middle East. None of the Muslim states in the region—Brunei, Indonesia, Malaysia or the Philippines (the latter has only a small Muslim minority) has seen the extensive level of Islamic militancy experienced elsewhere. It would not be correct to ignore the current resurgence of Islam in Southeast Asia as well.

Women in Traditional Asia

Although until recently women have lived in few societies that have afforded them even a semblance of equality with men, the women of Asia have often been particularly challenged by the limitations of their own unequal status. Nevertheless, the region covered by *East, Southeast Asia, and the Western Pacific* is large and it is difficult to make generalizations. In some traditional societies and especially hierarchical societies like those dominated by Confucianism, which has had such an important influence throughout much of the region, women are regarded as decidedly inferior to men. As elsewhere, they were commonly less valued both as infants and as adults. Female babies were less likely to be nurtured when young and more frequently experienced infanticide than males. They were raised to serve as a wife for a male chosen by others (if they were lucky). Too often, in times of financial distress, daughters found themselves sold into virtual sexual slavery by their parents.

Nevertheless, the specific nature of their unequal status has varied widely from region to region and from period to period. In China, for example, it appears that Chinese women were more influential early on and that their status deteriorated around the 8th century A.D. By about the 11th the horrendously painful practice of foot binding, that is of forcing the female child's foot into an artificially tiny shape, had emerged, a practice which would cause untold suffering among Chinese women until the 20th century. Elsewhere though, the status and circumstances were quite different. In early Japan, women appear to have been much more important than their latter status suggests and impe-

Women suffering foot binding in China

6

rial women of the court, individuals like Lady Murasaki, are credited with creating the modern form of the novel, most notably in works like the *Tale of Genji* written around 1000 A.D.

In Southeast Asia, peasant women remained much more important than their peers in either East Asia or South Asia and played an important role in the local economies. Even in places like Vietnam, whose elite were especially influenced by Confucianism, the peasant women's lives remained much less constricted than the elite women of the Confucian aristocracy.

The Impact of the West

One of the most dramatic aspects of modern world history was the enormous movement of colonialism and imperialism which saw the Western nations spread their influence and direct administrative control over a large percentage of the globe. From a period running from approximately 1500 through the early 20th century, the various Western powers, and eventually Japan, gained control over much of the world. Only a few nations remained outside of their control. In Africa the ages–old empire of Abyssinia, today's Ethiopia, managed to resist an Italian effort at conquest in 1896 and in Southeast Asia the kingdom of Siam, today's Thailand, survived albeit hemmed in by English and French colonies on either side.

It was that world of colonial and imperial control that brought the globe into the 20th century, and during much of the 1900s, the era emphasized by *East, Southeast Asia, and the Western Pacific*, deals with the reverse of that process as individual national communities eventually found their way to national freedom from colonial administrations. East and Southeast Asia were not exempt from this global phenomenon and in fact were the original region that had attracted the Europeans in the 15th century at the dawn of the modern colonial age.

The countries of early modern Western Europe, especially Spain, Portugal and the Netherlands, tried to reach East Asia and the Western Pacific in order to acquire the profits from the extraordinarily lucrative spice trade, to gain converts to Christianity and to acquire new territories for their respective governments. Especially significant in those early years were the Iberians, adventurers from Spain and Portugal, who had also led the efforts in the Western Hemisphere.

Ferdinand Magellan, a Portuguese in the service of Spain, was the first to lead Europeans to the region. He was killed in the Philippines in 1521. Half a century later Spain, operating from its bases in the

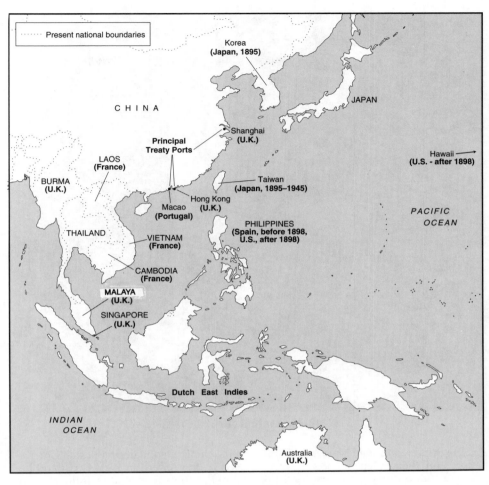

New World, began to colonize the Philippines, which it eventually held for three centuries. In the 16th century, Portuguese explorers, traders, and missionaries spread similarly from the Indian Ocean to Southeast Asia and the coast of southern China. They were not strong enough, however, to make much of an impact on the region, and most of their holdings soon fell to the Dutch.

The Dutch East India Company was the strongest European influence in East Asia and the Western Pacific in the 17th century. Its main theater of operations was the Dutch (or Netherlands) East Indies (now Indonesia), the richest in the region in the resources then in most demand in Europe (spices, coffee, etc.). Although the Dutch government eventually took direct control of the East Indies from the Dutch East India Company in the early 19th century, its rule was distinctly paternalistic and did little to develop the islands from either an economic or a political point of view.

The British impact on the region was less than they had in the Indian Ocean and South Asia, where they built up their enormous empire in India, but it was still significant. In Southeast Asia, the British colonial presence began first in Burma.

For the British, expanding control was usually a response to growing commercial interests. In Burma, territorial disputes and issues of sovereignty arose in the late eighteenth century. Anglo–Burmese relations deteriorated until 1823, when British forces captured Rangoon. By the end of the 1860's, the British had integrated all of the Burmese provinces into British Burma and into the Indian empire.

By 1826, they had established what was known as the Straits Settlements along the coast of Malaya (today, Malaysia). These settlements consisted of the island of Penang, just off Malaya's north coast, Malacca, formerly a Dutch possession on the central coast, and Singapore at the southern tip of the Malay peninsula. Over the next fifty years their control extended over all of Malaya. They obtained vast quantities of tin from the interior and commerce from the straits settlements. An Anglo–Dutch Treaty of 1824 recognized British dominance along the Malay coast and also acknowledged Dutch interests to the south. This resulted in the effective splitting up of the old Malay world. The Dutch eventually established their control over all of Sumatra and Java, and became the colonial masters of the future Indone-

Historical Background

A Chinese Opium "den" in 1898

sia. The British controlled Malaya and Singapore until their independence.

In the 19th century the British East India Company had also become a major commercial force along the South China coast, its main interest being Chinese tea, silk and porcelain. Merchants brought opium, usually bought from the Company in India, to the South China coast and sold it in defiance of an official ban. Machine–made British textiles eventually became a major Chinese import in the 19th century, especially after the British East India Company lost its legal monopoly of its share of the China trade early in the century.

The British government used armed force at intervals to compel China to lower its barriers to expanded foreign trade (including opium imports) and residence (including missionary activity). These pressures eventually culminated in the famous "Opium Wars" of the early nineteenth century and resulted in a series of unequal treaties with the Chinese that saw Westerners establish themselves along the China coast in a series of "treaty ports" which were outside of formal Chinese control.

Although the United States had been late to enter the competition for empire in the Pacific it eventually became very involved there. By the mid–nineteenth cen-

tury, the United States had established itself on the American West Coast and begun the effort to extend its influence into the Pacific. The Hawaiian islands came under American control in 1898.

Meanwhile, by the late nineteenth century, a number of educated Filipinos were moved by modern nationalist ideals to declare independence from Spain and cooperate briefly with the United States in expelling the Spanish during the Spanish American War of 1898. Unfortunately for them, after the defeat of Spain, the United States proceeded to take over the Philippines for itself. After crushing a spirited Filipino resistance, the U.S. set up a reasonably efficient colonial regime and did a good deal to prepare the Filipinos for self–government, but like the other colonial powers in the region it did not qualitatively develop the economy, which remained essentially an extractive (mining) and plantation one.

Earlier, the U.S. had, beginning in the mid–19th century, spearheaded the western entry into Japan. In contrast to many other communities in what became the colonial world, the Japanese, were much better able to control the process, and Japan never became a colony of the West. In effect, in attempting to avoid the fate of so many other Asian peoples, Japan decided to dramatically revolutionize their

society. Thus it borrowed from the West (mostly technology and organization) and combined it with the essentials of its own culture. In the process, Japan became a military and imperial power strong enough to defeat China (in 1895) and Russia (in 1905) and itself emerge as a major colonial power with control over the Chinese island of Taiwan and the Korean peninsula.

Certainly not content to be left behind their colonial rivals, Paris was involved in Southeast Asian colonialism. The Treaty of Saigon of 1862 established the French colony of Cochin China in southern Vietnam. The conflict leading to this treaty was in response to several decades of tension as a result of inroads into Vietnamese society by French Catholicism. The French seemed to be as much interested in the spread of their own religion as the potential for economic gain. Especially important, in the minds of the French, was the necessity of keeping up with their English rivals. French control of Cambodia and Laos followed and, with Vietnam, became French Indochina. The Laotians and Cambodians were more favorably disposed toward the French, having been under the authority of both Siam and Vietnam previously. For Vietnam, the period of French domination was culturally much more difficult.

Sandwiched between the British colonies of Burma and Malaya, and the French in Indochina, Siam (now Thailand) was able to survive under its own monarchy without being colonized by any European power. This was partly because the British and French were more interested in penetrating Southwest China from their bases in Southeast Asia than in colonizing Siam and because they both saw the benefit of Siam as a buffer between their respective territories. Siam also benefitted from a highly talented monarchy that earlier saw the need to learn about western institutions and governing methods. When the British did come, the Siamese showed considerable diplomatic skill in meeting the challenge.

An important product of western colonial rule in Southeast Asia was the influx (from about 1850 to 1920) of large numbers of Chinese immigrants, driven by poverty and chaos at home and drawn by the economic opportunities created by colonialism. These "overseas" Chinese have tended to be resented by the indigenous peoples and have never been allowed a share of real political power (except in Singapore, where they are the majority), but their economic activity and influence have been very great.

Major political and military trends of the twentieth century, culminating in Japan's launching of World War II in the

Pacific (see Japan), were to sweep away Western colonial rule in Southeast Asia, and make its restoration after the war a practical impossibility. As we shall see, during the post war era, colony after colony emerged out from under Western control though some anti–colonial struggles, like that of Vietnam, were to become particularly bloody as anti–colonialist momentum became entwined with the struggles of the Cold War.

The islands of the Western Pacific were no exception to this process and even as they were among the first communities absorbed into the Western colonial empires, many of them have only recently gained their autonomy. A few, like New Caledonia for example, still remain today as colonies.

Nationalism, Communism and Revolution in Twentieth Century Asia

One of the principal and predictable results of Western influence, which contained the inherent threat of domination because of advanced technology, has been resistance to the idea of external control in Asia. The desire to be independent of such influence is part of the structure of modern Asian nationalism. As long as Western political control over colonial Asia seemed unshakable, there was little basis for the emergence of nationalism. When Japan defeated Russia in 1905, however, the myth that the Western powers were invincible was shattered.

Japan also showed by its example that it was possible, however difficult, for an Asian country to modernize itself along the lines of Western nations. During the brief period that it controlled substantial portions of Southeast Asia, Japan weakened the prestige of the colonial powers to the point where it would be all the more difficult for them to reestablish themselves in the region after the war.

Next to the influence of the West itself and that of Japan's successes, the third great external influence on the emergence of modern Asian nationalism was the example of Soviet Russia. Before 1917 Marxism had almost no following in the area, but many Asian leaders became impressed with the seemingly rapid success of Lenin's Bolsheviks in seizing power within Russia in 1917. Of even greater importance was the loudly declared determination to modernize Russia along socialist lines, and to help the people of the non–Western world to throw off alien influence. The communism of Marx, prescribed for industrial nations of Europe and America, was billed as the medicine which would allegedly cure the ills of the poor, non–Western countries of Asia.

Lenin attracted great attention with his theory that the main obstacle to progress in the non–Western world was Western "imperialism"; he urged that local nationalists, supported by Soviet Russia, could make progress toward expelling this imperialism. This would be, according to him, a preparation for the day when "proletarian" parties, in other words, communist parties, organized along the disciplined and apparently effective line of the *Bolsheviks,* could emerge and seize power. The combination of the concept of *imperialism,* the exploitation of existing nationalism and the triumph in Russia of a communist party has had an enormous influence in Asia as well as elsewhere in the world. These ideas became part of the mental equipment of many, although by no means all, Asian nationalists, whether or not they consider themselves communists. Stated otherwise, many Asian nationalists adopted some communist ideas and techniques without becoming communists—or find it politically useful to act as though they have.

The result is a complex alignment of nationalist and communist elements, in which it is often difficult to see where the nationalistic spirit ends and the communist aims begin. The obvious communists are not hard to identify; Ho Chi Minh was a member of the Communist International, the founder of the Vietnamese Communist Party and yet a committed Vietnamese nationalist. Unlike the situation in Eastern Europe where communists and

Historical Background

nationalists were often bitter enemies for most of the 20th century, the dynamics of anti–colonial struggles in much of the world often saw the two groups not only closely aligned but united in the personalities of many of the anti–colonial leaders. Sadly, this reality was too often misunderstood by Western leaders and analysts, trained more in the politics of Europe than Asia.

Anti–colonial movements began to assume importance in the colonies of Asia about 1920. The spread of Western education and political ideas, the limited measure of self–government granted by the colonial powers, the influence of Woodrow Wilson's doctrine of self–determination—the idea that every people has the right to choose the form of government under which it will live—and the Bolshevik Revolution in Russia, all played parts in the spread of nationalism.

The Chinese communities living in Asian countries other than their homeland (the "overseas Chinese") were stimulated to nationalist activity by the revolutionary forces then at work within China, but usually preferred a continuation of Western political rule to the possibly oppressive rule of the native majorities where they lived. Non–Chinese nationalists usually resented the Chinese for their hard–earned wealth and economic influence, to the same degree that they also opposed the political control of the Western powers. As a result, their agitation was usually directed against both groups of outsiders.

Prior to World War II, there were no nationalist movements in Southeast Asia able to challenge the well–armed colonial governments. Nationalists were unable to gather sufficient support for the independence cause until the outbreak of the war changed the dynamics of the entire region. As will be seen in the individual national state sections, the combination of the Japanese temporary occupation of the region and the weakening of the colonial powers made a complete reestablishment of the former Western colonial world in East and Southeast Asia simply impossible. Certainly in some areas, like Indonesia and Vietnam the colonial powers attempted to reestablish their power but each in turn was eventually stymied in the face of the worldwide anti–colonial momentum. The age of formal colonies had passed. Only the rise of the Cold War in the late 1940s made this trend somewhat less certain as many nationalist and economic struggles became entwined with the politics of Soviet/American rivalries.

Communist challenges arose in the Philippines, in the form of the *Huk* rebellion in the early 1950's; in Malaya, under the "emergency" declared from 1948 to 1960; and in Indochina and Indonesia.

Burma, Thailand and even Singapore also experienced communist activities. In Indonesia, the movement was strongest in Central Java. The Indonesian *Communist Party* met its bloody demise in 1965 when it was destroyed by the Indonesian military under Suharto whose regime has continued to maintain stability under an authoritarian government through today.

Presently, Vietnam is the only surviving nominally communist regime in Southeast Asia, and that will be increasingly debatable as reforms move ahead. Laos no longer qualifies as a bonafide Marxist state. Laotian politics was for decades a family affair, and with the opening of the country in recent years, economic change will easily overcome the remnants of the past.

It is difficult to find a uniform explanation for the Asian experience with communism. One thing is clear, of the remaining communist states, the People's Republic of China and Vietnam did not begin to expand their GNPs until the decision was made to open up their economies more. And North Korea which has still not seriously done so remains mired in an ever sinking economic state.

Nevertheless, communism was often an essential ingredient in the emerging nationalism of the region. In some cases, it forced colonial and then newly independent governments to address social problems which they might have otherwise ignored. And in contrast to Eastern Europe, communism still remains a vital if certainly evolving force. The tensions of the old Cold War have dimmed in East Asia much slower than they have in Europe.

Post–Colonial Political and Economic Developments

As the new states of East and Southeast Asia began to emerge after the demise of colonialism, hopes were high, especially in the West, that many new economically vibrant democracies would emerge. In fact, many new states began their existence as free countries using models borrowed from the Western liberal democracies which had originally colonized them. Burma, Indonesia, Malaysia, the Philippines and Singapore were all thus born as democracies. Today Singapore and Malaysia survive as single party dominated systems, while the Philippines has only recently managed to reestablish a democratic tradition after a generation of authoritarian rule. Indonesia, and Burma to a much greater extent, have lived under clearly authoritarian governments. Thailand has not yet resolved its political fu-

ture and often mixes its military with elements of democratic rule. The communist states of course embraced a system of Party domination over both their countries' economies and political life.

In what became known as the East Asian NICs, the East Asian Newly Industrialized Countries, like Taiwan and South Korea, extended periods of strongman government lasted until the late 1980s. In Japan, although the occupation had seen the establishment of a parliamentary government, most of the period has seen the country ruled by a combination of a single party in domination largely led by an especially powerful bureaucracy.

Economically, after the war the hope was of course to see the region recover from the devastation of the war but sadly that was not be to be case. The economies were weakened by both the anti–communist struggles of the era, strife in places like Vietnam and Korea as well as by related struggles like those in the southern islands of the Philippines. That region's natural economic structure was undermined by the continuing turmoil within the PRC as well.

If the immediate post–war years were not very successful in establishing more democratic governments and economically open systems, the region's more recent record is much more promising. As we approach the end of the 20th century, East and Southeast Asia, so recently an area in constant turmoil, has emerged as the most economically dynamic area in the world. The Industrial Revolution that transformed Western Europe a century ago and has now dramatically hit East and Southeast Asia not only radically changed the economic life of its citizens but raised their educational and political aspirations. Not surprisingly, authoritarian regimes have been more and more challenged in their efforts to dominate the political life of their people. From South Korea to Taiwan new leadership has been elected democratically with the support of more politically involved middle classes, the very middle classes required and nurtured by economic changes. How these economic and political changes will ultimately transform the entire region is only just beginning to become clear. What is certain is that the entire region will play a much more significant role in the global arena in the 21st century than it did during the 20th.

Women in Modern East and Southeast Asia

Along with many women of the Western World, the women of the East, Southeast Asia and the Western Pacific have often made enormous strides during the 20th century. In China, although the dominant figure as the century began was a woman, the famous Cixi, the dowager empress, most women labored under both the physical pain of foot binding and the limitations of their educational and career possibilities. Yet within the first quarter century not only was foot binding outlawed and eventually suppressed, but those years saw women in large numbers begin to gain higher education and to take part in political activism as shown in their role in the famous May Fourth Movement.

When the communists came to power in 1949 one of their first moves was to legislate improvements in the lives of women which, if not creating a society of equality, have much improved the lives of millions of Chinese women.

In Japan, the century began with a few women striving to establish their own political and literary activities and more often ending up in trouble with the conservative governments of the time. Nevertheless, Japanese women gained the vote as a result of the changes brought about during the American Occupation of Japan and the end of the century has seen a woman emerge as the head of one of the major Japanese parties, the Japanese Socialist Party.

Throughout the world the development of better contraceptive devices and the growing perception that women need to be educated in order to contribute to the economic lives of their families has also spurred improvements in many areas of East and Southeast Asia. Not surprisingly the women of the more urban classes have gained the most from these changes while poorer women are less likely either to have the finances, access or education necessary to take advantage of the new technologies available for family planning. And in some areas, like the Philippines, where the Catholic Church is influential, there is considerable opposition to birth control.

Politically the single most important element to affect the lives of women of the region was probably the emergence of nationalism as a driving force. In many regions, especially in places like Vietnam, women played important roles in the anti–colonial struggles of the post war era. Moreover, in recent years women activists have been especially involved in encouraging democratic growth in the region. Corazon Aquino emerged triumphant in the struggle that saw the end of the Marcos dictatorship in the Philippines and elsewhere in the region, most notably in Burma, where Aung San Suu Kyi has led the democratic opposition. During 1996 Megawati Sukarnoputri the daughter of the late Indonesian ruler Sukarno, at-

tempted (unsuccessfully) to challenge the continuing dictatorship of Suharto.

Despite these changes, real improvements in the lives of women have never been even nor routine across the region. In some areas like China where recent economic liberalization has at times given more discretionary power to families and individual factory managers, we have

seen the emergence of more traditional values regarding the worth of daughters than was experienced under the height of socialist control. These new freedoms have sometimes actually worked against women's rights. And in some other areas a religious backlash against the secularism of the West has also challenged those gains already made.

Arriving from Hong Kong by train, these high rise buildings are the first evidence of new development seen by visitors at Shenzhen's commercial center, Luohu.

Courtesy: Caltex Petroleum Corporation

11

The People's Republic of China

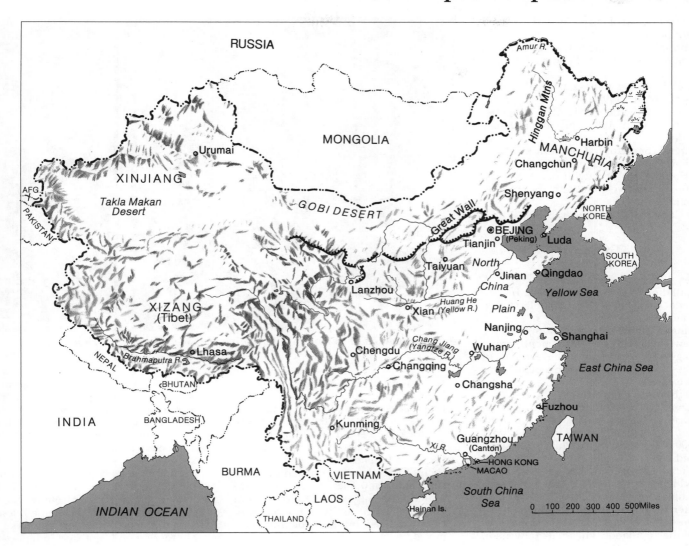

Area: Approximately 3.7 million square miles, including Inner Mongolia and Tibet. (As large as the 50 United States plus another Alaska).

Population: 1.17 billion (estimated).

Capital City: Beijing (Peking), Pop. 9.9 million, estimated. (pronounced Bay-jing.

Climate: Dry, cold with bitter winters in the mountainous West and North, temperate in the East, subtropical with rainy monsoons in the South.

Neighboring Countries: Russia (Northwest, North, Northeast); Mongolia (North); Korea (Northeast); Taiwan (Southeast); Vietnam, Laos, Burma, India, Nepal (South); Pakistan and Afghanistan (Southwest).

Official Language: Mandarin Chinese, the

←

Dragon pavement leading to the Gate of Supreme Harmony in Beijing's Forbidden City

Courtesy: Caltex Petroleum Corporation

dialect of the Chinese language spoken in Central and Northern China).

Other Principal Tongues: South and West Chinese dialects, including Cantonese, Hakka, Fukienese and Wu, the Tibetan language. Tribesmen of remote Xinjiang, Inner Mongolia and Manchuria have their own languages and dialects.

Ethnic Background: Chinese, sometimes referred to as *Han* (about 95%). Relatively small minorities of Mongol, Turkic, Tibetan, Thai and of other ancestry live in the remote regions of the interior.

Principal Religions: Confucianism, Taoism, Buddhism, Islam and Christianity, all of which have been intermixed to one degree or another. They have been severely opposed and suppressed by the communist government, but in recent years the anti–religious pressures have lessened and they are enjoying a revival.

Main Exports (to Hong Kong, Japan, U.S., Germany, Australia): Manufactured goods, agricultural products, oil and

minerals. Mineral resources have only been partially exploited, but are known to be substantial.

Main Imports (from Japan, U.S., Hong Kong): Grain, chemical fertilizer, steel, machinery, equipment.

Currency: *Renminbi* (people's currency) expressed in units called *Yuan.*

Former Colonial Status: Some regions

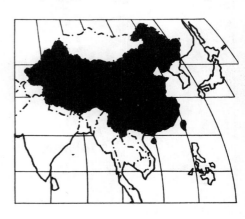

13

China

were briefly colonized by various Western powers.

National Day: October 1, anniversary of the founding of the People's Republic in 1949.

Chief of State: Jiang Zemin, President (since March 1993).

Head of Goverment: Li Peng, Premier (since April 1988; pronounced Lee Pung.)

General Secretary, Communist Party: Jiang Zemin (since June 1989).

National Flag: Red, with one large and four small five–pointed stars at upper left.

Per Capita GDP Income: U.S. $2,935

Taiwan

Area: 13,885 square miles.

Population: 20.5 million (estimated).

Capital City: Taipei (Pop. 2.8 million, estimated).

Climate: Subtropical and humid in the lowlands, with an eleven–month growing season; in the higher elevations of the central mountains the temperatures are cooler.

Neighboring Countries: The Republic of China has been on the island of Taiwan, located 100 miles from the southeast China mainland, since 1949. It is about 300 miles north of the Philippine island of Luzon.

Official Language: Chinese (Mandarin, which is spoken in Central and North China).

Other Principal Tongues: Amoy, a Chinese dialect, is spoken by the majority of the population, known as Taiwanese. Tribal aborigines in the mountains

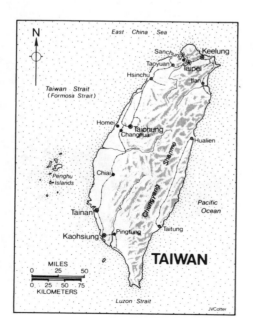

A mother and child framed in a decorative wall-window in Hangzhou

Courtesy: Jon Markham Morrow

speak a number of tongues related to Malay.

Ethnic Background: Chinese, sometimes referred to as *Han*. The highlands are occupied by a small group of Malayo–Polynesian ancestry who resemble the people of Indonesia.

Principal Religions: Confucianism, Taoism, Buddhism. These three, which migrated with the earliest Chinese from the mainland, have not been and are not clearly defined, but are generally intermixed.

Main Exports (to the U.S., Japan, Hong Kong): Textiles, clothing, electrical and electronic equipment, processed foods.

Main Imports (from U.S., Japan, Kuwait): Industrial equipment, automobiles, oil.

Currency: New Taiwan Dollar.

Former Colonial Status: Taiwan was a Japanese colony from 1895 to 1945.

National Day: October 10, anniversary of the Chinese Revolution of 1911.

Chief of State: Lee Teng–hui, President (1988); pronounced Lee Dung Hway.

National Flag: A red field with a blue rectangle in the upper left containing a 12–pointed white star.

Per Capita GDP Income: U.S. $14,295.

Note: At the beginning of 1979, The People's Republic of China officially adopted an already–existing system known as *Pinyin* for writing out Chinese names and terms in the Western alphabet. That system is now increasingly used in both the West and even on Taiwan. Thus the capital of China, once known commonly as "Peking" is now more often rendered "Beijing." The Pinyin system is used in the following text except where possible confusion might occur with terms already quite familiar, thus "Daoism," will also be followed by the less correct but more familiar "Taoism."

Occupying a land area larger than that of the 50 United States, China stretches for a distance of 3,400 miles from its Northeastern region adjacent to remote Russian Siberia to the mountainous regions of Tibet bordering on Nepal and India. As for temperature, altitude and roughness of terrain, fertility of the soil, and rainfall, there are two distinct regions. The invisible line that divides the two starts in the distant north at the Amur River and runs southward through the crest of the Great Khingnan Mountains. It follows the contours of the Huang He, or Yellow River, turning northwest and then west to accommodate that part of the river that arches toward Mongolia. Turning again southward, it searches out the upper part of the river, passing through the region around Lanzhou and Chengdu and finally becomes obscure in the hilly southern area of Kunming near the Vietnamese border.

To the south and east of this demarcation "line" lies China proper; to the north and west the area is referred to as "outer" China. The land is relatively fertile south and east of this "line." In the eastern region of central "inner" China there are few hills which break the monotony of the level land. In the south, the land is also fertile, but is more hilly.

In the West, on the left–hand side of the

rough demarcation line, the land is a combination of closely crowded mountains with rough surfaces possessing little greenery even in the warmer regions of the lower altitudes. The towering peaks are occasionally interrupted by expanses of flat territory that is also desolate and dry, being surrounded by a natural barrier that withstands the invasion of rain clouds. The mountains in the North on the edge of the "line" give way to the Gobi Desert, filled with shifting earth, harsh rock formations and severe extremes in temperature, all of which combine to exclude more than occasional visits of man and beast. The mountains envelop this desert which extends from Manchuria into southern Mongolia.

These areas of outer China are largely unmapped by Western standards. The thinly scattered people of Tibet, Xinjiang and Manchuria have traditionally relied on herds of animals as their principal resource, although great treasures of mineral wealth may lie buried below the surface of the earth. A short growing season provides the small amount of greenery available. The air is dry in both summer and winter, blowing out of Asiatic Russia (Siberia). The great distance the wind has traveled prior to its arrival in China has taken almost all moisture from the air. The absence of bodies of water in the endless expanses also make the dry winds cold—bitterly so, almost beyond belief, in the winter.

In the spring enough warmth arrives to melt the snow in the lower altitudes of the mountains. This is sufficient to support limited agriculture at the lower edges of the mountains bordering the Gobi Desert of western Manchuria and Mongolia in the area between the mountains and the Takla Makan Desert in Xinjiang and the valleys of Tibet, but only during the brief summer season.

To the south and east of the "line" the land changes into temperate farmland; it is relatively flat and somewhat drier in parts of northern China, notably in the North China Plain. The hillier and more mountainous areas found in southern China have more moisture and warmer temperatures, producing thick growths of forest on the land not under cultivation.

The three main rivers, the Huang He (Yellow), the Yangzi and the Xijiang (West River) have their origins deep within the remote territory west of the mountains, but flow through the more level eastern regions in a sluggish manner. Refreshed by the cool water of melting snow, they are quickly swollen in the spring by rains brought by the southeastern monsoon, and overflow their banks, spreading rich silt over the surrounding land. Flood control has been considerably improved in recent years, however. They also are a traditional source of communication and transportation in the region, but this is being replaced by railroads.

The lower valley of the Huang He is

From the surging waters of the Huang He (Yellow) River . . .

China

... to the parched wastes of the Gobi Desert

temperate and is the area in which the major aspects of Chinese civilization were born. The river itself is unpredictable. It left its old course south of the Shandong peninsula in which it had flowed for more than 800 years, and assumed its present course north of the peninsula in 1853, a shift of more than 500 miles. The immense quantities of silt it carries in its waters gave it the name "Yellow River" and also have built up a river bed over the years which is higher than the surrounding land. When it enters flood stage, the results have been catastrophic.

The growing season increases in the central and eastern region of China which is drained by the Yangzi River; it becomes almost continuous throughout the year in the southeastern area through which the Xijiang (Sikiang) River flows. If the rainfall in these regions was uniform from year to year, both would produce great quantities of food to feed the huge number of Chinese. The variations in rain, however, cause periodic loss of crops by either drought or flood. During a prolonged drought, even the violent summer rains are not of much help, since they run quickly into the rivers and flow into the sea rather than watering the land, which then dries out, unless there is further, preferably steady, rainfall.

The island of Taiwan has an elongated oval shape and its entire length is dominated by a chain of mountains rising with regularity to heights of 6,000 to 11,000 feet. These peaks lie close to the eastern side of the island and drop steeply at the coastline into the warm waters of the Pacific. The western slopes descend gently to a fertile plain that occupies almost one–half of the island's surface. The climate varies from tropical to temperate, depending upon altitude. As is true on the Chinese

mainland 100 miles across the Taiwan Strait, the summer winds bring abundant rain which supports intense agriculture. The smaller rivers do not cause the catastrophic floods of the three mighty rivers of continental China, so that bountiful harvests of a variety of produce, principally rice, are regularly gathered.

History

The Formative Era

China is the world's oldest continuous civilization in the sense that contemporary Chinese civilization recognizably resembles its earliest origins. Today's Arabic and Islamic Egypt, for example, is far more different from the civilization of the Pharaohs than China is from its early years. Still China is actually of much more recent vintage than the major early civilizations of Southwest Asia and North Africa.

Archeological evidence from north China, where its dryer climate better preserves artifacts, reveals neolithic communities based in several parts of the region dating from around 5000 B.C. These communities cultivated dogs and pigs and, even at that early date, silk.

By the period 1800–1000 B.C., the Chinese had begun to develop into a highly stylized, complex pattern. Advanced and very artistic techniques of casting bronze developed. The system of *ideographic* writing was refined and became the method of communicating and recording of ideas. But it did not and it does not now have an alphabet; it consists of a collection of thousands of symbols, each of which represents a word. Somewhat similar to Egyptian hieroglyphics, these characters have evolved far beyond their original graphic

origins. Today, merely looking at a character provides few clues to its meaning. For many hundreds of years this system of writing was known only to scribes and intellectuals and has only recently become more widely known among the general population.

Nevertheless, the Chinese, using this tremendously demanding writing system, developed quite early a society more dependant on a wide dispersal of learning than almost any other major civilization. The 20th century has seen many modifications to both the format and structure of the characters to make them more accessible to the average person.

The Early Dynasties

From around 1800 B.C. the Chinese were ruled by kings of the Shang, an apparently feudal and aristocratic dynasty. The Shang rulers were replaced by the Zhou (Chou) dynasty, which formally governed from about 1100 to 800 B.C., after which their power rapidly diminished until it was destroyed centuries later. Although the details of the fall of the Shang need hardly concern us here, what is astonishing is that from that collapse emerged one of the most significant Chinese contributions to political philosophy ever devised, The concept of the "Mandate of Heaven."

In originally justifying their conquest of the Shang, the Zhou leaders explained that the Shang, due to their degeneracy, had forfeited the "Mandate." According to their reasoning, which would dominate Chinese political thought down through the ages, "Heaven" was not viewed as a spiritual place of post–life salvation. It was a conscious entity that insisted that governments on earth must rule for the benefit of the masses. And leaders maintained the right to do so only as long as they continued to behave well toward the people. In a world where too often political power has derived more from the sword or inheritance, this provisional nature of power has been an important idea first developed in ancient China and eventually complementary to many modern democratic theories of government. Some early Chinese thinkers even went so far as to claim that the "Mandate" actually justified the right of the masses to revolt!

The real power of the Zhou dynasty lasted only a few centuries before North China then disintegrated into a number of feudal states led by "princes" who occupied their time and that of their subjects in a variety of wars against each other. The use of iron tools in agriculture during this period produced a high yield from the earth, which, together with irrigation and (after 1,000 A.D.) the widespread cultivation of rice, permitted a correspondingly high rate of population growth. As the people pressed outward, they came into greater conflict with non–Chinese people who inhabited central China around the Yangzi River. The stronger rulers subdued the weaker and smaller states, and the number of feudal princedoms became

less, gradually falling under the control of two major states: Qin, which ultimately triumphed in the 3rd century B.C., was in the west central and northwestern part of China and Chu in the central Yangzi valley. Graphically, this period is known as the "Warring States Period."

The Hundred Schools

Though China was divided during the later Zhou period, this diversity of political power proved to be a major benefit for its cultural development. In fact, one of the most interesting features of Chinese civilization is that, given its usual tendency toward centralization and successive government enthusiasm for promoting an orthodoxy of thought, it is most often during periods of relative weakness that Chinese intellectual life most dramatically has flourished.

Several points in modern history, the 1920s and most recently in the era before the clashes at Tiananmen Square in 1989, serve as good examples. The later Zhou was just such an era, a time when in the 5th and 4th centuries B.C. China enjoyed an intellectual blossoming comparable to that of Greece during the same period. Lit-

erature and the arts flourished, and the desire for knowledge and social order led to the creation and formalization of the two intellectual systems which originated in China: Confucianism and Taoism, the latter a mystical and contemplative system of belief and magical imagery (see Historical Background).

Confucianism, in contrast, is largely a system of social philosophy, and became a very influential source of satisfaction for the learned Chinese as well as providing a sense of imperial legitimacy and the security arising out of its emphasis on hierarchy and deference to authority, a feature many in East Asia today claim still plays an important role in their recent economic successes.

The First Empires

By 221 B.C. the Qin ruler, who led a highly organized and militarily strong state, conquered his rivals and established control over all of north and central China as well as part of the southern region. For China this was one of the darkest periods in their history. The Qin dynasty unified the empire in more ways than military conquest; the Great Wall of China

The 1,400 mile long Great Wall of China

Courtesy: Bruce Terry Howe

China

was constructed laboriously over a period of years to ward off the periodic raids by the nomadic central Asians from the North. Roads and other public works were built and the system of writing and weights were standardized. Obsessed with the needs of state power, the Qin leadership ignored the precepts of Confucianism, even killed many of its adherents, rejecting totally the idea that the state existed to serve the masses.

Not surprisingly the rule of the Qin was extremely oppressive and produced much discontent among the Chinese people. It was soon overthrown by a new dynasty that took the name *Han*.

These new rulers, successfully avoiding the arrogance which had brought down the Qin, eventually governed for almost 400 years (2nd century B.C.–2nd century A.D.) before and after the beginning of the Western Christian era. The people of China today are sometimes referred to as *Han* to differentiate them from the minorities that live in the outer part of what is modern China. In spite of a brief collapse at the halfway point of its reign, the Han Dynasty succeeded in making China into an empire of power, wealth and cultural brilliance comparable to the other great civilization of the same period, the Roman Empire.

Technologically, it was in fact far more advanced than its Roman counterpart on the other side of Eurasia. Its boundaries were pushed well into central Asia, where local leaders were awed by the brilliance of Chinese advances in learning and military prowess. Even if not directly supervised by the Chinese, rulers of the outlying states of Asia were often willing to acknowledge themselves tributary and vassal states of the mighty empire.

When the Han dynasty collapsed, the following four centuries were marked by frequent nomadic invasions from the North which resulted in a series of states in northern China ruled by non–Chinese. A few Chinese, or Han states, did survive in the South, however, under a series of weak dynasties. During this time of uncertainty, Mahayana Buddhism, sometimes referred to as northern Buddhism (see Historical Background), spread quickly following its arrival from northern India by way of Central Asia at the beginning of the Christian era.

The Middle Dynasties

China was reunited by the Sui and Tang dynasties after 581 A.D., and under an energetic succession of emperors it once more extended the area of its power far into Central Asia. For the first time in world history, a written examination was developed for civil servants, appointment of whom was based more and more on ability rather than family ties. Ironically, aspects of this movement away from aristocracy and toward a more individually based system of merit had begun earlier under the generally hated Qin dynasty.

Although the officials of the Tang Dynasty were largely Confucian in outlook, it was in this period that Buddhism reached the height of its influence in Chinese civilization. Nevertheless, that influence was not long lasting and the later Tang era saw many cruel persecutions of Buddhists. Though losing its hold on official Chinese thought to Confucianists and Daoists (Taoists), this South Asian belief system would nevertheless remain influential on the popular level into the modern period.

There was a short period of disunity following the decline and fall of the Tang dynasty in the 10th century A.D. The brilliant cultural advances of the ensuing three–century period centered chiefly on the art of painting and the discipline of philosophy. Under the influence of Buddhist theology, official Confucianism was modified by about 1200 into Neo–Confucianism which concerned itself more with abstract philosophy than had the original form of this belief.

The country was ruled by emperors of the Song (Sung) dynasty, and was continually threatened by a succession of powerful non–Chinese states that emerged along the northern border. The end of this era came with defeat by the most powerful northern force, the Mongols, who were able to succeed in their conquest only after a long and bitter campaign. The Song had withstood the Mongols longer than any of the other civilizations of the world into which the conquerors intruded, but ultimately became a part of a vast empire stretching from the Pacific to what is now the Middle East.

The Mongols finally unified all China in 1279 and ruled for a century, taking the name Yuan dynasty. Already disliked by the Chinese in a number of ways, the Mongols had but slight respect for Confucianism and the civil service examinations, factors which led to even greater opposition by the Chinese, particularly the upper classes. The rulers though were religiously tolerant, and permitted small communities of Franciscan missionaries to introduce Christianity into several parts of coastal China.

The Mongols were expelled from China in 1368 in a great upheaval with strong anti–foreign tendencies. This new, ethnically Chinese dynasty, which came to power, the Ming (1368–1644), at first ruled firmly and energetically, creating a powerful empire.

Following the momentum of the outward–looking Yuan Dynasty, the Ming Emperor even sent out huge overseas flotillas toward the west to explore and demonstrate the might of the Chinese Empire. Starting in 1405 the Ming Emperor Yong Le sent out an extraordinary series of naval expeditions which over the years eventually traveled throughout Southeast Asia and parts of India and ranged as far away as Aden in Arabia and Mogadishu in East Africa. The final expedition in 1431 even sent some ships as far as Jedda on the Red Sea! The efforts, whose motives are not exactly clear, certainly had its impact. The Chinese flotilla intervened in a number of local disputes and worked to further the prestige of the Chinese emperors.

However, they lacked the ongoing significance of the voyages Westerners mounted in the opposite direction several generations later in the 15th century. By the time the Europeans attempted similar voyages, memory of the early Chinese flotillas had been all but forgotten.

Within China, a period of decline began about 1500. Japanese pirates began to increase their activities along the coast. Internal weakness became an increasing

---

The Chinese Exam System

The Chinese examination system, which existed in various forms until the early 20th century, was truly remarkable for a traditional society. Rather than relying on birthright to choose the bulk of their elites, as was so common among the Europeans and even their East Asian neighbors, the Japanese, the Chinese eventually developed a massive system of offering Confucian–based exams to thousands upon thousands of males annually. Those that advanced beyond the first demanding tests went on to even more rigorous exams at the provincial and eventually imperial level. Although, few became great officials of the government, the system created an enormous pool of educated people who served the needs of society as local leaders, and for the lucky few, officially within the imperial bureaucracy.

Not surprisingly those who came from educated and reasonably well off households had a major advantage in the competition. Nevertheless, the record of graduates shows that it was a true system of social mobility that allowed many people year after year to rise beyond their families' earlier accomplishments.

Marble sculpture of a Ming soldier at the Imperial Tombs

problem which was transformed into an even greater liability by the rise in power of the Manchu rulers to the north. In 1644, a combination of domestic rebellion and Manchu might was sufficient to overthrow the Ming dynasty; Within a few decades, the Manchus had subdued all of China.

The Manchus

The new rulers took the name Qing (Ch'ing) dynasty, but are more commonly referred to in the West as the Manchus. Although Chinese culture was by this time static to a degree that made basic changes difficult, under the Manchus the country was once again united and became rapidly powerful. In an effort to consolidate their positions, the Manchus ruled through existing Chinese institutions, including the very formal civil service examination system with its Confucian orientation. For this reason, and others, they were accepted rapidly by their Chinese subjects.

Interestingly, they devised a system whereby major offices and responsibilities were shared by matched sets of Manchu and Chinese officials. After an initial period of wise and successful rule, the Manchus indulged themselves in a period of

energetic, but arbitrary and costly, warfare in the late 18th century which undermined the dynasty and coupled with internal corruption and a number of internal revolts combined to make China less able to deal with the challenges the nineteenth century would bring.

Arrival of Westerners

Although Westerners from the Roman era on had periodically visited China, the modern period of Sino–Western relations really begins in the 18th century when Europeans, principally British, started to seek Chinese silk and tea. Unfortunately for these early merchants they had, at first, little to offer, save silver bullion in exchange for the coveted Chinese goods. The Chinese seemed quite disinterested in Western products. In fact, the famous emperor Qian Long even explained to a Western visiting dignitary in 1793 that China had "all things" in abundance and was simply not interested in Western goods. Nevertheless, the trade did develop and at the insistence of the Beijing government it was confined to the southern port of Guangzhou known to foreigners as Canton.

For the English though, this "Canton

System" although lucrative enough, did cause problems. They were interested in trading further north in China where there might be a better market for their goods and in having direct contact with Chinese officials when various problems, legal and commercial, arose.

None of these things though was possible given the prevailing Chinese disinterest in any Western style foreign relations or commercial exchanges beyond those considered important to maintaining the dignity and universal legitimacy of Chinese imperial claims. For the Chinese, foreign relations as understood in the West did not exist.

The Chinese emperor was considered the "son of heaven" and people interested in having relations with China were expected to take part in the Chinese "Tributary System," largely a symbolic system whereby other communities recognized the supreme symbolic authority of the Emperor. On a technical level, that required a physical prostration before the emperor known as the *kowtow* and an exchange of various presents. In fact, the presents the Chinese gave away were not uncommonly more valuable than those they received. For the Chinese emperors, it was the symbolism of the relationship that mattered, not the cash transaction. England, the country that some had disparaged as the nation of shopkeepers, had met an empire completely disinterested in commerce. It was a bad match.

But by the late eighteenth and early nineteenth century two developments occurred which led to dramatic changes in China's relations with the Western powers. The British discovered that opium, grown in their possessions in India, could be sold at a handsome profit in China. Over the next decades the amount of opium imported into China by the British grew enormously until by the first quarter of the 19th century the drug was devastating Chinese society, especially in the south.

After first undergoing an internal debate in the late 1830s about how best to deal with the crises, the imperial government decided to force the foreign traders to give up their trade. To that end, an imperial commissioner, Lin Zexu, was sent to Guangzhou (Canton to the foreigners) in 1839 to attempt to suppress the trade. Although the imperial commissioner managed to confiscate the traders' opium stocks and destroy them, the British government, by then especially committed to the drug trade, declared war. Over the next generation and during two successive "Opium Wars" one of which culminated in the capture of Beijing itself in 1860, the British, and eventually their French allies, managed to impose a series

China

Traditional *Junk* on the China Sea

of "unequal treaties" on the Chinese. Those treaties would dominate Sino–Western relations until the middle of the 20th century.

What had gone wrong for China? For most of world history Chinese technology had far outshone the skills of the Westerners, but by the 18th century, the industrial revolution, especially centered in England, gave the British enormous advantages over the once self–sufficient Chinese empire. That advantage would last for more than the next hundred years with profound implications for our own century.

The Diplomacy of Imperialism

Under the series of "unequal treaties" signed under pressure in the first half of the 19th century, China lost a large part its sovereignty. The Westerners gained the right to dominate a series of ports, soon known as Treaty Ports along the coast. Hong Kong and Shanghai, are the best known of them. The treaties also gave the foreigners immunity to Chinese law and control over China's tariffs; especially important for later developments was the insistence that foreigners be allowed to preach Christianity in the interior of the country. Moreover, due to the concept of "most favored nation," the rights won by the English and French guns applied to all other foreigners in China including the Americans who had hardly taken part.

Cutting the Melon

The culmination of this era of imperialist greed occurred just as the 19th century was coming to a close. Known as the "Cutting of the Melon," one European power after another began demanding further spheres of influence in China. The British demanded an expansion of their influence in the region east of Shanghai and north of Hong Kong while the French pushed into southern China from their base in Vietnam. To the north the Russians and Germans made their demands while the Japanese insisted on gaining further rights in the Chinese coastal areas opposite Taiwan. In each of these, a particular Western power (with the exception of the United States) was granted sweeping and exclusive economic rights in its area, coupled with a great degree of political influence.

Russian domination was established in Manchuria, but the fertile southern portion of that region went to the Japanese in 1905 after their victory in the Russo–Japanese War. The Germans established themselves in the province of Shandong (Shantung); the British became the major power in the Yangzi valley region; the Japanese controlled Fujian (Fukien) Province and the French asserted their dominance over Southwest China.

Interestingly for readers of this year's edition of *East, Southeast Asia, and the Western Pacific 1997,* the new demands were often made in the form of forced 99 year leases. Although most of these arrangements have long since been terminated, the lease on the New Territories of Hong Kong continued. Only now ninety–nine years later has it run out. Thus the drama of last July's return of Hong Kong to the People's Republic of China.

That imperialistic high point known as the "Melon Cutting" did not stop at the century's end. Outside what had been China, places like Korea and Okinawa, which had paid tribute to the Manchu emperors, also became colonies or spheres of influence of Britain, France, Russia and Japan. Russian influence became paramount in Outer Mongolia, and penetrated into Xinjiang (Sinkiang) in the 1930's. The British became a powerful influence in Tibet and remained so until 1947.

These losses of territory and authority were dramatic demonstrations of China's basic weakness by the standards of the 20th century Western powers and were an insult to the sense of national pride of the Chinese. The economy of the coastal regions, traditionally more wealthy than the interior areas, was almost totally dominated by foreign trade and investment.

Although many among the Chinese tended toward an inwardness that made effective response to these pressures difficult, there were other more far sighted individuals within the Chinese leadership. They foresaw crises developing, and began, as early as the 1860s, to adapt to the various Western military techniques needed to maintain the country's sovereignty in that imperialistic age. Led by perceptive individuals at both the imperial and military level, most notably the Manchu Prince Gong, a period known as "Self Strengthening" was begun. He was aided at the provincial level by leaders like Li Hongzhang and Zuo Zongtang. Under this program, during an energetic era dating from the late 1860s through the 1890s, several military arsenals and dockyards were founded and scores of students sent abroad—to America and Europe—to learn Western military and engineering techniques. Sadly, though considerable effort was put out and significant gains made, they were overall too little to stem the flow of China's diminishing strength nor to equal similar but more energetic efforts like those of their neighbors, the Japanese, which were simply far more successful.

As seen below, in the first test of their respective efforts at mastering Western military techniques during the Sino–Japanese war of 1894, the Chinese accomplishments proved sorely lacking and the country experienced yet another massive humiliation. The significance of these humiliations and the various unequal treaties, cannot be underestimated. It is important to understand that even today many of China's leaders grew up when these special Western and Japanese privileges were still in effect.

The Heavenly Kingdom of Great Peace

Although the long term implications of the Western pressures on China were enormous, the larger issue at the time for the Chinese themselves was the outbreak in 1851 of an enormous rebellion which eventually devastated much of the country over the next fifteen years.

The origins of the Taiping Heavenly Kingdom, as the rebels called themselves, lay in the startling increases in population which had added enormous pressures on the land. Moreover, the Opium Wars themselves had disrupted economic life in southern China. It was in that disrupted environment that arose one of the more curious dramas of world history.

The story began in the early nineteenth century when a frustrated Confucian scholar, who had for years been unable to pass the demanding Confucian civil service exams, decided that he was the younger brother of Jesus Christ and developed a new "trinity" which included "God, the Father", "God, the Son" and in this new theology, himself, the "little brother."

For fifteen years, dating from the original revolt in 1851, China was divided between two governments, the ethnically Manchu, but Confucian–oriented Qing Dynasty, and the unique Chinese Taiping Rebels with their semi–Chinese–semi–Christian orientation. Following ideas found both in the Old Testament and drawn from mythic memories of early China, the Taipings established a theocracy with a communal economic structure. Life was organized, especially at their capital at Nanjing, around a religious military structure which at least on the surface seemed quite puritanical. Women, in sharp contrast to traditional Confucian practice, were far freer. Foot binding was not practiced and the women also took part in battle. But the assault on traditional practice had been too great and by 1864 the Heavenly Kingdom of Great Peace collapsed under pressures from Qing Militia leaders aroused by the struggle to preserve Confucianism (and assisted by Western military soldiers and advisors).

Following the death of the Emperor in 1861, his widow, referred to as the Empress Dowager Cixi, became co–regent during the reign of her son and wielded considerable influence. When he died in 1874 the throne then passed to Cixi's own young nephew and her power continued as before. Probably the most powerful woman in world history, Cixi dominated China, the largest population under a single government in the world, from the early 1860s through 1908. Her influence cannot be underestimated. Ruthless, able and extremely conservative, she embodied the traditions cherished by the Manchu court officials who clung to the security of the past. Nevertheless, under her reign, the first efforts to deal with the Western challenge in the form of the various industrial efforts known as "self–strengthening projects," were begun.

Cixi's power was so great that when she felt threatened by the Emperor Guang Xu's dramatic effort during the summer of 1898 to drastically reorganize the Chinese government and educational system, the better to make it able to withstand imperialistic pressures, she had him arrested. But if the Empress Dowager Cixi had intensely disliked the Emperor's response to the weakening of China, that did not mean that she failed to recognize the peril the dynasty faced. It is probably with that reason in mind that she soon pinned her hopes on yet another approach to the question of saving China. And in that case, one that arose from the popular masses' anger with the disruptions in their lives said to be caused by the foreigners. The results came to be known as the Boxer Rebellion.

At the popular level, there were many anti–foreign and anti–Christian outbreaks of violence in the years following 1870. Both sentiments joined to provide discontent resulting in the famous 1900 Boxer Rebellion a dramatic effort by thousands of Chinese to literally drive the Westerners out of China. In fact, the "Boxers" as the foreigners called them because of their ritualized style of physical and mental exercise, were encouraged by influential members of the Manchu court. For months, especially in north China, the Boxers terrorized Westerners and their Chinese converts.

Eventually, a joint military expedition was sent by the Western powers and crushed the Boxers. American and other foreign troops stormed Beijing in August 1900. Less than fifty years after the 1860 capture of Beijing by the Westerners, it was again under their control!

The Empress Dowager, who had fled the city as a young woman in 1860 was understandably shaken by the defeat and

American, British, and Japanese troops storming Peking (Beijing), August 1900

China

大清國當今慈禧端佑康頤昭豫莊誠壽恭欽獻崇熙聖母皇太后

The Empress Dowager Cixi

granted her reluctant assent to certain innovations in the imperial government. But it was too late. She died in 1908. The Manchu Qing dynasty had only a few more years to survive.

Trying to Save China

In the years after the 1839–42 Opium War several important officials and thinkers had come forward with theories and projects for reforming the Chinese empire. Some among them, as influential provincial leaders, put into place the various projects of the "Self–Strengthening Movement." More radical reformers later in the century played an important role in the Emperor's dramatic and failed reform effort of 1898, the so called "100 Day Reform." Nevertheless, as China moved into the 20th century its problems worsened and the ability of the imperial Manchu government to respond to the crises less and less significant. These early reformers were not unified; and their disunity prevented them from achieving any real influence on the Manchu court until it was too late.

As the situation deteriorated, the influences of these reformers became increasingly irrelevant, and leadership passed to those calling for more radical actions. It was in that context that a new generation of leaders arose, men not interested in reforming the Manchu Qing Empire but in replacing it with a republic more along the lines of Western models.

The most important of these radicals was Sun Yat–sen, who dedicated himself to the overthrow of the Manchus and to the modernization of China along semi–Western lines. Although he was eventually able to attract a relatively large following, Sun was not very effective in organizing his followers. Nevertheless due to the drama of Sun having been unsuccessfully kidnaped by Chinese agents in London in 1896, he became very well known in the West and eventually personified, in the minds of many Westerners, the goal of a Chinese republican revolution.

When the Empress Dowager died in 1908, the Manchu court installed the two–year–old Pu–Yi as child emperor. He reigned through regents appointed by the court until 1912. Later he was to serve as the "Emperor" of Manchukuo (Manchuria) when the Japanese attempted in the 1930s to colonize northern China.

The Revolution of 1911

In the fall of 1911, the ability of the Court to maintain the two–hundred and fifty year old Qing dynasty finally failed. A rebellion broke out in the city of Wuhan which, given prevailing frustrations with the Manchu leadership, spread rapidly across the country. One after another, various provinces declared themselves for the revolution. Sun Yat–sen, although at the time visiting the United States, emerged by December as the provisional president of a new Chinese republic. It appeared at first that China was about to take its place among the democracies of the modern world. But that was not to be.

If the forces of the old regime had been unable to maintain themselves, portions of their strength remained potent enough to direct the course of events over the next several years.

To avoid a civil war, Sun turned over power to Yuan Shikai, a former Qing general who still held considerable loyalty among many government soldiers. There was actually little choice. A civil war between the new revolutionary forces and those of Yuan Shikai would have only weakened China further. The compromise seemed necessary to save what had been already won. But sadly, Yuan was more interested in establishing a new dynasty than serving as a true democratic president, and within a few years China literally collapsed from the stress.

By 1916 China had disintegrated into a score of petty states run by individual military governors, usually referred to as "warlords." They had little governing ability and their rule was almost uniformly oppressive. The legal government of China in Beijing continued to be recognized diplomatically by the foreign powers. In reality, this "government" was an ever–shifting combination of one or more warlords, sometimes under the influence of foreign nations. Communications were extremely poor and there was a thin scattering of modern arms in the outlying regions, making it almost impossible to achieve any genuine national unity.

Sun Yat–sen, the "Father of the Revolution," embittered by his experiences in these developments, established himself in the south and tried in various ways, without success, to overthrow the shadow government at Beijing and to reunite the country. In the following years he devoted himself to the building up of the *Guomindang* (Kuomintang)—"National People's Party," or "GMD." But far to the north, an intellectual energy and nationalist momentum was growing that would go far beyond even Dr. Sun's revolutionary plans.

The May Fourth Movements

The May Fourth Movement of the years 1915 to 1921 was a multi–dimensional era

Dr. Sun Yat–sen addresses a crowd before departing with his troops on the campaign against Beijing

China

which embraced few central themes save a general disregard for China's traditional Confucian culture. On an individual level many of those involved loudly advocated a reorientation of cultural values. The young were told to become more independent, less tied to the more tradition–bound older generation. Confucianism, it was said, simply did not allow China the vitality necessary to withstand the aggressive modern world.

In addition to the trend toward economic modernization in the cities and coastal regions and cultural speculation during the 1920's, there was a marked growth of nationalism among the Chinese, who sought an end to foreign influence in their country. The "central" government was in the hands of a group under Japanese influence who cooperated with the latter's efforts to have their control over the Chinese province of Shantung formalized by the treaties that ended World War One. An outburst of patriotism, led by students, which became known as the May Fourth Movement, prevented the actual signing of the treaty and sparked an era of intense popular political activity.

On the national level the people of China, particularly the youth, desired the end of imperialism and internal disunity and came to believe that these goals could only be achieved through a major political and social revolution. Some chose the *Guomindang,* while a smaller number joined the infant communist movement.

Communism

The *Chinese Communist Party (CCP)* was founded in 1921 mostly by young Chinese intellectuals. The movement quickly came under the control of the Third International, more familiarly known as the *Comintern* of Russia under its energetic revolutionary leader, Lenin. The picture became even more complicated when the *Comintern* decided to enter into an alliance with Sun Yat–sen's *Guomindang* and ordered the local Chinese communists to do the same. This unstable union was produced by a common, overwhelming desire to expel Western and Japanese influence from China and to eliminate the power of the warlords.

To accomplish these aims, the *Comintern* reorganized and greatly strengthened the *Guomindang* through money and military aid, but it also hoped that communists could gradually acquire control over it by infiltrating top positions, and by putting pressure on the party through communist–dominated labor and peasant unions. Although there was considerable uncertainty about the collaboration of the *Guomindang's* nationalists and the commu-

nists, what mattered above all was that their cooperation help unify the country once more. In 1926 that great effort, known as the "Northern Expedition," began. For the next several years, sometimes by fighting, sometimes by negotiation, the nationalists marched north enthusiastically attempting to build a new, stronger and now unified China. The march was to prove ultimately successful, although tensions inherent in the nationalist/communist alliance eventually broke out.

While Sun Yat–sen had been alive, the effort to both unify China and to maintain the coalition of nationalists and communists continued fairly well. But after his death in 1925 he was eventually succeeded by General Chiang Kai–shek, who had become increasingly alarmed at the threat of Soviet domination of China and the

General Chiang Kai-shek

more immediate threat of potential communist revolution.

Chiang determined to head off these threats by military force and in 1927 sent his forces into the newly liberated Shanghai to slaughter his communist allies. The alliance between the Chinese nationalists and the communists was thus broken. For the moment the nationalists—the *Guomindang* forces, under Chiang—seemed triumphant.

Chiang captured Beijing in 1928, and proclaimed the renewed Republic of China with its new capital at Nanjing, a city which has often served as an alternative capital in Chinese history. Actually the *GMD* controlled only the eastern provinces of China and was faced with tremendous problems: a large army that had to be fed and clothed, floods, famine, and

political apathy. After a generation of struggle the *Guomindang* had finally come fully to power. But its ability to attempt a rebirth of China was soon to be severely curtailed when, in 1931, the Japanese began their effort to dominate the country.

The Japanese Invasion

Japanese efforts to establish an East Asian empire for themselves had begun in the late nineteenth century. By the early 1920s, their influence had grown considerably. Korea and Taiwan were already colonies and Japanese influence in Manchuria was considerable. China's weakness during the era of the "Warlords", 1916–1928, had given them even greater leeway to assert themselves. Moreover, the worldwide depression, which struck at the end of the 1920s convinced many Japanese nationalists that Japan's future lay in furthering their hold on northern China. That commitment lead to the Japanese Manchurian army's (see Japan) decision to provoke an incident which would allow them to take over Manchuria.

The Japanese seized it in 1931–32; the territory was renamed Manchukuo and the former Manchu emperor of the Chinese Empire, the youthful Henry Pu–Yi, took the throne as "Emperor of Manchukuo." This interesting character had been tutored in the Western classics by a Britisher after the ouster of the Manchus, who suggested that he take an English name. Having been enthroned as emperor and deposed while still a child, the possibility of once again becoming an emperor must have been exhilarating for the young man. Nevertheless, during his years as emperor over Manchuria, he would prove as powerless under the Japanese control as he had been as a child under the direction of the adults around him in the Chinese imperial court. His story is a fascinating one and it eventually became well known to millions of filmgoers through the movie "The Last Emperor."

To Chiang Kai–shek, the Japanese assault, while dangerous, was still not his most immediate concern. The Generalissimo was more concerned about what he saw as a disease of the "heart," the Chinese communists, who, while weakened by his assault in 1927, had remained a potent force. While Chiang had managed to weaken the city–based Shanghai communists, many others, most notably Mao Zedong in southeastern China, had managed to establish communist strongholds far beyond *GMD* control.

Chiang Kai–shek then made the poorest of choices. He decided to concentrate his energies on dealing with the Chinese communists rather than the Japanese invaders. That decision would eventually put into question whether the *GMD* really had any right to call itself the "Nationalists." His primary opponent, Mao Zedong, himself both a nationalist and committed communist, was often alienated from the leadership of the Chinese communist party; it often saw him as less orthodox in his ideological outlook. But these differences were hardly significant to the *Guomindang* which set out in the early 1930s to destroy the Chinese communist base known as the Jiangxi Soviet.

After long and difficult campaigns—the communist resistance was initially very effective—the communists were forced by overwhelming *Guomindang* military pressures to evacuate their base areas in Central and South China. Eventually , after a long dramatic trek of thousands of miles and extraordinary hardships later known as the "Long March", the temporarily defeated Chinese communists took refuge in the remote and desolate regions of Northwest China. During the march, after a crucial meeting at Zhunyi, Mao Zedong at last emerged as the leader of the Chinese communists, a position he would not relinquish until his death in 1976. While Chiang Kai–shek may have felt some satisfaction with the weakening of the communists, he had more pressing pressures to the north.

Mao Zedong (Mao Tse-tung) in 1945

World War II

By late 1936 in the midst of yet another effort to completely destroy the Chinese communists, Chiang was kidnaped by his own troops who were angry about his preoccupation with the communists in the

midst of the imminent Japanese threat. After a dramatic episode that came close to bringing China to civil war, the *Guomindang* and Chinese communists made yet another alliance. From Mao's perspective and that of many patriotic Chinese, it was absurd for Chinese to fight in the interior while Japan pressed forward in the northeastern part of the country. Moreover, Russia's Stalin had been urging the communists to enter into another alliance with the *Guomindang* in order to resist the invaders. Mao probably saw an opportunity not only to resist the Japanese, but to ultimately overthrow the Nationalists after they had been weakened by the enemy.

The new alliance came none too soon, for Japanese forces invaded eastern China in 1937 and started an assault of extraordinary brutality that at times foreshadowed later Nazi acts in Eastern Europe. The Japanese conquered the prosperous coastal regions of China, depriving the *Guomindang* of its major economic and political bases. Driven into the hills and mountains of southwest China, it became even more conservative and subject to corruption than before. Under Japanese control, cities like Nanjing, the Nationalist's capital, experienced a horror of mass murder and rape that went on for weeks. To the north, Japanese doctors would eventually establish a medical experimen-

Japanese troops in China, 1937

China

Silk tapestry   B. R. Graham

tation center that carried out live vivisections on hapless Chinese captives. Though less well known than the Nazi brutalities, they left a legacy of bitterness between China and Japan that still exists.

The expansion of the communists from that time forth was actually at the expense not only of the Japanese but also of the *Guomindang*. Inflation and weakness also sapped the strength of the Nationalists, enabling the Japanese to inflict further heavy defeats on it as late as 1944. Nevertheless, the Japanese were unable to prevent the communists, more skilled in the art of guerrilla warfare than the Nationalists, from infiltrating and setting up base areas within territory that was supposed to be Japanese. Partly in retaliation for this resistance, the Japanese committed more atrocities against the Chinese people in the occupied areas, driving many into sympathy with the communists and thus assisting them to seize political control on

an anti–Japanese, more than an anti–*Guomindang,* platform.

The Struggle for Power: nationalists and communists

Increasing numbers of Japanese soldiers were withdrawn from China starting in 1943 because of the defeats that were being suffered in the Pacific war. This permitted the communists to expand rapidly, so that by the end of the war they controlled nineteen base areas, in various parts of China, principally in the North and Northwest.

The elimination of Japanese troops from China at the end of the war brought a frantic flurry of political and military activity by both the *Guomindang* and the communists. In the immediate period after the war the U.S. was the major political power in the Pacific area and it attempted to bring about some sort of settlement between these two competing Chinese parties. The talks though, conducted under the encouragement of U.S. General George C. Marshall, special envoy of President Truman, completely broke down in 1946 because neither side had any real desire for an agreement. Each preferred a trial of armed strength. Neither had any interest in sharing China's future with the other.

Unfortunately for the *Guomindang*, the Nationalists, nominally more powerful, were plagued by their inability to deal with China's most serious problems: inflation, corruption and loss of political unity. The military leadership also employed very poor tactics against the communists, especially in the battle over Manchuria, and soon found themselves losing control over the mainland.

His Holiness The Dalai Lama of Tibet

By the end of 1949 the *Guomindang* was driven to the island of Taiwan. The Chinese communists under Mao then controlled all of mainland China except for Tibet which had been outside Beijing's control since the collapse of the Qing. They proclaimed the People's Republic of China and reestablished the Chinese capital at Beijing.

The next year the soldiers of the People's Liberation Army invaded Tibet. Although there was some initial resistance, the "roof of the world" was brought under Chinese control again; the Dalai Lama, spiritual leader of the Tibetans, who also was vested with rather wide governing powers, was soon made a figurehead. He eventually fled Tibet in 1959 after an unsuccessful uprising against the Chinese in the eastern part of the region.

The "People's Liberation Army" brought the new regime to power, and it remained important as a defense against possible enemies, both internal and external. The *Chinese Communist Party* however er was the real instrument behind Mao and his regime; its members held and now hold all important public offices. It has proven the only political force since the Manchus that has demonstrated itself able to hold China together. For the first quarter century of the People's Republic's existence, Mao Zedong played an overpowering role. He made himself into a cult–like father figure whom all Chinese, especially the youth, were taught to worship to a degree that would have created envy in the hearts of previous emperors.

Building a New China

The team of Mao, the *Chinese Communist Party (CCP)* and the army, held together quite successfully through the late 1950s and achieved results which were quite impressive considering how devastated the country was after generations of invasion and civil war. The majority of the people regarded the regime as the only hope of escape from the long nightmare of civil and foreign war, chaos and abject poverty, and gave it overwhelming support. Initially following the Soviet model of development, China's new leaders restored the defunct economy and launched an impressive program of heavy industrialization with Russian technical assistance and equipment. After igniting a frequently violent purge against the rural landowning classes, small plots of farmland were distributed to the peasants and then as the years went on collectivized. The lives of women were improved with the passage in 1950 of a new marriage and divorce law that gave women more marital and property rights.

In short, China progressed from war–

inflicted chaos toward a centralized, autocratic and rationally administered state. Traditional Chinese culture and society were forcibly changed in directions desired by the communists with widespread, fundamental and seemingly impossible effects. By 1956 the regime apparently felt confident enough to encourage the masses to voice their opinions on the many changes the *CCP* had brought about. "Let a hundred Flowers Bloom," Mao, the supreme leader, proclaimed though apparently what the *CCP's* leadership heard was not to their liking—by 1957 a cruel repression known as the "Anti–rightist Campaign" had commenced which was to destroy the careers of millions of Chinese intellectuals and others who had been naïve enough to actually speak out.

In foreign relations, the Chinese regime initially established a close alliance with the Soviet Union, still led by the aging Stalin. Doing so was not without its difficulties. The Soviet dictator would clearly have preferred a Chinese leadership more servile to Moscow and had even made Mao wait three days in Moscow before receiving him in November of 1949! Nevertheless the tie was formalized into a thirty year treaty of friendship. China also entered into diplomatic relations with all communist countries and with a number of neutral and Western nations. The United States, which had become protector of the Nationalists on Taiwan, refused to recognize Mao's government. With only slight success, the Chinese communists initially tried to promote revolutions elsewhere in Asia, but eventually retreated from this policy somewhat in order to be in a better position to cultivate the friendship of the neutral Asian nations.

The Korean War

Although the Chinese leadership may have wished to concentrate on solidifying their control over China in their first years of power, international developments became impossible to ignore. In June of 1950, the North Koreans, apparently with Soviet support, invaded South Korea with the goal of unifying the entire peninsula under their leadership.

Although the immediate Chinese reaction was somewhat restrained, the American decision to intervene through the United Nations aroused their ire. More to the point, after the American troops successfully drove the North Koreans back across the 38th Parallel demarcation line, they decided to invade North Korea with little thought to the consequences of moving toward the Chinese border. (see Korea section)

From the Chinese perspective, the

American troops (the apparent allies of their enemies the Chinese Nationalists) were pushing toward their borders and ignoring Beijing's warning that they would intervene if the Americans continued north. Unfortunately, the American forces *did* continue north and the Chinese, urged on and with the support of the Soviets, committed massive numbers of "volunteers" to stop the Americans and to the aid the besieged North Korean communist government. Whatever possibilities might have existed for a successful relationship between Washington and Beijing was destroyed in the explosion that followed and killed so many Americans, Chinese, and Koreans over the next few years. Happily, by July of 1953 an armistice was signed dividing the peninsula between the North Koreans and their

Harvesting in a *People's Commune*

communist allies in the north and the South Koreans and their American allies to the south. U.S. forces have remained in South Korea ever since.

The "Great Leap Forward"

By the mid–1950s, the Chinese leadership had at last successfully stabilized the economy and begun the long effort to recover from so many decades of war and civil war. The Soviet model of a command economy with its five year planning models was being used and significant progress was made.

But Mao wanted more; he wanted China to literally leap forward toward a more industrialized and socialized future, not at some distant point in the future but *immediately* with one giant effort of the

Chinese people united in the endeavor. By 1958, new and far more ambitions plans were announced for the country. Mao declared that China should catch up with industrialized England within 15 years.

The "Great Leap Forward" as it was known was to have two fundamental aspects, one industrial, one social. Toward the first, enormous industrial goals were announced. Each work unit was, among other things, expected to create "backyard furnaces" to boost iron production. Every industry was expected to dramatically increase its output of goods using an emphasis less on industrial know–how than the cumulative willpower of the energized population.

On the "communitarian/socialist" side Mao's planners herded people into what would become known as "People's Communes," which would dominate almost every aspect of their lives from child care to the use of their labor. Moving far past the Soviet model of state farms and limited private plots, the peasants were now told to live in completely egalitarian communities where there was literally no room for individual family initiative (or privacy). Even such mundane activities as growing a pig and raising it for market were branded "capitalist" and made impossible to carry out.

Most of these programs were terrible failures. Industrial production collapsed. The famous "backyard furnaces" often produced completely useless materials. The harvest revenues plummeted horrendously. Amidst the propagandistic circus of claims and boasts, a very real food dis-

China

Mao Zedong in 1966   AP/World Wide Photos

aster developed which turned into an enormous famine. Millions of people died in the following years due to this man–made disaster.

Late in the decade, policy differences and political tensions began to appear between the aging Mao and some of his colleagues who were more pragmatic than he and obviously worried about the suffering brought on by the failures of the Great Leap Forward. Few though were willing to challenge the Great Leader openly. Moreover, problems with their enormous socialist neighbor were as well beginning to develop.

Relations with the Soviets

By the late 1950s, relations with the Soviet Union, the principal source of economic and military aid, were becoming severely strained. The Soviet leader Khrushchév cut off all aid in 1960. Actually a clash between Mao and Nikita Khrushchév was probably inevitable—the former regarded the younger Khrushchév as an upstart and at the same time Khrushchév, blessed with an over abundance of ego, considered Mao a fanatic and an adventurer. China's enthusiasm for considering itself, rather than Moscow, the leader of their world revolutionary movements hardly endeared it to the Soviet Union either.

Soon growing Chinese political pressures on the Soviet Union, calculated to prove the correctness of Mao's brand of communism and the error of the Soviet "deviation," produced serious and fundamental tensions not only between the Soviets and the Chinese, but within the entire communist world. Over these years relations with the Soviets, never close, would continue to deteriorate until by 1956 they seemed in competition for leadership of the communist world.

In the summer of 1958, Mao engaged in another unsuccessful gesture—the shelling of the islands of Quemoy and Matsu, controlled by the Nationalists, close to mainland China in the Taiwan straits. Whatever his original intentions had been, nothing more than an artillery and air–power duel occurred, notwithstanding the alarm of other nations because of the possibility of a Chinese–U.S. confrontation. The Soviet Union's unwillingness to be supportive during the crises, and later when tensions developed with India, further alienated Beijing's leadership from Moscow.

The Soviet Union was accused of being as great if not greater political enemy than the United States. The task of struggling against the supposed imperialistic designs of the U.S. was in effect assigned to other revolutionary movements in Asia, Africa and Latin America.

The revolutionary zeal of the Chinese, and their tendency to urge radical and nationalistic movements to greater tasks than were possible, with endless quantities of advice and of Mao's "thoughts," coupled with quantities of arms, did not produce the desired results. A number of moderate nationalist and socialist leaders of Asia and Africa became rapidly aware of the not yet serious threat, and took steps to expel Chinese agents. There were especially serious setbacks in Indonesia and in sub–Sahara Africa, which had seemed promising to the Chinese in the years 1963–1965. After the fall in 1964 of Khrushchév, who had handled the revolutionary impatience of the Chinese rather clumsily, his more practical successors offered China a limited agreement, which was spurned by Mao. With this refusal, Mao worsened his relations with some of his critics at home and abroad who wanted a less antagonistic attitude toward Russia.

By the early 1960s, tensions within China's leadership had become more obvious. Mao had withstood the direct criticism of former allies like Peng Dehuai regarding the disasters caused by the Great Leap Forward. But by the early 1960s his influence over events within China was being lost to the more pragmatic bureaucratic leadership of the *Chinese Communist Party*, most notably individuals like Liu Shaoqi and Deng Xiaoping. For the aging leader Mao Zedong, this development was completely unacceptable.

The Great Proletarian Cultural Revolution

By the last half of 1965, Mao became convinced that the time had come to silence his critics within the party. Thus began another mass campaign: the "Great Proletarian Cultural Revolution." His first obstacle, the reluctant municipal boss of Beijing, Peng Zhen, was soon overthrown by a combination of political pressures and military threats. Mao then proceeded to call on the revolutionary young people, organized into "Red Guards" to root out his enemies. Moreover, in his struggle with the leadership of the *Chinese Communist Party,* Mao also had the support of Lin Biao, the commander of the People's Liberation Army. The youthful Red Guards attacked and terrorized Mao's real and imagined opponents in the universities, in the party structure and anywhere else they were thought to be found.

The victims ranged from party officials to teachers and other professionals in almost all fields from medicine to religion. Almost anyone the young enthusiasts could accuse of being insufficiently Maoist was in danger. The students created their own kangaroo courts to punish their victims and broke into homes looking for anything considered counter–revolutionary. Those found with materials ranging from books by Confucius to Western writings, even possession of materials written by the now purged former leadership of the *Communist Party,* could cause an individual serious problems.

Throughout the country, former officials and others who had held authority previously were beaten and humiliated as they were marched through the streets wearing banners proclaiming their supposed guilt. The lives of countless millions, were affected by the malicious chaos of the era.

The struggle was as much an assault on the full heritage of Chinese tradition as it was against Mao's enemies. Throughout the country the "Red Guards," aroused as they were against almost any object connected to China's imperial past, destroyed or defaced materials of enormous beauty. Practitioners of traditional arts, from Buddhist monks to magicians and fortune tellers, were hounded from their professions.

Eventually even central power began to break down in many parts of the country as Mao's "Cultural Revolution" went far beyond what even he had envisioned. By early 1967, it was necessary for Mao to urge the army to intervene in order to prevent chaos and yet to keep the Cultural Revolution moving. The army quickly discovered that these two tasks were inconsistent and increasingly began to emphasize the restoration of order in place of the

China

disorder created by the unruly Red Guards. In 1967, Mao was brought, willingly or unwillingly, to endorse a turn towards a more conservative line. After that time, the impact of the Cultural Revolution on everyday life lessened. During 1968 the army acquired more and more local power, and with Beijing's consent, it forcibly suppressed the Red Guard movement. The young Red Guards were banished to the countryside to "educate" themselves among the peasants.

Though how much they actually "learned" is less certain, what is clear is that a huge percentage of the young people of that era lost their opportunity for higher education and a better life. If many of their older contemporaries, those they had been persecuting, were able, once calm was restored, to resume their former lives, that was not true of many of these youth who were in many ways the real victims of the Cultural Revolution. Not only were they as individuals to lose, but China itself ultimately lost out on the professional skills they would have potentially made available to build a new, more modern China.

The Vietnam Wars

While China itself was going through the chaos of the Cultural Revolution, just to the south one of the longest struggles of the twentieth century, the Vietnam war, was entering an especially critical stage. (See the Vietnam section). For China, despite the eons of tension and ambivalence which separated the Chinese and Vietnamese, there was no question but that Beijing would support North Vietnam in its struggles against the Americans during the Vietnam War (approximately 1965–1975 for the American stage). But here, unlike in Korea, China did not play a major role.

China sent some arms (mainly infantry weapons) to North Vietnam, cooperated for a time in transshipping Soviet weapons by rail to it and sent railway engineering units to help keep the main Vietnamese railway lines open in spite of American bombardment. After the American withdrawal in 1973, China stepped up its flow of arms to Hanoi and in this way contributed significantly to the rapid fall of South Vietnam in the spring of 1975.

But by that time, however, Hanoi had already begun to show signs of abandoning its neutrality in the Sino–Soviet disputes, and was "tilting" toward Moscow. By 1977 Vietnam was involved in a border war with Cambodia, where the pro–Chinese rather than the pro–Vietnamese wing of the Khmer Rouge (the Cambodian communist movement) had come to power in 1975. When China began in 1978 to put

pressure on Vietnam in support of Cambodia, Hanoi expelled several hundred thousand "boat people," many of them of Chinese ancestry, and moved still closer to Moscow. At the end of 1978, Vietnam invaded Cambodia and installed a puppet government in Phnom Penh. Accordingly, China then experienced its own Vietnam War for a time by invading Vietnam briefly in February–March 1979 with the announced purpose of teaching Hanoi a lesson.

The lesson though did not take. Vietnamese forces did far better than expected against those of their giant neighbor and relations were tense for decades. And not surprisingly, despite the alliances of the war, centuries of animosity that existed between China and Vietnam were revived.

Tensions have continued for years in the vicinity of their common border, as well as in naval rivalry in the South China Sea. Nevertheless, the collapse of the Soviet Union eventually led to a slight defrosting of relations between China and Vietnam.

A Basic Shift in 1971–2

The military clash along the Sino–Soviet border in early 1969, which turned out badly for the Chinese, eventually led to some astonishing shifts in East Asian politics. Given the reality that China was finding itself "squeezed" between two different antagonists, the jealous Soviets to the north, and the Americans struggling against communism in Vietnam, many in China felt it was time to rethink China's international position. A moderate coali-

tion, led by Premier Zhou Enlai and some of the military, tried to restore a greater degree of domestic stability and more workable foreign relations.

Zhou felt it advisable, after several months of Soviet threats, to enter into negotiations on border problems and related matters, and to downgrade disputes concerning communist theory. Nevertheless, by the end of 1970, it appeared that the negotiations had resulted in a deadlock.

Internal politics also played a role in bringing about the new international alignment when Lin Biao, the long–time leader of the contentious *PLA*, who had supported improved Sino–Soviet relations, conspired against Mao. He was eventually killed in a 1971 abortive plan to flee the country. The way was clear to open relations with the United States, a relationship many in the Chinese leadership hoped would serve as a balance to the potential threats posed by the Soviet Union.

To the surprise of the Americans, China extended in 1971 an invitation to an American ping pong team to visit. This was quickly followed by a visit by Dr. Henry Kissinger in July 1971 and later by President Nixon in 1972. For the Americans, of course, better relations with Beijing offered the possibility of finding a new tool to end their frustrating involvement in Vietnam. Beijing's help did eventually prove significant in developing the treaties which allowed for the United States to withdraw, even though that aid hardly affected the ultimate outcome of the Vietnam war itself. For, despite the hopes of many, by 1975 Vietnam was again united but under the direction of Hanoi.

President Nixon contemplates the Great Wall, 1972   AP/World Wide Photos

China

Nevertheless, American ties to China continued to improve and by 1978 President Carter of the United States formalized diplomatic relations with Beijing. At the same time, the United States terminated its formal diplomatic relations and defense treaty with the *Republic of China* on Taiwan. Other important ties, however, remained intact and the U.S. continued to sell arms to Taiwan and to offer considerable "moral support." Once Beijing and Washington began to improve their relations Taiwan's international position began to deteriorate. In a humiliating move, Nationalist China was expelled from the United Nations and the People's Republic of China became the official representative of China at that organization.

The Emergence of Deng Xiaoping

In the mid 1970s an upsurge of political ferment reflected radical dissatisfaction, especially from the individuals eventually known as the "Gang of Four" which included Madame Mao, Jiang Qing, as its most prominent representative. They were clearly dissatisfied with Premier Zhou Enlai's more moderate policies, desiring another dose of Mao's sloganeering agitation. In spite of this, Zhou, a highly skilled and educated person, though suffering from cancer, remained in power until his death, counterbalancing the influence of the waning Mao, who though physically frail was still perceived as supporting, or at least protecting, the more radical Maoists.

Zhou Enlai was still effectively in charge, though in a hospital, possibly hoping that an early demise on his own part would not give the radicals an opening to resume their initiatives. Whatever his goals, Zhou died in January of 1976 more than ten months before Mao Zedong passed away. The timing appeared to allow Madame Mao and her radical allies their opportunity to come to full power at last.

The death of Zhou Enlai deprived the world of one of its most astute statesmen and placed the future of the moderates in Beijing in jeopardy for a time. Vice Premier Deng Xiaoping, Zhou's main assistant since 1973, had badly antagonized the Maoist radicals and did not remain in office long; he was forced out by April, presumably with Mao's approval. The new premier announced at that time, however, was not formally a radical, but a compromise choice, Hua Guofeng, whose record suggested a closer affinity with the moderates than the radicals.

A major earthquake in July 1976 tightened the political ties between Hua and the army, which handled most of the relief work. Given the trauma and demands required to recover, it was apparent that China needed a breathing spell away from the political bickering of the communist era.

Frail, senile and moribund, Mao died in September 1976. His death removed the main shield of the leading radicals, including his widow, Jiang Qing. They were purged by Hua a month later. The so-called "Gang of Four" soon came to be seen as central symbols of the suffering experienced by so many during the previous decade's Cultural Revolution. After their purge, propaganda against them continued unabated.

Deng Xiaoping, the leader of the more pragmatic communist officials was "rehabilitated" and soon became the most powerful man in the country. Deng's general

Deng Xiaoping
(pronounced *Dung Shou–ping*)

approach could not be more in contrast to Mao Zedong, his long–time leader. Mao had been committed to an ideological approach to governing that often excluded basic realities, thus making possible movements like the "Great Leap Forward." In dramatic contrast, Deng was more concerned about emphasizing a pragmatic approach to issues, preferably devoid of ideology. And it was with that approach that he set about, in what in hindsight turned out to be an incredibly successful effort, to build a new China.

Building a New China

Under Deng Xiaoping's leadership China underwent an extraordinary series of changes almost unprecedented in Chinese history. Famous for his comment that "it did not matter if a cat were black or white,

as long as it caught mice," Deng, while committed to the political power of the *Chinese Communist Party* was first and foremost a pragmatist. Early on he forced the retirement of Premier Hua Guofeng. He ultimately was replaced by Hu Yuobang. Deng then successfully went forward with the trial of the "Gang of Four," thus neutralizing radical opposition, some of which was within the army, making it easier to move against the ideas and policies they and Mao had represented.

The purge of radicals continued in both the party and the bureaucracy during the early 1980s. In 1985, 64 members of the Central Committee "resigned" under pressure from Deng. Zhao Ziyang was named General Secretary of the party in 1987, replacing Hu Yuobang. Eventually, he in turn, after the crises of Tiananmen Square, was replaced by the present party leader, Jiang Zemin, in 1989.

Deng was also the driving force behind significant agricultural reforms during the 1980s, which led to partial decollectivization. In 1984, control over industry was eased, giving local managers more authority. Prices were set at the local instead of the national level (at least in theory), and food and housing subsidies were reduced for urban dwellers. In 1985, the economy grew by 15%. That astounding leap in GNP would begin a pattern of growth that has continued well into the 1990s.

Unfortunately, inflation and corruption also exploded. Attempts by more conservative forces to reign in the freer economic environment were not successful. Deng also took a more "open" approach toward the outside world. Relations with the U.S. improved after the issue of American arms sales to Taiwan was aired in 1982. A cautious move to improve relations with the Soviet Union was also undertaken.

In 1987, the Thirteenth Party Congress signed off on a policy of moderate political and economic reform. Deng held on to most of his authority. But in 1988, probably as a reaction to rapid uncontrolled growth in the south, a two year suspension of further price reforms was enacted.

1989—Tiananmen Square

The death of Hu Yaobang, once considered the likely successor to Deng, in April 1989, ignited demonstrations by students who had long idolized him as a true reformer. By early May they had turned out by the hundreds of thousands in the larger cities, particularly Beijing, waving banners with statements unheard of in China: "Down with Corruption! . . . Long Live Democracy! . . . Press Freedom!" . . . "Down With Rule By Men, Long Live The Rule Of Law!" A level of student and public activism emerged that had not been

May 21, 1989: *A People's Liberation Army* **convoy is engulfed by demonstrators in Tiananmen Square, Beijing.**   AP Wide World Photo

seen since the most heady days of the 1919 May Fourth Movement seventy years before.

Tiananmen Square was literally taken over by a huge encampment of protesting students some of whom gained even more support by going on a hunger strike to demonstrate their commitment. Not only students but workers in cities throughout China became involved and their demands ranged from moderate calls for further democratization in China to protests against political and economic corruption. A shaken *Communist Party* leader, Zhao Ziyang, mingled with the student demonstrators and made some vague concessions, but was swept aside by Deng Xiaoping and the more conservative Premier Li Peng.

There were clearly conflicting opinions among the leadership on just how to deal with the protesters. Moreover, the leadership itself appeared divided on larger issues of policy regarding the economy. Should it continue its rapid growth or reign in the increasingly open economy toward a more party-dominated one? Who would win in the leadership struggle thus had clear ramifications for China's entire economic future as well. But the more immediate crisis was in the streets and for the moment, the hardliners both political and economic were in the ascendance. For weeks, during a period of leadership indecision complicated by the visit of the Soviet leader Mikhail Gorbachév, the crisis grew and the humiliation of the government leaders along with it.

Suddenly on June 4th tens of thousands of well-armed troops smashed their way through Beijing to the heart of the city, Tiananmen Square. The tanks crushed many in their path; estimates of those killed and wounded were in the thousands. There were reports of soldiers firing indiscriminately into the crowds, invading hospitals to yank out life-support systems of the wounded, attacking doctors and engaging in other violent acts. The hardliners had won, at least for the time being.

The massacre in Beijing was followed by a massive nationwide campaign of political repression involving many arrests. This evoked outrage abroad and some limited, largely temporary, sanctions on the part of China's major trading partners, which had little effect on the hardliners dominant in Beijing.

Parallel with this political crackdown, Deng Xiaoping's economic reform program went into reverse. In fact, some have surmised that the economic conservatives among the leadership had used the confrontation for their own ends, to return to a more Soviet style command economy at almost the same time that the Soviet Union was unraveling. Central control over the economy was strengthened, prices were more closely controlled and there was even talk of the "voluntary" recollectivization of agriculture.

Whatever senior leader Deng's commitment to stopping the political challenge and chaos of the streets in 1989 had been, he himself clearly remained convinced that China needed more, not less, economic freedoms. Thus in early 1992, Deng Xiaoping and his supporters prevailed over conservatives to reinvigorate the eco-

nomic reforms again. The private sector received encouragement and the free market concept was legitimized in the Constitution in 1993. The "open" policy toward the outside world remained in effect, and foreign investment continued to flow in, from the United States as well as from other sources.

In 1990, Beijing tried to improve its international image by taking a moderate public position on the Cambodian and Kuwait crises. It undid much of this, however, by taking advantage of the distraction created by the war in the Persian Gulf to sentence a number of political prisoners accused of involvement in the 1989 demonstrations. That policy of greater international economic involvement, alongside a continuing internal repression of those who would challenge the regime, has continued throughout the 1990s.

Although opposition continued to be sternly repressed, China in the early 1990s experienced one change with important political possibilities. The provinces were gaining in autonomy and authority at the expense of the center. This was especially true of the comparatively prosperous and dynamic provinces along the coast. Nevertheless political discontent in China was prevented from assuming serious proportions partly by the state of the economy, which was doing well in both the private and cooperative sectors although poorly in state-directed enterprises.

The Death of Deng Xiaoping

After years of waiting, the world heard of the news of Deng Xiaoping's death in

China

Deng Xiaoping with the Reagans, Beijing 1984

February 1997. While he had not been influential in decision–making for years, many had waited for word of his death with trepidation. After all, more than once before, the death of a senior leader had set off dramatic developments in the People's Republic. In 1976, both the early death of Zhou Enlai in January and Mao's death in October had set off dramatic changes in the leadership of the country. Indeed, it was only with Mao's death that the forces were released that brought Deng Xiaoping to supreme power. And more recently, the death of the former party Chairman Hu Yaobang, had set off the chain of events that eventually brought on the Tiananmen Crisis of June 1989. But in the first weeks after Deng's death it appeared that nothing of the sort was likely to occur this time around.

Chief among the differences was the very success Deng had brought about. When Deng first emerged in real power in the late 1970s he led a weak China with a military that would soon embarrass itself in the expedition against Vietnam, one which hardly made a dent on the international, political or economic scene. A generation later the China of Deng has been drastically transformed.

In 1978 when Deng's authority began to be significant, Chinese exports to the world were U.S. $9.8 billion, by 1995 they were U.S. $149 billion! Steel production had tripled and urban Chinese lived increasingly in cities that often resembled huge construction sites which were the product of a building boom. More than a decade of double digit growth rates had transformed China. Even the World Bank estimates that the number of people living in poverty had been cut by two thirds!

Thus by the time Deng died an enormous percentage of Chinese felt invested in the new changes. And while there were clear differences between some of the top leaders, the sort of issues that had divided the leadership in 1976 and for a time in 1989 seemed much milder. With even the conservative military making billions from their role in the surging economy there was clearly no turning back from the world that Deng had built. China would be an involved player in the world community. Only the details needed to be worked out. The dramatic and sometimes deadly struggle between the Maoists and the Pragmatists that had characterized aspects of the earlier Mao years seemed to have passed. There was far more general agreement on the new China that Deng had set in motion.

Nevertheless, many in the Western news media, aware of developments which had occurred in the aftermath of the death of other preeminent leaders, had spoken of potential dramas after Deng's death, but long–time observers generally agreed that the lines of succession seemed to have already been in place. Jiang Zemin, 70, appears likely to continue to dominate the political arena as the general secretary of the *Communist Party*. Real change seems more likely to come within the State Council where Li Peng, a more conservative leader, has held the position of Premier. Premier Li will be required to step down from his position during the spring of 1998 when his term expires. Many expect Li's position to be assumed by Zhu Rongji, the respected economics expert who has been in charge of the economy in recent years. Both leaders, Jiang and Zhu, are clearly committed to continuing the general lines of reform though not surprisingly from a more sophisticated perspective than Deng whose education had been from an earlier era.

Another important player in Chinese politics is the National People's Congress. Under its influential chairman Qiao Shi, it has gained more influence in recent years. In 1995, it successfully modified changes in the education system and banking reform sponsored by party leaders. The body also became the locus for increasing popular expressions of opposition to government policy. Perhaps most importantly under Qiao Shi, the body has been especially involved in moving toward a more modern legal system.

At the local level it is now more possible for non–party members to hold important positions of influence, something that would have been practically impossible in the past. Even more interesting has been the decision to allow local elections and to even invite former President Jimmy Carter to serve as an election poll watcher. The *Chinese Communist Party* in recent years has made it clear it intends to remain in ultimate control. Nevertheless it has been willing to allow extraordinary freedoms in the economic arena and on the local level even some political freedoms.

But retaining control does not preclude seeking competence over ideological purity or party cronyism. It looks like China plans to return to some of the roots of its own civilization for help in recruiting qualified personnel. Since 1994, China has moved to return to the time honored system of examinations to recruit candidates for government jobs. High officials have been quoted as saying that China hopes to abolish the current system of appointment by seniority, personal recommendation or degrees with a more regularized civil service examination for all potential civil servants.

The year 1997 is likely to be an especially remembered one for the People's Republic for it will have included not only the death of the patriarch Deng Xiaoping and the return of Hong Kong to the People's Republic but the meetings of the 15th national congress. That and the meeting of the National People's Congress to convene in the spring of 1998 are likely to set the agenda for years to come.

But will the People's Republic simply

President Jiang Zemin

proceed on the path Deng laid out a generation ago? That seems unlikely. Deng Xiaoping was trying to "jump start" an economy that had been artificially wounded by impractical economic leadership. His goal was to reinvigorate the economy through internal reforms and an external opening to the world. But those initial goals were accomplished and his heirs, especially Jiang Zemin, seem committed to refining the economic and social message that dominated Deng's years. Given the current weakness of communism as a unifying message, that seems especially important, thus Jiang's recent efforts to promote what he calls a new spiritual civilization which combines elements of economic growth with both communitarian and nationalist elements.

Jiang has even been heard speaking positively of Confucianism, whose memory had become so defamed during the height of the revolutionary era. But is a greater opening toward democracy on the national level likely? At this point it seems not at all probable. In fact President's Jiang's image of "spiritual civilization" seems to indicate even a lessening of some freedoms. Word has gone out to journalists and others to emphasize support of patriotism and the *Communist Party*. If Beijing is influenced by any outside models at all, it is probably the example set by people like Lee Kuan Yew of Singapore who has been one of the most influential spokesmen for an Asian vision of social and economic governance and a frequent visitor to China.

More than likely the immediate future will be dominated by an economically energetic China led by a reinvigorated *Communist Party* which will be unwilling to accept challenges to its leadership. Although

the vast majority of Chinese have reason to be satisfied with the general flow of developments in China, those that challenge Beijing are likely to feel its wrath. Areas to watch will be developments from Xinjiang in Western China where outbreaks against Chinese rule have resulted in riots and then retribution and summary executions by Chinese officials. More subtly, will be pressures on those in Hong Kong who challenge Beijing's authority under the assumption that the promised autonomy will allow them the same freedom to publicly criticize Beijing they enjoyed under the British. Such an assumption might well be very much in error.

The Rise of Shanghai

In recent years there have been other important changes at or near the top which may effect the future direction of the country. In September 1994, at the fourth plenum of the Fourteenth Central Committee, Huang Ju became a member of the Politburo, the highest major decision–making body in the *Communist Party*. He is now the fourth member of the Politburo from Shanghai. The others are Jiang Zemin, Zhu Rongji, and Wu Bangguo. The four have either served as mayor or party secretary for Shanghai. In addition, several other Politburo members have their roots in Shanghai. Even the new Chinese governor of Hong Kong, Tung Chee Hwa has origins in Shanghai and speaks the local dialect! This suggests

that at a minimum the interests of the region will not be overlooked.

The enormous effort the government has put into building up Pudong, the new economic area just across the river from urban Shanghai, also indicates the central leadership's interest in the city as do the other major projects that have sprung up in recent years. Today, Shanghai is fast returning to its previous position as the preeminent city of the Chinese economy, a development which will no doubt have an impact on how important future Chinese leaders will consider Hong Kong.

Foreign Relations

In many ways the People's Republic has moved to play a more cooperative role internationally. It made offers to host the Olympics in the year 2000 as well as to serve as the site for the 1995 UN–sponsored Fourth World Conference on Women, and a parallel conference of non–governmental organizations (NGO's). Unfortunately, the Olympic bid was ultimately unsuccessful and aroused unneeded tensions during the competition ultimately won by Sydney, Australia. They were able to host the Second United Nation's Conference on Women. The meeting though itself aroused considerable controversy. Some of the advertised facilities were not ready. The NGO meeting was moved and some delegates were prevented by various means from attending. Interestingly, the Western media's

Young workers exercising in the Shanghai Petro-Chemical Works

China

emphases on problems at the conference clouded over the important work that many delegates actually reported upon after their return. Two years later, of course, China had its own revenge of sorts as it enthusiastically took part in the widespread international criticism of American mistakes in running the 1996 Atlanta Olympic games!

It is true as well that China has entered a potentially more assertive period in its foreign relations. The PRC's economic success has created conditions where the country's leaders feel it possible and appropriate for China to assume a higher profile internationally. In effect after more than a century of weakness, Beijing appears ready to to assume its former place of significance in the world. Moreover, as mentioned previously, with the weakening of communism, nationalism remains the best means of unifying the Chinese people, something the central government needs to survive. Thus recent events have shown they are quite willing to play the nationalist "card" to ensure their continuing legitimacy before the Chinese public.

The attempt by Japanese extremists to assert their control over the islands known in Chinese as the Diaoyus last year is a good example of the complexities of nationalism in this new era. On one hand Chinese from all walks of life and throughout the Chinese world literally from Hong Kong to Taiwan and the People's Republic were united in anger against these Japanese efforts. From Beijing's perspective issues with such nationalist sentiment can be helpful as they continue to justify their leadership in the vacuum left by the weakening of communism. On the other hand, when mainland Chinese students used the Internet to create their own networks dedicated to protesting the Japanese acts, the leadership became uncomfortable and closed them down. Arousing popular sentiments can be a complicated matter. Once aroused there isn't always an easy way to control the results!

It was also clear in early 1997 that in many other ways China's new international connections had produced a more complicated foreign policy. Last winter it found itself caught between its old ally North Korea and its new friend South Korea in a struggle over a senior North Korean official who had successfully sought asylum in the South's embassy in Beijing. Beijing obviously wanted to find a solution to the dilemma but it wasn't easy. In the end ties to South Korea proved more influential and the new defector set off indirectly for Seoul.

UNITED STATES–CHINESE RELATIONS

A significant part of China's foreign policy in recent years has centered on resolving issues with the United States. During the early Clinton administration, the United States government's policy was geared toward exacting concessions in the area of human rights from China before economic relations could progress; this included holding up most favored nation (MFN) status, favorable tariff concessions, for China.

In May 1994 however, Washington realized that little headway was being made

Solitary Beauty Peak (Du Xiu Feng) in Guilin, one of hundreds of such peaks along a 50–mile stretch of the Li Jiang River valley of southern China. Many of these limestone formations have caves with intricate Buddhist carvings   Photo by Miller B. Spangler

and the policy modified. Despite his early campaign statements, President Clinton changed his approach to one of "comprehensive engagement," in many ways assuming the same approach to China as the previous Bush Administration.

President Clinton had come to understand that the People's Republic was simply too large and too important to withdraw from economically and diplomatically. Moreover, the previous emphasis on linking trade issues with human rights had simply not worked. Far too many economic and geo–political issues required Beijing's cooperation. China was critical to dealing with issues ranging from North Korea's nuclear aspirations, to progress on nuclear non–proliferation, to working within the United Nations' Security Council where China held a permanent veto. Thus Clinton's new policy delinked China's human rights policy from MFN. Soon afterward the late Commerce Secretary Ron Brown flew into Beijing with a planeload of American businessmen. When they left, they took with them over $6 billion in contracts. In October 1994, Washington ended the ban on hi–tech exports to China, which responded with an agreement not to sell ground–to–ground missiles to other countries.

A major sticking point in China–U.S. relations in the early years of the Clinton administration was the former's desire to be admitted to the GATT and to be a founding member of the new World Trade Organization (WTO). It has not yet been able to meet the conditions set by the developed countries so Beijing's participation remains uncertain. The principal problem was whether China would be admitted as a developing nation or as an already developed one. The definitional issue was important in that each carried with it different requirements about a country's economic obligations to the rest of the world. The Chinese wanted to be admitted as a developing nation. The West insisted it adhere to the standards set for the developed world. Obviously, China, given its enormous size and diversity represents aspects of both. Eventually, after a series of successful trade agreements were signed, the United States finally agreed to work for China's admission to the WTO as a founding member, though the specifics of the obligations it would incur under the world trading system would remain to be established.

By mid 1997 the United States remained supportive of China's entrance which has helped reduce some aspects of Sino–American tensions. Newly reelected President Clinton was talking enthusiastically of building a strong and more positive relationship with the People's Republic. Nevertheless, some issues, like the future of Taiwan and the United States' commit-

ment to the improvement of human rights in China often added to the tension.

As the United States slowly recognized the reality of China's growing strength, many felt compelled to warn of a growing Sino–American Cold War. The reality though was more complicated. As former Secretary of State Henry Kissinger counseled in the days after Deng Xiaoping died, the United States needs to clearly differentiate what in Beijing's future activities represent the natural behavior of a newly powerful great nation and what might more specifically be a real threat to the United States. Clearly they are not necessarily the same thing, but it requires a more sophisticated view than many are willing to apply to understand the difference. As so often in the past, careless errors of perception could end up being a major problem for future generations.

During upcoming months the two most important features of Sino–American relations may well be American concerns about developments in Hong Kong—to what extent Beijing interferes in matters there, and the scandal associated with possible official Chinese contributions to President Clinton's reelection.

American legislation passed in 1992 specifically requires the United States to officially monitor whether Hong Kong is "sufficiently autonomous". This is likely to be cause for considerable disagreement over the coming years. Secondarily, in the early spring of 1997 reports have surfaced in the press about possible Chinese efforts to "purchase" influence within the White House. While no reports were iron–clad as of this writing, Beijing's long frustration with Taiwan's well–known influence in Congress is just the sort of thing that might have encouraged such an effort.

The Triangle

As discussed in the introductory part of this volume, from Beijing's perspective, Taiwan remains the single most important issue in Sino–American relations. Offering a constant counter–weight to Taiwan's efforts to officially rejoin the international community, Beijing continues to apply pressure to any country which cooperates with Taiwan's efforts to integrate itself more formally into this community. The results of such pressure are myriad; the Japanese uninvited President Lee of Taiwan from an Asian games meeting in response to pressure from Beijing. In May 1995, the Chinese Minister of Defense postponed a visit to the United States because President Lee was granted a visa to attend his college reunion at Cornell University.

Under pressure from the Republican majority in Congress, the Clinton Admin-

istration had agreed to allow Lee's June 1995 visit to Cornell. On the surface the visit might appear to have been no more than a personal visit by a former student to his alma mater, but all involved knew it was much more. The visit was a conscious effort by Taiwan's government to continue their quest for international recognition as an entity apart from the People's Republic of China. On both sides of the Taiwan straits it was understood what granting the visa would imply, and within the Clinton administration its rejection was strongly encouraged. Nevertheless, Taiwan has long nurtured allies within the American Congress and they vociferously and successfully insisted that Lee be allowed to visit the United States.

From the perspective of Beijing, granting the visa was a clear indication that the United States had sided with those who encouraged Taiwan's independence. Thus, Lee's visit was viewed as another step toward Washington's abandonment of the "one China policy" which had dated from the Nixon era. From Beijing's especially nationalistic perspective of late, that decision was absolutely unacceptable and relations between the United States and China entered into one of its most difficult periods. Over the next year the situation got worse rather than better.

By the spring of 1996, U.S.–China relations were at an all time low. As Taiwan's first presidential election campaign was going on, Chinese naval forces initiated very provocative military maneuvers off the coast of the Republic—actually firing live shells vaguely in the direction of Taiwan's leading port. As the March election decision drew near Beijing kept up the threatening stance, clearly hoping to weaken the popularity of those who were calling for Taiwan's independence from the mainland.

Washington responded by sending two carriers into the waters off Taiwan. The election took place with a smashing victory for Taiwan's President Lee who had maneuvered his campaign brilliantly between those on the island emphasizing independence and those who wanted reunification with the mainland. China had not succeeded with its scare tactics and in fact probably played into the astute President Lee's politics of ambiguity vis-à-vis the mainland. While Washington and Beijing both publicly stated that conflict was not imminent, it remained for them to withdraw from a needless confrontation.

U.S.–China Economic Relations

Sino–American relationships took on a new potentially burdensome problem in 1996. Although arguments about differing methods of registering trade balances per-

China

Open air market, Shanghai

sist, it is clear the trade imbalance between the United States and China finally appeared poised to pass that between the United States and Japan, thus opening the door to the sort of public confrontations and accusations that have so often strained Japanese–American relations. In fact it actually did so during some periods in 1996. This time, though, the United States seemed committed to base these newly established economic ties on a more equal footing than had evolved over the years with Japan.

Led by the office of the U.S. trade representative, the U.S. and China signed two agreements, the first providing for the protection of copyrights in China, and the second which further opened up Chinese markets for American business. These agreements came only after Mickey Kantor, the U.S. trade representative at that time, threatened Beijing with a 100% tariff increase on over a billion dollars of Chinese exports to the United States. Unfortunately, the success of the agreements too often relied on success in other areas of the complex relationship.

Nevertheless, early 1997 did appear to offer some promise for improved economic relations. The United States and China negotiated a new economic agreement on textile trade early in the year which appeared likely to allow easier sale of American textiles in China in the future. And doing so remains an important goal given the realities of contemporary U.S.–China trade in textiles. As relations stand now, China sells 1000 times more textiles to the United States than the U.S. sells to China!

Defense issues of the People's Republic

The military is enjoying the fruits of economic expansion. One estimate is that about one fifth of all domestically pro-

duced consumer goods in China are produced in factories owned by the military. The army apparently keeps the profits. The army also handles foreign military sales. And, because of its support of the government during the demonstrations of 1989, the defense budget has steadily increased. The Party may be attempting to hedge its bets by insuring the loyalty of the defense establishment.

As a result of this new–found wealth, China may have purchased as much as $2 billion in military hardware from Russia in 1992, and was also able to buy computer equipment from the United States. Now China has begun to worry its neighbors, who are concerned about the possibility of military expansionism. Of particular concern are the Chinese claims to the South China Sea's Spratley Islands with their oil wealth. While an agreement with Vietnam was recently reached to put aside the claims in favor of cooperation in developing under–sea oil deposits, military officials in the region are continuing their own plans for upgrading naval and air capabilities.

The recent spending and especially the purchase of former Soviet equipment adds to the overall effectiveness of the Chinese military. Clearly the surging Chinese economy is giving the People's Republic the ability to strengthen its forces, but for the immediate future its effectiveness remains limited.

Nevertheless, Beijing has been willing to assert itself in disputes regarding many islands in the region. These disputes have ranged from the Diaoyu islands in the East China Sea mentioned previously to the Spratley Islands and Mischief Reef in the South China Sea.

In early 1995, China landed personnel on Mischief Reef, a small speck of land in the Spratley Islands about 110 miles off

the Philippine coast. Philippine patrol boats responded by blowing up Chinese markers in the area. Sixty–two Chinese fisherman were also detained by Manila. Then, in May, a Philippine vessel carrying an international group of journalists was blocked from approaching Mischief Reef. These events led up to the ASEAN Regional Forum and an apparent modification in China's position.

China's occupation of Mischief Reef in the South China Sea galvanized the ASEAN states of Southeast Asia. Beijing made moves to smooth relations with the Philippines, which claims Mischief Reef, and agreed at the Forum to negotiate the issue of the South China Sea on a multilateral versus a bilateral basis, and in accord with international law.

Happily, when Japanese nationalists attempted to assert their claims to what they call the Sankaku Islands (known as the Diaoyus to the Chinese) Beijing played a cautious role even as Chinese nationals from Taiwan to Beijing and Hong Kong were aroused in anger.

Economy

As China moved into 1997 its economic planners had plenty over which to feel satisfied, although its GDP had slowed somewhat. Reports had set the 1996 GDP at 9.7, a very enviable figure for most of the world but slower than China's heights in recent years, but that "slowdown" reflected the government's much discussed interest in a more manageable growth rate which would lessen inflation. And they appear to have succeeded. Inflation which caused so many tensions in recent years seems under control. In fact since 1994 it has come down from 22% to a more manageable 6%. Foreign reserves have climbed to over U.S. $100 billion. No doubt this calmer growth rate played a role in attracting more direct foreign investment; it rose by 7% in 1997 to a record $40 billion. The People's Republic even passed Japan as the world's largest crude steel producer for the year!

This rosy picture masks a fundamental and significant problem facing the Chinese leadership: the cost and inefficiency of state owned enterprises (SOEs). Of the approximate 100,000 SOEs, only about 1/3 of them are profitable. The total cost of propping them up may be as high as $50 billion. About 100 million workers or about 70% of the country's industrial work force is employed in the state sector. With unemployment already high and underemployment at perhaps 20% in the state sector, only token layoffs are politically possible. According to one estimate, to make the state sector profitable, massive closings and a reduction in the work force of at least 30% would be required. However, this would spell disaster for the government. On the other hand, the continued drain on the national economy will eventually produce a crisis of major proportions. The best that Beijing can do is encourage partnerships between profitable and nonprofitable enterprises. A few enterprises did take a more radical approach. For the very brave, there are currently four SOEs on the New York Stock Exchange.

China has long wanted to simply grow past the problem of the state owned enterprises and in many ways they have been making progress. In 1978 they were 77% of the industrial economy. By Deng's death they were only a bit more than a third. Nevertheless, that one third, employs millions of people and remains a major drain on the economy. But given the reality that simply laying off that many people would release unacceptable social tensions, the leadership is unlikely to do anything very drastic to deal with the problems.

Another serious and related challenge to the economy and the political leadership in 1997 was the growing migrant worker population. Neither the state nor the party could control this mass of people. The private sector is not growing fast enough to meet the demand for jobs. And, as economic growth slows as it must to insure stability and stem inflation, the situation will worsen. Urban areas are feeling the influx of poor, less educated, rural Chinese, and are reacting negatively. There is little that Beijing can do.

The biggest issue remains China's effort to join the World Trade Organization. Nothing was certain yet as this book went to press for 1997, but the People's Republic was showing signs of a willingness to revise or abandon some of its own regulations to meet the objections of outsiders. One issue that China was reported willing to modify was a requirement that foreign investors export the vast majority of what they manufactured in China. Having the right to sell locally–produced material in the People's Republic would obviously be helpful to foreign investors, and China's willingness to abandon such restrictions may signal progress on its application to join the World Trade body.

CULTURE AND SOCIETY

The twentieth century has seen extraordinary changes in culture and society in China. Ironically, Chinese communities in Hong Kong, the PRC and Taiwan spent much of the late 1900s moving farther apart while during the last decade of the 20th century, their societies have started to appear more similar again. Keeping up with these changes is breathtaking for the outside observer, actually living them would be astounding.

In 1900 when our century began most Chinese were rural peasants living very simple lives as farmers. The fundamental and lasting institutions of family life and farming completely dominated Chinese culture for thousands of years; this was certainly true throughout most of Asia, but these two foundations were developed to a higher level within China. Agriculture combined the careful cultivation of cereal grains, skillful efforts to control water by the construction of levees and irrigation ditches, and the return of all available fertilizer, including human waste, to the soil. This permitted high nutritional content of the harvests, which in turn permitted a rapid rate of population growth. The family was the basic social unit—above it stood the village, governed usually by the heads of the leading families; contact with central government officials was avoided by the elders with varying degrees of success.

The society was dominated by an intellectual elite known as gentry who were very influential on the local level and supplied most of the personnel for the imperial bureaucracy which ran the empire. The traditional upper class culture was also based on the family and on the group of related families which together formed a

In 1996, China became the largest steel producer in the world.

China

The Great Wall of China, still one of the world's major tourist attractions

clan. Ancestor worship, involving sacrifices to dead forebears, who were not considered to be actually divine, had begun among the upper classes and spread to the lower classes. The wealthy avoided manual labor and regarded literacy and education (especially in the Confucian tradition), ownership of land and public service, as the highest social goals and symbols of status. This upper crust, dominating education, government service and land ownership, was not so exclusive that the lower classes were entirely excluded from it. Unlike India, China never had a caste system as part of its culture, but in reality, it was highly unusual for a person of peasant origin to acquire enough education, wealth or influence to move to the top of the social scale.

In spite of tendencies toward conservatism and anti–foreignism, traditional Chinese culture was probably the richest, and certainly the longest lived and most continuous of the great civilizations, ancient and modern, of the world. It was relatively free from the religious bigotry and intolerance that was evident in much of Western history. In contrast to the principles of decaying despotism of France under the Bourbon kings, China's traditional philosophy and culture greatly impressed well–educated Jesuit missionaries

who came to China in the 17th century. Through his writings, the French writer and philosopher Voltaire communicated some of these Chinese ideals to the education of Europe.

The decline of the traditional Chinese political system in the late 19th and early 20th centuries brought a loss of confidence in many aspects of the traditional Chinese cultural values. Education was increasingly altered to conform to Western ideals; literature began to be written in the vernacular, or conversational language, rather than in the old, more difficult and formal literary language.

By the early years of the 20th century new groups of elites and workers became significant. On the elite level, new types of soldiers, business people, and intellectuals emerged as well as the formation of a new industrial working class that lived in the Western ports. China was starting its extraordinary century–long transformation.

During the 1920's, the new ideas and values including Marxism were gaining ground among intellectuals. At the level of the uneducated, the solidarity of the family was greatly weakened by the beginnings of economic progress toward industrialization, which created jobs for women, drawing them away from their families to the factories in the cities. The Japanese in-

vasion in 1937 and the ensuing chaos uprooted millions of people and heavily contributed to the further breakdown of the traditional social and cultural order.

In the first generation after the second world war, society in the several parts of China began to diverge. Both Taiwan and Hong Kong were aligned with the Western capitalist economies and each saw tremendous economic changes in their respective communities over the years. Economic growth was significant and people's lives were dramatically altered by the changing circumstances.

Within the People's Republic in contrast, while economic growth remained the principal goal, Mao Zedong's ideologically driven approach, as demonstrated in the Great Leap Forward and the Cultural Revolution, failed to economically raise people's living standards; indeed at times the situation simply deteriorated dramatically. Even a casual visitor to the area in the late 1970s and early 1980s could see a great difference in the life style of these different parts of the Chinese community.

But again, the revolutionary cycle has changed and since the late 1970s under the direction of Deng Xiaoping, the People's Republic has itself chosen to enter and compete in the world market. And it has done so with enormous success. Real gains have been made in people's economic possibilities. Individual citizens can now purchase their own apartments, and professionals like lawyers are free to privately organize themselves to develop clients.

Although the West hears much about the harsh repression of individual dissidents who have chosen to challenge the state, the reality of a more general improvement in human rights is also true. Unlike in the past, criminal lawyers are now officially allowed to represent their clients rather than the state; and people have successfully sued the government for false arrest and detention.

Chinese Women

Chinese women have often been among the biggest winners of the 20th century changes. Beginning the century with almost no rights or education they were more often than not controlled partly through the painful process of foot binding. Yet by the early years of the century, women's education, even at the college level, was much more common, and foot binding less and less practiced. The Communist Revolution of 1949 moved as well to improve their status and the next year passed laws giving them more rights. At the height of Mao Zedong's influence, the circumstance of women and men did not widely vary. Neither had much personal freedom. On the other hand it was difficult for those who controlled the factories to dismiss anyone, so at least more economic security was possible.

More recent changes though have again altered the circumstances of many women. Given the decision–making powers to hire and fire, many employers have made it clear they preferred males as workers to avoid the expenses associated with maternity leave; industries which have been especially associated with female labor have been particularly hit by cutbacks.

Women have as well been especially impacted by the efforts to control the population. With a burgeoning population of more than one billion people, China has not surprisingly been pursuing since 1979 an energetic program to reduce population growth to zero or below. A very real system of "carrot and stick" has been employed under the title of the "One Child Policy" though that has never been an absolute goal for the entire country. Stringent regulations have been promulgated which include stiff taxation, forced abortions and economic penalties against couples who exceed the established limit of one child, while significant financial and other incentives have been offered to those who cooperate. Not surprisingly there have been abuses. Local officials have often forced pregnant women to abort. The program has been relatively successful according to the government, but this is impossible to verify.

This program is very controversial both inside and outside China; yet no one would argue against the importance of China maintaining a stable rather than constantly rising population. But the burden of adhering to the population control measures more often affects women than men. They are of course the principal targets for efforts to monitor fertility and are most responsible for pressuring people to adhere as well.

———— • ————

Like so much of the rest of the world Chinese society ends the 20th century grappling with the meaning of the emergence of the personal computer and the networking of much of the globe through the Internet. Even in the People's Republic, which initially lagged behind in computer use, sales are booming as parents buy P.C.s hoping to give their children an edge in the future job market. Over 1.8 million computers were sold in China last year, many of them into the homes of the emerging middle class.

The Internet

Not surprisingly the government, well aware both of the importance of the emerging global networks and of its own insistence on retaining ultimate control, is experimenting with means to have it both ways. The year 1997 saw many reports of PRC officials hoping to incorporate a more controlled model of telecommunications—an "intranet" model designed for the more closed corporate environment—to give political decision makers more control over what is available to Chinese users of the Internet. But regardless of the details, it seems highly unlikely that Beijing will be able to shield its citizens from the global telecommunications revolution that is enveloping the planet. Chinese society will, as many other societies, be dramatically impacted by changes which the most perceptive among us can only vaguely speculate at this point.

THE FUTURE

For much of human history China was at the forefront of the human experience in both the arts and sciences but that extraordinary series of accomplishments ground to a halt in the late 18th century as the West, newly invigorated by the Enlightenment and the Industrial Revolution, surged ahead. For almost two hundred years, dramatic internal problems and external pressures ranging from Western imperialists to Japanese invaders kept China from regaining its traditional place at the forefront of the human drama. But things have now changed. The generation long surge of economic building set off by Deng Xiaoping has helped China pull itself out of the two century long doldrums within which it had fallen. The central reality of our time is that China is back and ready to resume its place of importance. The ramifications of that development are monumental.

Some have warned about the potential dangers of China's industrialization on the world's environment or food supplies. Others speak of a flood of industrialized goods overwhelming the world's economic system and some even talk of a new "cold" and even possibly "hot" war with China. The only thing that is really certain is that one of the world's great peoples have found their way into the modern industrialized world. Adjustments will have to be made.

Billboard encouraging family planning   Photo by Miller B. Spangler

39

HONG KONG:
Special Administrative Region of the PRC
since July 1997

Area: 398 square miles.
Population: 5.7 million (estimated).
Administrative Capital: Victoria.

The former British Crown Colony of Hong Kong consists of three parts. The first is the island of Victoria (or Hong Kong Island) on the north side of which the city of the same name is located. The second part is the small area known as Kowloon, at the tip of the peninsula jutting from the Chinese mainland toward Victoria. Between Victoria and Kowloon lies one of the world's busiest and most beautiful harbors. The third part is composed of the New Territories, which extend northward from Kowloon to the Chinese border, and also include some islands in the waters around Victoria. Kowloon is connected by rail with the Chinese city of Guangzhou (Canton).

Most of the area of Hong Kong consists of hills and low mountains, but there are enough level lands in the New Territories for large quantities of food to be harvested; Hong Kong is actually dependent for much of its food and water on the mainland of China. The population is almost totally Chinese, many of them having arrived since 1949 in order to find greater safety, freedom and economic opportunity than was allowed on the troubled mainland of China. The climate is subtropical and monsoonal in the summer, but relatively cool in the winter.

Realizing the potential value as a naval base, although not seeing at first the commercial possibilities of Hong Kong, the British annexed it from the Manchus in 1842, after the first Opium War. Under an effective British administration, and sharing in the increase of British trade with

and investments in China during the nineteenth and early twentieth centuries, Hong Kong experienced rapid growth as a port. Kowloon was annexed in 1860, after Anglo–French forces again attacked China. The New Territories were added in 1898 in order to provide agricultural land and living space for the growing population but were held on a 99–year lease. It is of course that lease that ran out in the summer of 1997.

Given their large population, Victoria and Kowloon could not survive without the New Territories.

During the damaging Japanese occupation of Hong Kong from 1941–45, and the Communist takeover in China in 1949, Hong Kong's "trade" with the mainland of China was increasingly confined to the import of food, water, and consumer goods.

40

Nearly forty–five per cent of the mainland's foreign trade passes though Hong Kong. The former colony has excellent port facilities and commercial relations with the rest of Asia. In the 1960's, foreign capital, including that from America and Japan, poured into Hong Kong, building apartments, erecting office buildings and light industrial plants in particular.

Toward Unification with the Mainland

Much of Hong Kong's recent economic success is directly tied to the changing policies of the People's Republic of China. The ideologically driven PRC of Mao Zedong hardly needed Hong Kong's economic strengths, but Deng Xiaoping's arrival to power in the late 1970s brought change. Deng was determined to open China up to the world and to begin the effort in the southernmost parts of China. Under the circumstances, the British colony, with its abundant knowledge of both China and the Western world was in a perfect position to contribute to and take advantage of Beijing's changing economic policies.

Just north of the Hong Kong border, Beijing established special economic zones which would eventually become the earliest engines of China's resurgence in which Hong Kong was able to take part. Hong Kong's economy, which had earlier been less tied to the People's Republic, actually began the first steps, at that point economic, in its reintegration with the mainland. Thus China's economic accomplishments became Hong Kong's as well and the momentum toward 1997 already begun.

Ironically, given some of the tensions which arose in the years before the 1997 hand–over of Hong Kong to the PRC, it was the British who had pushed for treaties to resolve the impending end of the 99–year leases of 1898. In Beijing's perspective, none of the nineteenth century treaties imposed on China by the imperialistic West had any validity, so there was no reason to consider 1997 any different.

But the British wanted the fate of their colony, the last Asian remnant of their once enormous Asian colonial system, resolved, and insisted on negotiations. Happily, during those years the two powers worked well together and the Sino–British Joint Declaration on Hong Kong was signed in 1984. The United Kingdom even agreed somewhat later to coordinate its changes in Hong Kong with the People's Republic. Thus, Britain unilaterally gave up the right to change the Hong Kong political system which for the colony's entire history had meant being ruled undemocratically by a series of governors sent from London.

Within the agreement Beijing promised

to leave the existing economic and social systems essentially unchanged for at least fifty years after 1997 as well as to permit a degree of self–government. Although there will be no way to compel Beijing to honor this pledge if it chooses not to do so, most of the population of Hong Kong—who have nowhere else to go—appear to have resigned themselves reluctantly to a future under the Chinese flag. White collar and professional workers however have emigrated in considerable numbers, over 500,000 alone in the last twelve years. The British announcement that many of the more elite Hong Kong families would receive the right to live in the United Kingdom if they so chose was made to help shore up confidence in the aftermath of the Tiananmen Square demonstrations of 1989.

Ironically, during the last years before 1997 both Beijing and London have shown an increasing willingness to violate the spirit of the 1984 treaty. Britain on its part, long happy with governing Hong Kong under its own benign colonial dictatorship, moved aggressively, especially under its last colonial governor, to transform Hong Kong into an increasingly democratic political entity, something Beijing had hardly agreed to. Even a bill of rights was introduced by 1991.

With the appointment of former Conservative Party MP, Chris Patten, to the post of Governor of Hong Kong in 1992, the British had apparently decided to take a stronger hand in determining the future of the colony's government prior to their withdrawal in 1997. Even before Governor Patten's appointment, the British had taken some steps to strengthen the democratic process in Hong Kong. In September 1991, elections were held for 18 of the 61 seats on the Legislative Council (Legco). Sixteen of these seats were won by pro–democratic candidates. This election gave a considerable boost to the pro–democracy movement, though it did not make the Chinese on the mainland happy. The first truly free election did not occur until 1995—only two years before the turnover.

Not surprisingly these last minute British changes have aroused the anger of the Chinese government. The basic disagreement between the British and the Chinese had to do with the type of government Hong Kong would have. Beijing had in mind an executive–dominated government for Hong Kong, where the legislature plays the role of an adviser. The British in contrast moved to establish a strong, elected legislative assembly and more freedoms than they themselves had ever tolerated.

In December of 1996 Tung Chee Hwa, a shipping company magnate, was elected by the 400 member selection committee to be the first chief executive for Hong Kong after the transition. Almost 6000 people had applied for membership in the committee and a final 400 eventually selected Tung. Tung Chee Hwa to many seemed an especially appropriate choice. His personal background has well prepared him to deal with challenges ahead. A Shanghai–born Chinese who speaks the same dialect as many of China's new leaders, Tung lived for a decade in the United States and has many ties there. He has been involved with the United States Chamber of Commerce, the Hoover Institution and the Council of Foreign Relations.

He is said to count former president

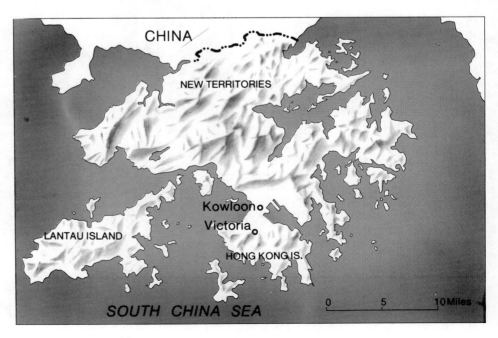

CHINA

NEW TERRITORIES

Kowloon
Victoria

LANTAU ISLAND

HONG KONG IS.

SOUTH CHINA SEA

0   5   10 Miles

China

Chief Executive Tung Chee Hua

how little the two groups had come to understand each other despite more than a century of interaction.

The British efforts toward democratization clearly complemented Western political and social values though one might ask sarcastically why Britain had waited so long to introduce them. What they did not complement was efforts to make a smooth transition from Hong Kong's earlier status as a colony to its future as part of the People's Republic which, despite Western preferences, continues to be controlled by an authoritarian, single–party government. Thus the fact remains that the real legacy of these last minute's efforts to transform Hong Kong into a democracy may not be democracy itself but of having gotten Beijing into the habit of intervening in Hong Kong's affairs. Such a legacy will hardly be helpful for the people of Hong Kong.

The other big question of course is the future of Hong Kong's vibrant economy which is intimately linked both to the Western economies and that of the People's Republic. For the moment Hong Kong seems likely to continue economically as it has before, but there are potential problems looming on the horizon. Much of Hong Kong's recent strength came from it's role as an economic intermediary between the global economy and China. But now that Shanghai has been allowed to resume its place as an economic powerhouse in the People's Republic, and Taiwan is moving toward more and more direct economic ties with the mainland, one has to ask for how much longer Hong Kong will remain important. The short term economic situation seems relatively assured. The long term issue though is something quite different.

Bush among his personal friends. Moreover he had already served as an advisor in the British administration of Hong Kong. That China's leader Jiang Zemin favored him was also known previous to the selection.

Following Tung's selection, Rita Fan, a former legislator and advisor for the British colonial administration, was chosen to lead the new provisional legislature with which China planned to replace the current Hong Kong legislature. She, too, is from Shanghai, another example of the growing influence of that city in Chinese politics.

A Difficult Transition

Throughout early 1997 tensions ran high regarding the upcoming transition. Beijing, following through on its long standing rejection of those political changes Britain had made, planned to repeal many of the new laws. Most controversial was Beijing's plan to reinstate provisions against demonstrating without government approval and the ban on ties with foreign groups. The reinstatement of these laws, which had been part of British colonial controls and ironically are common in many other Asian governments, became, given the tense environment, a major cause of international concern.

There was as well considerable talk of the undemocratic aspects of Tung's election though with little appreciation that he was actually the most democratically elected leader in Hong Kong's history and the first Chinese! If anything, these tensions during the hand–over underscored

View from the Peak on Hong Kong Island looking towards the North Point

MACAU
Portuguese Dependency until 1999

Senate Square, Macau

Area: 6 square miles.
Population: 450,000 (estimated).

Portugal's only remaining overseas territory, Macau, is divided about equally into Macau proper, which has a common land frontier with the Chinese mainland, and two nearby islands. The terrain is mostly flat. The offshore waters are muddy with silt carried by the Pearl River. The climate is subtropical, with a summer monsoon and a relatively cool winter. Except for a small community of Portuguese (officials, soldiers, police, missionaries, businessmen, etc.) and other Europeans, the population is overwhelmingly Chinese.

Portugal acquired Macau in the mid–16th century for use as a base from which to trade with nearby Canton by an agreement with the Ming dynasty of China. It became prosperous in this way in the 18th century, but during the 19th century it was rapidly overshadowed by Hong Kong. It was not occupied by the Japanese during World War II, however, as was Hong Kong. From its earlier days of prominence, Macau has retained some beautiful old buildings and something of

a Mediterranean flavor. It has a reputation, partly justified but also somewhat exaggerated, as a center of opium and gold smuggling and assorted vice. Gambling is unquestionably a major feature of the economy, and auto racing and bullfighting have recently been introduced as well.

The new government of Portugal after 1974 wanted to return Macau to China, but Beijing would not accept it, because of the disturbing effect that such a transfer would have on Hong Kong. Portugal did agree to allow more internal autonomy to its former colony in 1976 and granted it increased powers in 1990. Once the Sino–British agreement was reached on Hong Kong in 1984, however, negotiations began in 1986 between Lisbon and Beijing for the reversion of Macau to Chinese control. It was agreed in April 1987 that reversion would take place in 1999, along lines similar to those already worked out for Hong Kong. Certain concessions were granted to Macau's leaders. For example, it was agreed recently that capital punishment, common in the People's Republic, would be employed in Macau.

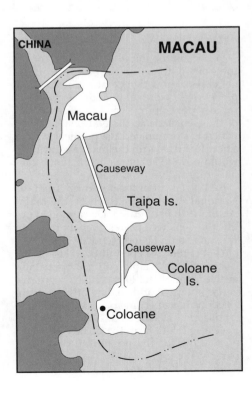

43

Taiwan: Republic of China

For BASIC FACTS on Taiwan: Republic of China, see page 14

Downtown Taipei

Politics in the Republic of China constitutes one of the more clear and encouraging cases of how democratization can take place over time alongside a modern, rapidly developing economy. Even critics of the Guomindang, the Nationalist Party which has dominated the political system since the break with the mainland in 1949, would have to acknowledge that substantial progress has been made.

By 1991, most of the holdovers from the National Assembly elected on the mainland in 1948 had retired. Discussion of politically sensitive issues such as whether Taiwan should be independent of the People's Republic was permitted at last by the Guomindang. A viable political opposition in the form of the Democratic Progressive Party emerged, and free, relatively clean, elections have become part of the political landscape. Disaffected GMD members have also left to form the Chinese New Party, making for the possibility of a three party system.

Much of the contention among the par-ties has centered on the independence versus unification issue. The New Party was more representative of the old line GMD which claimed the right to rule over one China. President Lee's GMD took a centrist approach, while the DPP was openly supportive of an independent Taiwan. The Chinese New Party was not able to establish itself nationally.

Further evolution of the political system also came about when steps were recently taken to strengthen the position of the president. Constitutional amendments provided for the direct election of the president and also granted the president the authority to appoint and dismiss high government officials without the consent of the prime minister. The GMD dominated legislature also strengthened presidential power over three important agencies. The position of president has become far more than ceremonial.

On March 23, 1996, Taiwan held its first ever presidential election. The incumbent president, Lee Teng–hui, was elected with 54% of the vote. The voters rallied around their serving president who had skillfully raised Taiwan's diplomatic profile by meeting with several ASEAN heads of state, and visiting the United States. Peng Ming–min, the Democratic Progressive Party candidate, came in second with 21% of the vote. Peng is an open supporter of Taiwan's independence.

Beijing, no doubt concerned about the rising popularity of efforts to disassociate Taiwan further from the mainland, made a crude effort to intimidate voters there by staging military maneuvers in the weeks leading up to the election. While Beijing's exact motives are not completely clear the result of their threats was to complement President Lee's efforts to fix his candidacy in the middle of the Taiwan political spectrum. Thus he became the election's big winner while the votes of both those advocating declaring formal independence and those encouraging closer ties to the mainland went down. Beijing ended up with a newly strengthened Taiwanese

President with something of a mandate to continue his politics of ambiguity toward the mainland.

Taiwan's Foreign Relations

The fundamental goal of Taiwan's foreign policy is to gain international recognition. This is seen as essential to the island's survival as an independent state; it has become more important each year. Taiwan is drawing economically closer to mainland China because of huge investments flowing in that direction. Thus its leaders know that they will need a counter–balancing political legitimacy capable of preventing the country from being swallowed up. There is no question that Taiwan is an independent entity in economic terms. The question of its official political standing has not yet been settled. Nevertheless Taiwan, with its NIC (Newly Industrialized Country) size economy has long been viewed as an independent actor by much of the global community. But politically things are less certain and Taiwan's efforts to gain further international recognition have regularly met with Beijing's active opposition.

In January 1994, the prime minister visited Singapore and Malaysia. President Lee then visited the Philippines, Indonesia and Thailand. The Thai prime minister, under pressure from Beijing, did not meet with the president. The meeting in Indonesia was unofficial. President Ramos of the Philippines did meet the Taiwanese head of state. A major disappointment was that the president was not able to attend the second APEC meeting in Indonesia in November. The APEC nations' deference to Beijing does not change the fact that Taiwan is a major economic player in Asia. Nor has Taiwan been able to make any real progress on gaining admission to the United Nations. Everyone thinks China is just too big to ignore.

From Taiwan's perspective, some progress was made when officials from the American Institute in Taipei, the unofficial American presence in Taiwan, were allowed to meet with Taiwanese officials. For Taiwan itself, the struggle remains an ongoing one. South Africa late in 1996 withdrew its recognition and opened relations with Beijing. The German government, much to President Lee's frustration, has refused to sell the Republic of China the submarines it has sought to buy.

There have been successes of course. One very important one occurred in the spring of 1995 when President Lee left for the United States for a speaking engage-

President Lee Teng–hui

ment at Cornell University. It was made possible when the Clinton Administration gave in to pressure from Taiwan's supporters in the Congress to grant the Taiwan president a visa.

The ramifications of that success though came at a high price for many involved. Relations between the People's Republic and the United States were at an all time low for a time, and if allegations surfacing by 1997 about Beijing's efforts to influence the 1996 elections prove true, they may originally stem from the People's Republic's frustration with its inability to compete with the Taiwan lobby within the United States Congress!

Taiwan's Economy

While official political relations with the mainland continue to be discussed in at times harsh terms, the reality is that Taiwan is growing more and more close to the mainland economically. Taiwan has invested billions in the mainland and connections between the two grow more and more common. This last winter plans were finally formalized to allow direct shipping between Taiwan's largest port at Kaohsiung to Xiamen and Fuzhou. For the time being the arrangement is only for the ships of foreign nationals and no direct cargo will be carried from the mainland to Taiwan, but that day is surely coming.

For 1995, GDP advanced 6.4%, slightly below expectations. In spite of President Lee's efforts, unemployment remained at 8%, rising to 10% in 1995. (Most countries would consider this as full employment) Although still doing very well, Taiwan may be moving into a situation where it is the victim of its own success. As the economy matures and wages rise, it is harder to maintain competitiveness with the "younger," booming economies of Asia. The country was also rocked by significant financial scandals during the 1995. In addition, slumping real estate prices, a sagging auto market, and a business downturn resulting from tensions with Beijing all combined for a less than spectacular 1995.

Like so many rapidly developing countries, there is a problem with infrastructure. Because domestic investment was not all that strong, the government held up many projects needed to modernize the country. While the outflow of investment funds signaled opportunities for Taiwanese businessmen to reap substantial profits, some of these funds could have been used at home to directly benefit the domestic economy. Hundreds of construction projects outlined in the Six Year Plan were curtailed, including a high speed rail system. Taipei's mass rapid transit system (MRTS) also ran into serious trouble which will result in delays and loss of funds.

In 1996, the economy repeated the performance of previous years with growth at about 6.6%. Per capita GDP was $14,295. Economists worried about a possible slowdown—rising wages, costs of land and increasing concern for the environment are all important factors.

Taiwan's Future

Taiwan needs to continue on its quest for international legitimacy. Its economy is sound and its politics is evolving in the right direction. If it can protect itself against shock waves coming from the mainland, its future can be bright. The biggest challenge will remain gaining as much political legitimacy as possible in the international community without arousing Beijing too much. Continuing to involve itself in the international community is important. Declaring independence would probably be counterproductive.

East China Sea

Sanching
Keelung
Taoyuan
Taipei
Hsinchu
Ilan

Taiwan Strait
(Formosa Strait)

Homei
Taichung
Changhua
Hualien

Penghu
Islands
Chiai

Pacific
Ocean

Tainan
Kaohsiung
Pingtung
Taitung

TAIWAN

MILES
0   25   50

0   25 50   75
KILOMETERS

Luzon Strait

Tokyo's shopping district, the Ginza, at night. *Courtesy: Japanese Embassy.*

Japan

Area: 142,726 sq. mi (370,370 sq. km.)

Population: 125,449,703 (est. 1996).

Capital City: Tokyo (Pop. 9.5 million, estimated).

Climate: Subtropically warm in the extreme South, becoming temperate in the North. The high elevations have much lower temperatures than the coastal areas. There is a rainy monsoon from June to October.

Neighboring Countries: The islands of Japan are closest to Russia (North); Korea (West); and mainland China (Southwest).

Official Language: Japanese.

Ethnic Background: Overwhelmingly Japanese—99.4%—and some Koreans. There is a very small community of *Ainu* on Hokkaido Island who are physically very different from the Japanese, possibly descended from the earliest inhabitants of the islands.

Principal Religions: Shinto, the earliest religious tradition, and Buddhism. The latter is especially widespread and split into many old and new sects; Christianity.

Main Export (to U.S., nations of Southeast Asia and Western Europe): Products of heavy industry, including ships and autos, products of lighter industry, including consumer electronics, cameras, and a wide range of other items, i.e., textiles, iron, steel, fish.

Main Imports (from nations of the Middle East and Southeast Asia): Oil, raw industrial materials, foodstuffs.

Currency: Yen.

National Day: December 23 (birthday of the Emperor).

Special Holiday: April 29, called "Green Day" to honor the late Emperor's interest in the environment.

Chief of State: Emperor Akihito.

Head of Government: Ryutaro Hashimoto, Prime Minister (January 1996).

National Flag: White, with a red disk representing the rising sun in the center.

Per Capita GDP Income: U.S. $21,300.

The island nation of Japan consists of four larger bodies of land, Hokkaido, Honshu, Shikoku and Kyushu and the smaller Ryukyu Islands south of Kyushu. The southern half of Sakhalin and the Kurile Islands to the north, which Japan possessed at the height of its World War II power, were lost to the Soviet Union at the close of the conflict.

Geographically, Japan is part of an immense hump on the earth's surface which extends from Siberia on the Asian continent through Korea and Japan southward, rising above water again in the areas of Taiwan and the Philippines and extending further south into the eastern portions of Indonesia and Australia. As is true in oth-

er portions of the ridge, Japan is geologically unstable and subject to frequent and sometimes violent earthquakes. Thermal pressures from deep in the earth escape periodically through the many volcanoes which are interspersed among the mountains. Mt. Fuji, its lofty crater surrounded by a mantle of snow, is visible from the streets of Tokyo on a clear day—one of the most beautiful sights in Asia. It has not been active since 1719. All of the mountainous areas, volcanic and non–volcanic, are scenic—the taller peaks on Honshu have justly earned the name "Japanese Alps."

The mountains leave little level space; only about 15% of the total land area is level, and much of the only large plain is occupied by the huge and busy capital of Tokyo. As a result, farms are located in the hilly areas of the islands and are made level by the labors of the farmers, who have constructed elaborate terraces in order to

win more land for their intense cultivation. Japanese farming is actually better called gardening, since the small units of land, an average of 2–1/2 to 5 acres per farm, are tilled with such energy that none of the soil or available growing season is wasted. This tremendous agricultural effort produces almost enough to feed the people, most of whom live in densely packed urban areas.

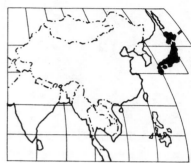

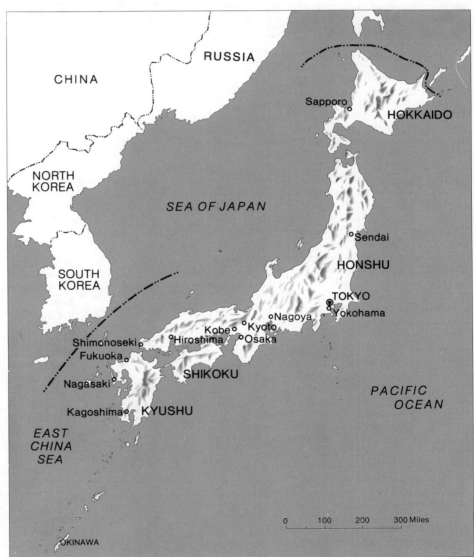

Japan

"Bullet" train streaking commuters home against the majestic background of Mt. Fuji

The climate of the islands is totally dominated by the seasonal winds, or monsoons. Cold winds blowing from the Asian continent invade the land beginning in September each year. All of Hokkaido and a substantial part of Honshu lie buried in snow from December to March. In the spring, the winds shift, blowing from the warm equatorial South Pacific; the growing season of Honshu and Hokkaido then commences.

The subtropical island of Kyushu remains warm all year around, permitting two or three harvests of paddy rice each year. Only one crop of dry, or field rice, grows in the much shorter summer of Hokkaido. In the last half of August and in September, the southern monsoon brings typhoons (hurricanes), laden with rainfall and often destruction from the Pacific to the shores of Japan.

Rainfall and weather are also affected by the oceanic water currents which envelop the islands. The warm southern *Juro Siwo* dominates the summer months; the arctic *Oya Siwo* descends as far south as Tokyo in the winter. Both currents bring a huge number of fish to the off–shore areas on the Pacific side, and an even larger number to the Sea of Japan. Depending almost wholly for animal protein upon this bounty from the sea, the Japanese raise only an insignificant number of livestock on the islands.

History: The earliest known inhabitants of the Japanese islands were probably the Ainu, a people who are physically very different from the Japanese. For much of Japan's history the Ainu people were driven steadily northward by the people arriving from mainland Asia. The Ainu exist today in small reservations on the island of Hokkaido where in recent years they have launched efforts among them to revive their ancient culture. The men have much more body and facial hair than the Japanese. Archeological evidence reveals the existence of a neolithic culture in Japan from about 10,000 B.C. known as *Jo-man*, from the rope patterned ceramics they produced. This community was apparently displaced around 300 B.C. with the arrival of other people from mainland Asia who introduced a rice–growing culture known as *Yayoi*.

The people who eventually formed the community we know as "Japanese" had themselves come primarily from the mainland of northeast Asia, by way of Korea, and are of the same linguistic ancestry as the Koreans. They were mainly of Mongolian stock whose ancestors had lived a nomadic existence on the continent

An Ainu elder   Courtesy: Jon Markham Morrow

of Central and Northeast Asia. This ethnic group became the predominant one, but there were also other elements from the South China coast and the Southwest Pacific.

All of these elements gradually blended into a people possessing very similar physical characteristics, considering the large size of the present population. In the first centuries A.D., the Japanese lived mainly around the Inland Sea, a body of water almost completely enclosed by three of the four large islands. They were organized into many warring clans and had no writing system with which to express their language, which is derived from dialects originally spoken in what is now Manchuria, Mongolia and Siberian Russia.

Japanese tradition tells of the creation of the islands by the sun goddess whose descendants founded the Yamato clan which eventually emerged as the Japanese imperial family. Actually, there is considerable evidence to suggest that the real origins of the imperial elite are to be found, not in Japan itself, but in Korea. In fact, some authors, going beyond the more vague references to "continental influences" have argued succinctly that the original Japanese ruling family was founded by the early southern Korean kingdom of Paekche. Whatever the specific ties to Korea, it is certain that the evolution of Japan was fundamentally altered by its leadership's decision to immerse itself in the culture of the continent in the 6th century A.D.

Encounter with China

The Japanese were greatly impressed by the tales told of Tang (618–907 A.D.)—China's power, wealth, prestige and culture. They quickly set about importing many aspects of Chinese civilization. Religiously, Buddhism was at its height and it was through that medium that a range of cultural, linguistic and political elements of Chinese civilization entered Japan. On a political level, the Yamato clan was interested in borrowing the Chinese imperial system since it offered the possibility of greatly enhancing their power far above the influence the clan had long held.

In an attempt to imitate the Tang dynasty, the Japanese imperial court built a capital at Nara, near the waters of the Inland Sea on the island of Honshu; they worked to establish a centralized governing system along Chinese imperial models. For a time the influence of China was enormous. The Chinese language was adopted as the official writing system and played a role similar to that of Latin in the medieval west. Later Kyoto emerged as the new imperial capital in the late 8th century and became the home of a brilliant culture. Histories were produced to "prove" the divinity and supremacy of the Yamata imperial clan. The 7th century B.C. was selected as the time that the sun goddess was said to have given the blessing of creation to Japan and established the reign of her descendants on the islands.

Imperial Court Life

Within court life at Kyoto, the arts flourished, especially a particularly distinctive literature which many believe to have been the world's first formal novels. The physical form of the novels, produced by women of the imperial court, was influential as well. Interestingly, although literary production was considered a fundamental talent for both men and women of the imperial court, the men largely wrote in the adopted language of Chinese. Women, who in contrast, wrote using a system of modified characters known as Kana to represent the sounds of Japanese, went on to write these profoundly influential works.

The best known of them, the *Tale of Genji,* a thousand page work about the romances of Prince Genji of the imperial court, is a sophisticated novel which deals with an extraordinary range of human emotions and sentiment. It is a far more personal and introspective work than the romances that had preceded it either in Japan or elsewhere. Written by Murasaki Shikibu during the early 11th century, the work ultimately became the model of refined behavior for educated Japanese, a literary influence that could only be compared to that of Shakespeare in the West.

As time passed and Imperial Tang China itself faded, the more direct links to China were severed. After the tenth century no more formal missions were sent to the Chinese court. By then the Japanese aristocracy was ready to build their own syntheses from both earlier Japanese traditions and the more recent borrowing from the court. If however, many aspects of the period of tutelage continued to influence Japan over the centuries, the Yamata imperial family's efforts to establish themselves as Chinese–style emperors failed.

The creation of a true central government was not possible because many

clans, particularly those in central and northern Japan, were strong and independent—preoccupied with battling the Ainu people and each other. These clans did not attempt to overthrow the imperial court, however. They contented themselves with largely ignoring it. Moreover many had ties to powerful court factions which gave then additional autonomy.

Although the more martial, semi–independent clans outside the capital admired and imitated the cultural achievements of imperial Kyoto, they were primarily interested in the military power. The Taira, one of the two most powerful military clans, defeated the other, the Minamoto, in 1160 and then temporarily seized control of Kyoto. Shortly afterward, the Taira were in turn defeated by the Minamoto, whose leader Yoritoma was appointed as the first *Shogun,* or Generalissimo, of Japan by the

Japan

Shogun in Court attire

emperor. Thus was founded the Kamakura Shogunate which remained in power for 150 years and an entirely new system of ruling.

The Shoguns

With the emergence of the Minamoto family and the Kamakura *shogunate* they founded, Japan moved into a new phase of its development, one that would last in various forms until the 19th century. Although it varied over the centuries, it usually operated as a generally feudal society dominated by successive shogunal families best thought of as military dictators. For the next seven hundred years real power usually existed in a somewhat precarious balance between regional lords and various shogunal families that emerged from time to time.

The imperial court remained largely irrelevant to the real issues of power. In fact, not until the nineteenth century, and then more in symbol than reality, would power appear to gravitate once again around the imperial court. For the feudal era even that appearance of power was gone.

Japan's feudal era has often been compared to feudalism in Western Europe, and indeed there were many similarities. Although Japan's feudal experience developed later than that in Europe it too was characterized by the dominating presence of an aristocratic military elite loyal to various regional lords or *daimyo* as they were known in Japan. In both regions, feudalism reflected the decentralized nature of power and a system that was built upon the labors of peasant farmers. Nevertheless, there were clear differences as well. The ties between the military elite, *samurai,* and the *daimyo* tended to be more personal and based on kinship than that of the more contractual minded Europeans who developed elaborate contracts to cement feudal relationships. And, of course, Western Europe never developed the institution of the *shogunate* which eventually became a sort of "halfway stage" between feudal society and the centralized governments of a modern country.

The Kamakura *shogunate* was soon faced with the external threat of the powerful empire established by the Mongol emperor Khubilai Khan in China in the 13th century. Two attempted Mongol invasions were defeated by a combination of Japanese military resistance and timely, violent typhoons. Interestingly, the Japanese perception that they had been saved by the intervention of divine winds, i.e. *Kami Kazi,* was an inspiration under far different circumstances many centuries later as young Japanese suicide bombers attempted once again to save their country from invasion during the last days of the Second World War.

In the centuries after the 14th A.D., the fall of the Kamakura *shogunate* led to other weaker powers moving into the breach to establish their own dominance for a time. More importantly, the powerful regional lords known as *daimyo* came to dominate the life of the islands. These feudal lords were supported by highly trained and loyal *samurai,* who followed a warrior's creed of honor and loyalty known as *Bushido.* It was the bloody struggles among these regional leaders that made the late 16th century an exceptionally violent time in Japanese history.

The Tokugawa System: 1603–1868

Japan disintegrated into a state of feudal warfare in the 16th century resembling that of the Wars of the Roses in England. Commercial interests continued, however, to promote trade and build roads. Warfare was gradually brought under control in the later part of the century by two persons—Oda Nobunaga and his brilliant general, Toyotomi Hideyoshi, who succeeded Nobunaga as dictator when his overlord was killed by a dissident general. After two unsuccessful attempts to invade China (see Korea section), Hideyoshi was assassinated. Though things were a bit unsettled for a time, Japan was about to enter into one of its most stable eras, the *shogunate* of the Tokugawa.

In 1603 Tokugawa Ieyasu, a feudal lord from the region around present day Tokyo, then named Edo, emerged triumphant and established a new *shogunate* which lasted until the nineteenth century. The Tokugawa developed a complicated system which can be described as a sort of "centralized feudalism." On one hand the Tokugawa retained very considerable power, yet the regional lords, the *daimyo,* controlled their own domains. To retain power, the Tokugawa insisted that the lords maintain a residence and the permanent presence of themselves or family members at Edo. In short, the Tokugawa maintained control through a formal hostage system.

For generations thereafter, anyone on Japan's main thoroughfare was treated to the vision of aristocratic lords and their *samurai* entourages regularly traveling through the countryside to and from Edo. There is a curious irony to this system, sometimes known as the "alternative attendance" system. The Tokugawa *Shogunate* had been powerful enough to impose it on the many feudal lords of Japan, yet weak enough to need such a system to maintain control. Moreover, the system, designed to freeze the political and social structure of Japan under the Tokugawa, ironically had the unexpected effect of vastly improving the resources of the despised merchant class which served this enormous and peripatetic nobility.

The Arrival of the West

It was in the 16th century that the western ships, Spanish and Portuguese, began to arrive in Japanese waters and the various Catholic missionaries, from the aristocratic Jesuits to the more populist Franciscans, began to build commercial and religious ties to the islands. The Jesuits converted a large number of people, particularly in the island of Kyushu and its largest city, Nagasaki. Their position was enhanced by the conversion of a leading feudal lord of the island, which led many vassals and followers into the arms of the Church. Firearms and other Western methods of violence were introduced and eagerly adopted by the Japanese.

Spanish Franciscans, who arrived in 1593, began a period of even greater efforts toward conversion of the Japanese and also complicated the situation by periodic bickering with the Jesuits. If the missionaries were at first well received, the tensions among the Westerners and the Japanese' knowledge of their role in colonizing the Philippines, soon combined to arouse Japanese suspicions. Hideyoshi, who was in domination by the 1580s, became convinced that Christianity was nothing but a veil concealing a future European invasion and embarked on a course of persecution of priests and their converts. Later, also concerned that the Westerners could threaten their own power, the Tokugawa authorities moved not only to persecute Christians but to close the entire country to the outside.

For the next two hundred years the only Westerners allowed into the country were those on a yearly Dutch ship permitted to trade at Nagasaki. Ironically, Japan under the Tokugawa chose to isolate itself just as the West was beginning to dramatically emerge.

During this period of isolation, the clans, each ruled by a powerful *daimyo*, built ornate castles around which towns arose. Agriculture prospered, sporadically interrupted by revolts of the peasants, who lived in abject poverty. Trade flourished and the population increased. A merchant class emerged which quickly acquired a great deal of influence over the *daimyo* and the martial *samurai* by making loans to them. There was much intellectual activity, which was conservative, to the extent that it advocated that the imperial clan, which had survived over the centuries, be restored to full power and replace the "usurping" *shogunate*.

Over the next centuries sporadic attempts by the Western powers to "open" Japan to foreign trade were largely unsuccessful until the mid nineteenth century when the Russians, British and U.S. developed more serious plans to penetrate the

Commodore Perry's fleet in Tokyo Bay

islands. For the United States, which was to take the lead in Japan's departure from isolation, the effort was a logical extension of its generation–long thrust toward the Pacific and beyond. In 1846 San Francisco had been taken and an eye clearly directed to the possibilities of commerce beyond. Though Japan itself was of less interest than the riches of China, it was seen as a stepping stone to the Asian continent. Ironically, if the Americans who wanted to open the islands knew very little about Japan, many in Japan itself were quite knowledgeable about the outside world— they had had access to Western materials smuggled into Japan during the periodic visits of the Dutch ships at Nagasaki.

The Opening of Japan

The uncertainty among the Japanese when Commodore Perry of the United States sailed his fleet into Tokyo Bay in 1853–1854 is understandable. They had a good understanding of the military power the Westerners had demonstrated against China in the Opium War a decade earlier and knew they did not have the weapons to match the West. On the other hand, the policy of exclusion, now more than two centuries old, had become the accepted custom. No mere request by the arriving American flotilla could easily change that. The situation was even more complicated by the continuing antagonism of the southwestern domains of Satsuma and Choshu and the growing impe-

rial sentiment which itself undermined the authority of the Tokugawa *Shogunate*.

Uncertain how to respond to Commodore Perry's demands, the *shogun's* government took the unprecedented step of asking the several hundred *daimyo* for their advice. Even though the answers received were not unanimous, they did demonstrate a generally anti–foreign tone. Nevertheless, the *shogun's* government, facing the potential military power of the Americans, signed the foreign treaties anyway thus even further alienating them from many of the feudal lords over whom they had so long dominated. Commodore Perry was therefore able to get the treaty desired by the U.S., and other powers soon had their own agreements. All of these were patterned after the "unequal treaties" that were then being imposed on the waning Manchu dynasty of China.

The opponents of the Tokugawa, especially the powerful clans of the Southwest, accused the government of weakness and continued an anti–foreign campaign under the slogan "Honor the Emperor—Expel the Barbarians." But their enthusiasm for driving the Westerners out proved militarily impossible. Western naval bombardments at Kagoshima in 1863 and Shimonoseki in 1864 convinced them of the folly of their demands. Eventually they did an about–face, becoming eager advocates of learning as much as possible from the West in order to be better equipped to resist its influence and power.

The immediate problem though was

Japan

frustration with the Western pressures. The Shogunal court found itself caught between the Western demands and the aroused *samurai* class. After a series of confrontations, the two–hundred and fifty year old Tokugawa *shogunate* collapsed in the face of a coalition of forces which included the southern domains of Satsuma and Choshu in alliance with the Kyoto–based imperial court. This truly revolutionary development known perhaps inappropriately as the *"Meiji Restoration,"* due to the reemergence of the imperial court as a player, was to be the central turning point in modern Japanese history.

The Meiji Restoration

The *Meiji Restoration* was ostensibly the restoration of the Japanese emperor to power by the southern regions of the islands. What really occurred though was the arrival to power of an oligarchy of extraordinary young mid–level *samurai* mostly from the Southwest who were fundamentally committed to modernizing Japan in the face of the Western challenge. The leadership set up a strong central administration and governed in a style that nevertheless made some concessions to the concerns of those *samurai* elite left outside of the new constellation of power. Their fundamental goal was to build a "rich country and strong military" and to have Japan enter the Western family of nations as a full partner rather than, as was the case so often elsewhere, yet another victim of Western colonization.

Determined to make a dramatic break with the past, the new leaders issued a series of goals known as the "Charter Oath" which outlined their hope of reforming the social structure of Japan and to learn as much as possible from the outside world. The period of feudal isolation was clearly at an end. These new *Meiji* leaders wiped out the old clan system of authority and at the same time modernized land tenure. The landowning peasants were heavily taxed, however, yielding greater funds for modernization. Modern communications were established and new machinery was imported to manufacture textiles and other goods. An entirely new system of banking and other modern industrial techniques were imported and many "foreign experts" were temporarily engaged to help in the transformation.

A modern education system, eventually geared to the production of literate and obedient subjects of the Emperor, was created. An effective army and navy and a modern legal system also emerged within a short time, eventually permitting the Japanese to renegotiate the "unequal treaties," but the leadership avoided foreign military adventures at first. On a political

Entrance of a Shinto temple at Nagasaki, c. 1880

level, the *Meiji* oligarchies continued to dominate, though by the 1880s they found themselves pressed by a "popular rights" movement led by wealthier members of the peasant class and former members of the *samurai* elite. Eventually, after studying Western governmental systems, the leadership adopted a modified version of the imperial German parliamentary system.

A *Diet*, or parliament, was created under a constitution of 1889 that proclaimed the emperor as the supreme ruler. Nevertheless, behind the scenes the governing oligarchy continued to rule. The period of

indiscriminately adopting foreign institutions and techniques diminished and practically ended by 1890. After that, although the interest in Western science and technology continued unabated, more emphasis was now placed on traditional Japanese institutions and customs. The emperor became the object of still greater glorification, even though he possessed little more than nominal power. This veneration interestingly was less a product of traditional Shinto imperial myths than Japan's search for modernity. The oligarchies who created the new governing system felt that the nation needed some sort of unifying principle to support its modernization and the ancient system of the imperial dynasty seemed to suit their purposes.

Economically, a small group of *zaibatsu* (large family–owned holding companies) arose which dominated the beginnings of industry in Japan in a manner reminiscent of Carnegie, Harriman and Morgan in the United States, but there was abundant room for small business as well. This balance between central control and local initiative, coupled with the rapid urbanization of Japan, its fairly low rate of population growth and the fact that the people demanded little in personal comforts, permitted a rate of modernization unparalleled in history.

By the end of the *Meiji* period (1868–1912), Japan had largely achieved its goal of modernization, a feat not duplicated by any other traditional nation in the world in such a brief period, or indeed anywhere on such a tremendous scale. Nevertheless, despite the changes in the material circumstances of Japan, many martial feudal values from the Tokugawa era would continue to be influential for generations.

The Rise of the Japanese Empire

The international arena that Japan had chosen to enter during the late nineteenth century was an aggressive one of imperialism. After centuries of colonialization, the imperial urge had continued to grow at an even faster pace. Africa and Southeast Asia were being carved up by the Europeans, and the Americans were beginning to turn an eye toward the Hawaiian islands and eventually the Philippines. In central Asia, the Russians and English were competing for influence and China, the giant of traditional East Asia, was struggling to maintain even a modicum of influence. Within Japan many would argue that they too had to take their place among the imperial powers and begin to assert themselves abroad.

For many, the first goal was obvious, the Korean peninsula. In fact, as early as the 1870s some in government had forcibly argued for a move against the then closed "hermit kingdom" of Korea. That early effort had not been carried out but by the 1890s the Japanese were aggressively competing with China for influence on the peninsula. By 1894 a full scale war had broken out. The Japanese army and navy seized control of Taiwan and conquered Korea, which was annexed in 1910. In its war with China, Japan fought alone, without the support of any of the major Western powers and aroused the antagonism of the Russians who had their own interests in the area. Working with other European powers, they forced the Japanese to give

up at the bargaining table much of what they had won on the continent itself.

This lesson left a lasting impression on Japanese leaders. In their minds, the "Western imperialists" had their own set of rules; outsiders, like the Japanese, were not part of their "club" and were not permitted the same freedom of action as other world powers. Nevertheless, in 1903, the Japanese concluded an alliance with Britain that lasted until the 1920's. The ensuing period saw a tremendous growth in Japanese military and political power at the expense of its neighbors, in part a result of its strengthened position as a member of a Western alliance.

The Japanese, of course, did not conquer territory from the Chinese alone. By the turn of the century the dramatic episode known as the "Cutting of the Melon," had begun which saw the Western powers grabbing even more power for themselves throughout China. The Russians' actions particularly aroused Japanese anger. The two were competing for influence in northeast Asia. The Russians had established a "sphere of influence" in Manchuria dating from 1898. By 1904 The Japanese felt ready to challenge them and launched a victorious land and sea campaign (the Russo–Japanese War) and thereby established themselves as the

The late Emperor Hirohito at his coronation, 1926

Japan

leading power in East Asia—in fact, one of the world's major powers.

A decade later Japan did not waste the opportunity offered by the vulnerability of Germany during World War I. It quickly declared war and seized its holdings in Shandong Province in China, as well as several small island groups in the Pacific. At the same time, it shipped considerable quantities of munitions to the Allied Powers, including Russia, its former enemy. At the end of the war, and after the Bolshevik Revolution of 1917, Japan sent a large military force to occupy eastern Siberia to see if the region could be added to the growing Japanese empire. Internal and external pressures though forced them from Siberia and also from Shandong by 1922.

Taisho Democracy

The post–World War I period in Japan was one of transition. The original *Meiji* Constitution of 1889 had not worked quite as anticipated. The cooperation of the parliamentary parties had become more necessary than expected for the smooth operation of government and they had thus gained in power. Party leaders such as Hara Kei emerged in power as prime ministers and Japan entered an era where more experimentation was carried out in democratic decision making. The voting lists were enlarged to include the whole of the adult male population. The political parties became more influential than ever before. By the 1920s two political parties rotated in power and a system of formal parliamentary government seemed to be at hand.

Nevertheless, the parliamentary leaders found much of the real power needed to run the country still denied them. The military and bureaucracy remained extraordinarily influential and the aging oligarchic leadership still powerful. Internationally these parliamentary governments were more inclined toward negotiation and signed a treaty limiting the growth of the navy much to the irritation of the Japanese right wing.

But the speed of modernization in Japan left unsolved some problems and created many others. The rural population remained isolated from urban progress, while continuing to pay for it by increased taxes, rents and difficult conditions in the countryside in the 1920's, all of which created much discontent. Moreover, Japan had changed greatly since their days of isolation. The country's economy was far more integrated into the international order than ever before. Thus, not surprisingly, the onset of the great depression hit the country very hard and the rural peasants especially so. The cause of the peasants was championed by ambitious army offi-

The newly installed *Orchid Emperor of Manchukuo* reviews Japanese troops at Dairen in 1934

cers, partly in sincerity but also for political reasons. The officers, who were often of rural origin, found allies among some civilian nationalists. They adopted the position that rural poverty had two basic causes: poor government by the political parties and economic practices by the large combines. They criticized the political parties, who were more influential during the 1920's than at any previous time.

The *zaibatsus*, also came under fire for their devotion to the goal of high profits. The military and civilian nationalists also blamed injurious and "insulting" tariffs and discriminatory trade policies of some foreign nations for the adverse conditions of the peasants. The answer to Japan's dilemma was, in their eyes, usually further expansion into the mainland which was seen as a "new frontier" which could be developed for Japan's benefit and receive its excess population.

This line of argument had a broad base of appeal, and the rightists strengthened their position by taking forceful action in the form of assassinations and coups. The extreme right wing did not succeed, but it was able to force the parliamentary parties from power.

Toward War With China

From the early 1930s, though the extremists failed to gain power, Japan was again controlled by conservative leaders often drawn from the military. All political parties were abolished in 1940. Within China, Japan took advantage of the conflict between the nationalist forces of

Chiang Kai–shek and the Chinese communists. Increasing pressures, both diplomatic and military, were brought to bear in order to give Japan great influence over China. The Japanese army seized Manchuria in 1931–1932, soon after the local authorities had threatened Japan's interests by accepting the authority of Chiang Kai–shek's government.

Renaming the area Manchukuo, the Japanese military established the youthful Henry Pu–Yi, the "last emperor" of the Manchu dynasty, as its puppet emperor. Frequent military clashes with China led to an invasion of eastern China in 1937, in the course of which a multitude of atrocities were committed by the invading soldiers. The best known of these came to be known as the "Rape of Nanjing" for the reign of terror the Japanese soldiers inflicted on that city's hapless residents. With that development World War II had begun in Asia. Within two years it would be expanded by Hitler's invasion of Poland.

Merciless bombing of the mainland cities alienated the Chinese completely and enabled both Chiang and Mao to rally support for their separate struggles against the Japanese. Eventually an uneasy truce emerged between the two Chinese leaders because of the Japanese threat. Nevertheless the Japanese forces remained in occupation of the major cities of eastern China. These Japanese efforts at expansion led to increasing criticism and pressure from the outside world, including the United States. Unfortunately for the Chinese, only the Russians initially offered any significant official help.

Eventually though, in an effort to limit the capability of the Japanese war machine, the U.S. gradually cut down shipments of oil and scrap steel. This reduced shipment of strategic materials caused the Japanese to look for sources elsewhere, particularly to iron in the Philippines and oil in Indonesia. By the 1940s the successful German victories provided an example of the rewards of aggression and weakened those Western colonial powers the Japanese were soon also to challenge. Fortunately for the rest of the world, cooperation between Nazi Germany and Japan was always very unsteady even though they and Italy formed an alliance in 1940. All three, but most of all the European "Axis" powers, had the habit of making bargains with other nations without consulting or informing their allies.

World War II in the Pacific

In late 1941, Japan decided to force the issue with the Americans. They demanded an unfreezing of its assets in the United States, a measure which had been undertaken in response to the July 1941 Japanese invasion of Indochina. Washington refused to continue oil and scrap steel shipments, and in addition, encouraged the Dutch in Indonesia to withhold their oil unless the Japanese agreed to a political settlement, which would have involved an end to aggression and withdrawal from China. The Japanese had no interest in such a dramatic retreat. The Americans were unwilling to compromise with a nation many felt would not dare attack. The die was cast for an even greater extension of the developing world war.

Believing that the U.S. would oppose any Japanese seizure of the resources of Southeast Asia, the Japanese decided to destroy the U.S. Pacific Fleet stationed at Pearl Harbor in Hawaii. On December 7 Japanese airplanes without warning almost completely wiped out the U.S. battleship fleet stationed at Pearl Harbor. The imperial forces of Japan then quickly attacked the many Western colonies in Southeast Asia. Initially, their superior might in the Pacific was impressive enough to cause fear of an imminent naval attack on California. While that threat never materialized, it did arouse enough popular sentiment on the American west coast to round up the region's Japanese–American population, regardless of their U.S. citizenship, and relocate them to prison camps over the next several months.

The Japanese army met its greatest resistance in the Philippines, where the people cooperated with the U.S. defense force led by General Douglas MacArthur. But ultimately the islands fell. Apart from unwise attempts to gain still further territories from Australia and India, the Japanese military settled down to occupy and exploit their newly won empire. The only land resistance during this period was sporadic and weak, from Chiang Kai–shek's forces, which were contained in southwest China, and from Mao Zedong's troops in the northwest.

Although many Japanese convinced themselves that they were on a great mission to free Asia from Western colonialism, their own brutality against the local peoples very quickly alienated these communities and created an anti–Japanese sentiment in parts of the region that continues to this day. In the later years of the war, active resistance to the Japanese formed in most Southeast Asian lands they had conquered.

As the war economy of the United States came into full production, the Japanese suffered increasing defeats in naval and air battles with the U.S. Australia initially served as the main base for the Allied campaign; it and New Zealand also contributed fighting units to the war. Island after island fell to American Marines and Allied Army units. U.S. aircraft and warships, principally submarines, cut the Japanese islands off from Japanese Southeast Asian and the Southwestern Pacific conquests by sinking tremendous amounts of shipping and by defeating the Japanese navy. By 1944 General Tojo, who had led Japan to war with the U.S., was deposed as premier and disappeared from the circle of military officers who were in control. Important persons in the imperial court and the government saw that the war was lost and believed that peace should be negotiated as soon as possible in order to save the Emperor and avoid a communist revolution. The military however insisted on continuing the losing battle; the Emperor might have overruled them but chose to remain silent fearing that a move on his part might create an even more destructive civil war. The stage was set for the Americans to force a surrender without invading the Japanese home islands.

The Atomic Bombs

On August 6, 1945, the sky above Hiroshima was lit by the fiery destructiveness of the first atomic bomb used in the history of the world. The Japanese were already hard pressed by the Allied troops, who were being reinforced by soldiers that arrived in the area after the fall of Germany earlier in the year. On August 8, the Soviet Union declared war on Japan. It had agreed to do this the preceding February in exchange for postwar control of Outer Mongolia, and territories like southern Sakhalin Island and the Kurile Islands. A second atomic bomb was dropped on Nagasaki on August 9; the next day the war and peace factions went to the Emperor and submitted the choice of war or surrender.

The Emperor, in an act of great moral courage, chose surrender. The final terms of capitulation were agreed to by August 14, 1945, and the formal agreement was signed aboard the U.S.S. Missouri in Tokyo Bay on September 2, 1945. The is-

Japan's Foreign Minister Shigimitsu signs the documents of surrender aboard the *U.S.S. Missouri*, while General MacArthur broadcasts the ceremonies

lands had been terribly battered and exhausted by the war. National morale was almost completely crushed; some army leaders and high government officials chose *seppuku*, a formal suicide which eliminated the necessity of facing their conquerors or the people they had led.

The American decision to use the atomic bombs has continued to arouse heated controversy more than a half century after their use. Some have argued that Japan was already defeated—that the bomb was used more to intimidate the Soviets than to end the Pacific War. Considerable documentation exists to suggest the usual combination of mixed motives on the part of the American leadership. Nevertheless, regardless of the decision–making process then going on in Japan, which American leaders were not privy to, many believed

Japan

His Imperial Majesty Emperor Akihito with Empress Michiko   AP/Wide World Photos

then and now, however correctly or not, that the use of the bombs would eliminate facing a bloody invasion of the Japanese home islands with an accompanying loss of lives which was incalculable. Whether the war could have been ended without resort to either atomic weapons or an invasion we will never know.

The Postwar Occupation

The American occupation of Japan after World War II was initially an ambitious attempt to remake Japan's political, economic, and educational institutions in a way that would prevent the future reemergence of militarism. In reality, the occupation can be divided into two distinct periods, the period of the transformation of a defeated enemy and the period, after the commencement of the Cold War, of working to revive their former foe and transform it into a loyal ally in the struggle against communism. During that early phase, the Supreme Commander of Allied Powers (SCAP), MacArthur's headquarters, rewrote the Japanese constitution, began to break up the powerful *zaibatsu* business conglomerates, and completely revamped the Japanese educational system.

In many respects, some of the reforms forced on Japan in the war's aftermath

were more liberal than many comparable U.S. policies. Most importantly, the circumstances of the rural Japanese were vastly improved as the occupation forces moved to lessen tenancy and help establish the peasantry as a land–owning class.

Moreover, the right wing of both the military and civilian sectors were purged with the goal of rebuilding Japanese governance on a new more peaceful basis. The pre–war parliamentary system, which had been largely suppressed during the 1930s, was revived and this time its authority was more clearly established and codified. Unions were encouraged as never before as the Americans sought to rebuild Japan largely in its own image. Women were granted the vote during this restructuring as well.

The American efforts were as much the product of ignorance, however, as they were of a concerted effort to remake Japanese society in America's image. And as the Cold War developed by the late 1940s many American reforms were abruptly curtailed as the U.S. hastily sought to firmly anchor Japan as an anticommunist bastion in the Far East. Union activities, earlier encouraged, were now often suppressed in the name of the supreme struggle with communism.

The war in nearby Korea also had a profound impact on the course of the occupa-

tion. The socialists, who naturally supported some of the liberal reforms proposed by the Americans, were now eyed with suspicion and many were purged from government positions by SCAP authorities. Japanese moderates were genuinely frightened by prospects of political unrest and they feared a communist takeover right on their Korean doorstep. Discredited conservative politicians, removed from office due to their support of Japan's war effort, were rehabilitated as anti–communist allies. The war had a number of other effects as well. While the Japanese adhered to the constitutional prohibition against maintaining armed forces, under U.S. pressure a national armed constabulary was formed. Heavily armed, these "police" effectively replaced U.S. occupation troops, freeing them for combat on the Korean peninsula. Japan's devastated industries were slowly revived by the Korean war boom, providing supplies and equipment for the U.S. war effort. Almost overnight, the nature of the U.S. occupation and U.S.–Japanese relations had changed dramatically.

A peace treaty was signed with the United States and some other Western and Asian nations in 1951, but the communist bloc refrained from concluding formal peace accords. Under the U.S. treaty, Japan regained its independence, but lost all of its empire outside the home islands. Further reparations were left to be determined between Japan and each individual country concerned. A security treaty was signed with the U.S. under which America was to maintain military bases in Japan and to administer Okinawa in the Ryukyu Islands, where the U.S. had established its largest military base in the western Pacific. This treaty was renewed in 1960, but was modified at that time by the inclusion of certain concessions to Japan. It was renewed a second time in 1970. The island was finally returned to Japanese jurisdiction on May 15, 1972.

The Structure of Postwar Politics

The new constitution introduced in 1947 under the occupation had established a constitutional monarchy and a parliamentary system resembling those of Britain. It also provided (in the famous Article Nine) that Japan forever relinquished the right to make war and or even to maintain armed forces. This article, which on the surface would appear to ban even self–defense, has been gradually loosened over the years. Japan created an armed constabulary in the early 1950's, which, after being armed with heavy weapons, aircraft, and tanks, expanded into the Japan Self Defense Force. Japan's deepening commitment to the U.S. alliance and growing

Japan

global importance have today expanded the role of self–defense to include responsibility for shipping lanes out to a 1,000–mile radius from the Japanese islands; Japan's navy (Maritime Self Defense Forces) is one of the largest in Asia.

The constitution failed to mention, and in this way repudiated, any divine attributes or political power on the part of the emperor. In spite of this, or perhaps because of it, Emperor Hirohito remained a generally respected symbol of the nation. In 1986 he celebrated his 85th birthday and also the sixtieth anniversary of his accession to the throne—one of the longest reigns in modern history. He adjusted remarkably well to the tremendous changes in Japan since World War II—essentially from a military–dominated authoritarian state to a parliamentary democracy. He was kept informed of political developments by the prime minister.

After one of the longest reigns in history, and after a lengthy illness, Emperor Hirohito died on January 7, 1989. He was succeeded by his modern–minded son Crown Prince Akihito (sometimes referred to as the Rising Son), who took the title *Heisei* (Achieving Peace) for his reign. This transition evoked a great deal of soul searching in Japan about the responsibility for World War II in the Pacific and about Hirohito's role in that war. The fairest verdict seems to be that Hirohito had not favored Japanese aggression but had felt bound as a constitutional monarch (although theoretically divine) to accept the advice of his officials. At the end of the war, he certainly showed great moral courage in dealing first with his

Suburban Washington, D.C.? No, suburban Tokyo! Courtesy: Alfred Magleby

own militarists and then with the American Occupation authorities. New information available after his death suggests that the Emperor had feared an earlier intervention on his part might well have provoked a civil war within Japan.

Ironically, the parliamentary parties that had represented the official left wing of Japanese politics in the pre–war era became in the post war years, after the militant ultra–nationalists were purged, to represent a conservative front of big–business, pro–American politicians. Merging

in 1955 into the *Liberal Democratic Party*, the domination of the *LDP* was so great that the opposition parties had no realistic chance to come to power. In fact, real politics revolved within the *LDP* where the party's many factional leaders competed for power within the party and thus over the Japanese government itself. They continued to dominate the political scene until the 1980s when their power began to weaken. Nevertheless, though the *LDP's* influence was enormous in the decades after the war, even its power was dramatically limited due to the extraordinary control of the entrenched Japanese bureaucracy.

Moreover, Japan, like so many other countries, has been dominated by "money politics." Politicians have very heavy expenses, since they are expected to make presents to many of their constituents and to make outright gifts of money to their supporters. The funds for these transactions come mostly from business, in one form or another. For this reason, the political clout of the enormously wealthy business community has increased greatly over the years.

During the post–war era much of the wind was taken out of the opposition's sails by the remarkable growth of the Japanese economy which began in the 1960's. Premier Hayato Ikeda (1960–4) avoided the controversial behavior of his predecessor Kishi, cultivated a "low posture" in politics and launched a program to double the gross national product by the end of the decade, a goal that was more than achieved.

His successor, Eisaku Sato (1964–1972),

Seaweed, widely used in cooking, is gathered off the rocky coast.
Courtesy: Marilynn and Mark Swenson

Japan

Former Emperor Hirohito addresses the opening of the Diet.
Courtesy: Japanese Embassy

was more "high posture" and created considerable controversy, mainly by staying in office for the unusually long period of eight years and by being perceived, especially in Beijing, as being too pro–U.S. and too pro–Taiwan. In 1965 Sato announced his determination to regain jurisdiction over Okinawa, and after prolonged negotiations with the U.S., the island, as well as the rest of the Ryukyus, reverted to Japan in 1972. Sato also cooperated with the U.S. to a degree during the first several years of the Vietnam war, from which Japanese firms made large profits by selling supplies and equipment to the U.S. for use, as they had during the Korean War.

Japan's special relationship with the United States did not save it from the geo–political dramas of the early 1970s. Long supporters of the pro–Taiwan stance of the United States, the Japanese were shocked when the White House, without any advance warning, set out to improve relations with the People's Republic of China. Although Prime Minister Sato hesitated, his successor moved quickly to establish relations with Beijing.

Kakuei Tanaka, a farmer's son and popular politician was elected president of the ruling *Liberal Democratic Party* in 1972, thus assuring him the prime ministership. He then paid a successful visit to Beijing and established diplomatic relations with the People's Republic of China. But in 1973 a series of political and economic setbacks badly eroded the Tanaka government's popularity. Inflation, pollution and ever–present corruption continued to be major issues.

Japan's international vulnerability due to its limited national resources was especially demonstrated in late 1973 when there was a temporary Arab oil embargo against Japan arising from the Middle East war. The *LDP* government had long supported American policies in the Middle East that had usually meant a generally pro–Israeli position. But Japan was importing 80% of its oil from the Middle East. The price of oil quadrupled. Recognizing the situation, the government made statements critical of Israel and began to woo the Arab states, in particular, by promising them $3 billion in aid. Moreover, it set about, as the United States was doing as well, to attempt to create a strategic oil reserve which, it was hoped, would make Japan less vulnerable in the future.

This crisis reduced Japan's economic growth in 1974 roughly to zero and further weakened the Tanaka government. In order to recover, the ruling *LDP* spent large sums of money received from business contributions in an effort to influence elections in mid–1974 for the upper house of the Diet, the House of Councillors. The party emerged with only half the seats (126 out of 252), however, and suffered a further setback—business contributions began to decline. Several leading figures resigned from the cabinet, and the feeling grew that if Tanaka stayed in office until his term expired in 1975, he would bring disaster to his party in the next elections to the lower house of the Diet, also scheduled for 1975. The Watergate affair in the United States and President Nixon's resignation in 1974 had heightened the attention of the Japanese public on the behavior of their own leaders. The final blow fell

in October–November 1974, when a series of press articles exposed Tanaka's personal wealth and the questionable means by which it had been obtained.

Feeling that it might be facing its last chance to save itself from losing power, the *Liberal Democratic Party* dispensed with the usual jockeying for the premiership and entrusted the selection to the party's Vice President, Etsusaburo Shiina, whose surprising choice was the moderate Takeo Miki. The latter published a list of his personal assets (an unprecedented step in Japan) but could not persuade his colleagues to do the same.

Miki's political position was weaker than that of several other leaders of his party, including Tanaka. Miki tried with some success to improve his image and strengthen his position by a number of initiatives. One was a trip to the United States in 1975, following which Emperor Hirohito also made a similar visit. In late 1975 he participated with five West European premiers in a conference on economic matters, the first time a Japanese premier had done this. At his insistence, a general strike of government workers was called off.

However, in early 1976 it was revealed in the United States that over the previous twenty years the Lockheed Aircraft Corporation had paid about $21 million in bribes to various Japanese officials and politicians to promote the sales of various types of military aircraft. The U.S. Central Intelligence Agency was probably already aware of these, but other agencies of the government, including the U.S. Securities and Exchange Commission, cooperated with the Japanese government's investigation of the scandal, which rocked Japan. Miki's investigation aroused the anger of some of his senior colleagues in the party, who evidently feared that they and their friends might be implicated. As a result, Miki was in danger of being forced out of office even before the general election of November/December 1976. Nevertheless the inquiry proceeded, and resulted in, among other things, the trial and conviction of Tanaka. Following the election, Miki resigned and an able, experienced conservative leader of the party, Takeo Fukuda, became Premier.

A new system was introduced for selecting the leader of the party, who at that time automatically became Premier. This consisted of a direct vote by all members of the party for two candidates, with the final choice made by the party members in the Diet. When the primary was held in November, it resulted in an upset victory for Masayoshi Ohira. Fukuda resigned in his favor without waiting for the final vote in the Diet. But in May 1980, Ohira lost a vote of confidence arising from charges of corruption in office; he died on June 12th of a heart attack. He was in turn succeeded by the virtually unknown Zenko Suzuki as head of the party, which then won the June 1980 Diet elections with a surprisingly solid majority (284 seats out of 511). Suzuki's performance was weak, and in late 1982 he was replaced by the able and energetic Yasuhiro Nakasone, who began to try to improve relations with the United States which had become frayed by economic issues and by American pressures on Japan to strengthen its military posture at a faster rate.

Nakasone was a controversial figure, partly because of his desire for a larger defense budget and partly due to his close connection with former Premier Tanaka— they were sometimes referred to collectively as "Tanakasone." Nevertheless, the *LDP* did well in the elections to the House of Councillors in mid–1983. In spite of its successes, the party continued to have a major burden—Tanaka remained in the Diet (even though he had nominally resigned from it) and controlled the largest faction of the party. Worse yet, he was convicted and sentenced to four years in prison, although he never went to jail.

The party dropped from 286 to 258 seats in the lower house in late 1983 elections, holding on to a bare majority. The main opposition parties, other than the communist, made gains; Tanaka was reelected. The party had to enter into a coalition for the first time to ensure continued control in the lower house; the political marriage of convenience was with a small independent party, the *New Liberal Club*.

Without opposition, Nakasone was reelected to a second term as president of the party and, therefore, prime minister in late 1984. However, he faced some continuing, serious problems. He was still dependent on the support of the disgraced Tanaka. Further, it was only after considerable delay and great effort that he was able to push Japan's defense budget to a level above 1% of the gross national product. He did not take effective steps to reduce the huge trade and payments imbalance in Japan's favor as requested by the United States. The prime minister also faced a rising level of political activity by opposition parties, especially the *Socialists* under their new, moderate leader, Masashi Ishibashi.

Prime Minister Nakasone maintained a rather high profile abroad as well as at home. He visited the United States in January 1983 and Southeast Asia the following May. President Reagan returned the visit in November. Nakasone threw his considerable prestige and popularity in 1985 behind an appeal to Japanese business and the Japanese public to import and buy more foreign (especially American) goods, so as to reduce Japan's huge payments surplus. This appeal had little effect, except to worry the Japanese about their economic relations with the United States and the possibility of American "protectionism."

Early in 1986, Nakasone decided to call an election for the lower house of the Diet for July, to coincide with the regular election of one–half of the upper house every three years. He apparently wanted a third two–year term as President of the *Liberal Democratic Party* and as Prime Minister. The issue he selected to campaign on was the denationalization of the efficient, but unprofitable, Japanese National Railways, a very controversial move. In reality he appeared to be trying to distract public attention from a potentially even more controversial issue, certain legislation, including an Official Secrets Act, that he was trying to get through the Diet so that the United States would consider the Japanese government able to maintain security on sensitive information and thus eligible to take part in the lucrative American effort to develop the "Star Wars" defense initiative.

In the 1986 elections, helped by the premier's good image, the *LDP* won 309 seats in the lower house, more than ever before. Its main gains were in the cities and at the expense of the *Japan Socialist Party*, which dropped to 87 seats in the lower house. In an effort to make a fresh start, the *JSP* then elected a woman, Takako Doi, as its chairwoman, an unprecedented step for a major Japanese political party.

Nakasone then got a one–year extension of his premiership (until the summer or fall of 1987) and moved ahead with two of his favorite projects—a tax reform bill (modeled partly on the one in the U.S., and introducing a 5% sales tax), and the

Tokyo's expressways curve and divide as they crisscross the city.

Courtesy: Japanese Embassy

Japan

privatization, or denationalization, of the major government monopoly corporations, including the railways.

These moves aroused much opposition to Nakasone, who in any case had never been really popular with the politicians in his own party. He also damaged his prestige with some remarks he made in 1986 to the effect that Japan's relatively homogeneous population gave it a marked advantage over the U.S.; he disparaged the abilities of Black and Hispanic Americans. Thus, in spite of the July 1986 electoral victory, Nakasone's political future suddenly seemed insecure.

He resigned in 1987 in favor of Noboru Takeshita (pronounced Tah–*kesh*–tah), a "low profile" politician who had just taken over the leadership of former Premier Tanaka's sizable faction in the Diet. Takeshita moved quickly to try to improve relations with the United States and China, which had cooled somewhat during the late Nakasone years.

The End of *LDP* Domination?

With the advent of the Takeshita government in 1987, Japanese politics began to change. The years of domination and corruption charges had clearly taken their toll on the *LDP*. No longer were they the masters of Japanese politics, and an era of instability, of revolving door prime ministers and governments, began that would continue until the mid 1990s.

As the accompanying table illustrates, there were seven prime ministers in the period from October 1987 to January 1996, with the longest term in office being just over two years.

Japan's Revolving Door Politics

Prime Ministers:
Noboru **Takeshita**, Oct. 1987–Apr.1989
Sosuke **Uno**, Apr. 1989–Jul. 1989
Toshiki **Kaifu,** Jul. 1989–Oct. 1991
Kiichi **Miyazawa** Oct. 1991–Jun. 1993
Morihiro **Hosakawa**, Jul. 1993–Apr. 1994
Hata **Tsutjoma**, Apr. 1994–Jun. 1994
Tomiichi **Murayama**, Jun. 1994–Jan. 1996 (Socialist)
Ryutaro **Hashimoto**. Jan. 1996–

It can be argued that many of the fundamentals of Japanese politics during this revolving–door period differed little from what came before. That is, factionalism, corruption, the dominance of big business and "money politics" still pervaded the system.

While the Japanese political spectrum had been dominated by an essentially conservative majority, factions built around prominent and powerful individuals within the *LDP* were common. Thus,

the *LDP* could not be thought of as an extremely homogeneous party. As described below, these factions eventually broke to form new independent parties.

The country's electoral system also has contributed to the instability. Until the changes in the electoral law in 1994, Diet members were elected entirely from multi–member districts. The presence of factions and more political parties guaranteed a large number of candidates and that candidates from the same party would have to compete against each other. Essentially, under this system, the way to get elected was to buy enough votes. Since each voter had only one vote, there was a fixed number of votes to be divided up. It is obvious, therefore, what a significant infusion of campaign spending could do. A new structure of voting patterns would not emerge until after the 1994 reforms were implemented in the elections of late 1996.

The roots of the government's problems had begun as early as 1984, when a rising but "outsider" firm, the Recruit Cosmos Company, began to try to buy its way into the inner circle by making interest–free loans to some eighty politicians (from all parties except the communists) and senior bureaucrats with which to buy stock that was cheap because it had not been publicly listed. Two years later, the stock was listed, and its value appreciated rapidly, much to the benefit of the purchasers. In July 1988, one of Japan's most influential newspapers, the *Asahi Shimbun*, began to expose this transaction, which although not necessarily illegal (since no political favors were known to have been done in return for the benefit), it was certainly corrupt. Finance Minister Miyazawa, who was implicated in the scandal, resigned in December. Premier Takeshita promptly reshuffled his cabinet, but some of the new ministers also soon had to resign. In February 1989, a series of arrests began to be made as a result of the Recruit Cosmos affair. Growing public disgust with "money politics" reached new heights when it became apparent that about 160 politicians and bureaucrats, previously perceived as honest, were implicated in the Recruit scandal. The apparent collapse of *LDP* domination had begun.

CONTEMPORARY GOVERNMENT

Japan is a constitutional monarchy, with the constitution dating to May 3, 1947. Administratively, the country is divided into 47 prefectures. It has universal suffrage at age 20. The legal system is modeled after European civil law with some English and American influence. The Supreme Court has the power of judicial review over legislative acts.

The Emperor is the ceremonial head of state. The Prime Minister heads the government and has the power to appoint the cabinet.

The legislature, or *Diet*, is bicameral, consisting of the upper House of Councillors and a lower House of Representatives.

New electoral laws took effect on January 1, 1995 but were not tested until the fall of 1996. The reforms left untouched the upper House of Councillors which is less significant in the legislative process. Under the new system, the lower house consists of 500 members. Of these, 300 are elected from single member districts. The remaining 200 are chosen through a system of proportional representation.

Parties with at least five Diet seats and which received at least 2% of the vote in the last national election will receive government funding. Candidates can receive funds from their party, may accept a corporate contribution up to $5,000, and must report contributions over $500. The original bill banned corporate contributions, but the *Liberal Democratic Party* changed this. The reforms on campaign spending resemble those implemented in the U.S. in the 1970's. If the American experience is any example, then it may be assumed that big business will still find a way to use its money.

The results of the October 1996 elections suggest that Japan's era of revolving door governments may finally be over. As expected the new rules weakened the ability of the small parties to compete. The strongest parties are now once again the *LDP*, plus the *Shinseito* and the *Minshuto* parties. In contrast, the *Socialists*, and the *Komeito* both are weakened.

The several years of instability, which had followed the collapse of the *LDP's* longtime dominance, now appear over. The *LDP* has reasserted itself again. Prime Minister Hashimoto still lacks a clear majority (his party holds 239 seats out of 500 *Diet* seats) and thus needs the support of smaller parties. Nevertheless, he has the authority now to offer a level of political stability that Japan has lacked in recent years. But will things now return to the politics of the past? That seems less likely.

For much of Japan's modern history, despite the domination of the *LDP*, the real governors of Japan were the prestigious bureaucrats that controlled the major government ministries. But recent trends within the *LDP* and in the population at large suggest that the reign of the bureaucrats is at long last about to be challenged. Hashimoto himself understands that he has a clear mandate from the electorate to lessen the control of the major ministries, and his party has its own memories of negative bureaucratic treatment when the *LDP* was out of power Moreover, so much of recent Japanese politics was driven by the success of the economy, but those more certain years seem to be products more of the past than the future. There has appeared a stronger conviction that over–regulation has not only added impediments to the economy but made day–to–day life for Japanese citizens harder as they struggle with extraordinarily high prices on consumer goods.

Especially interesting is that these recent calls for profound reform of the country's system of regulation are coming not, as usual, from foreigners, but from the Japanese themselves who appear increasingly interested in making whatever changes seem necessary to revive the economy after a period of weakness. Ryutaro Hashimoto himself seems posed to be a far more long–lasting prime minister than his weak predecessors. He first became prime minister in mid–January 1996, having previously served as Minister of Trade. This was the fourth change in government since the July 1993 elections, and it had temporarily returned the *LDP* to control of the premiership. It fell to Hashimoto to build on that temporary return to power.

Hashimoto, 58, is known as a sharp dresser and a man with a temper. He is admired for his strong stand against former American Trade Representative Mickey Kantor in discussions over automobile imports and other issues. The new Prime Minister also handled the difficult negotiations over the American bases in Okinawa. In the end (see below) he built an agreement that managed to satisfy at least some of the demands of each side.

New Stresses

The last several years have not gone well in Japan. The political and economic weakening has been "complemented" by other even more disturbing events and trends. The country experienced a "reality check" of sorts when its long assumption of being well prepared for earthquakes was severely challenged by the government's often poor performance in responding to the Kobe Earthquake of January 1995. The quake had measured 7.2 on the scale and the death toll eventually climbed over 5,000, with 26,000 injured and 300,000 left homeless. Offers for assistance poured into the country which in some cases the government was very slow in accepting. But that was not the only trauma of recent years.

In mid–1995 Japanese prosecutors secured the indictment of cult leader Shoko Ashara for masterminding the poison gas attack which killed 12 people on the Tokyo subway earlier in the year. Since the incident, numerous cult officials and members

have been detained; there have been scares of additional gas attacks. One observer referred to the matter as Japan's spring of terror. *Aum Shinrikyo*, the cult which had masterminded the gas attack has now been shown to have had far more ambitious projects in mind. Investigations have revealed efforts to obtain samples of the deadly Ebola virus in Africa, the employment of nuclear engineers in Russia and an apparent effort to mine uranium in Australia. How much more terrifying their effort might have become for Japan and the world is only just now being assessed.

By late 1996 the sense that Japan was somehow free from the social ills that beset much of the rest of the world was crumbling. During a holiday party in the

Prime Minister Ryutaro Hashimoto

Japanese embassy in Lima, Peruvian leftists broke in and took dozens of guests hostage. That the rebels had singled out Japan, whose ties with Peru had grown since President Fujimori came to power in Peru, was something quite new for the Japanese. For so many years such international incidents had been the problems of other nations, not Japan. One writer, commenting on the full range of Japan's recent experiences, even went so far as to write an article about Japan finally becoming an "ordinary" country.

Foreign and Defense Policy

Several issues dominated Japanese foreign and defense policy over the last year

and both had their origins in Japan's World War II experiences. One, the struggle over the renewal of the American bases in Okinawa, harkened back to the era of American occupation of the islands after the war, and the second, the effort by right–wing Japanese to strengthen their claim to the Daiyous Islands, (known to the Japanese as the Senkaku Islands) harkened back to even more emotional memories of the pre–war era. As always the tensions over Japanese–American trade balances continued to complicate matters as well.

For years resentments have grown in Japan over the presence of American bases. These sentiments are especially strong in Okinawa where the bulk of the bases are located. Several factors have added to the tensions, some tied to a more general evolution of the international arena and others linked directly to events in Okinawa. Support in Japan has dramatically lessened for a continuing American presence in the country. The Cold War has been over for almost a decade and the general public is no longer as supportive of the American presence.

On June 9, 1993 Japan's attention was riveted on a solemn but joyous event. Concern for political scandals and economic troubles were set aside. For this was the day on which the son of Emperor Akihito, Prince Naruhito, was to marry American–educated career woman Masako Owada. The ancient ceremony was watched by millions of Japanese throughout the country on high definition TV (HDTV). The ceremony, which takes the better part of a day, involves several costume changes and rituals performed in different locations. The Prince's parents did not attend the ceremony but received an official report from the Prince at the end of the day informing them of the marriage. For weeks prior to the wedding, the newspapers and television carried stories about the princess–to–be, complete with interviews of friends she hadn't even seen in a decade or more.

But the excitement regarding the wedding of the crown prince in 1993 was embarrassingly complemented by published reports in Japanese newspapers during 1996 of sexual escapades within the imperial family— a public treatment of the Japanese family more typical of media behavior toward the British Royal Family than anything the public has been previously used to in Japan.

Japan

Within Okinawa, American insensitivity and domination of some of the island's best lands has added to the problem. The American establishment of an artillery range which fired over a public road is only one of the most egregious examples. But the rape in 1995 of a young Japanese girl by soldiers from one of the American bases dramatically increased the anger of the Okinawans.

For a time the Governor of Okinawa refused to cooperate with the effort to renew the bases and only with considerable difficulty was Prime Minister Hashimoto able to find a solution to the tensions. The final treaty signed last year will see a significant reduction of the American presence in Okinawa and the creation of a new off–shore helicopter landing facility to be used by the Americans (paid for by Tokyo).

For decades the trade imbalance has also been a constant irritant in Japanese–American Relations. Over the last decade Japan has consistently had a sizeable trade surplus with the United States. In 1994 it was over $67 billion!

In an earlier attempt to address this problem the U.S. Congress passed the Omnibus Trade and Competitiveness bill in 1988. The "Special 301" section of that bill provided a powerful weapon in the form of heavy tariffs on U.S. imports from countries deemed to be engaging in unfair trading practices. "Special 301" was used with limited successes by both Presidents Bush and Reagan. The Bush Administration introduced the Structural Impediments Initiative (SII) to be used with Special 301. SII talks were aimed at eliminating the fundamental economic differences between the two countries that resulted in large trade deficits. These areas included the high Japanese savings rate and low level of support for public infrastructure, high land prices, and Japanese business practices deemed unfair by the Americans. There was little effect on the overall trade deficit.

In a somewhat curious irony from the usual American association with "free trade" the Clinton Administration opted for an aggressive "managed trade" approach which insisted on establishing set targets. In 1994 and early 1995, the major issue was access to the Japanese market for American autos and auto parts. On May 6, 1995, talks collapsed. The Clinton Administration responded with a plan to place a 100% tariff on the major Japanese luxury cars. The Japanese did not accept the U.S. concept of managed trade. Nevertheless, enough progress has been made to lower the level of rhetoric.

By the end of 1995, there was hard evidence that the large deficit in U.S. merchandise trade with Japan was shrinking rapidly. The deficit for 1996, having gone down for two years in a row was a lower $47.7 billion. This was because of the high value of the Japanese yen, because of an opening of some markets and a more subtle dispersal of Japanese manufacturing throughout other parts of Asia which made the specific Japanese–American relationship look somewhat more in balance. Moreover, newer developments are likely to improve trade relations The long term weakening of their economy has added to the Japanese consumer's interest in less expensive goods, and the drop in land prices have combined to allow the introduction of more American style superstores. Changes in regulations regarding such investments have also facilitated this development. It seems likely as well that more international marketing over the Internet is likely to transform international trade in ways we have not yet even begun to imagine.

Lastly Japanese American economic issues are less likely to make waves in the media. China is rapidly becoming the country with which America has its largest trade imbalance. Thus, "Japan bashing" may well give way to "China bashing" as the U.S. deficit with that country grows. But relations, economic and political, with the United States, for so long the most important aspect of Japan's foreign relations, have now become less important as its role in Asia grows.

Japan's relationship with China was especially in the spotlight in 1996. Japanese ultra–nationalists made more efforts to stake claims on the disputed East China Sea Daiyous Islands during the summer of 1996. Not surprisingly, Chinese from all walks of life, from Hong Kong to Taiwan and the People's Republic, were angered.

Crown Prince Naruhito and Princess Masako visit a nursing home.

Unfortunately the Japanese government's rather casual attitude about the affair only helps reinforce some of the remaining fears of Japan. Happily, the government of the People's Republic seemed more concerned than Tokyo that the situation not get out of hand.

Beyond Asia and the Pacific, Japan has continued to expand its international role, assuming more of the posture expected of a major power. This was most evident in the country's participation in UN sponsored missions. Japan sent forces to Rwanda to perform a human relief operation. Air self–defense forces served in Kenya in September ferrying supplies to the Rwanda operation. Japan continued to be a major aid–giving country.

Japan defeated India for a coveted rotating seat on the U.N. Security Council and continues to work toward gaining a permanent seat.

CULTURE

Before the arrival of Chinese influence, Japanese culture was rather simple; it was centered around the Shinto belief in spirits existing everywhere in nature. With the adoption of so many aspects of Chinese civilization Shinto was somewhat overwhelmed by the growth of Buddhism. In the modern era Shinto experienced a revival of sorts with the Meiji Government's decision to use it as a feature of its enhancement of the role of the emperor.

After the Second World War, that "official Shinto" as it is sometimes called, was again de–emphasized. Today both Shinto and Buddhism are somewhat eclectically interwoven in Japanese society.

Today it is acceptable for a Japanese to marry in a Shinto shrine, to venerate his ancestors at the Buddhist Temple and at the same time to celebrate the Christmas holidays even if in reality he has little faith in any religion. The emphasis at Christmas is actually on gathering at the family home for fun and fellowship.

The Japanese were the first non–Western country to attempt to industrialize along Western models and thus faced earliest a dilemma that communities around the world continue to deal with—how to modernize one's society without simply becoming "Western." Today, the older cultural patterns are not dead—in fact they are often creatively blended with modernity.

The increasingly urban life of the Japanese is a distinctive one. The business sections of the city are usually constructed of reinforced concrete, but the outlying buildings are simple, yet attractive, wood and paper structures. The people who work in the central city during the day go

Marunouchi, Tokyo's business district

Courtesy: PANA, Japan

to the suburbs in the evening—thus the morning and evening commuting hours are as frantic as those in the cities of the United States. Very long commutes are the norm and the common pattern is one that Americans who commute by rail into cities like New York could easily identify with.

Happily for the Japanese their transport systems, particularly rail, are as modern as can be found in the world. The *Bullet* trains between Tokyo and Osaka, as known around the world, are traveling as fast as 160 miles per hour. By contrast, Metroliner service between Washington and New York runs at the same speed it did 25 years ago (although plans are now being carried out to speed this up by using new equipment).

Television, radio and computer games are widely enjoyed, and while not yet as enamored of the Internet as many Americans, its use is growing quickly. All of the fine arts are widely found in the cities, particularly Tokyo. Traditional European and Western musical works and ballet are heavily attended, as are cultural expres-

sions which are distinctly Japanese such as the Kabuki and Noh theater performances.

On another level, blue–grass and country western music *sung in Japanese* has a large following. And today, McDonald's and Kentucky Fried Chicken are the top two restaurant chains in Japan. Underlying this shift to Western food is a far more significant outcome. Rice consumption is down 50% in the last quarter century. Consumption of meat and dairy products is skyrocketing, and Japanese young adults are definitely growing taller and bigger.

On paper Japanese women have rights that American women are still struggling for. More than a decade ago, a Japanese law similar to the American Equal Rights Amendment was passed, and now efforts are underway to strengthen its provisions against sexual discrimination. Laws are even under consideration to legally allow them to retain their maiden names after marriage. (A curious irony since in some Asian countries that has always been the case).

Nevertheless women still earn only

Japan

Yokozuma **Akebono holding young boy aloft**

art of Japanese *Sumo* wrestling, a highly stylized, ritualistic and beloved sport of Japan. Learning Japanese and taking the name *Akebono,* in 1993 he vied for the championship, winning when he heaved his opponent out of the ring in less than 5 seconds. Conservatives in the Sumo hierarchy debated furiously before reluctantly awarding him the title of *Yokozuma* ("grand champion").

As we approach the end of the 20th century, the single most important aspect of Japanese society is the reality that it is aging rapidly. Today, more than 14% of the population is over 65. By 2020 more than a quarter will be. How more and more pensioners are going to be supported by fewer and fewer workers will be the challenge Japan and many other developing countries are soon going to have to face. Japan though is facing this graying of its population sooner than others.

EDUCATION IN THE U.S. AND JAPAN

The growing importance of the United States and Japan to each other has led, on both sides of the Pacific, to comparisons of many aspects of the two countries, especially their economic ties. Another frequent subject of comparison is their respective educational systems.

On the U. S. side, the public school system below the college or university level is highly decentralized thus making it very difficult to generalize about the American system as a whole. Control rests with state and local officials and boards, including popularly elected members. The system is permissive in many ways, the most obvious being with respect to dress. Academic standards vary widely. There are often serious disciplinary problems (violence, drugs, and pregnancies) especially in the big urban schools.

The comparatively less official pressure in the U.S. toward conformity produces a typical situation in which the general level of achievement has markedly declined compared to other countries such as Japan. However, there are incentives and opportunities, at least in the better schools, for able students to do original and reasonably advanced work. Private (including parochial Catholic) schools charge tuition rather than being tax–supported, and on the average have higher standards than the public schools, although not higher than the best public schools.

At the college level the situation also varies widely, to the point where few generalizations are possible here either beyond the observation that there are both public and private universities and colleges, with a wide qualitative gap between the best and the worst. A student

about 62% of what a man earns and hold only 23 seats in the lower house of representatives among a total possible of 500. Happily, there is more common agreement today that these issues need to be addressed than there was in the past. Japan has finally begun to make progress in dealing with its responsibilities toward the "comfort women" it enslaved during the war. Government sponsored private charities are now funneling funds to its wartime victims though the government's unwillingness to officially confront its treatment of women during the war is still a subject of considerable anger in some parts of Asia.

Despite Japan's obvious accomplishments in engineering and technology, there are curious ironies in its delivery of modern medicine. Only recently has the country departed from its traditional definition of life: the presence of a beating heart, regardless of the condition of the patient's brain. This definition made it practically impossible for Japanese medicine to offer its patients transplant procedures common in the rest of the world. This will now rapidly change. In contrast to the United States, procedures like abortion are not controversial in Japan while the use of the birth control pill is still illegal.

Chad Rowan from Hawaii studied the

64

usually spends the first two years completing his or her general education, and the last two (or perhaps three) specializing ("majoring") in some particular subject or field. At the graduate and pre–professional levels, there is less variation in the quality of programs offered, and American institutions offering such programs are widely admired abroad and attract large numbers of foreign (including Japanese) students. One of the signs of the creativity that is not only permitted, but encouraged, by the American system, is the high proportion of all Nobel Prizes gained by their graduates. Only at the graduate and professional school levels are standardized admissions tests, such as the LSAT and the GRE, important.

On the Japanese side, the situation is quite different, in spirit and outcome as well as in form. The system is much more centralized and on a practical level easier to generalize about. At all levels the public schools, and to some extent also the private schools, are under the control of the Ministry of Education in Tokyo.

From the kindergarten level through high schools, Japanese students and their parents are under tremendous competitive pressure, mainly because ultimate career success is assumed to require graduation from some prestigious university (ideally Tokyo University known as *Todai*). Below the college level, students generally wear uniforms, and conformity is expected as to hairstyles, behavior and effort. Students who rebel, as some do, are usually severely dealt with—and that in a system where corporal punishment administered by teachers is still common. The emphasis in education is on memorization. Individuality and creativity are discouraged and even penalized.

Very competitive entrance examinations for schools are common, even below the college level. Parents and students spend an enormous amount of time and energy on special programs and "cram" schools to improve their chances of admission into the better schools. Not surprisingly, there are frequent reports of students committing suicide from the pressures imposed

upon them and their families. Fees of $400 a month were not uncommon for after–school training, and a week–long cram school program for entrance into middle school could cost as much as $5000!

Although hard to get into, Japanese colleges are not hard to stay in. The instruction generally adds little to what the student has already learned. There is slightly more scope for originality, but not much. The real accomplishment more often than not is admittance and graduation from a particularly prestigious college rather than the material learned. Professional training, except in law and medicine, tends to be received on the job rather than in graduate school. By the "Nobel test", the Japanese system of higher education does not stand up well; relatively few of these prizes have been won by graduates. The growing awareness of the problem has been especially highlighted by reports of Japanese successes in science earned by those who have worked outside of the system in other countries.

By comparison, however, U.S. employ-

Morning traffic on Uchibori–dori Avenue

Japan

ers seeking technical job applicants and even clerical help in virtually every field find the potential employees often lack basic skills they should have learned in the first eight years of education. These include clear handwriting, good research, writing, organizational skills and mathematical proficiency.

In short, the strengths and weaknesses of the two systems vary dramatically from each other. American society at its best has been able to create a world class system of higher education, but has all too often fallen dramatically short at the lower levels, while Japan's system has been much more able to supply a uniform level of accomplishment through high school but less so at the university and graduate levels.

ECONOMY

The experience of Japan in the half–century since World War II has been one of extraordinary sacrifice, accomplishment and more recently of disappointment. World War II brought on the virtual destruction of Japan's physical plant, but not of the human qualities that had built that plant. Among the most important of these were (and are) energy, persistence, a high level of education and basic technical skills, a high rate of saving and a willingness (somewhat declining at present) to accept relatively modest living standards.

The American occupation helped the Japanese economy by not imposing war reparations or other excessive burdens on it. The Korean War gave it a major shot in the arm (as did the Vietnam war in the next decade) in the form of official U.S. "offshore procurement" of supplies other than weapons from Japanese firms for use in connection with the war. By that time, various American specialists were beginning to advise Japanese industry how it could increase its productivity, which was then low; it was not long before Japanese efficiency began to approach the highest world levels.

As suggested above, the Japanese government, after the end of the Occupation in 1952, systematically pursued an Asian capitalist style of "industrial policy" aimed at stimulating Japanese recovery on the basis of "export–led growth." Anti–trust policy in Japan is much less severe than in the U.S., and this made it possible for Japanese industry to "rationalize" itself to a high degree in the mid–1950's. The government, through the Ministry of International Trade and Industry, MITI, was much more involved in economic planning than is common in the United States (at least at the federal level), and more concern was put on retaining workers and markets than shareholder's profits.

"Sunset industries," such as textiles,

were de–emphasized, although not necessarily phased out entirely; industries using "leading edge" technologies were promoted: steel, automobiles, electronics, etc. This "rationalization" process had a spectacularly beneficial effect on Japan's industrial production and its export position beginning in the early 1960's. So did such domestic factors as political stability, social cohesion and a low defense budget, held by treaty to a little bit under 1% of the GNP until 1987. External factors such as the relative openness of the vast U.S. market also helped greatly.

These elements were coupled with relatively high tariffs imposed by the Japanese government on imports and a maze of import regulations which were actually barriers, a generally stable international scene (due in large part to U.S. policy) and the conscious undervaluing (at least until 1971) of the yen, with its stimulating effect on Japanese exports.

But even from the Japanese point of view there have been some real drawbacks to this process. The cost of living has been kept unnecessarily high due to many factors ranging from the undervaluing of the yen and the extensive system of middlemen in the distribution system through barriers to imports, including agricultural products. The Japanese agricultural population (about 12% of the total) is guaranteed high prices and protected from foreign competition for political reasons, so that food is very expensive. The distribution (retail) system is very inefficient; it is divided between chains of large, expensive department stores and a huge number of mom and pop corner stores, also expensive. Housing, public utilities and the like have been the victims of cumulative under–investment, so that the average Japanese lives under conditions considerably less pleasant than the overall wealth of the country (with currently a GNP of well over one trillion U.S. dollars annually) would suggest. Energy costs, especially for oil (all imported) are necessarily high; Japan is developing a major nuclear power industry (also based on imported raw materials) as a partial solution.

In spite of these problems, Japan is an industrial giant, second only to the United States. It has proved better able than other industrial economies to cope with the rise (since the end of the 1960's) in the cost of imported oil. Its large trading companies have proved very effective in penetrating foreign markets, especially that of the U.S. It copes with import quotas, when imposed by foreign governments, through "up scaling" (keeping the number of exported units within the quotas, but improving their quality and increasing their price, while staying somewhat below the prices of competitive goods

Refrigerator inspection line.

Courtesy: Japanese Embassy

A steel mill.

produced in the countries of destination). Having accumulated enormous foreign exchange surpluses through exports and domestic savings, Japanese firms and banks have long been in a position to lend and invest abroad on a massive scale.

Japan is as well in the forefront of advanced technology; its main competitor is the U.S. There is a race between them, for example, to develop the next "generation" of computers, ceramic engines, etc. In short, for much of Japan's recent history, while the individual consumer was often hard pressed to make ends meet, the economy as a whole has done well. But that situation has changed in recent years.

Bank failures have grown, the stock market has weakened and the economy has lost the momentum which made it seem invincible only a few years ago. The bubble has burst on land prices and they too have begun to decline. The Japanese economy grew at less than 1% in fiscal 1994, which ended on 31 March 1995. Reports of 3.6% for 1996 sounded better, but forecasts in early 1997 showed more weakening. Overall, since 1992 the Japanese economy has only risen by 6% while that of the United States has gone up by 22%.

Low consumer demand has also hurt the economy. Ironically, given the years of tension within the international auto in-

dustry, the American Ford Motor Company has just taken a controlling interest in Mazda. *This is a the first time a Japanese company has ever been directed by foreigners.*

But these changes have had some positive aspects—if not for Japanese corporations, then for the Japanese public. Japanese consumers have long shouldered the burden of artificially high prices for most of the goods they consumed from rice to electronics. The Japanese model seemed to be one of excellent service coupled with high prices regardless of what people actually wanted. But those days may be passing. The declining price of land coupled with changing consumer attitudes and regulatory changes have made it possible for the larger American style super store and malls to make significant inroads into Japan. These developments may not please the Japanese corporations or small businesses but will certainly have a positive impact on consumer satisfaction and U.S.–Japanese trade balances.

Japan's regional role in Asia has been growing significantly over the past decade. In fact, Asia is the principal area of Japanese trade these days rather than the United States. And Japanese corporations have turned to Southeast Asia to solve some of their own economic problems. Facing a tendency for Japanese workers to demand higher pay and shorter hours,

Japanese industry has moved much of its production, usually toward the lower end of the technology spectrum, off–shore, especially to China and Southeast Asia (Thailand in particular). This Japanese investment, coupled with the opening of China under Deng Xiaoping, has spurred economic growth in much of Southeast Asia and even northern Australia. Japan is also becoming a leading investor in Vietnam, a country that because of the former U.S. embargo, was unable to obtain U.S. investment.

THE FUTURE

The face of Japanese politics continued to change in 1996, but not its substance. Changes in the electoral system have had a significant impact on the House of Representatives and appear to have allowed the *LDP* to resume its leadership of the country. But if the *LDP*'s problems have lessened, those of Japan as a whole have not, and today's *LDP* will lead not an insular economic giant, as it did in an earlier era, but an aging industrial nation with greater responsibilities and enemies abroad than Japan has been used to in the post war era.

Korea

Sketch of a street scene in Seoul about 1880

The Republic of Korea (South Korea)

Area: 38,452 sq. mi. (98,919 sq.km., somewhat larger than Indiana).

Population: 44,600,000 (1993 est.).

Capital City: Seoul (Pop. 9 million estimated).

Climate: Temperate, with a short winter, hot and humid in the summer with a rainy monsoon from July to September.

Neighboring Countries: North Korea (North); Japan (East).

Official Language: Korean.

Other Principal Tongues: Japanese, spoken by many older Koreans; English, spoken by many of the educated Koreans.

Ethnic Background: Korean, related to Manchurian and Mongol.

Principal Religions: Buddhism, Confucianism, Christianity.

Main Exports (to U.S. and Japan): Textiles and clothing, electrical machinery, footwear, steel, ships, fish, automobiles and electronics.

Main Imports (from Japan and U.S.): Machinery, oil, transport equipment, chemicals, grains.

Currency: Won.

Former Colonial Status: Korea was a tributary state of the Chinese empires for certain periods until 1895; Japanese protectorate (1905–1910); Japanese Dependency (1910–1945); it was occupied by the U.S. from 1945 to 1948.

National Day: August 15, 1948 (Republic Day).

Chief of State: Kim Young Sam, President, (since February 1993).

Prime Minister: Lee Yung Duk.

National Flag: White, with a center circle divided equally by an S–curve into blue and red portions; there is a varying combination of 3 solid and 3 broken lines in each corner.

Per Capita Income: U.S. $11,750.

The predominantly mountainous peninsula of Korea is actually an extension of the mountains of southern Manchuria, from which it is separated by the Yalu and Tumen Rivers. The spine of the mountains runs from northeast to southwest, but remains close to the eastern coastline area of Korea—eastern Korea is thus rugged, containing many scenic mountain peaks. The famous Diamond Mountains (*Kimgan–san*) in North Korea are particularly spectacular, reaching their greatest height in the Changpai San at the northern border, where the peaks are snow–covered all year.

From these immense mountains, streams gather to form the Yalu River which empties into the Yellow Sea, and the Tumen River which flows into the Sea of Japan. The steep descent of these rivers provides one of the world's best sources of hydroelectric power, with a great potential that has only begun to be developed. The western coastal regions contain most of the peninsula's level plains, interspersed with frequent rivers—this is the agricultural belt where rice predominates, raised in wet paddies in the South, where two crops are harvested each year, and grown in the North on dry plantations, where only one crop matures at the end of the summer.

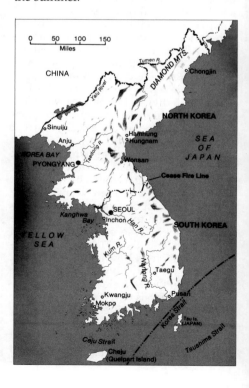

Skyline of modern Seoul. The grounds of the Duksoo Palace, built in the 15th century and carefully preserved, are seen in the foreground, surrounded by the bustling city.

The Democratic People's Republic of Korea (North Korea)

Area: 46,814 sq. mi. (121,730 sq. km., somewhat smaller than Mississippi).

Population: 22 million (estimated).

Capital City: Pyongyang (Pop. 1.2 million, estimated).

Climate: Temperate, with a longer and much colder winter than in the South; summer wet season from July to September.

Neighboring Countries: China (North); Russia (Northeast); South Korea (South).

Official Language: Korean.

Other Principal Tongues: Japanese, spoken by many older Koreans; Russian, spoken by many of the educated Koreans.

Ethnic Background: Korean, similar to both Manchurian and Mongolians.

Principal Religion: Buddhism, Confucianism. The government discourages religious activity.

Main Exports (to Russia, China, Japan): Minerals, meat products, fish.

Main Imports (from China, Russia, Japan): Petroleum, machinery, grains.

Currency: Won.

Former Colonial Status: Korea was a tributary state of the Chinese empires for most of its history up to 1895; Japanese protectorate (1905–1910); Japanese Dependency (1910–1945); from 1945 to 1948 it was under Soviet occupation; after 1948 it developed an independent communist regime allied with both the Soviet Union and with China.

National Day: September 8, 1948.

Chief of State: Kim Jung–Il (not officially announced, but probable), President.

National Flag: Two blue stripes on the top and bottom separated by two thin white stripes from a broad central field of red which contains at left center a white circle with a 5–pointed red star.

Per Capita Annual Income: About U.S. $200.

Tidal variations along the west coast are extreme; there is sometimes a difference of 30 feet between low and high tide. The offshore islands, numbering about 3,500, are the remnants of the mountain chain, standing with their shoulders above water. The long coastline and the nearness to some of the richest fishing grounds in the world have made the people, especially in the South, skilled fishermen and have led to frequent squabbles with individual Japanese and with Japanese governments, because the people of the over–crowded neighboring islands desperately need the same protein which the Koreans harvest from the sea.

The cooler climate of North Korea resembles that of Manchuria. It is better endowed with minerals, hydroelectric facilities and capacity, and the lower regions of the mountains support thick stands of timber. South Korea has a warmer climate, which supports a greater agricultural production. In December, the temperatures in Pusan may be mild at the same time that frigid blasts of below–zero arctic weather envelop the remote mountains of the North. The Siberian black bear and leopard mingle with fierce wild boars, Manchurian tigers and smaller Korean tigers in the thinly populated northern region. As the warmth increases to the south, the animal life becomes more nearly tropical, dominated by herons, gulls and other birds with colorful plumage.

History

From their appearance and language, the Koreans appear to have similar origins to the Turkic–Manchurian–Mongol people who have inhabited northeastern Asia for more than 4,000 years and migrated to the island of Japan as well as to the Korean peninsula. By the 2nd century B.C. they began to undergo a series of waves of Chinese influence; the northern part of the country became a part of the Chinese empire.

For most of the first nine centuries of the Christian era, Korea was divided into three states: Koguyro in the North, Silla in the Southeast and Paekche in the Southwest. All of these were under strong Chinese cultural influence, including Ma-

Korea

A game of *Go–ban*, or oriental chess. Korean Minister of War, Yun–Woong–Niel, is on left. (1900)

A young Korean and his wife in street dress, Seoul, 1902.

hayana (northern) Buddhism, Confucianism and the Chinese written language. There is considerable evidence to suggest that the original Yamato Japanese state may have been an offshoot of the Paekche kingdom. From the 10th through the 14th centuries, the entire peninsula was united under the Buddhist Koryo dynasty, which although theoretically independent, was dominated and paid tribute to the nomadic Mongol empires of northeast Asia which had overrun part or all of China.

In 1392 the area came under the control of the Confucian Yi dynasty which ruled from an imperial capital established in Seoul. For several decades the Yi showed great creativity, wisdom and artistry, advancing in the field of astronomy and inventing an alphabet based on symbols which could be expressed by a movable metal type also devised during the period. Although ruled by a local line of rulers, Korea remained a faithful tributary of the Chinese empire and devoted to Confucian civilization. Chinese military assistance enabled the Koreans to withstand, but with great difficulty, a major Japanese invasion from 1592 to 1598. The drain and exhaustion of the war though rendered the prostrate Koreans an easy

mark for the powerful Manchus from Manchuria, who after conquering the peninsula, seized China itself.

There was a general decline of cultural and political activity in Korea, which became an intensely isolationist vassal of the Manchu empire in China for the next two centuries. Occasional Europeans who were shipwrecked on the rough coastline were held captive. Shortly after the mid–1850's the major Western powers became interested in the region. China was weakened by its own efforts to resist domination by the same powers and expressed no reaction when the Japanese recognized the "independence" of Korea in 1876. Japan did not win this concession from China—it was merely taking advantage of the weakness of Korea and the Manchus.

Despite its almost extreme preoccupation with anti–foreignism, the Yi rulers were compelled to sign a series of "unequal treaties" with the major powers, beginning with Japan, similar to those which had been and were being extracted from China and Japan. Inside Korea, nationalists and modernists at the royal court and the more educated youth looked to Japan as a source of inspiration and direction. On the other hand, the elderly conserva-

tives remained attached to the traditional Confucian empire of the Manchus. China still insisted that it was overlord in Korea. The Japanese, who had rapidly modernized their armed forces, therefore, declared war on the Manchus in 1894.

With little resistance, Chinese forces were driven out of Korea, but the Japanese were not able to establish undisputed control after defeating the Manchu forces—the Russians had also started to exhibit considerable interest in the peninsula.

A Japanese Colony

The short Russo–Japanese War of 1904–1905 resulted in a Japanese victory and the establishment of a protectorate over Korea, which had been the biggest issue in the conflict. With no opposition, Japan simply annexed the peninsula in 1910; Korea became the largest dependency of the growing Japanese empire. Japanese rule was harsh and military, devoted to creating investment opportunities for Japanese capital, raising rice to feed Japan and establishing military bases for further expansion on the Asian continent.

The modern techniques of the Japanese and the advanced education which they offered created in the long run a dramatic and beneficial change from the extreme isolationism which had prevailed under the Yi emperors prior to the advent of Western powers. Angered by open Japanese exploitation and inspired by newly learned democratic slogans used in World War I, thousands of Koreans, many of whom had been converted to Christianity, staged a massive, peaceful demonstration in favor of independence in 1919 which was brutally suppressed by the Japanese.

Independence movements fled to bases outside the country or went underground; they split into a communist wing located in eastern Russia, Manchuria and northern China and a nationalist wing located mainly in eastern China. Relaxing their rule briefly because of adverse Korean and world popular opinion, the Japanese intensified their exploitation when they undertook the conquest of Manchuria and China in the 1930's. In an effort to avoid further unrest, they attempted to absorb the Koreans by forcing them to adopt Japanese names and to speak the language of their conquerors. This had no lasting effect and actually served to further embitter the Koreans against the Japanese.

At the close of World War II, when Japan had all but surrendered to U.S. and British forces, the subject of the future of Korea was considered by the leaders of the "Big Three" at the Potsdam Conference in mid–1945. Russia's Stalin reaffirmed his promise that the U.S.S.R. would declare war on Japan, which it had refrained from doing prior to that time, and proposed that it would secure the Korean peninsula from the Japanese armies. It was ultimately decided that Soviet forces would occupy the northern part of Korea and accept the surrender of the Japanese troops in that region, and the U.S. forces would do the same in the southern portion. The American expectation was that the whole peninsula would come under the supervision of the then infant UN.

This decision, made half way around the world from the helpless Koreans, was to be the basis of continued conflict and friction for years, and also was to cost the loss of thousands of lives. It also ultimately was to result in an economically harmful division of the peninsula. Two days after the first atomic bomb had burst with a terrifying effect on the Japanese city of Hiroshima, the U.S.S.R. declared war on Japan. The Japanese accepted the Allied surrender terms on August 14, but during the few intervening days the Soviets had easily occupied North Korea. The boundary between U.S. and Soviet troops was fixed shortly afterward at the 38th parallel.

In the North, the Russians promptly installed a satellite regime run by Korean communists under the control of the Soviet occupation forces. In the South, U.S. occupation forces followed a shifting policy primarily devoted to economic recovery and to the creation of a democratic government. There were seemingly unending negotiations between the two powers in 1946–1947 on the formation of a provisional government for the entire peninsula; these broke down when it became clear that the Soviets would not settle for less than one rigged in favor of the communists, who were actually a small, predominantly northern minority.

The United States laid the issue before the UN, which tried in 1948 to hold free and supervised elections in both halves of the country as a first step towards reunification. The Russians excluded the UN mission from the North, whereupon the UN authorized elections only in the South. Syngman Rhee, a venerated nationalist figure who had been popular for decades, became the first president. The southern based Republic of Korea was declared independent and was admitted to the UN. The American occupation came to an end. The Russians promptly reacted by establishing the "Democratic People's Republic of Korea" in the North and withdrew their occupation forces. Soviet control and support of local communists were sufficient to maintain North Korea within the Soviet bloc with little or no Russian military presence.

Though the two regimes were poles apart on economic matters, and the nations they chose to associate with during the developing Cold War, each was led by committed nationalists who were determined to reunite their nations.

The Korean War

In January 1950 the American Secretary of State, in a public discussion of American interests in East Asia, excluded South Korea as part of the area. Such words were no doubt encouraging to those in North Korea who hoped to unify the peninsula under their control. Thus after careful preparations, in mid–1950, bolstered by a heavy dose of Soviet military aid, North Korean forces invaded South Korea. Having the advantage of surprise, they were barely prevented from overrunning all of South Korea. Angered by the North's invasion, President Truman reversed the previously announced U.S. policy on Korea and ordered military intervention on the side of the South Koreans.

Choosing to work within the structures of the newly formed United Nations, President Truman then arranged for the UN to condemn the aggressive acts of North Korea and to order military sanctions against the Soviet satellite. Ironically, the representative of the U.S.S.R., who could have employed its veto power was not there to do so. They had been boycotting the council due to controversies surrounding the question of who should hold the China seat; the People's Republic or the Nationalists on Taiwan. The counter–attack itself, while nominally carried out by a UN force, was primarily an American military effort. General Douglas MacArthur commanded the UN forces. Demonstrating

U.S. Marines in Korea, November 1952

Korea

the same energy and self–will he had shown during World War II, MacArthur planned an aggressive campaign to drive the Northern forces out of South Korea.

A combination of mass bombing of the North and a flank attack by an amphibious landing at Inchon, a coastal town near Seoul, succeeded in driving the North Koreans from the territory they had conquered. Then having successfully driven the northern troops from South Korea, MacArthur insisted, and found support among his superiors, for an attack on North Korea and yet another unification drive, this time from the south. Even as the American forces were moving closer and closer to the Chinese borders, MacArthur, ignoring Beijing's warnings, was certain that the forces of the People's Republic would not intervene. Sure of his judgment, MacArthur continued to order his forces toward the Yalu River, the border which divided Korea from China.

MacArthur was wrong. China was not prepared to accept foreign and probably hostile troops within its border. Moreover, both Moscow and Beijing wanted to save the communist regime in Korea. Chinese forces, pretending to be "volunteers," crossed the Yalu River into Korea. Beijing's forces struck with great force, using the same successful guerrilla tactics they had learned in their battles with the Chinese Nationalists during the decades of their civil war. Their effort to drive U.S. and UN forces out of North Korea succeeded, but they could not mount a successful invasion of South Korea.

MacArthur, realizing he had been put on the defensive, very publicly advocated a wider war effort, including the bombing of Chinese Manchurian bases. Eventually the famous general's utterances caused a public break between him and President Truman who had lost faith in his judgment. MacArthur was replaced, but the war itself waged on. Chinese forces tried to retake Seoul in April and May 1951, but their supply lines had become too long to support the effort. Armistice negotiations began in July 1951, but since neither side had won a clear victory, the talks dragged on for two years, while fighting continued.

Each side sought to obtain a defensible position, and gradually the lines of battle hardened with heavy fortifications which would have made a major break–through by either side almost impossible. A crisis over the repatriation of prisoners also prolonged the conflict—the Chinese and North Koreans disliked, and refused to recognize, the proposition that their soldiers—many of whom were former Nationalist soldiers—might not want to return to their homelands. An armistice was reached on July 27, 1953, a few months af-

ter the death of Stalin had led to a reduction of Soviet support for the Chinese role in the Korean war. About 70% of the Chinese prisoners held by the UN forces refused to return to China, and they were soon released, mostly to the Nationalist Chinese on Taiwan.

American politics contributed heavily to this armistice. The popular military hero of World War II, General Dwight Eisenhower, was chosen by the Republican Party to oppose the Democratic Party's nominee. Eisenhower's promise during the campaign to use his influence to end the Korean War greatly influenced the American public.

Privately, President Eisenhower threatened to use nuclear weapons to settle the dispute. The eventual armistice was a stalemate of military might—the demarcation is along about the same line as it was prior to the conflict. The real result of the struggle was the loss of several hundred thousand lives and an almost utter devastation of both Koreas. The fighting may have ended but the two parts of Korea then settled in for a generation long struggle for domination of the peninsula. Over the years that new struggle would take many forms.

Economy of the Two Koreas

Shortly after the armistice, the Soviet Union and China embarked on policies of substantial economic aid programs to North Korea. As a result, it acquired a broad industrial base and a per capita industrial production which rose to a level higher than that of China. Kim Il Sung, the political leader selected by the Soviets in 1945 to lead North Korea, soon acquired exclusive control over the local communist party at the expense of his rivals.

Eventually the Korean War and subsequent Russian–Chinese ideological disputes over what is "true communism" gave Kim a much wider degree of freedom of action within the communist sphere. For a few years after 1960 Kim tended to favor the Chinese without being totally dominated by them. After 1964 he swung back toward the Russians, then again toward the Chinese for a time, and after 1983, toward Moscow until the Soviet Union collapsed.

In South Korea, despite massive American aid the postwar economy floundered and the elderly President Rhee grew senile, autocratic and unpopular. He resigned in 1960 and left the country in the face of rebellious student demonstrations which the army made no effort to suppress. There followed a year of political ferment and regrouping under a weak government which ended in 1961 when the army seized control of South Korea.

South Korea Emerges Economically

After the initial period of direct military rule, General Park Chung–hee, the leader of the military junta which had seized power, nominally became a civilian and was elected president—he was reelected in 1967. In 1972, not satisfied with his authority as the elected president of South Korea, Park pushed through legislation which allowed him to become the dictator of South Korea. With that development, the entire peninsula had fallen under the control of autocratic governments, the communists in the North and Park's supporters in the South. Park justified his actions by citing the need to retain national unity in the South in the face of the northern threat. But if the political situa-

General Park Chung–hee

tion of the two Korea's was growing more similar, the beginnings of their modern economic divergence was also gaining momentum.

The roots of South Korea's modern economic miracle are diverse—ranging from both external to internal factors. What is clear is that from an economy that saw the average per capita income in 1963 at around $100, became by 1990 over $5000! And as the century reached its termination some Korean laborers were earning salaries comparable to American workers in the Midwest.

Previously such an economic transformation is caused by myriad developments but for Korea certain key factors can be noted. Especially important among the external factors were ties with both the Americans and the Japanese. The United States, since the decision to intervene during the Korean War, had been committed to a stable South Korea, and helped create the conditions there conducive to such a condition. By the 1960s, the Korean willingness to align themselves with the internationally unpopular American effort in Vietnam was especially helpful and lucrative. In fact some of the most important South Korean construction firms profited greatly from the projects they carried out in South Vietnam during the war. Their role in some ways resembled that of the Japanese during the similar American involvement in Korea itself during the Korean War. And it was ties to the Japanese themselves that also helped.

Though the memories of the Japanese occupation remained bitter, the reality as well was that the Koreans, and especially many in the elite, were well positioned to take advantage of the economic growth then going on in Japan. These Korean leaders including General Park himself were fluent in Japanese and quite willing to gain the advantages of close economic ties to a growing Japan. And that strategy worked quite well as Japan invested enormously in South Korea. For example Mitsubishi owned about 10% of the South Korean automobile company Hyundai and supplied many of the most important parts.

These advantages would not have been realized if the Park government had not chosen to move his committed and inexpensive labor force into the world export market, an economic path already well trodden by Japan itself. President Park's economic policy and the advantages it gained from the international environment, especially after the early 1960s, was eventually a major success. One has only to look at the modern industrial skyline that Seoul has become or to recognize the very real improvement in living standards today to understand how much was accomplished in those years on the economic front. But on the political level Park's leadership was much less successful.

The talent in North Korea was no more successful. Insisting on maintaining a million–man armed force to hopefullly crush South Korea, the country survived only because of Soviet and Chinese assistance. When the Soviets departed, Chinese rivalry with them in this part of the world waned. North Korea is now bankrupt and starving. It still has its armed force, but dares not to use it for fear of nuclear retaliation by the U.S.

President Park's increasing personal power aroused considerable opposition, especially from the intellectuals, students and the powerful Christian churches. This opposition was cruelly suppressed on the ground that it gave aid and comfort to North Korea at a time when American protection of South Korea was becoming increasingly unreliable. An opposition

leader, Kim Dae Jung, who had received a large minority of the popular vote for the presidency in 1971, was kidnaped in Japan by the South Korean Central Intelligence Agency in 1973 and brought home. President Park's widely beloved wife was fatally shot in mid–1974 in what was officially described as a attempt on the life of the president himself. Since the assassin had some Japanese connections, the government launched a dispute with Japan, but there were reasons to believe that this quarrel, as well as tensions in North Korea–South Korea relations which existed in 1974, was at least partly an effort by the Park government to distract attention from its domestic difficulties.

Despite his easy victory in a rigged referendum held in February 1975, it appeared that Park's heavy–handedness

General Chun Doo Hwan

might cost him the crucial support of the army leadership. Although President Ford visited South Korea in late 1974, it appeared that the U.S. Congress would force budget reductions leading to a partial or even total withdrawal of American forces from South Korea. Subsequently, the Carter administration decided to withdraw all American ground forces by 1982—but changed its mind in 1979 in view of the threat from North Korea. The fall of Indochina to communism in 1975 left South Korea the only non–communist nation on the East Asian mainland and intensified the sense of danger felt in the U.S. This was exploited by President Park to increase his rigid control through repressive measures.

Human rights critics in the U.S. urged withdrawal of economic aid and military support. The ruling Korean *Democratic Republican Party* came closer to defeat in a

1978 election when it won 68 seats in the National Assembly to 61 for the opposition *New Democratic Party*; 22 seats went to independents. President Park reorganized his cabinet and released a number of political prisoners, including the *New Democratic Party's* leader, Kim Dae Jung.

President Park's Death

President Park was assassinated by the head of the South Korean Central Intelligence Agency in October 1979 because of his heavy handedness, particularly towards students and some of his own officials. After an interlude of confusion, the army, under General Chun Doo Hwan, seized power in December 1979. In mid–1980 it proclaimed martial law and viciously crushed a revolt in a southwestern city, Kwangju. The Kwangju Massacre, as it was to become known, was one of the most violent incidents in recent South Korean history and has continued to affect the course of South Korean politics ever since. Chun then became Acting President and began to install a new government. Martial law was finally lifted at the beginning of 1981.

He then launched a policy of "national reconciliation" under which thousands of people imprisoned or barred from public life were pardoned. Even Kim Dae Jung, the best known leader of the democratic opposition, was released at the end of 1982. Nevertheless, he was forced to go into temporary exile in the United States. Despite the repressive measures used by the government to retain and control South Korea, surging economic figures during the 1980s helped retain a reasonable level of satisfaction among the population. Seoul's international prestige was helped as well when it was chosen to serve as the site of the 1988 Olympic Games.

In many ways the assassinated President's emphasis on economic growth was allowing the Republic of Korea to surpass its northern rival without a military confrontation. It was increasingly able to demonstrate by virtue of its accomplishments that its own economic system was stronger.

A Weakened Dictatorship

By the mid 1980s President Chun faced serious political problems. There were mounting student demonstrations against the government, and the leading opposition politician, Kim Dae Jung, had returned from the U.S. Although he was placed under house arrest, a new political party with which he was affiliated, the *New Korea Democratic Party*, did unexpectedly well in National Assembly elections held shortly after his return, winning 50

Korea

out of 276 seats. The overthrow of Marcos in the Philippines in 1986 also had a considerable impact on South Korea, particularly because the U.S. had withdrawn support from him in spite of its large strategic interest in the country. If the United States, reacting to popular Philippine democratic pressures, could turn its back on a long–time ally like Marcos, this might just as easily occur in South Korea as well. The military generals who dominated South Korea clearly decided it was time to move toward opening the system more.

An intensified dialogue ensued between the government and the legal opposition centering on the *New Korea Democratic Party (NKDP)*. A deadlock soon developed,

General Roh Tae Woo

however. It related to the desirable nature of a new constitution. The government and the ruling party, the *Democratic Justice Party (DJP)*, wanted a cabinet (parliamentary) system, with the real power vested in the premier who would presumably be a *DJP* member; the opposition insisted on a directly rather than indirectly chosen (as prevailed at that time) president. He was, it was argued, to be the effective head of the government. The opposition however was hampered by disunity within the leadership of the *NKDP*. Other elements of the opposition, including Christian clergy, lay believers and activist students, demonstrated from time to time against the government. The demonstrators, although fairly numerous, were generally outnumbered by the huge forces of police that the government deployed to cope with them.

South Korea's huge ally, the U.S., clearly favored compromise between the govern-

ment and the opposition, and a democratization of the political system, as Secretary of State Shultz, for example, made clear during a March 1987 visit, but its influence was limited. The activist elements of the opposition tended to view the U.S. as the mainstay of the hated South Korean "establishment," which they regarded as a military and police dictatorship. Many also blamed the United States for the continuing division of their country caused by the tensions of the Cold War.

In the summer of 1987, Chun's *DJP* was preparing to hand over the reins of power to his designated successor, fellow former general and *DJP* politician Roh Tae Woo who had been named head of the ruling *Democratic Justice Party* in early 1985. The public outcry reached even higher levels than those of the spring. Facing potential disaster, Roh called for free elections, counting on a loyal (but minority) *DJP* rural political base and a divided opposition to salvage victory. His assumption that he could still win the election given the splits in the opposition proved correct.

The first direct presidential elections in more than 16 years were held in South Korea in December 1987. The candidate of the ruling *DJP* was Roh Tae Woo. The two top opposition leaders, Kim Young Sam and Kim Dae Jung, were unwilling to cooperate, and the result was predictable: the winner was Roh Tae Woo with 39.9% of the vote, while the two Kims split the majority opposition vote 27.5% and 26.5%. Amid anti–government protests, erupting into severe street rioting, Roh Tae Woo was sworn in as president in February 1988. For the moment Roh, the former general, had prevailed, but the momentum toward a more open system had nevertheless begun. The system was beginning to open up. In an election for the National Assembly held in April of 1988, the ruling *Democratic Justice Party* won only 125 of the 299 seats.

Flexing its new power, the opposition then held hearings on various abuses of power during the tenure of former President Chun Doo Hwan, and especially on the Kwangju massacre of May 1980. Chun himself refused to testify, and President Roh refused to compel him to do so. Chun did make a public apology, turned over his assets to the state, and retired to the countryside. Dissatisfied, a number of opposition politicians and radicals continued to demand that he be put on trial. That demand though was to wait until more progress was made in the democratization of the country. Nevertheless, early in 1989, approximately fifty people, including two brothers of Chun's, were arrested on charges of corrupt practices under his administration.

President Roh himself had a better im-

age than his predecessor, but the opposition in the National Assembly hoped to pass a vote of no confidence in his administration and compel his resignation. In March 1989, Roh canceled an earlier promise to submit his administration to a popular referendum after one year in office. The several years leading up to the 1993 presidential election was an important transitional period. Many did not trust the ruling party or President Roh Tae Woo. It was believed that he might seek illegal means of holding onto power. The new constitution was untested and the opposition was, for the most part, weak.

President Kim Young Sam

There was also concern that the United States might significantly downsize its commitment to the republic. In spite of these concerns, 1993 did mark the beginning of a new, more democratic era for the country.

Contemporary South Korea—Political

South Korea is composed of fifteen administrative subdivisions including nine provinces and six special cities. The current constitution became operative on February 25, 1988. The legal system is derived from both Western and Chinese sources. Suffrage is universal at age 20. The president is the chief of state, while the prime minister is the head of government. The State Council (cabinet) is appointed by the president with the recommendation of the prime minister. South Korea has a unicameral (single house) legislature, the *Kukhoe*.

Major political parties include the: *Democratic Liberal Party (DLP)*, headed by President Kim Young Sam; the *Democratic Par-*

ty (DP), under Yi Ki–taek; and the *United People's Party (UPP)*, Kim Tong–kil, chairman. The *DLP* was formed when the *Democratic Justice Party (DJP)*, *Reunification Democratic Party (RDJ)*, and *New Democratic Republican Party (NDRP)* merged in February 1990. Both the parties and their membership are fluid, with frequent name changes and membership re–alignment.

South Korea also has a number of functioning special interest groups such as the National Council of Churches, National Council of Labor Unions, and the Korean Trade Association.

The Latest Elections

The election of 1993 finally brought to power Kim Young Sam, a long time democratic reformer who along with Kim Dae Jung had been especially involved in trying to bring about democratic reform. His election represented the arrival to the presidency of the first civilian elected leader in a generation. His *Democratic Liberal Party* continues to be the dominant political party though by early 1997 its leadership was being severely questioned.

Upon coming to power, the new president, who was initially quite popular, put forward three specific goals: achieve civilian control over the military and depoliticization of the military, a more caring

government, and an anti–corruption program. By 1994 President Kim had initiated reforms to improve the political process. In a bi–partisan move, the National Assembly passed bills dealing with campaign spending, election procedures and local government. Government subsidies for political parties and candidates were increased. The overall limit on campaign spending was lowered. Strong penalties were introduced. The legislation did not place a limit on how much *a party* could spend on a candidate. Overall, these changes made it easier for the opposition to compete on even footing with the ruling party (unless South Korea applies the lesson of the U.S. in its 1996 election).

Legislation dealing with local government provided for the election of mayors to begin in June 1995. The legislature also was given increased authority over the budget and actions of the *National Security Planning Agency (NSPA)*.

President Kim also succeeded in obtaining the agreement of all top military officials not to interfere in the political process. Charges of corruption were brought against top military figures and several were relieved of their positions, including the army chief of staff. Army personnel who were members of the *Hanahoe* (One Mind) organization were removed from office. The new government also moved

to dismantle the *National Security Planning Agency*. A further significant move involved the release of almost 40,000 criminals and political prisoners. Helmeted riot police withdrew from the streets and the number of student demonstrations decreased.

Anti–corruption measures were initiated against a number of high ranking government officials. After some thirty years of military participation in the political process, it is somewhat remarkable that the new president has had as much success as he has. South Korea had changed a great deal since President Park had ruled with an iron hand! President Kim was even named the winner of the Martin Luther King Prize for his contribution to building democracy and human rights in South Korea. To the astonishment of many who had watched the long time domination of South Korea by the military, President Kim even put on trial his two predecessors, Chun and Roh, for their roles in both the coup that brought them to power and the subsequent 1988 Kwangju Massacre. The trials ultimately concluded with former President Chun sentenced to death and President Roh to life imprisonment (lessened on appeal to life sentence and 17 years respectively).

If President Kim had thought the trials would work to his advantage, he may

South Korea's National Assembly in session. Housed in the nation's new building, legislators enjoy all modern technological innovations including electronic voting.

Courtesy: Embassy of Korea

Korea

Mechanized rice harvesting in Korea. Although Korean rice yields are among the highest in the world, mechanization has become necessary as demand rises with the standard of living, and agricultural workers leave the land for jobs in industry.

have guessed wrong because they uncovered the depth of corruption inherent in the South Korean political system. That public airing of the Chun and Roh years eventually spilled over on to Kim's own associates.

Economic Corruption Scandal

A flow of corruption revelations has swept over the political landscape in recent years. Former President Roh Tae Woo admitted to receiving over $600 million in contributions from businesses during his term in office. Roh's admissions came after two of his associates, one of whom managed the secret fund, revealed its existence. It then became apparent that in return for the huge payments, large corporations such as Hyundai, Samsung, Daewoo, and Lucky Goldstar received large government contracts. Another revelation was that Kim Dae Jung, an unsuccessful candidate for the presidency in 1992, had received over $2.5 million from Roh for his campaign.

The corruption charges, however, were not exclusively the problems of the former Presidents Chun and Roh or even President Kim's long time democratic rival Kim Dae Jung. Early 1997 saw charges of collusion between President Kim's closest

advisors and even his son with the *Hanbo* Group. The President was struggling, as spring of 1997 unfolded, to find a way out of the growing scandal with his own reputation intact. And with the recent memory of his two predecessors in jail, President Kim has plenty of reason to do so. But corruption scandals which were rocking South Korea by mid 1997 were not the only thing that weakened President Kim's prestige.

Well aware that South Korea's soaring economy of the 1980s had stalled, the President became convinced that new economic laws needed to be implemented to give South Korean businesses more flexibility over their work forces. That in itself might have been an understandable conclusion, but when President Kim's supporters called an early morning meeting of the Korean Parliament on December 26 and passed legislation allowing businesses to lay workers off or adjust their hours more easily, this stirred up a hornet's nest of civil disobedience movement. For weeks, in late December and January of 1997, the world watched as South Korea's democratically elected president was challenged by thousands of workers for reducing their economic security and acting undemocratically. Eventually, President Kim, his earlier insistence on holding firm not with-

standing, agreed to allow the parliament—including the opposition parties—the opportunity to review the legislation.

Worrisome to many though in the aftermath of the compromise was the fact that enhanced security legislation passed during that same early dawn meeting was allowed to go into effect. Many feared it would have a chilling effect on South Korea's new freedoms.

Recent Relations with North Korea

In the years since the collapse of the Soviet Union and the more recent death of Kim Il Sung, the long–time leader of North Korea, people in the south have been divided about how to deal with their northern neighbor. On one hand it has been clear that the North Korean economy has been failing and the regime losing its grip on the its citizens. Most important, food production has been plummeting in North Korea. That the regime is likely to continue to weaken seems apparent but how the South should react remains less clear. Basically three different approaches seem to be in the forefront of public thought.

First, the regime might collapse suddenly. That such an eventuality might please those in the South who have spent their lives struggling against the North is

76

certainly likely. On the other hand such a collapse would leave the Republic of Korea the enormous and sudden burden of integrating the much less sophisticated infrastructure of the North into that of the South. The financial burdens would be enormous as demonstrated recently when West Germany basically had to do the same thing regarding East Germany. But South Korea does not have the same resources as Bonn did, and its current economic weakness would only make the burden more difficult.

Second, others hope to work for a smoother transition, a so–called easy landing to North Korea's assumed collapse, emphasizing those programs which allow a smoother and less dramatic transition. Third, some aware of the enormous complexities of following either strategy have understandably hoped for a simple relaxation of tensions that had prevailed on the Peninsula. But that is often as difficult as incidents keep occurring that highlight both these difficulties and the North's weakness.

The problem is not one that consideration of which can be postponed. Investigations are now underway into the actual conditions within North Korea, where some children are reported to be limited to three ounces of rice per day.

Among other prominent incidents in recent months was the landing, apparently forced, of a North Korean mini–submarine in South Korea. In that September 1996 incident a mini–submarine was accidentally beached in South Korea. Recognizing the dangers of their circumstances, the sailors on board appear to have killed themselves while the soldiers set off into the interior of South Korea. Before the incident was over 26 North Koreans and several people from the South were dead.

Eventually the North apologized for the incident but not before another round of incrimination had developed between the two sides. But the North's apparent attempt to infiltrate the South even while it accepted its food aid was only one more example of the North's inconsistency regarding relations with Seoul.

... and the United States

A large number, although not a majority, of South Koreans, not all of them radicals, have become strongly dissatisfied with the status of the relationship with the United States. The major issues are the American responsibility for the partition of Korea in 1945 (even given that the alternative was Soviet domination of the entire peninsula), American support for a series of authoritarian governments in South Korea, and the alleged lack of American enthusiasm for reunification of the country. Somewhat less serious irritants are American control of the Combined Forces Command, under which South Korean forces serve; American military facilities including a golf course not far from the center of Seoul; American pressures to increase Seoul's financial support for the American forces in South Korea and to open its markets further to American products, especially agricultural commodities and, finally, the alleged tendency toward protectionism in the United States.

The recent weakening North Korea has added to the differences which divide these two long–time allies. Chief among them is the ambivalence among the South Koreans regarding the appropriate policy to take towards the North. For some Koreans this is believed to be the best time to push toward a complete collapse of the Northern regime regardless of the short term difficulties involved in absorbing the communist government. Washington however, with thousands of troops on the peninsula, has been much more interested in lowering the level of rhetoric and moving toward a much smoother transition toward the future. These two views have often dictated different attitudes toward events and decision–making on the peninsula.

Culture

Korean culture, although distinct from that of Japan, resembles it in many respects. And of course they have both also been exposed to Chinese influences over many centuries. Not surprisingly there are many cultural features that all three Confucian–influenced communities share in common. Nevertheless, Korea like Japan has also developed along its own unique cultural lines. The ancient pre–Chinese aspects of Korean culture, such as shamanism—the belief in occult sorcerers and worship of demons—have a Northeast and Central Asian derivation. On this base the ingredients of Chinese culture, including Buddhism and Confucianism, were superimposed as a second layer.

Since the 19th century there have been many conversions to Christianity. In fact, due to the support many foreign Christian missionaries gave to the Koreans during their years as a Japanese colony, the religion has an association with Korean nationalism not generally found elsewhere in East Asia.

Today, the Christian community is a large and influential group which exerts a profound influence in the peninsula. Like most of Asia, Korean society remains a strongly patriarchal society. Traditionally some women's roles as shaman–like priestesses in the traditional religion of the peninsula did give them levels of influence not always possible elsewhere.

In recent years, partly as a result of women's activism, laws have been passed improving their status when the South Korean Family Law was amended to give women more property and divorce rights. Today, they have access to higher education as do young men though few hold positions of executive level responsibility in the country's businesses. Women have served in positions of influence in the government bureaucracy and as elected officials, and more efforts have been made to expand the opportunities available to them. The Korean military has even been involved with efforts to have women serve as pilots.

Economy

The last 18 months have been a period of serious trauma for the South Korean economy. After spending a heady period as one of the exciting Asian Tigers, South Korea, like Japan before it, is seeing its economic energy lessening. Its wage bills have been going up faster than its competitors and have not kept up with a corresponding growth of productivity.

Koreans have been losing markets to newer emerging economies like that of the People's Republic of China. Early last year, hoping to inject new life and flexibility into the system, President Kim reverted to a very undemocratic method of decision–making. In the early dawn hours after Christmas his party arranged for a secret parliamentary meeting where they used the absence of opposition delegates (who had not been informed of the meeting) to pass legislation that would have given Korean employers more flexibility in firing workers. The act, which on purely international economic grounds might be defensible, only further undermined the reputation of the government while doing little to add strength to the economy. By January 1997 President Kim had been forced by weeks of street demonstrations to allow the entire parliament, including the opposition, an opportunity to amend the document. These moves may have strengthened democracy in the long run but they did nothing to make South Korea more economically able to meet the demands of the 21st century, nor to compete with other Asian economies with lower wage demands.

NORTH KOREA

Political System

The Democratic People's Republic of Korea (DPRK) is one of the world's few remaining hard line "communist" states.

Korea

Assembly line at the Hyundai automotive company in Seoul—the *Excel*

The constitution was adopted in 1948 and was revised most recently in 1992. The legal system is built on communist jingoism and German civil law. The judiciary has no authority to review acts of the legislature. Suffrage is universal for everyone 17 years of age and older. The government has both a President and a Premier. The State Administration Council (cabinet) is appointed by the Supreme People's Assembly. For most of its history the state was dominated by one individual, Kim Il Sung, who died in 1994.

Since then his son Kim Jung–Il has assumed the mantle of authority. Hong Song Nam is the acting premier. The Supreme People's Assembly is the national legislature and has one house. Candidates for office are chosen by the *Korean Workers' Party (KWP)* and run unopposed. Minor parties are tolerated and hold a few seats in the People's Assembly. As a matter of practicality, all government structures exist only with the permission of the military and, to a lesser degree, the party. Kim Jung–Il has remained largely in seclusion, either voluntary or arranged.

The 1990s have been a disaster for North Korea. The decade began with the collapse of their long–time supporter, the Soviet Union, and continues to today with Beijing, their only significant international friend insisting that they dramatically transform their economy to survive. Despite North Korea's long–time reputation as the most isolated of national states, evidence of its dramatically faltering economy are everywhere. Recent years have seen disastrous floods that have devastated important farm lands while the once proud regime has had to request food aid from outside agencies. Bluster aside, the defection of respected leaders, and even deals to house Taiwan's nuclear waste, all attest to the desperate situation Pyongyang finds itself in.

In 1994, Kim Il Sung, the long time exalted leader, died just before he was to meet with South Korean President Kim Young Sam.

Economy

The government of North Korea did not release a budget for 1995–1996. Massive floods and mismanagement of the economy were responsible for a disastrous year. It can be estimated that for 1995, the country was three to four million tons short on its grain supply. Even in 1993, the government launched a "let's eat two meals a day" campaign. Per capita GNP for 1994 was put at about $900 by one South Korean estimate. The same estimate suggests a decline in trade of some 20%, to about $2.1 billion. For 1995, trade was probably below $2 billion. Between 1990 and 1994, the economy is estimated to have shrunk almost 20%. Far too late North Korea has been attempting to follow the path long ago trodden by its huge northern neighbor the People's Republic of China, that of opening the country to global trade while liberalizing the economy. Following China's lead North Korea has finally established a free trade zone at Rajin–Sunbong. Like those established a generation ago by China near Hong Kong, the goal has been to attract foreign investment with promises of cheap labor and tax incentives.

However, investments since 1993 have been slow and remain disappointing from the government's perspective. The effort to find new funds has ranged widely from agreeing to allow international flights over North Korea to gain overflight fees from the airlines to the more controversial offer to accept some of Taiwan's nuclear waste. That deal will bring in millions of dollars into North Korea and calls for Pyongyang to accept and bury on their territory thousands of barrels of radioactive material from Taiwan. While not of potential use for military purposes the agreement has aroused considerable tension with South Korea which was especially unhappy with the decision to place the material in mine shafts near their common border! Tensions between North Korea and South Korea have made it much more difficult for southerners, the most logical investors, to play much of a part in the new economic zone.

Theoretically, though, the North is in a reasonable position to arrest its drastic economic downturn. After all, just to their south lies the Republic of Korea with which they share a common language and heritage. Economically the two are a fine match, reminiscent of the relationship between China's Guangdong province and Hong Kong. The South has international economic sophistication but is burdened by wage bills that are moving ahead faster than both that of their competitors and their own productivity. In theory an economic accord between Seoul and Pyongyang would help both but examples of such logical cooperation are few. Daewoo, the huge South Korean industrial giant, has set up a textile facility in North Korea. But tensions on the peninsula have made this potential avenue of relief quite unlikely.

North Korea has had few options as it attempts to survive in the post Cold War world. It needs to stabilize the economy and improve its relations with outside powers. Its efforts though in that direction have been at best inconsistent. On one hand it has made gestures toward improving relations with both South Korea and the United States, yet concurrently it has carried out provocative acts ranging from sending troops into the demilitarized zone to the submarine incident mentioned above which so aroused southern fury. It has also refused the play the "beggar" it has actually become in recent years. Instead it has used the "nuclear card", i.e., threatening that it will move toward developing nuclear weapons unless the outside world supplies it with needed supplies and facilities and most prominently a new series of more modern nuclear reactors. After considerable discussion the U.S. and North Korea have reached an agreement in Geneva which provides for the building of two light–water reactors.

South Korea will be the builder and pay the bulk of the costs. These new facilities will not produce by–products which can be used in the manufacture of nuclear weapons–grade material. North Korea has, however, refused to publicly acknowledge South Korea's central role in the construction and financing of the reactors. The money could be spent more profitably in development of additional hydroelectric resources lying idle in the North.

The U.S. will also contribute funds along with other countries for the reactors. The accord also opens the way for the establishment of diplomatic relations between North Korea and the U.S., and the easing of trade restrictions against the latter. The U.S. has delivered tons of heavy fuel oil to North Korea. But despite the real progress already made the regularity of incidents usually provoked by North Korea keeps derailing efforts to lessen tensions on the peninsula. Clearly North Korea wants to improve its relations with the outside world, if only to strengthen the regime, but its inconsistent behavior and frequent resorts to aggressive statements such as continuing to berate Japan, provoking incidents with South Korea, etc., accomplish very little. Nor have its efforts to drive a wedge between Seoul and Washington had significant effect. In November 1995 South Korea, Japan and the United States agreed to redouble their efforts to work together in approaching North Korea. This was a defeat for the North's desire to gain recognition, while dealing South Korea out. It seems a certainty that U.S. and Japanese relations with North Korea will not advance significantly until North–South interaction improves.

The Future

South Korea faces many challenges in the decade ahead. Its first civilian elected president seems likely to leave office far less popular than he was when he arrived. And the economy while still impressive has lost much of the momentum that carried it through the 1980s. More ominously, it seems likely that the continuing weakness of North Korea may bring enormous challenges. Whether North Korea continues to limp along, suddenly collapses or simply withers over time, it will be South Korea that will have the principal responsibility for picking up the pieces. There are also those who fear that the North in a desperate effort to enhance the leadership's credibility may actually provoke some sort of confrontation with the South. While they would be unlikely to benefit from such aggression it will still be South Korea that would bear the principal brunt of such a move. Nevertheless, South Korea, which began the 20th century as an oppressed colony of Japan is ending it as an increasingly important player in the world economy, in fact the 11th largest economy and with a population which has seen its living standards improve enormously over the last few generations.

North Korea, in contrast, is clearly in major trouble. The economy is a disaster and major supporters have been defecting. The drama of early 1997 was the spectacle of the chairman of the Foreign Affairs Committee of the North Korean Workers Party, Hwang Jang Yop, defecting to South Korea's Beijing embassy. It probably is too late for the regime to reform itself sufficiently to survive into the 21st century. One major factor preventing North Korea from joining the international community is an exalted sense of "pride." Both China and the U.S. are shipping grain to North Korea, where some children are limited to seven ounces of food per day.

To survive it needs to stabilize relations with South Korea and that is something it is unable to do. To the contrary, Hwang Jang Yop said in April 1997 that war is more imminent than is generally recognized. Kim Jung–Il's control of the army is tenuous; most of the one million troops are massed along the border with South Korea.

View of the port of Pusan, South Korea

WORLD BANK Photo

Mongolia

Celebrating the 750th anniversary of the 13th century volume, *The Secret History of the Mongols,* a book devoted to the Mongolian Empire and to the exploits of Chingis Khan

Courtesy: Government of Mongolia

Area: 604,247 sq. mi. (1,564,619 sq. km., somewhat larger than Alaska).

Population: 2.5 million (estimated).

Capital City: Ulan Bator (Pop. 450,000, estimated).

Climate: Dry, with bitterly cold winters.

Neighboring Countries: Soviet Union (North, Northwest); China (South, East).

Official Language: Mongolian.

Other Principal Tongue: Russian.

Ethnic Background: Mongol (about 97%); Turk (about 3%).

Principal Religion: The Lamaistic sect of Buddhism; religious practice is not discouraged.

Main Exports (to Russia): Beef, meat products, wool, minerals.

Main Imports (from Russia): Machinery, equipment, petroleum, building materials, clothing.

Currency: Tugrik.

Former Colonial Status: Tributary of the Manchu Dynasty of China from end of the 17th century until 1912; Soviet influence since that time. Nationalist China recognized Mongolian independence in 1946, but withdrew recognition in 1952.

Communist China recognized the Republic in 1949.

National Day: July 11th, in recognition of a communist revolution in 1921.

Chief of State: Natsagiyn Bagabandi, President (since May 1997).

Prime Minister: M. Enkhsaikhan.

National Flag: Three vertical bands of red, blue and red. The band closest to the pole has a set of traditional symbols with a five–pointed star at the top all in yellow.

Per Capita Annual GDP: US $2,185.

Mongolia is located in an area of extreme contrast in terms of geography. The arid rocks of the Gobi Desert in the southeast region of the country support almost no vegetation, and have a variation of temperature that splits the craggy rocks which interrupt the monotonous landscape. Proceeding northward there is a gradual change, punctuated by the presence of mountains rising to heights of more than 13,000 feet. The desert gives way to mountainous forest which ceases its thick growth in the heights where continuously present snow dominates the landscape.

Water also becomes more abundant in the North, but the rivers are uncontrolled and rough, descending in cascades over rocky beds and resembling the swirling waters of the Pacific Northwest and Alaska.

It is in this somewhat inhospitable part of the country that most of the people live in a thinly scattered existence devoted to animal husbandry. Their dwellings are constructed of felt from their animals stretched over rickety frames. Although possessing an international currency, the rural people still think that one horse, yak or ox equals seven sheep, fourteen goats or one–half of a camel.

History: Prior to the 16th century, the people who inhabited Mongolia had an aggressive, warlike character which enabled them periodically to conquer vast areas as far away as eastern Europe. This was principally due to the greatly superior horsemanship and cavalry techniques of the Mongols, acquired as a necessity due to the organization of their society which was traditionally nomadic. This pastoral existence contributed to the superior stamina of the fierce horsemen.

Several Mongolian leaders became well–known; the most famous was Chingis (Genghis) Khan; he and his successors were able to lead his men in the conquest of vast areas of eastern and southern Asia as far as Baghdad, now the capital of Iraq. However, the Mongols were eventually "conquered" by the people they had subdued. Their empire broke up in the 16th century and they were converted to Lamaist Buddhism, a pacifist religion, by contact with Tibet. At about the same time, they became dominated economically by the industrious Chinese, who possessed skills in manufacturing and trading unfamiliar to the Mongols. They soon found themselves trapped between Russia and China, two large wealthy empires, equipped with newly discovered firearms and other instruments of modern technology which rendered the skills of horsemanship and prowess in cavalry warfare obsolete.

The Mongols were soon reduced to the status of a tributary of the mighty Manchu Empire which had come to power in China. Russian interest in the area awakened to a greater extent in the 19th century; considerable economic and political power was gained in what was then called *Outer Mongolia* by the end of that century.

The numerous and hard–working Chinese pressed northward in the first decade of the 20th century, settling what was Inner Mongolia to the edge of the Gobi Desert, and creating a threat to the people of remote Outer Mongolia. For this reason, when the Chinese Manchu Empire collapsed in 1912, the princes and lamas of Outer Mongolia refused to recognize the claim of the Republic of China to the lands within the region.

In order to gain support for their independence, they appealed to the Russian tsar for protection. An agreement was reached in 1913 whereby China was to administer Inner Mongolia, and its legal "sovereignty" over Outer Mongolia was "recognized," but actually the region was to remain autonomous under local administration.

China took advantage of the collapse of the government of the Russian tsar in 1917 and attempted to seize absolute control of Outer Mongolia in violation of the 1913 agreement. This attempt was initially successful, but in 1921 Outer Mongolia was invaded by a force of White (anti–Bolshevik) troops from Russia. Control was then wrested from the White Russians by the Bolshevik (communist) forces, who remained until 1925.

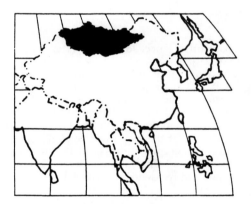

The Russians quickly organized a communist regime, built around Mongols who were either communist or pro–communist—Mongolia became the first satellite of Soviet Russia. From the Soviet point of view, Mongolia served as a buffer against an increasingly powerful Japan, and now also serves as a buffer state, separating it from any threat posed by China to the south. It also has been cited as a model of the possibilities of achievement under communism.

In the succeeding decades the communist regime brought the nomadic tribes and lamaist monasteries under increasingly centralized control. Occasional resistance was easily crushed by Soviet troops armed with modern mechanized equipment. State services, previously unknown in the region, were provided, including badly needed shelters for livestock to provide protection from the bitter winter wind and snow.

A defensive alliance between Mongolia and Russia, signed in 1936 and renewed every ten years since, was used by the Russians in 1939 to drive a force of invading Japanese from eastern Mongolia. The troops of both nations joined in 1945 to fight Japanese troops remaining in Inner Mongolia; at the same time, Stalin was able to obtain the promise of the Chinese to recognize Outer Mongolia's independence if a vote of the people showed that this was their desire. The plebiscite was held under carefully regulated conditions in October 1945, resulting in a unanimous vote for independence from China. The Nationalist Chinese subsequently recognized Mongolia's independence in 1946,

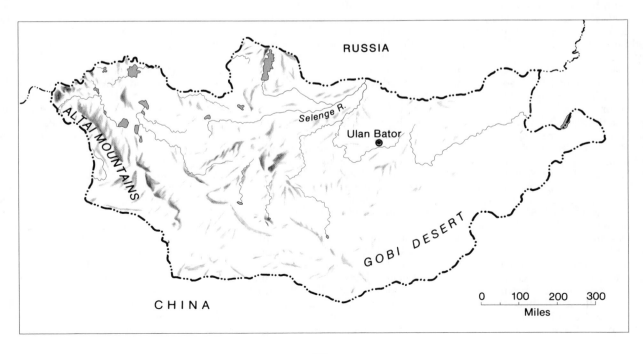

Mongolia

Former President Ochirbat's oath–taking ceremony   Courtesy: Government of Mongolia

but withdrew this in 1952, claiming that the Soviet Union had violated the commitments made to the Nationalist Chinese under the treaty of 1945.

The communist Chinese, with some hesitation due to their reluctance to abandon traditional claims of sovereignty over Mongolia, recognized Mongolia in 1949, and subsequently signed a boundary treaty with it in 1962. But China has occasionally shown some signs of wishing to increase its influence. These pressures caused Mongolia to cling to Russia for protection—it sided with the Soviet Union in all phases of the ongoing Sino–Soviet dispute. It received in return substantial economic aid, which permitted the beginning of industrialization in the country.

Mongolia sought and was granted admission to the UN in 1961, and at about the same time it started to establish diplomatic relations with a small number of "neutral" nations such as India and Indonesia. Japan recognized the Mongolian People's Republic early in 1972.

A boundary treaty with the Soviet Union was signed in late 1976. But because of tensions along the Sino–Soviet border, Soviet troops had entered Mongolia ten years earlier. In 1981, as a gesture to Mongolian nationalism, a Mongol cosmonaut was allowed to take part in a Soviet space flight.

Tsedenbal, Mongolia's long–time leader, was removed in 1984 allegedly because of age and illness, but also apparently because of his colleagues' discontent over his autocratic behavior and his subservience to the Soviet Union. Jambyn

Batmunkh succeeded him later in the year.

As part of its effort to improve relations with China, the Soviet Union began in late 1986 to withdraw one of the estimated five divisions it had maintained in Mongolia. Diplomatic relations with the US were established at the beginning of 1987; Mongolia opened its embassy in Washington in 1989, and the U.S. had already rented office and residence space in Ulan Bator.

New Directions

Under the influence of developments in the Soviet Union, especially the ascendancy of Mikhail Gorbachev, the Mongolian leadership had begun to move toward political liberalization in 1985. By the end of 1989, the dramatic events in Eastern Europe led to the emergence of an opposition party in Mongolia, which calls itself the *Mongolian Democratic Union* (MDU). Led by Soviet–educated intellectuals, it demanded an end to the communist monopoly of power. Surprisingly, this position won increasing acceptance from the communist leadership, beginning with an official statement in early 1990. This decision was the outcome of a debate within the Politburo during which some members urged the use of force against the demonstrators. When Batmunkh said he would agree only if all members signed the order, the idea collapsed.

In early 1990, Batmunkh promised free elections for April. The *MDU* tried to maximize its appeal to the voters by emphasizing nationalism, including praise for the medieval conqueror, Ghengis Khan, in

opposition to communism. A few weeks later the entire five–man Politburo of the ruling *Mongolian People's Revolutionary Party* resigned and was replaced by reformers; Batmunkh remained as chief of state for the time being. The ruling party formally gave up its monopoly of power at that time. The new General Secretary, Gombojavyn Ochirbat, was a relatively unknown figure.

In July, while the communist ruling party won about two–thirds of the seats in an election for the Great People's Hural, the opposition parties achieved a recognized place in Mongolian politics. The beginnings of a new era of reform seemed imminent. Changes came quickly. By 1992 a new constitution was in place that allowed for multi–party voting and even the term *People's Republic* was dropped and the country was renamed simply "Mongolia."

Political ferment and liberalization continued after these dramatic events. Freedom of the press brought a mushrooming of new newspapers and magazines. Freedom of religion led to a widespread resurgence of Buddhism and even to some extent of Christianity.

The constitution provides for a popularly elected president and a Western–style parliamentary system of government, with a 76–seat unicameral legislative chamber, the *Hural*. The president may introduce legislation before the *Hural*, and has a veto. The prime minister is the leader of the dominant party or parties in coalition, which control the *Hural*. A Constitutional Court has the authority to review the legality of laws.

The new constitution also allows for private property, but pastureland continues to be under public ownership. After the mid–1992 elections, the former *Communist Party (MPRP)* still controlled 71 of 76 seats in the *Hural*. But their domination was beginning to weaken.

In mid–1993, Mongolia held its first presidential election. Candidates for the post had to be over forty–five years of age and only political parties that held a seat in the parliament could select a standard bearer. The old line *Mongolian People's Revolutionary Party* (MPRP) nominated L. Tudev, over the incumbent President Ochirbat. The opposition *Mongolian National Democratic Party* (MNDP) formed a coalition with the *Mongolian Social Democratic Party* (MSDP) and selected President Punsalmaagiin Ochirbat, himself, who had been turned down by his own *MPRP*, to be their candidate.

In the election, Ochirbat was elected president with 58.7% of the vote. Perhaps as high as one–fourth of the *MPRP* supporters defected to support their old president. The newly reelected president

Mongolia

promised to speed privatization but also to protect those who were hurt most by the process.

During 1994 the *MPRP* continued to rule under Prime Minister Puntsagiyn Jasray, but not without challenges. Street demonstrations broke out in April. The primary issue was apparently corruption in the *MPRP* which reached as high as the prime minister. Demands that the government resign were ignored. Perhaps as a way of making peace, the *MPRP* sat down with the opposition parties in the Great *Hural*, the *Mongolian National Democratic Party* (*MNDP*), and the *Mongolian Social Democratic Party* to create important reform–oriented legislation. One part of the agreement between the three parties was to require electoral reform to allow for a fairer representation among the parties in the Great *Hural*. The *MPRP* also agreed to the creation of an independent media, not under government control.

A Non–Communist Start

The weakening of communist control which had been going on since the early 1990s was finally fully realized during 1996 when in the July elections a coalition of democratic parties swept the communist *Mongolian People's Revolutionary Party* from power. The *MPRP*, which had been in power since 1921 saw its legislative control destroyed as its opponents won 48 of the 76 seats in the parliament! With that vote Mongolia took its place along side other former socialist states which have attempted to find a new future beyond their communist past.

The new prime minister was the 41 year old M. Enkhsaikhan, leader of the Democratic Union Coalition. Moving beyond the economic liberalization which had already begun, the new prime minister promised to reform the economy to attract more foreign investment.

And the new prime minister certainly had his work cut out for him, for within months of his election, in May 1997, Mongolian voters, frustrated by recent economic problems, elected Natsagiyn Bagabandi, leader of the formerly dominant *MPRP*, into office as president. He had run on a platform promising to slow down reforms. Although the new president has

few real powers within the Mongolian system, Prime Minister Enkhsaikhan needs to heed well the message of the voters who put Bagabandi into power with 60% of the vote.

Foreign Relations

The new Mongolia has been moving to improve its relationship with the outside world. Meetings have been held with Bill Clinton, François Mitterrand and Boris Yeltsin. Not surprisingly relations with Russia have been especially important though not always as smooth as one might have anticipated. Officials from both countries have met to discuss the terms under which Mongolia would repay its debt to Russia. The two parties disagree on the amount and the terms. One estimate puts the debt at about $15 billion. A second on–going problem, cross–border smuggling and rustling, is being addressed jointly.

Without doubt, the most prominent visitor to Mongolia in recent years was that of the Dalai Lama. People came from all corners of the country to hear him speak,

Ulan Bator—modest modernity comes to a proud, isolated society

Mongolia

A factory worker packs camel wool for export   Courtesy: Government of Mongolia

Women have long been respected in traditional Mongolian society. The socialist state carried out proactive efforts to raise their status further. Today, the vast majority are literate and they constitute almost half of the graduates of higher education. Women play important roles in the professions, and represent the majority of the physicians and academics and over forty percent of the agronomists, public servants, economists, and engineers.

Although recent years have seen a greater openness in the country's political system, the end of the formally free health care system has especially hurt women, particularly pregnant and nursing women. Not surprisingly the maternal mortality rate has risen. Moreover, as with other collapsing socialist regimes, the withdrawal of state child care facilities have added additional burdens on women.

Economy

Agriculture and livestock production have been and remain the backbone of the Mongolian economy. Much of the country's industry, including wool production, clothing and leather goods, is tied to this sector. The mining of gold, coal, copper, molybdenum, tin and tungsten also figure significantly in today's economy.

The transition from communism has not been easy. The break–up of large collective farms had a negative effect on production in 1995—livestock production (28.6 million animals) was only slightly larger than the previous record set in 1941. But the country's population is three times larger than it was in 1941. In 1995, the country experienced a significant shortage of meat in urban areas. Chicken and pig breeding suffered from shortages of supplies and labor, as a result of de–collectivization. The production of cereal grains also fell, though at least the production of gold has doubled.

Inefficient state–run businesses are still in operation, and foreign investment has been slow to come into the country because of the uncertainty of government regulations. The national stock exchange in Ulan Bator averaged about $20,000 per day in volume. The director of the exchange, Naidansurengen Zolzhargal, an American trained Mongolian, is working on a cellular phone system which will allow herdsmen to trade directly with the exchange from horseback. As a result of the collapse of communism and the privatization movement, some one million Mongolians own stock. Because the exchange is starting from scratch, it is likely that the new state–of–the–art systems will be far more advanced than exchanges in many developed countries.

Inflation fell during 1996 to 30%; high,

and his presence signaled a rebirth of a part of the country's culture which had been suppressed under communism. During his 10 day visit the "God King of Tibet" conducted a mass initiation to replenish the dwindling number of Buddhist monks. One source estimated a crowd of 37,000 people (or about 2% of the population) greeted the former leader of Tibet.

The major foreign policy initiative for 1995 was launched in August when Natsagiyn Bagabandi, chairman of the People's Great *Hural* (national assembly) publicly expressed Mongolia's desire to join the Asia–Pacific Economic forum. The country's former and current leadership feels APEC membership is essential to open the door wider for foreign investment and economic cooperation. That same year an agreement was reached in Washington, D.C., for military assistance for Mongolia.

The country is wisely attempting to reach out as far as it can. The more friends it has, the more secure it may be with its closest neighbor, the People's Republic. Indeed, Mongolia is very concerned about China which is so large that it could easily overwhelm Mongolia through trade and migration. Beijing was hardly likely to have been pleased with the warm reception the Mongolian people offered its long time nemesis the Dalai Lama.

Culture

The nomadic pattern of life of the Mongols, reflecting a need and desire for mobility, has slowed the growth of substantial cities until recent years. Likewise,

there have been no buildings of any great size except for the monasteries within the country.

The traditional literature of the people is ancient—it first consisted mainly of oral epics passed down from generation to generation. In the 13th century the Mongols developed a system of alphabetical writing based on the Tibetan script which served to record the epics as well as being a tool for later literary efforts. The indigenous religious tradition was relatively simple until the advent of lamaist Buddhism in the 16th century. Though the communist era no doubt weakened the religious establishment the recent visit of the Dalai Lama demonstrated a clear interest in their religious heritage.

While the processes of industrialization and modernization intrude into the solitude of the people with increasing frequency, the Mongolians are still excellent horsemen, fond of festivals which stress the traditional skills of horsemanship, particularly racing, archery, wrestling and physical stamina. They actually bear a strong resemblance to rodeos in this country.

Today's Mongolia is undergoing the severe stresses common since the collapse of communism around the world. During this transition, as efforts have begun to build economic systems based on more open markets, the day to day lives of people have been shaken by the increase in unemployment. In the last several years the numbers of people living below Mongolian poverty line standards has risen sharply as have related problems such as alcoholism and spousal abuse.

but at least down from the over 50% in recent years. The tugrik, which is the local currency, declined to 475 to one dollar and Mongolia's trade surplus increased from $109 million in 1994, to $123 million in 1995. The economy remains dependent on international organizations and foreign countries to the tune of approximately $200 million a year. This situation is not likely to change much in the near future.

Mongolia is currently receiving more aid per capita than any other Asian country because the outside world does not want the country to fall under Chinese influence. A group of donors headed by Japan has put up over $750 million, while the United States has pledged $10 million.

The Future

Mongolia has made remarkable progress in the last several years toward the goal of creating a politically more open society. Unfortunately, the economic transition from a communist economy to a more open market society is likely to be slower and the rewards less obvious in the near future.

This circumstance is not likely to change significantly soon. Its strategy of trying to find as many international friends as it can is important. The greatest challenge is probably just across the border. Maintaining good relations with the increasingly powerful People's Republic, especially in the face of Russian weakness, is likely to occupy much of the leadership's energy over the next few years.

The pastoral life of Mongolian sheepherders

Brunei Darussalam

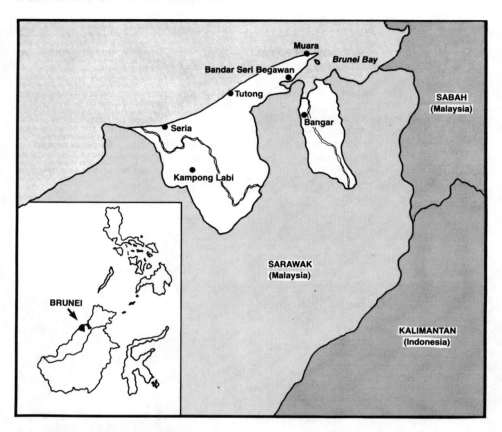

Area: 2,226 sq. mi. (5,765 sq. km., about the size of Delaware).

Population: 292,000.

Capital City: Bandar Seri Begawan (named in honor of the present Sultan's father, Pop. 121,000, estimated).

Climate: Tropical.

Neighboring Countries: The East Malaysian states of Sarawak and Sabah enclose Brunei on the large island of Borneo, also known as Kalimantan, two thirds of which is Indonesian.

National Language: Malay. English is the second language.

Other Principal Tongue: Chinese.

Ethnic Background: Malay (64%), Chinese (20%), Other (16%).

Principal Religion: Muslim (60%, official State religion); Buddhist, Christian, traditional native beliefs.

Main Exports: Crude petroleum, liquified natural gas, and wearing apparel.

Main Imports: Aircraft, electronics, other manufactured goods, and foodstuffs.

Currency: Brunei dollar.

Former Colonial Status: Previously independent, it was a British protectorate (1888–1983).

Independence Day: January 1, 1984.

Chief of State: His Majesty the Sultan and Yang Di–Pertuan of Brunei Darussalam, Sultan Hassanal Bolkiah Mu'izzaddin Waddaulah (b. 1947).

National Flag: A yellow field crossed diagonally by single white and black stripes upon which is centered a red crest.

Annual Per Capita Income: U.S. $16,000 (1993 est.).

Brunei *Darussalam* (meaning "abode of peace") is one of the most unusual nations in the world. Having two distinct parts, with Malaysia's state of Sarawak plugging a 15–mile gap between the two, it is also one the wealthiest sovereign nations *per capita* on earth.

Much of inland Brunei is dense jungle scattered with remote villages and alive with brilliantly–plumaged birds, but its gleaming capital city, Bandar Seri Begawan, on the Brunei River about nine miles from its mouth, is sleekly modern, has several international–class hotels— and no slums! The country's main port is bustling Muara.

Malays form the majority of the population, but there are also about 70,000 non–Malays, most of them Chinese involved in trade and commerce. In 1961 Brunei passed a law allowing non–citizen Chinese to become Brunei citizens if they had resided in the country for 20 of the previous 25 years and could pass a Malay language test. There are also small groups of British, Dutch, American and Australians associated with the oil and gas industry. Education is free up to a doctorate if one's scholarship takes him that far. There are three "streams" in the educa-

tional program—Malay, English, and Arabic; students may pursue advanced studies at schools at government expense. Over 2,000 students are enrolled in foreign universities.

Brunei has many splendid beaches, and hotels provide excellent service and delectable foods, often combinations of rice, meat and vegetables. The country's cattle are raised on a ranch in northern Australia, which as it turns out, is larger than Brunei! The cattle are flown into the country and slaughtered according to Muslim customs. Television is common in most households.

History: From the 14th to the 16th century, Brunei was the cornerstone of a powerful Muslim empire which encompassed most of northern Borneo and the Philippines. However, the advance of the Dutch and the British, internal corruption, and warfare took their toll as the 17th century dawned. Brunei's rule was confined to an area today formed by Sarawak and part of Sabah. Towards the middle of the century, in 1841, in a rather desperate move to secure military help against marauding South China Sea pirates, the Sultan ceded to the English adventurer Sir James Brooke the entire region of Sarawak. Brooke styled himself *Rajah* ("prince" or "king") of the area and was succeeded by his nephew and the latter's son until 1946. By 1847 the British secured from the Sultan the island of Labuan off the northwest coast of Borneo, which they speculated could become an imporant naval base, although the plan never came to realization.

There were further concessions and further treaties. In 1865 the United States government under President Lincoln's administration, concluded a treaty with the Sultan. The *American Trading Company of Borneo* was created and granted vast land holdings, but this venture was soon thought worthless and was abandoned. Sixteen years later the British set up the *North Borneo Company*, which acquired the assets of the U.S. firm and pushed further land concessions from the Sultan who had little power to refuse the mighty British Empire. Brunei was thus reduced to its present size.

With a fragile economy and no way to defend itself against the many European powers which were continuing to colonize the entire area, Brunei chose British protection in 1888 and, later in 1906, permitted a British commissioner to take up residence in the country; the Sultan was required to take his advice in all matters involving defense and foreign affairs, but not the Islamic faith and Malay customs.

During the next few years the country's economy began to grow, first with the cultivation of rubber. Then the economic picture drastically changed as vast oil reserves and natural gas were discovered in the 1920's in the western part of the nation followed by offshore deposits in the 1960's. Brunei was on the road to enormous wealth.

Brunei's 1959 constitution allowed for a measure of shared political decision–making beyond the royal family, but that experiment in more open politics was short–lived. In the aftermath of a 1962 rebellion led by a pro-Indonesian leftist, a state of emergency was imposed which allowed the banning of all political parties. The state of emergency allowed the sultan to reestablish absolute control. That mandate has continued until the present. In fact, those powers were last renewed in July of 1996 more than thirty years after they were first imposed.

When the Federation of Malaysia was established in 1963 to be composed of Malaya, Sabah, Sarawak and Singapore, the Sultan of Brunei was urged to join. The then sultan rejected the plan, fearing for the erosion of his political position and determined that Brunei's oil and gas revenues would be reserved for the benefit of native Bruneians rather than becoming available to the proposed federation at large.

Brunei regained its independence after almost a century of colonialism on January 1, 1984. A member of the British Commonwealth, Brunei has since joined the UN and the Association of Southeast Asian Nations (ASEAN) among others. At the Sultan's request, the Gurkha army units from Nepal stationed in Brunei while it was under British protection have stayed on to aid the Royal Brunei Armed Forces. The government continues to pay

His Majesty The Sultan of Brunei, Hassanal Bolkiah Mu'izzaddin Waddaulah

for their maintenance, but they are still under British command. Given the end of the British control over Hong Kong, where the Gurkhas also served, the role of the Gurkha units in Brunei is now being revaluated.

The present Sultan, Hassanal Bolkiah, heads the government, serving as prime minister, defense minister and more recently as finance minister. Other key government posts are held by members of his immediate family. The Sultan, born in 1946, has, as Muslim custom allows, two wives; he has three sons and six daughters. Educated in Brunei and Malaysia, the Sultan then enrolled as an officer cadet at the Royal Military Academy at Sandhurst, England.

He was crowned the 29th ruler of Brunei by his father in 1968 upon the latter's abdication. Easily one of the richest men in the world, the Sultan controls the finances not only of his own family but that of the state itself. With such resources he can be quite lavish. For example, last year to celebrate his fiftieth birthday, the Sultan threw a party that cost over $25 million dollars and included Prince Charles, an old friend, as a guest, and the American performer, Michael Jackson, as the entertainment.

Politics and Government

According to its constitution Brunei is a "democratic Islamic Malay monarchy." However, while it is clearly a monarchy it does not constitute a true democracy. The Sultan and his family completely dominate the political life of the country. Although the constitution of 1959 did allow some sharing of political decision–making, much of it has been suspended since the early 1960s. Additional modifications have occurred since independence in 1984. Freedom of speech is limited and political activity severely restricted.

Sultan Hassanal Bolkiah, chief of gov-

The Omar Ali Saifuddien Mosque

Brunei

A marketplace in Bandar Seri Begawan

ernment and head of state, rules the country with the help of the Council of Cabinet Ministers, most of whom are family members. The unicameral legislature, *Majlis Masyuarat Megeri,* has been an appointed body since 1970. The traditional system of village chiefs was modified in 1992 to allow all adults to vote for them by secret ballot. It is through these chiefs and their various organizations that the government expects the population to present their concerns.

In February 1995, Haji Abdul Latif Chuchu was elected president of the *Brunei Solidarity National Party,* the country's only legal political party. He and other party officials then called for democratic elections in a meeting with the Sultan. He was later banned from all political activity. The party does not appear to have much of a following and most citizens seem content with the Sultan's rule.

The Sultan's father, who still had considerable power, died in September 1986. After his father's death the new Sultan reorganized the cabinet and began to play a more active political role. To reinforce its rule, the government devised an ideology designed to reinforce the monarchy. Known as *Malaya Islam Beraja* or *MIB* it is mainly an affirmation of Islam and the monarchy.

MIB was brought into the secondary schools in 1992. Christian and Chinese mission schools may also be subject to some exposure to Malay and Islam in the classroom, causing some concern for the multi–ethnic future of the country. Undoubtedly the country's leadership sees *MIB* as a mechanism for strengthening its continued leadership role. Yet, forcing Islam and the Malay language on non–Malays could bring about the very opposite of the desired results: political instability.

Defense

While tiny in size, Brunei has a modern and capable defense force. Internal and external security are under the control of the Royal Brunei Armed Forces (RBAF), the Royal Brunei Police, the Gurkha Reserve Unit, and the British Army Gurkha Battalion. Recent defense expenditures have been around 10% of the national budget. The RBAF has about 4,000 personnel and includes several hundred women who were recruited beginning in 1981.

The air force and navy are small but well equipped. Joint military exercises have been held with Malaysia, Thailand and Singapore; the latter trains its troops in Brunei's jungles. An option for Brunei would be to join the Five Power Defense Agreement (Singapore, Malaysia, New Zealand, Australia and Britain).

About 1,000 British Gurkhas rotated between the country and Hong Kong. The Gurkha Reserve Unit of some 900 men is directly under the control of the Sultan and is composed of retired British army personnel. The Royal Brunei Police Force of approximately 2,000 is the fourth component of national defense.

Negotiations over a Memorandum of Understanding (MOU) with the United States on national defense matters were initiated in the early 1990s; Brunei could enhance its security substantially with such an agreement. The United States could be interested in using the country as a staging point for air surveillance in the region.

Foreign Relations

Brunei foreign policy stresses the security of the nation. A true mini–state, the country must rely to a considerable extent on the goodwill of its neighbors. The fact that it is surrounded by its two Muslim brother states, Malaysia and Indonesia, is advantageous. Brunei joined the Association of Southeast Asian Nations (ASEAN) just after independence in 1984. Membership has helped the country establish close diplomatic and military ties with the other ASEAN states; Singapore is a particularly good example.

In 1995, Brunei was the venue for several important ASEAN meetings. On July 29, the 28th ASEAN Ministerial Meeting (AMM) opened in Bandar Seri Begawan, the Bruneian capital. The Sultan of Brunei, called on the ASEAN member states to push up regional trade liberalization by three years to the year 2000. He demonstrated that Brunei is not timid about approaching delicate regional matters matters. Brunei also takes part in the ASEAN Regional Forum (ARF), a consultative body which focuses on Asia–Pacific security matters.

Brunei became the first Muslim state in the region to recognize Israel. Earlier in the year, it established ties with the Palestine Liberation Organization and opened an embassy in Iran. In August, President Fidel Ramos of the Philippines visited Brunei. A rift over the possible involvement of Philippine entertainers with Bruneian royalty was apparently patched up. A more important topic of discussion concerned the establishment of an East ASEAN Growth Area, comprised of Brunei, southern Philippines, East Malaysia and part of Indonesia. Brunei has offered significant investments to get the project off the ground.

Culture

The royal line goes back some twenty-nine generations. Brunei Malays are similar to the Malays of Malaysia and Indonesia. All are followers of Islam, have a preference for living in coastal areas and speak the Malay language. They differ significantly from other ethnic groups. Traditionally Brunei Malays were fisherman, traders and craftsmen.

Today's generation is seeking more "modern" means of employment. About ten percent of the Brunei Malays claim royal blood, having been descended from one of the Sultans. Many live in Kampong Ayer, the Malay community consisting of about thirty–five villages. Marriages were once arranged by the village headman and the family. Now, however, more modern methods prevail. Although under Muslim law a man is permitted to have up to four wives this is actually rare.

Contemporary life in Brunei for its citizens is one that many would envy. Perhaps to keep dissatisfaction with the Sultan's political control to a minimum the state

Brunei

has used its oil resources to create a cradle to grave social security system. Almost every urban family owns at least one car, often more, and there is no income tax. Both education and health care are free.

The Kedazans are the second most populous indigenous group and are similar to Malays in their practice of religion, language and appearance. The greatest difference is that they have tended to be rice farmers. They do not have the same status in society as the Malays. Other smaller indigenous groups include the Bisayas, who follow traditional religions; the Penans, nomads of the jungle. The smallest group is the Muruts, who once populated the military for the Sultan, and the Ibans (whose numbers are increasing compared to the other smaller groups, and who are known in the past for head hunting activities).

The Chinese are far more important than their numbers would suggest and dominate the Sultan's commercial sector. They also provide the managerial and technical talent for the country. The older generation follows Taoist–Buddhist traditions. Less than ten percent of the Chinese in the country have been granted citizenship. While they have lived in the country long enough, they have difficulty passing the Malay language requirement. Some would argue that the Chinese are made to feel unwelcome in Brunei.

As is the case elsewhere, the experience of women in Brunei is a mixed one. While no women hold leading positions in the bureaucracy, large numbers hold positons at the lower levels. Today nearly two–thirds of the student body at the national university are women. They also serve in the military though not in combat positions.

However, since Brunei is officially a Muslim society Islamic domestic law governs the life of women. Women have fewer rights in such important areas as divorce and inheritance and, as is common in the region, they cannot pass on their citizenship to their children. Men also have considerable advantages over women in the government's civil service jobs.

Economy

Oil and gas provide Brunei with more than 90% of its export earnings; it is the third largest oil producer in Southeast Asia after Indonesia and Malaysia. The Seria oil field was discovered in 1929 and by the 1950's it was producing 115,000 barrels a day. Offshore production began in 1964 and there are today over 200 rigs operated by Brunei Shell Petroleum Company, jointly owned by the government and Shell. Production in 1995 was about 60 million barrels, less than in previous years, since

Brunei wants to conserve this source of income for the future. Most oil is exported to Japan—almost half—and the rest goes to other nations, the United States receiving about 10%. Brunei uses only about 3% of its production for domestic use.

Brunei is also the world's fourth largest supplier of liquid natural gas, a venture owned by the government, Royal Dutch Shell Group and Japan's Mitsubishi Corporation. Five million tons are exported annually to Japan alone. The petroleum sector still accounts for around 50% of Brunei's gross domestic product (GDP). This figure was over 80% in the 1980's. Another growing source of revenue is foreign investment which is now producing almost as much money as the petroleum sector ($2.5 billion according to one estimate). Given enough time, Brunei's estimated $36 billion in overseas investments (as of 1993) could become the major source of revenue for the mini–state.

In 1992, the government announced its Sixth National Development Plan for the 1991–95 period. The largest chunk of the B$5.5 billion plan is devoted to social services—education, health, housing, and religious affairs. The main focus of the plan is to steer the economy away from dependence on oil and natural gas. However, this attempt to diversify the economy has been less than a smashing success. It is made especially difficult because the government employs more than half of the labor force. A new joint–venture garment manufacturer was forced to import Philippine and Thai workers because locals were either too few in number or not interested. Brunei is not subject to quotas on garment exports. Thus, an opportunity to expand is at hand.

The government has frozen civil service pay in an attempt to make state employment less attractive. However, in a coun-

try where health care and education are free, and where subsidized loans are readily available, there is little pressure to change. There may be some ambivalence on the part of national leaders concerning economic change. An influx of foreigners and new ventures will surely disturb the confortable and traditional environment. Nevertheless, in June 1995, Brunei applied for membership in the World Bank and the IMF. It is unlikely that Brunei needs to borrow funds. The government does appear to be looking for assistance in broadening the economy.

The Future

With a per capita Gross Domestic Product (GDP) of $18,900 per year, the country faces no serious economic problems. The discovery of new oil deposits insures that the country will be pumping petroleum for many decades to come. Self–sufficiency in food is a worthy, but not essential goal. The country's wealth has spawned growing environmental problems. Local waterways are being clogged with styrofoam, old refrigerators, and even cars. This is a serious problem that can only get worse until the government takes action.

Although Brunei has good relations with its neighbors, long term defense requirements need attention. Brunei probably should join the Five Power Agreement to strengthen its international security. Finally, domestic tensions could rise if MIB is forced too aggressively. Like Malaysia and Singapore, Brunei is a multiethnic society which can only survive with a good bit of tolerance and acceptance of diversity. For the foreseeable future democratic reform is not likely. If it does occur, it will originate in the royal palace and not from the streets of Bandar Seri Begawan.

An early morning traveler swings through the towering trees in Bardar Seri Begawan
Courtesy: Sarah Cassell

A Burmese newspaper

The Union of Burma
(The government has renamed the country *Myanmar*)

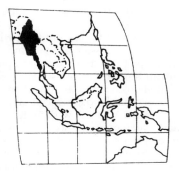

Area: 261,700 sq. mi. (676,600 sq. km., almost as large as Texas).

Population: 45 million (estimated).

Capital City: Rangoon (Yangon, Pop. 3.5 million, estimated).

Climate: Tropical, with torrential rains during the summer monsoon (June–November) in the coastal areas.

Neighboring Countries: China (North and East); India, Bangladesh (West); Laos (East); Thailand (East and South).

Official Language: Burmese.

Other Principal Tongues: English, Chinese, Karen, Shan.

Ethnic Background: Oriental Mongoloid mixtures, including Burman (72%) in the central valley area, Karen (7% in the Pegu Yoma and Karen States), Shan (6% in the Shan Plateau and Chindwin Valley), Chin and Kachin (5%) in the western mountain and extreme north, Wa (2%), a very primitive group along the Chinese border; Chinese, Indian, Bengali and other (8%).

Principal Religion: Buddhism.

Main Exports (to Singapore, China, Thailand, India and Hong Kong): Beans, teak, rice, hardwood.

Main Imports (from Japan, China, Thailand, Singapore, Malaysia): Machinery, transportation equipment, chemicals, food products.

Currency: Kyat.

Former Colonial Status: British dependency (1886–1947)

Independence Day: January 4, 1948.

Chief of State: General Than Shwe, Chairman, State Law and Order Restoration Council (since April 1992).

Secretary, SLORC: Kin Nyunt.

National Flag: A red field with a blue union in the upper left–hand corner containing a large white gear (representing workers) superimposed with a sheaf of rice (representing peasants) surrounded by 14 small white stars symbolizing the states and divisions of the country.

Annual Per Capita Income: U.S. $930 (1994 estimate).

The long western coastline of Burma faces the tropical waters of the Bay of Bengal in the North and the Andaman Sea in the peninsular southern regions. The northern part of the country is actually a moist and hot basin—it is separated from India and Bangladesh by high, forested ridges and lower valleys, and from China, Laos and Thailand by the mountains and by the Shan Plateau, which combine to form a crescent enclosing Burma.

The mountains of the plateau region are not particularly high when compared to those in other countries of southern Asia; they reach a maximum height of about 9,000 feet. The Irrawaddy River originates in the mountainous region of the north, turbulently descending to the lowlands where it is transformed into a sluggish, muddy stream of water. It is along this river and also along the Sittang River that the largest cities of Burma are located, including Rangoon and Mandalay.

The northern mountains are inhabited thinly by people who are mostly non-Burman; they live principally in the thick forests where teak and other valuable trees grow. Many are primitive and non-Buddhist—rumors of head–hunting in this area have persisted for centuries.

The great majority of the people live in the crowded central valley where great quantities of rice are raised each year, much of which is exported. The comparatively cool and dry season, which starts in November, ends in about mid–February when the wind changes from the north and begins to blow from the Bay of Ben-

Burma

Rush hour in Rangoon with Longgyi-clad men clinging to bus entrance

AP/World Wide Photos

gal. The air becomes hotter during April and May, and periodic storms appear on the horizon.

In June the full force of the southwest monsoon rains inundate the coastline. It is in this region that an average of 200 inches of rain fall each year, but the further inland regions receive less rain as their distance from the coast increases. The rains abate in late October; the wind again comes from the North; providing a cooler and drier relief from the oppressive moisture of the preceding months.

History

In the early centuries of the Christian era, the fertile coastal region of Burma was inhabited by the Mons, who had cultural characteristics quite similar to those of India. In about 1000 A.D. they became converted to *Hinayana* Buddhism which had come from India by way of Ceylon (Sri Lanka); they in turn transmitted this sect to other people living in the region, including the Burmans.

The adjective "Burmese" is used by Americans to describe all of the people living within the country; "Burman" is used to designate the largest ethnic group; the British usage is exactly the opposite. Burmans are closely related in terms of language and appearance to the Tibetans, and seem to have moved southwest into Burma from the remote regions of eastern Tibet beginning about 800 A.D. Although

they have the characteristic oriental flat nose, they usually do not have the eyelid fold of their Chinese neighbors; the color of their skin varies from deep brown to extremely light in color.

The Burmans emerged as the most powerful force in the country by the mid-11th century under King Anawrata, who established a national capital in the central city of Pagan, from which most of the country was subdued. The Shan (Thai) people, who lived in the northeastern part of Burma, disliked Burman rule, and in the late 13th century requested the protection of the Mongol empire which ruled China. The emperor Khubilai Khan sent a large force of cavalrymen who invaded Burma, totally destroying the Burman kingdom.

The Mongols did not remain for any great length of time; when they left the Shan established a number of states which were under Burman influence, but which governed the nation. From about 1300 to the mid–18th century, Burma's history is one of repeated destructive civil wars among the Burmans, Mons and Shans. No one emerged victorious; these wars served only to limit the development of Burma.

European merchants and explorers appeared along the coast after 1500; although the Dutch had trade bases for a brief period, there was no early colonization of Burma. In 1753 a new Burman kingdom emerged, rapidly reuniting the several small states into which Burma had been split by civil war. This warlike king-

dom raided Thailand, fended off two invasions by the Manchu dynasty of China and in the early 19th century invaded Assam to the west.

The British East India Company, which was in control of Assam at that time, sent British troops to push the Burmans out of the area in the First Burmese War (1824). The British took over the Arakan and Tenasserim coasts and advanced up the Irrawaddy River. Faced with defeat, the Burmans surrendered those coasts and permitted the British to maintain a minister at the Burman capital of Ava. However, they treated the British with contempt and interfered with colonial commerce, which led to the Second Burmese War of 1852. Trade relations were eventually established in a commercial treaty in 1862 giving the British the right to trade throughout Burma.

Thibaw became king in 1878, and rapidly alienated the British by again interfering with their trade and establishing relations with the French. This resulted in the Third Burmese War (1885–1886) which ended Burman rule. The country was governed as a province of British India until 1937 when it became a Crown Colony.

The emphasis during the British colonial period was on profitable trade and not on the welfare of the various ethnic groups in Burma. In depriving the Burmans of control, the British aroused the hate of this largest group; the minority Karen, Shan, Chin and Kachin people looked to the British for protection from the Burmans, and thus were less antagonistic towards their colonial rulers. The British also undermined the influence of the Buddhist monasteries and imported large numbers of Indians to perform skilled and semi–skilled tasks rather than training the Burmans for these jobs. Thousands of Chinese also entered to engage in trade. These foreign minorities caused anti–Indian and anti–Chinese riots in 1931. The anti–foreign Burmans resisted adoption of European skills and cultural patterns more successfully than the people in almost all of the other British colonies.

There was considerable economic growth during the colonial period. Burma became the chief rice exporter of Southeast Asia; the lower Irrawaddy valley was cleared of its dense forests and brought under cultivation. Burmese labor was used for the cultivation of the huge crops.

The British granted a degree of self-government to Burma in 1937 which included an elected legislature and a cabinet. The lack of experience in government on the part of the Burmans created a basic instability in the government; there was little support among the people for the elected members and officials.

When the Japanese invaded Burma in 1942, they were welcomed by the people, including many Buddhist monks. Chief Minister Ba Maw of the colonial government accepted leadership in a puppet government established by the Japanese in 1943. Even though the people had welcomed their conquerors, the Japanese quickly set up a very oppressive administration designed to exploit Burma's capacity to produce rice. Active resistance soon formed around the *Anti–Fascist People's Freedom League (AFPFL)*, a political movement composed of left–wing nationalists and some communists, leading a guerrilla army under the Burman popular hero Aung San. The Allied forces, in an effort to establish a supply route to southwest China, in order to support the war against the Japanese in that country, slowly fought their way through Burma in 1944–45. The country was eventually liberated by mid–1945.

The British tried to establish a government along prewar colonial lines, but friction erupted immediately with the *AFPFL* led by Aung San. The British, controlled by the *Labor Party* government of Prime Minister Attlee, was anti–colonial and nearly bankrupt; it was in the process of giving up its control over India and Pakistan. It agreed in 1947 to give Burma its independence; the *AFPFL* chose then to leave the British Commonwealth entirely.

Aung San was assassinated in 1947 at the instigation of U Saw. (In the Burmese language, "U" is a title, not a name.) U Nu, an attractive and fervently Buddhist member of the *AFPFL*, took control of the government. Burmese communists threatened the government of Burma in the years following 1948—in 1949 the government controlled little of the nation outside Rangoon. The lack of cooperation among the insurgents enabled the Burmese army under Ne Win to reduce the rebellion to a much lower level by 1951, although it was not eliminated.

China, Burma's largest neighbor, fortunately was not involved in the civil strife. The Burmese, although independent, were not experienced in operating an effective government; the *AFPFL* split and became a coalition of parties with a high degree of inefficiency, corruption and factionalism. The leftist–socialist group was led by U Nu; the more conservative wing was led by Ba Swe. The split between the two factions resulted in the forced resignation of U Nu in the fall of 1958; Burma was then ruled by the military commanded by Ne Win until February 1960. Little progress was made toward solving the political problems of the country, or toward getting the sluggish economy moving during this period of military rule.

Elections were permitted in 1960 which resulted in U Nu's faction being returned to office, but in 1962 adverse political and economic conditions again caused the military to intervene. This time, Ne Win abolished the existing political parties, imprisoned a number of political leaders, including the highly popular U Nu, and established a military dictatorship under the *Union Revolutionary Council* which he led. He dramatically announced that he would make Burma a completely socialist—although not a communist—state. The revolts had continued, particularly in rural areas during the post–independence years. Ne Win was unsuccessful in negotiating an end to these revolts in 1963 and then launched military operations and jailed a number of communist leaders. Relations with China, which formerly were polite and sometimes even cordial, deteriorated in the spring of 1967, principally because of the effects of Mao's "Great Cultural Revolution" on ethnic Chinese living in Burma, who are regarded with some distrust by the Burmese.

However, by 1968 it became increasingly evident that the Burmese had acquired greater confidence in their ability to withstand the displeasure of China. Contributing to this awareness were the good harvest, the reported killing of a communist leader, Than Tun, and a tendency of some of the tribal insurgents to draw closer to the government because of pressures from the Burmese communists and the regime of Mao Zedong and his supporters in China.

Ne Win invited some of the former political leaders in early 1969 to advise him on Burma's political future. They urged a return to elected government instead of military rule. When Ne Win refused, U Nu went into exile and announced that he would try to lead a political movement for

Lord Louis Mountbatten, supreme allied commander in Southeast Asia (1943–46), later *Earl Mountbatten of Burma*, talks with British troops near Mandalay in April 1945

Burma

the overthrow of Ne Win; however, he gave up the plan and returned to Burma in July 1980. Ne Win launched a process of making Burma a one–party state, controlled by the *Burma Socialist Program Party,* a leftist movement with some communist elements, headed by himself. The military government of Burma was repressive and unpopular; the army proved unskilled and ineffective in managing the economy.

A new constitution was adopted by referendum at the beginning of 1974. Burma was renamed the *Socialist Republic of the Union of Burma.* Real power was exercised by a 29 man Council of State, chaired by President Ne Win. However, the government remained repressive, unpopular and inept.

Inflation, shortages of rice, and floods contributed to political unrest in 1974. In December, the funeral of U Thant, former Secretary General of the United Nations, provided the occasion for Buddhist and student organized riots which were quickly suppressed by the military. Ne Win survived an attempted *coup* in 1976. In May 1983, the President purged his security chief and other officials for offenses including drug smuggling.

The resulting confusion probably made it easier for North Korean agents to plant a bomb in a public monument which killed 17 visiting South Korean officials and journalists on October 9th. High Burmese officials were narrowly spared from this terrorist attempt. Infuriated, Ne Win again shook up security services and broke diplomatic relation with North Korea.

The army improved its position against insurgency somewhat in 1985 as China reduced its support for the communists in the Wa and Shan states and as a number of Karen insurgents were driven across the border into Thailand. On the other hand, the so–called Shan United Army, which in addition to defending the interests of the Shan tribes in Burma and Thailand involved in the opium trade, transferred its operation from Thailand to Burma in 1982.

The *National Democratic Front,* a coalition of ethnic insurgent groups, attempted to engage the government in talks on the key issues of ending military rule, restoration of parliamentary government and autonomy for ethnic minorities.

In August 1987, Ne Win made an unprecedented public admission that he and his government had made some mistakes. These included authoritarian policies that led to demonstrations which in turn caused the closing of all educational institutions at the secondary and higher levels.

In March 1988, a long series of massive demonstrations against the ruling regime by students, monks, and urban residents seemed to promise a democratic or liberal

Aung San Suu Kyi (pronounced *Chee*) with a youngster

Photo by Leslie Kean, The Burma Project USA

revolution like those in the Philippines and South Korea. The army proved too strong and determined, however, to permit such an outcome. Another problem was that although Ne Win resigned in July as chairman of the ruling *Burma Socialist Program Party,* he stayed in the Rangoon area and continued to give orders to the army from behind the scenes.

At the end of July, Ne Win was succeeded by a close associate and tough former general, Sein Lwin, who also became president of the Union of Burma. He proclaimed martial law in Rangoon and tried to control the demonstrations by military force but failed; he resigned on August 12. His successor in both posts was a relatively moderate civilian, Maung Maung, who pledged multi–party elections in which none of the current leaders would run for office. There was great popular joy at this, but also widespread demand for an immediate interim government; former Prime Minister U Nu proclaimed such a government, composed largely of opposition leaders, on September 9.

To end the growing confusion, Defense Minister Saw Maung seized power on September 18 and assumed both the chairmanship of the ruling party (now the *State*

Law and Order Restoration Council (SLORC) and the presidency of the state. Protest demonstrations were dealt with by many arrests and much shooting on the part of the army, which succeeded in clearing the streets of the major cities. Press censorship was reimposed. On the other hand, the new regime tried to cope with the country's perennial economic stagnation by promising limited privatization of the heavily socialized economy. Multi–party elections were still promised for 1990.

Several foreign governments, including that of the U.S., protested the military coup and suspended economic aid to Burma. The opposition, calling itself the *National League for Democracy,* discarded U Nu and accepted as its leader Aung Gyi, a retired general. A more popular figure, however, was Aung San Suu Kyi, the daughter of national hero Aung San (assassinated in 1947); she benefited not only from his name and memory but from the atmosphere surrounding the funeral of her mother on January 2, 1989, which amounted to a peaceful demonstration against military rule.

In preparation for the supposedly free election scheduled for May 27, 1990, the military leadership disqualified the most prominent opposition figure, Aung San Suu Kyi, from running (January 1989) and placed her under house arrest in July of that year, together with other leading members of the opposition. One of the control techniques used by the military was the forced migration of about half a million people from the cities to the countryside, where they experienced serious hardships.

The opposition parties won 80% of the vote for the National Assembly in May 1990 elections. The army refused to surrender power, however, and intensified its campaign of repression. In December, Aung San Suu Kyi's party and the Karen guerrillas proclaimed a coalition government in opposition to the army–dominated one.

In spite of brutal repression by the military, unrest continued to grow, both in the cities and in the rural areas. The government closed the universities in December 1991. The army, strengthened by purchases of more than $1 billion in arms from China, launched a series of offensives in ethnic minority areas. One result was a stream of refugees out of the country, including Muslims fleeing to Bangladesh.

In 1994 and early 1995, the State Law and Order Restoration Council (SLORC) neutralized much of the opposition by signing individual ceasefire agreements with rebel groups. Their support was thus denied to anti–government democratic forces in urban areas. Supporters of democracy had to go underground. In Janu-ary 1995, government forces captured Manerplaw, the legendary Karen rebel base located on the Thai border. This was made easier by the death of Saw Maw Reh, President of the Karen rebel state, in March 1994. In April 1995, the Karen National Union (KNU) sent a letter to the head of SLORC seeking peace.

Government and Politics

After independence from the British at the end of 1947, the Burmese political system which emerged was nominally a parliamentary democracy under the leadership of Prime Minister U Nu. However, the multi–ethnic nature of the state, the lack of experience with the Western–style government and the inability to confront important political, social and economic problems, led to the entry of the military into government in both 1958 and again in 1962.

The early assassination of the country's popular independence leader also complicated the situation. The independence struggle had been led by Aung San, the man often spoken of as the father of modern Burma. Aung San had been an effective leader of the nationalist movement and was expected to lead the first post–colonial government, but his death ended that possibility. Later, of course, his memory would help galvanize Burmese behind the pro–democracy movement of his daugther Aung San Suu Kyi.

Today the country is best characterized as a military dictatorship. The dominant political figure has been General Ne Win, who still commands great loyalty, though by 1997 apparently no longer holds any direct power. He ruled from 1962 to the end of 1987 through the country's only political party, the *Burmese Socialist Program Party (BSPP)*. This was, however, only a front for military rule. The period from 1988 to the present, as described in the previous section, was one of crisis, in which the military sought a way to maintain control and regain legitimacy even going as far as ignoring the results of the 1990 election which had been overwelmingly won by the country's democratic party, the *National League for Democracy.*

The political culture of the country is both rigidly organized, but paternalistic. There is almost no real experience with democratic institutions despite the strong public support for Aung San Suu Kyi's efforts to create a democratic Burma. Effective control of the government now rests with the military junta officially known as the *State Law and Order Restoration Council (SLORC)*, created in 1988. Effective power within *SLORC* rests with its chairman, General Than Shwe, who also serves as Prime Minister.

The People's Assembly *(Pyitha Hluttaw)* was never convened after the May 27, 1990 elections because of the victory of the democratic forces. The judicial branch is subject to the power of *SLORC.*

The major political event of 1995 was the July 10 release of Aung San Suu Kyi,

The pavilion of the Shwe Dagon pagoda, Rangoon

WORLD BANK photo

Burma

Worshippers inside the Shwe Dagon pagoda   Photo by Jon Markham Morrow

military rule. The latter have managed to combine military rule with a vigorous economy, a combination that is attractive to the leaders of Burma. They, however, must have found the spectacle of Jakarta struggling with its own ongoing democratic movement during 1996 sobering!

Defense

Much of Burma's defense policy is internally directed against the various ethnic groups which seek either total independence or some degree of autonomy. Continuing progress in reducing the tensions between Rangoon and the Shan rebels is one of the regime's most important recent accomplishments.

On January 14, 1996, the *SLORC* further improved its hold on the country when Khun Sa, the number one opium and heroin producer in the Golden Triangle, surrendered his 10,000 man Mong Tai army to Burmese officials. The "triangle" refers to the area where the borders of Burma, Thailand and Laos meet. In return for the surrender, Khun Sa has apparently been assured that he will not be extradited to the United States, where a grand jury would like to talk with him. Amnesty from Rangoon and the right to maintain control over part of the Shan state with a downsized army may have also been part of the deal. Of course, business as usual will continue. Such a deal will make it hard if not impossible for U.S.–Burmese relations to improve.

The Burmese government signed an agreement in mid–1995 with the *New Mon State Party (NMSP)*. The military agreement gave Mon rebels control over 20 designated areas in their home state in return for a ceasefire. Rangoon also initiated new military action against remnants of the Karen National Union which had signed an agreement with the government after the fall of Manerplaw in the spring. A new offensive was also launched against the *Karen National Progressive Party*. These actions are a clear indication of Rangoon's determination to put an end to rebel activities in the country. Success, however, is not assured. The military situation along the Thai–Burmese border was tense during 1995. Rangoon accused Thailand of providing sanctuary and help to the Karen rebels, the *SLORC* was also angry about a March attack by Khun Sa's army on Tachilek, a Burmese border town. The attackers allegedly used Thai territory to their advantage. Burmese military forces also conducted raids against refugee camps across the Thai border. General Chawalit Yongchaiyut, Deputy Prime Minister and Minister of Defense for Thailand visited Rangoon in early September at the invitation of the Burmese Deputy

the most famous opposition figure in the country. She had been under house arrest since 1989. But despite her release from formal house arrest it has been clear that the government has no interest in allowing her to carry out her political activities. Throughout 1996 her efforts to address her supporters were constantly interfered with and confrontations between students, monks and the government forces were a constant feature of life in the capital. The *SLORC* even refused to allow the former president of the Philippines, Corazon Aquino, to visit her.

After her 1995 release, the *National League for Democracy (NLD)* MP's who fled the country when the 1990 election results were not upheld, met in Sweden to decide

the opposition's course of action. One result was that they recognized the *National Coalition Government of the Union of Burma,* which should have taken power in 1990. During the fall of 1996, the *NLD* even attempted to hold an official meeting within Burma which not surprisingly resulted in hundreds of arrests.

The *SLORC* created the *Union Solidarity Development Association (USDA)* as a front organization. It has set up branches throughout the country in an effort to channel support to *SLORC. USDA* appears to be modeled after Indonesia's *GOLKAR,* a political party which supports the role of the military in Indonesian society. The Burmese military apparently is more than a little interested in the Indonesian style of

Prime Minister, Vice Admiral Maung Maung Khin, to smooth things over.

The People's Republic of China is also important to the Burmese defense equation. Since 1993, Burma has reportedly received some $1.2 billion in military equipment from China. An agreement was signed for another $400 million in equipment in late 1994. There is also the recognition that with military equipment comes technical assistance and a limited presence.

Both India and Indonesia as well as the other ASEAN states appear concerned about Chinese access to three strategic islands (Ramree, Coco, and St. Matthew's), off the Burmese coast. St. Matthew's island is less than 200 miles north of Malaysia. China may well have an irreversible foothold in Burma.

Foreign Policy

As Burma emerges from its self–imposed isolation, it faces a complicated international environment. Its effort is especially complicated by a split between many Western nations and Burma's more immediate southeast Asian nations. External to the region its international support is dwindling. The fame of Aung San Suu Kyi is spreading throughout the Western world, no doubt helped by the success of the film "Beyond Rangoon." In early 1997 she even made it on the cover of the influential Parade Magazine, a newspaper magazine that reaches millions of Americans every Sunday. In the eyes of many Westerners, Burma is emerging as the "South Africa" of the 1990s. Within the United States, individual states like Massachusetts have moved to bar their governments from working with any corporation active in Burma and efforts to boycott the developing tourist trade have begun as well.

Not surprisingly, Burma's relations with its neighbors are even more complicated. Overall the closer nations, especially those in ASEAN, are interested in a policy of "construtive engagement" which has seen Burma move closer and closer to entering ASEAN as a full member. They gained official observer status within ASEAN last year. If all goes well, full membership could be achieved in several years. ASEAN is keen on bringing Burma into the organization as a means of providing Rangoon with other alternatives to China which has established strong ties with the country. Nevertheless, by early spring 1997 it still looked like Laos and Cambodia where likely to enter ASEAN before Burma did. Regionally it has countries with whom it must retain acceptable relationships: China, India and the ASEAN states (Thailand and Singapore are the most important within ASEAN). Chinese penetration of the country is already significant through military assistance described above and because of significant immigration and trade from the provinces north of Burma. India cannot accept an unchecked Chinese presence in Burma, and especially on its offshore territories. Recently India has attempted to warm relations with the SLORC perhaps to balance Chinese influence.

The United States, along with other Western nations as mentioned above, has become even more critical of the SLORC's domination of the country. Madeleine Albright, when she was still United States Ambassador to the United Nations, visited Rangoon and delivered the message that there would be no significant change in U.S. policy toward Burma until the SLORC changed the way it treats the Burmese people. Since she has become the first American woman to serve as the Secretary of State Dr. Albright has not indicated any change in the position.

Society and Culture

While Burmans constitute the largest ethnic group in the country, other groups such as the Karens, Shans, and Kachins are important. Much of modern Burmese history has been dominated by the efforts of these groups to gain greater autonomy from the Burmese Government.

Hinayana Buddhism pervades almost every aspect of Burmese culture. In fact, the military junta in recent years has made efforts to link itself to Buddhism as a way to reinforce its legitimacy. Monks are numerous and influential; most Burmese males spend at least part of their lives in monasteries. The countless temples and shrines have been constructed with great care and with precious materials which combine to create structures of exquisite beauty; the best known of these is the huge and ornate Shwe Dagon in Rangoon.

Although the Buddhists teach the normal traditions of Buddhism, there is still among the people a widespread belief in animism, especially with respect to the existence and activities of "nats" which are spirits within objects. But Buddhism is not the only tradition found in Burma. Christian and Muslim groups both exist though they operate under heavy controls imposed by the government.

In clear contrast to the customs of both traditional India and China, Burmese women have enjoyed a high degree of freedom and social equality; they can inherit property, keep their native names after marriage and have equal rights in contracting marriage and suing for divorce. Reports of spousal abuse are infrequent.

Young monks contemplate lottery tickets, Rangoon. Photo by Jon Markham Morrow

Burma

Nevertheless, for many young Burmese women, especially among minorities that live near the borders, life can bring great trials. There are frequent reports of young women lured across the border to Thailand for jobs, which, in contrast to the original claims, see these young women forced to work as prostitutes in Bangkok's brothels. Moreover, the government's policy of demanding forced labor from its citizens often leads to abuses.

Politically there are no independent women's rights organizations nor government ministries responsible for women's issues. With the exception of Aung San Suu Kyi, women play almost no role in the political life of the nation.

Despite the economic gains made in recent years Burma remains a poor country. A new Burmese middle class appears to be emerging but the average per capita cash income is between two and three hundred dollars a year and few get any advanced education. Forty percent of its children never attend school and 3/4 never get past the fifth year of schooling.

Economy

The government has continued to work successfully toward the transformation of its earlier centrally planned socialist style economy into a market economy. In doing so they have probably moved to lessen at least some of the dissatisfaction the population has felt toward the junta. In March 1994 the government announced that it would do away with the old 45 and 90 *kyat* notes in favor of more conventional denominations: 20, 50, 100 and 500 *kyat* notes. While the Burmese, who have been accustomed to thinking in nines, may find the change difficult, Western businessmen and investors, whom the government is now courting, will feel much more at home. In an effort to stimulate the inflow of foreign currency and to improve hotels and tourism ($565 million), seventeen hotels were under construction in Rangoon at the end of 1994. The government dubbed 1996 as "visit Myanmar year." Unfortunately for the junta their marketing campaign has weakened by the efforts of Aung San Suu Kyi and her supporters around the world to discourage tourism so as to avoid inadvertently helping the junta in its domination of the country.

The GDP for 1996 was 7.7%, a healthy rate that compares favorably with other South East Asian economies though the real per capita income remained at about $930 dollars. Foreign investment grew to over $2.6 billion by mid–1995. A major gas pipeline project accounted for a good proportion of this investment. Foreign banks are now allowed to operate in the country, and foreign businesses can in theory repatriate profits. Thanks to British colonialism, a workable legal system including patent and copyright law is in place.

Nevertheless, the bottom line is that Burma remains a very poor country and faces a number of significant challenges in the economic sector. These problems include a significant foreign debt, a continuing trade deficit, high inflation, an unrealistic exchange rate, a very poor improvement possibility, a failed educational system, and the prospect of no immediate assistance from the international community as a result of the *SLORC's* anti–democratic behavior. And many Western companies, including Eddie Bauer, Pepsi, Carlsberg, Heineken Beer, Liz Claiborne, Apple Computer and Levi Strauss have discontinued or lessened their operations because of the country's international reputation. Investment from the ASEAN states, such as Singapore, however have been growing.

The really significant economic gains though have been made in the illegal but lucrative narcotics trade. Since the *SLORC*

Rangoon: Procession in front of the Shwe Dagon pagoda

Photo by Jon Markham Morrow

came to power Burma, has become the world's main producer of opium and heroin.

The Future

Burma's move toward ASEAN in 1997 is encouraging. However, Southeast Asia needs an independent, economically stable Burma. For the moment the government has strengthened itself through its ties to the People's Republic by efforts to attract more investment. Democracy is only a distant hope at this time. What is likely though is that Burma, which has for so long remained on the "back burner" of Western human rights campaigns, is likely to become far more an issue in the future than it has been in the past.

A major shake–up in the Burmese military, which replaced many of the hard–liners in 1995, is also encouraging. A more pragmatic and hopefully less ruthless generation of leaders may be easier to work with and more open to slow change. Nevertheless, a more optimistic view of Burma's future is at this time unrealistic.

Two young boys in Buddhist ceremonial attire
Photo by Jon Markham Morrow

The State of Cambodia

The temple of Angkor Wat built by Khmer warrior kings a thousand years ago   AP/World Wide Photos

Area: 68,898 sq. mi. (181,300 sq. km.; slightly larger than Missouri).

Population: 9 million (1993 est.).

Capital City: Phnom Penh (Pop. 450,000, estimated).

Climate: Tropically hot with a rainy monsoon season during the summer from May to October.

Neighboring Countries: Thailand (North and West); Laos (Northeast); Vietnam (East).

Official Language: Khmer (Cambodian).

Other Principal Tongues: French, Chinese, Vietnamese.

Ethnic Background: Cambodian (Khmer, about 80%) Vietnamese (semi–permanent or permanent, about 12%), Chinese (5%), other, including primitives, (about 2%).

Principal Religion: Buddhism (Hinayana sect, but religious observances have not until recently been permitted.)

Main Exports (to China): Natural rubber, rice, pepper, wood; export trade is almost nonexistent.

Main Imports (from China, North Korea, Vietnam and Russia): International food aid and some economic development.

Currency: Riel.

Former Colonial Status: French protectorate (1863–1949); Associated State within the French Union (1949–1955).

Independence Date: September 25, 1955.

Head of State: Norodom Sihanouk, King (Sept. 24, 1993).

Heads of Government: Prince Norodom Ranariddh and Hun Sen, First and Second Prime Ministers.

National Flag: A plain red field upon which is centered in gold the ancient temple Angkor Wat.

Per Capita Income: US$130 (estimated).

Cambodia has a rather short coastline which runs about 150 miles along the warm waters of the Gulf of Siam. The land stretches from this coast in a wide plain, which is traversed in the eastern part by the broad waters of the lower Mekong River. The western part of the plain is dominated by a large lake known as Tonle Sap, twenty miles wide and one hundred miles long—a body of fresh water that produces a heavy annual harvest of fish needed by the Cambodians, who do not eat meat because of Buddhist beliefs.

The borders with Laos and southern Vietnam run through thickly forested foothills that rise to highlands at the demarcation lines. The greater part of the northern border with Thailand consists of a steep series of cliffs; the part of Thailand closest to Cambodia is a plateau which is situated about 1,500 feet above the plain. The western border with Thailand and most of Cambodia's coastline is occupied by the Cardamom, Kirimom and Elephant

Cambodia

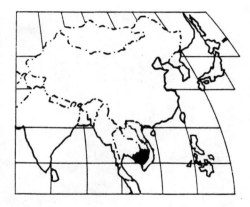

Mountains, which rise to heights of 5,500 feet.

Much of the central plain, which is the largest by far and is economically the area of prime importance in Cambodia, is regularly flooded by the mighty Mekong River in an uncontrolled fashion—there are no elaborate dikes to contain the waters such are are found along the Red River in northern Vietnam. The rains which begin in May are the first cause of flooding; melting snows in Tibet and China in July add to the volume of water, which is also joined by monsoon waters from Thailand and Laos. By mid–September the flood water may cover as much as 8,000 square miles of land. These are not violent waters—they deposit a fine silt which enriches the land and they also bring huge quantities of fish to the Tonle Sap lake, permitting annual harvests of up to 15 tons per square mile of water surface.

The waters recede in October and the winter season begins in November, bringing slightly cooler and much drier weather except in the western and southern mountains, where there is sporadic rainfall.

History: The Khmer people, from whom the modern Cambodians (Kampucheans) are descended, first organized themselves under a state usually known by its Chinese name of Funan, which emerged about 500 A.D. in southern Cambodia. This was apparently a result of trade with, and immigration from, India to Cambodia via the Kra Isthmus which is now the southern part of Thailand. In the early 10th century a powerful state known as the Khmer Empire arose, with its capital at Angkor, north of Tonle Sap, where huge and complex palaces were painstakingly constructed during the course of several centuries and are a major tourist attraction during periods when there is no civil or military strife.

The people were converted after 1000 A.D. to the southern school of Buddhism which originated on the island of Sri Lanka and is referred to as *Hinayana* Buddhism. At its height in about 1200, the Khmer Empire controlled much of what is now Vietnam, Thailand, Laos and Burma. For a number of reasons, including the over–extension of its resources and attacks by the Thai from the North, the empire declined a century later and was ultimately destroyed by the Thai about the end of the 15th century. For the next three and one–half centuries, Cambodia was sandwiched between the Annamese of Central Vietnam and the Thai to the north and west, and was almost continuously dominated by one or the other, or both.

French interest in Cambodia was stimulated in the late 1850's by British advances in Burma. Both powers thought of

Southeast Asia principally as a stepping stone to the supposedly vast treasures and markets of southwest China. Although it established a protectorate over Cambodia in 1863, France did not dethrone the reigning family; the area was increasingly drawn into the Indochinese colony created at the end of the century in an attempt to rival the much larger British Indian Empire. The French prevented the Thais from moving against Cambodia and protected it also from its other traditional overlord, the Vietnamese, who had also become part of the French Indochinese empire.

This protection was welcomed by the Cambodians, and as a result, there was not the violently anti–French attitude that existed in neighboring Vietnam. As in other parts of South Asia, the existence of a stable colonial administration attracted a sizable number of Chinese immigrants, who quickly emerged in a virtually dominant position in profitable ventures as commercial middlemen.

Japan quickly overran Cambodia in 1941, and as a token of appreciation, two of the Cambodian border provinces were awarded to Thailand, by then the official ally of the Japanese. Although they were returned after World War II, the Cambodians have a lingering suspicion that the Thai still covet them.

Politics in Cambodia was dominated after the return of the French in 1946 by a single popular and unpredictable man who ruled until 1970: Prince Norodom Si-

hanouk. He had been made king by the French in 1941, but became impatient with the conservative traditions of the monarchy and interested in the liberal political movements within the country; he abdicated in 1955. Freed of the burdensome ceremonial duties and able to play a free role in politics, he became premier and quickly took advantage of the French defeat in Vietnam (see Vietnam) to declare the independence of Cambodia.

Sihanouk abolished the monarchy in 1960 and became the titular as well as the actual chief of state. Nationalistic, but not anti–French, he had an immense popularity with the people of the nation. He skillfully used this popularity to cope with what he regarded as major domestic problems—the traditional aristocracy, the part-

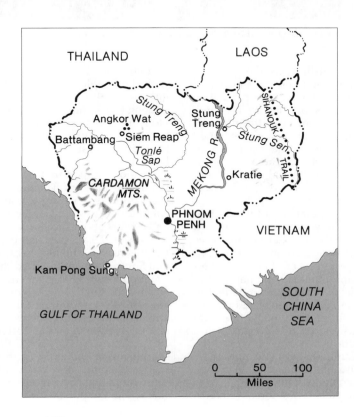

Cambodia

Days of the monarchy: young King Norodom Sihanouk, 1946

ly westernized intellectuals, the businessmen, the small communist movement and a segment of right–wing opponents who he believed were supported by Thailand. His efforts were almost uniformly successful at first. He founded and continued to lead the *Sangkum,* or the *Popular Socialist Movement,* which was the only significant political party. He did, however, allow his Premier, General Lon Nol, to exercise some power.

But for the popularity of Sihanouk at home, Cambodia would never have been able to deal with the external pressures with which it was faced. In order to keep open the largest number of possible alternatives, Sihanouk remained "neutral" in the international "cold war" and aloof in the hot war in Asia. He engaged in active and skillful diplomacy which often puzzled the most astute foreign ministries. His view after independence was to the effect that Cambodia was surrounded by potentially hostile forces and neighbors, with the exception of Laos.

To counter–balance the threat of North

Vietnam, he established close relations with the People's Republic of China beginning in 1956—the government of Mao Zedong (Tse–tung) was not anxious to see Ho Chi Minh's Vietnam dominate Cambodia, and apparently restrained its southern ally sufficiently to satisfy Sihanouk.

Sihanouk hoped that he could rely on the senior allies of Thailand and South Vietnam to restrain any ambitions of the communists toward Cambodia, but also had doubts about the sincerity and effectiveness of U.S. support of those countries. For this reason, and also because the U.S. and South Vietnam resented the fact that Cambodia served as a sanctuary for and an area through which North Vietnam supplied the communist forces in southern Indochina, relations between Sihanouk and the U.S. were strained after the early 1960's. Complaints by the U.S. increased sharply in late 1967 as the fighting in South Vietnam became more intense; there were some hints that the United States would claim a right to pursue the communist *Viet*

Cong into the eastern provinces of Cambodia. Prince Sihanouk announced he was willing to discuss the possibility of pursuit of the Viet Cong with a U.S. emissary, but when the diplomat arrived back in the U.S., he was denounced by the Prince, who proclaimed that the only item on the agenda was the "territorial integrity of Cambodia." The whole situation was made more complicated by Cambodia's claims to areas in South Vietnam, which were used at the bargaining table repeatedly when dealing with the U.S.; he refused to grant the U.S. any concessions unless it recognized the validity of Cambodian claims. When the U.S. agreed in 1969 to recognize Cambodia's existing frontiers, diplomatic relations, severed four years earlier, were restored.

The ever–changing and shrewd diplomacy of Sihanouk impressed the U.S., its allies, Britain, France, China and the Soviet Union to the extent that its Asian neighbors did not constitute a direct threat to the survival of Cambodia. There was a significant increase in communist–led revolts in the provinces bordering Thailand and Laos in the latter part of 1968, as well as the number of *Viet Cong* illegally present within Cambodia. The displeasure of anti–communist Cambodians grew so great that in 1970, while Sihanouk was out of the country, major anti–Hanoi demonstrations broke out in Phnom Penh. General Lon Nol and Prince Sirik Matak proclaimed the ouster of Sihanouk and a new government under their leadership. The communist problem, however, was not the only issue—there had been disputes over Sihanouk's socialist economic policies.

North Vietnamese and Cambodian communist forces promptly began to expand their military activities in various parts of the country; at the end of April 1970, American and South Vietnamese forces entered to clean out the "sanctuary" areas along the border from which the communists had been conducting raids into South Vietnam. A secondary objective was to give some support to the new Cambodian government.

American ground forces were withdrawn in mid–1970 and South Vietnamese soldiers left soon afterward. The country suffered severely as a result of this military campaign.

Although in poor health and under heavy military pressure from communist forces, Lon Nol remained in power until 1975. He dissolved the National Assembly in late 1971 and began to rule by decree. He then proclaimed himself President, reshuffling his cabinet drastically and excluding Sirik Matak from it.

During the following years, public confidence in the government eroded badly and the communists (with North Vietnamese support) made major military gains. The American military role included continuous bombing in support of Lon Nol's army, but with no advisors in the field and no ground forces. The bombing was halted in mid–1973 because of U.S. Congressional action.

The communist rebels, often called the *Khmer Rouge*, and at the time supported by North Vietnam, claimed to be loyal to a government headed by Sihanouk and based in China, but in reality they had their own local leadership. Communist military efforts came close to isolating Phnom Penh by early 1975. Undermined by his own shortcomings, political bickering, uncertainty as to continuing American support and communist military gains, Lon Nol's government evaporated. The rebels refused to negotiate with it, leaving it no alternative but to surrender amid ominous proclamations of a collection of "blood debts" from the leadership. The final collapse came in early May 1975, when Phnom Penh fell to the communists. The United States confined its active role in this situation to the rescue of an American merchant ship seized by Cambodian communists and the transport of several thousand refugees to safety.

The policies of the new regime, which was pro-Chinese and soon became anti-Vietnamese, reflected the guerrilla mentality of its leaders and personnel. The major cities, including Phnom Penh, were forcibly evacuated to a considerable extent, allegedly on account of food shortages. There were executions of supporters of the former regime and widespread atrocities, mainly against persons of middle class background.

Sihanouk returned from China in 1975; most of his entourage, however, chose to go from China to France the following month. Cambodia was actually run not by Sihanouk, but by a shadowy leadership of the Cambodian Communist Party known as the *Angka* ("organization"), of which Pol Pot was Secretary General. An election held in 1976 filled 250 seats in the *People's Representative Assembly*. All 515 candidates were picked by the *Angka*. Sihanouk resigned, together with the rest of the government. He was placed under house arrest. An entire communist government was announced, with Pol Pot in actual control.

Then began in 1976 one of the horror stories of the 20th century in "Democratic Kampuchea." Once a happy, rather carefree society, Cambodians found themselves brutalized by one of the harshest governments known, and a veil of secrecy shrouded the nation. The formerly beautiful capital of Phnom Penh with 1.3 million was left with 90,000. Boarded-over store fronts and virtually deserted streets told the story. The new regime wanted to stifle religion, wipe out any education system conflicting with the hopes of the "new order," and stamp out family ties.

Families were driven from the cities to labor from dawn to dusk in the fields. First priority was the destruction of the *intelligentsia* and *middle class*. Reports indicate that more than 3.4 million Cambodians were killed. The method of execution even saved the cost of a bullet: a skull–penetrating blow to the rear of the head by a pick axe used on a kneeling person. Silent, massive piles of bones throughout the country attest to this grisly activity. Others simply starved to death.

The new regime had immediate friction with all of its neighbors, the most serious with Vietnam, which erupted into continuing border warfare from early until late 1978 when a massive assault was launched on Cambodia. By early January 1979, Pol Pot had fled to western Cambodia, and a new pro–Vietnamese government known as the *People's Republic of Kampuchea* had been set up in Phnom Penh. Pol Pot's forces continued to fight a guerrilla war. This was one of the main reasons why China staged a brief invasion across the Vietnamese border in early 1979 with the announced purpose of "teaching Vietnam a lesson."

For a decade after 1979 there was fighting in western Cambodia between Vietnamese troops and Pol Pot's forces, as well as tension between Vietnam and Thailand over the Cambodian refugees grouped near the border. A coalition under Sihanouk, including what was left of Pol Pot's regime, emerged in opposition to the Vietnamese–dominated government in Phnom Penh. This group retains Cambodia's seat in the UN. The membership of ASEAN tried to negotiate a settlement of the Cambodia conflict and a Vietnamese withdrawal.

The unpopular Pol Pot "retired" as commander of the forces of the Khmer Rouge, the strongest faction in the anti–Vietnamese coalition. Son Sann, the head of another faction, survived a challenge by some of his colleagues in December 1985.

The Phnom Penh government, which was very repressive, continued to be dominated by the Vietnamese. The estimated 160,000 Vietnamese troops in Cambodia appeared to be concentrating on the resistance forces within Cambodia rather than putting pressure on the Thai border, as they had been doing earlier.

In March 1986, the anti-Vietnamese coalition, with the approval of China and ASEAN, softened its position somewhat by agreeing to negotiate with the pro–Vietnamese government in Phnom Penh. By the end of the year, it appeared that Hanoi, probably under Soviet pressure, was modifying its objection to the inclusion of the Khmer Rouge in any such talks.

Except for helping to keep the anti–Vietnamese coalition in possession of the Cambodian seat in the United Nations, ASEAN has tended to become less and less relevant to the conflict and its potential resolution. The initiative passed in 1987 to Sihanouk, who, under the sponsorship of Indonesia, held some inconclusive talks with the pro–Vietnamese regime but was frustrated by lack of support from his partners in the coalition. Accordingly, he resigned as head of the group in January 1988.

In May 1988, Hanoi announced that it would withdraw 50,000 of its 120,000-odd troops then in Cambodia by the end of the year, with the others to follow by first March and then September 1990. The reasons for this major policy shift included the dismal state of the Vietnamese economy, the small chances of aid from abroad while the Cambodian occupation continued, and Soviet pressure or at least persuasion; it is probably not a coincidence that only the month before Moscow had formally agreed to remove its troops from Afghanistan by February 15, 1989. Hanoi also tried to improve its relationship with the U.S. by agreeing to let more refugees out of Cambodia and to try harder to account for MIA's (Americans missing in action during the Vietnam war).

The prospect of Vietnamese withdrawal naturally accelerated the pace of political and diplomatic activity relating to Cambodia, both within and outside the country. The main problem was that the Vietnamese evacuation might lead to a second seizure of power by the Khmer Rouge, who had been heavily armed by China and were apparently still as bloodthirsty as they had shown themselves to be fifteen years earlier. They intended to dominate the four-party coalition government (the parties to the resistance coalition loyal to Sihanouk, which include the Khmer Rouge, plus the pro–Vietnamese regime in Phnom Penh, headed by party chief Heng Samrin and Premier Hun Sen) that everyone agreed in principle should be created to end the conflict. Prince Sihanouk, the titular head of the resistance coalition and the most likely leader of the future government, was torn between his fear of his ferocious Khmer Rouge "allies" and his detestation of the regime installed by the invading Vietnamese. He tried negotiating with Hun Sen, but without much success; on the whole, he managed as best he could having been more or less stuck with the Khmer Rouge.

As the Vietnamese began to withdraw from western Cambodia, Khmer Rouge troops followed them from bases near the border with Thailand. They herded Cam-

Cambodia

Jakarta, Indonesia, July 1988: Another fruitless meeting with (l. to r.) *Khmer Peoples National Liberation Front* leader Son Sann, Cambodian Prime Minister Hun Sen, and Prince Norodom Sihanouk

AP/Wide World Photo

bodian refugees back into Cambodia from camps in Thailand, to provide themselves with a labor force and a population they could claim to rule. They stockpiled arms in various places and attacked other forces, including those of their "allies." At times the Vietnamese relaxed their evacuation, turned back, and fought the Khmer Rouge.

Under these conditions, it was hard to see how the Khmer Rouge could be prevented from dominating Cambodia after the Vietnamese left. There were many efforts to do exactly that, however. In mid–1988 China agreed to cut off its arms transfers to the Khmer Rouge when the Vietnamese finished withdrawing and conceded in principle that the Khmer Rouge could not be allowed to dominate the future Cambodian government. In late July, an informal meeting ("cocktail party") of the four Cambodian parties was held in Indonesia, the first of a series to be convened under the auspices of ASEAN; the results were inconclusive, mainly on account of the extreme hostility between the Khmer Rouge and the Hun Sen group. In August, the Khmer Rouge tried to improve its image by agreeing that the future unified Cambodian army should be under international supervision, while continuing to insist that the existing pro–Vietnamese government in Phnom Penh be dissolved. At the end of August, a series of Sino–Soviet talks in which Cambodia was the main single topic were convened. The Chinese supported the Khmer Rouge position and wanted the future international (UN) peacekeeping force to be armed; the Soviet side favored an unarmed force and

the formation of the future coalition government around the existing Phnom Penh regime as its core. In the fall the UN General Assembly passed a resolution opposing a return to power by the Khmer Rouge alone; China voted for it. In November, Philippine Foreign Minister Raul Manglapus visited Hanoi. Indian Prime Minister Rajiv Gandhi's visit to China in December 1988 marked the beginning of an effort to put India forward as the mediator in Cambodia; the idea seemed to be acceptable to ASEAN and Vietnam.

Early 1989 saw a further flurry of diplomatic activity relating to Cambodia. In January, the Thai Foreign Minister visited Hanoi, and Hun Sen went to Thailand; Sino–Vietnamese talks, principally on Cambodia, were held in Beijing. February saw a visit by Chinese Premier Li Peng to Thailand and a meeting in Beijing of the three parties to the resistance coalition. U.S. authorities said it might support a government headed by Sihanouk and even provide armaments toward that end, provided it did not include the Khmer Rouge, now backed by about 40,000 heavily armed guerrillas.

Hanoi announced in April 1989 that it would withdraw the remainder of its troops from Cambodia by September 1990, but in reality they were out a year earlier than that. This withdrawal, as well as major negotiations held from time to time, had the effect of escalating the fighting in Cambodia. The two sides, the Khmer Rouge and its non–communist allies (who tended to become increasingly dependent on it for arms as only a limited supply reached them from other sources,

including the United States), and the pro–Vietnamese regime in Phnom Penh, tried to improve their strategic positions prior to a possible future cease–fire. Several thousand Vietnamese troops returned to Cambodia covertly in late October 1989 to help the Phnom Penh regime defend cities in western Cambodia which were threatened by the Khmer Rouge.

Both sides tried to improve their images at home and abroad. In mid–1990 Phnom Penh, for example, dropped the name *Kampuchea* in favor of the former Cambodia. The Khmer Rouge announced, not for the first time, the "retirement" of its notoriously murderous leader, Pol Pot.

Phnom Penh's objection to the inclusion of the Khmer Rouge in a coalition government tended to freeze various negotiations and conferences. By 1990, however, pressure from the Soviet Union, and probably Vietnam as well, had compelled Premier Hun Sen of the Phnom Penh regime to Khmer Rouge participation.

The Australian government proposed in late 1989 an enhanced role of the UN in a prospective settlement for Cambodia. The contemplated election would involve a contest among all four of the parties on an equal footing. This was done in spite of the fact that the UN officially recognized three of them (the anti–Vietnamese coalition) as the legitimate government of Cambodia, even though the Phnom Penh regime had been claiming that status itself. This complex formula, however, failed to win a level of acceptance at a conference held at Jakarta in February 1990. Agreement (and even the usual "joint communique") was impossible.

In March the five permanent members of the UN Security Council began trying to get the parties to accept an increased UN role along the lines of the Australian proposal.

In mid–1990 the United States withdrew recognition from the anti–Vietnamese coalition and began to negotiate with Hanoi in the hope of moving the "peace process" along. The situation continued to be seriously complicated by Chinese arms shipments to the Khmer Rouge, via Thailand.

In October 1991, nineteen nations (including the four Cambodian factions, signing as one nation) signed a treaty in Paris providing that, under United Nations supervision, and with the presence of a UN peace–keeping force, a ceasefire would go into effect and elections would be held when feasible. Meanwhile, the four Cambodian factions would participate in a Supreme National Council, under Prince Sihanouk.

The following month, the three coalition parties began to return to Phnom Penh. Sihanouk promptly aligned himself with Hun Sen, announced that he favored trying the Khmer Rouge leaders, and tried to keep the Khmer Rouge out of the coalition government. For its part, the Khmer Rouge claimed to support the Paris settlement but, alleging that there were still some Vietnamese troops in Cambodia, it continued fighting in the hinterland against the Hun Sen forces.

On October 23, 1991, the Paris International Conference on Cambodia adopted an agreement on a Comprehensive Political Settlement of the Cambodia Conflict, which created the United Nations Transitional Authority in Cambodia (UNTAC) with a force of 16,000 military and 6,000 civilians to begin arriving in Cambodia in early 1992. UNTAC's function was to disarm the Cambodian warring factions and create a political climate where free elections could take place.

The Current Outlook

Since 1993 Cambodia has operated under a democratic government formed in the aftermath of the 1993 United Nations sponsored election. After more than a generation of civil war and totalitarian governments this has been a remarkable change. The current coalition government, the result of the elections of 1993, is a constitutional monarchy nominally headed by the long time Prince Norodom Sihanouk. In the run up to the elections, UNTAC, the United Nations Transitional Authority in Cambodia, had placed many of its representatives into positions of influence as it attempted to move Cambodia toward a more representative governing system.

In order to split political power between *FUNCINPEC*, the "royalist" party and the *PPC*, (the Khmer Rouge Party of Democratic Kampuchea) the government has been formed with two Prime Ministers! Prince Norodom Ranariddh holds the position of 1st Prime Minister. He is a son of King Norodom Sihanouk, who had been sworn in as the constitutional monarch in September 1993. The second Prime Minister is Hun Sen. The cabinet also features dual ministers representing both parties. Although officially second prime minister, Hun Sen, who has long been dominant in Cambodian politics, wields greater influence.

The country operates as a parliamentary system though the judiciary is not as independent of the government as the constitution requires. The unusual system of two prime ministers certainly helped get the coalition going though the more common pattern of having rotating prime ministers as has occurred in Israel and Turkey might have worked more efficiently. The two prime ministers are largely estranged and actual fighting has broken out between their supporters.

Norodom Sirivudh, half brother to King Norodom Sihanouk, was even arrested for allegedly planning to kill co–prime minister Hun Sen. He is now living in exile in Paris. Many believe the Prince was framed in an attempt to silence his criticism of the government. However the murder in 1996 of Hun Sen's brother–in–law clearly shows the level of tension and does not bode well for the government's future efforts to accomplish anything.

Many observers, however, have been impressed with how well the coalition has managed to operate despite the obvious problems.

The *Khmer Rouge* and what to do about it has, of course, been the major issue which faced the government. Attempts to end the fighting have taken different forms over the years. The approach has ranged from the regularity of fighting to occasional efforts to reconcile with the *Khmer Rouge*, despite its bloody record of mass murder during its totalitarian reign from 1975 to 1979. There were many efforts to find a way to reconcile the *Khmer Rouge* to the changes in Cambodia. For example, in May 1994, the King called for peace talks with the *Khmer Rouge* which had refused to go along with the United Nations election efforts. There was also a move to have Sihanouk form a provision-al government. In June 1996, while in Beijing, he announced that he would be willing to return to be the head of government as well as head of state, and that he would form a government of reconciliation which would include the *Khmer Rouge*. The Hun Sen faction opposed the plan and Sihanouk withdrew his offer. Nevertheless, by 1996 real change appeared to be coming about.

Khmer Rouge Crumbling?

Happily, 1996 saw major progress in the government's efforts to end the long time insurrection of the *Khmer Rouge*. In August, Ieng Sary, the long time senior leader of the *Khmer Rouge,* said to be second only to the infamous Pol Pot, broke ranks and offered to end his role in the insurrection. The offer, while largely greeted as an important step in the final reconciliation of the country, was complicated by the former *Khmer Rouge* officer's direct role (vehemently denied) in the genocide of the 1970s. After complicated negotiations, he was granted a royal pardon by the fall of 1996.

That Ieng Sary's defection indicated a clearly weakening *Khmer Rouge* was highlighted by the remaining leadership's allowing of a formal radio talk show dis-

H.R.H. Samdech Krom Preah Norodom Ranariddh

Cambodia

Their Majesties the King and Queen of Cambodia

cussing the necessity of maintaining *Khmer Rouge* solidarity—a remarkable step to take for a party with one of the most totalitarian records of the 20th century. These developments highlighted a blow to the *Khmer Rouge* as profound as their earlier loss of power after the Vietnamese invasion of 1979.

The United Nations activities in Cambodia have in themselves had profound international significance. In some ways their role could be considered a test case of the "new world order" that some have written about. And while Cambodia remains a country whose politics are still driven more by factional politics than democratic decision–making, they have nevertheless been far more successful than many had thought possible.

Progress toward democracy, however, is clearly limited. The judiciary is not independent of the government and many newspapers have been harassed for criticizing the government. Such incidents, though, seem to be less than in previous years. Opponents of the government have not fared well. Sam Rainsy, the former head of the Ministry of Finance, returned recently to Cambodia to lead the *Khmer Nation Party (KNP)*. It had been under a ban by the government and continues to feel the heavy hand of government unhappiness with its efforts. Nevertheless, Rainsy has fought an uphill battle to keep his party legal and politically active despite these pressures.

Foreign Relations

Throughout its history, Cambodia has been in the unfortunate position of being caught between contending forces beyond its borders. In the precolonial era both Thai and Vietnamese empires occupied parts of Cambodia. The country was also caught between the United States and the Vietnamese during the Vietnam war. The North Vietnamese used overland routes through Cambodia to transport war materiels to the south to carry out the war against the South Vietnamese and their U.S. allies. The U.S. used the North Vietnamese supply lines through Cambodia for target practice. Prince Sihanouk, could neither prevent the North Vietnamese from using his territory, nor satisfy the United States that his policies were not pro–North Vietnamese.

During the Vietnamese occupation which was backed by the Soviet Union, Cambodia was a pawn between the Vietnamese and their ally on the one hand, Chinese, who backed the *Khmer Rouge*, and the United States which recognized the *Khmer Rouge* for a time as the legitimate authority over the country. With a new government in place the country's leaders must sort out with both the Thais and Vietnamese possible territorial boundary alterations which may have taken place in recent years.

Maritime boundaries in the gulf of Thailand may also cause difficulties in Phnom Penh's foreign relations. International drug trafficking through Cambodia is also a serious and growing problem. Relations with Bangkok showed some positive signs in 1994, although allegations continued that Bangkok was still aiding the *Khmer Rouge*. The Phnom Penh government was given access to *Khmer Rouge* assets in Thailand and there was increased cooperation along the Thai–Cambodian border. It should be recognized that Thailand has legitimate national security concerns over the future of Cambodia, and therefore Bangkok is likely to press its interests with those in power in Phnom Penh. The most important event for Cambodian foreign relations in 1995 was the securing of "observer status" with the Association of Southeast Asian Nations (ASEAN) in midyear. Malaysia and Singapore, both ASEAN members, are important investors in Cambodia. It can be expected that ASEAN will do what it can to help Cambodia prepare for eventual full membership in the seven–member organization which will greatly benefit Cambodia.

Relations with Thailand improved with the signing of several border security agreements. Bangkok also appeared to be controlling cross–border activities of the *Khmer Rouge*. Moreover Cambodia and Laos are involved in joint development of transport and telecommunications along the Mekong River

Overall, perhaps the most dramatic change in Cambodia's international situation is its increasing integration into the new more economically dynamic and politically stable world of Southeast Asia. Thus Cambodia's relationship with its immediate neighbors is becoming more important as its ties to the former major powers from Beijing and Moscow and the United States lessen. The days when Cambodia's relations with the superpowers was more important than those they maintained with their own neighbors are probably over.

Culture

The art and culture of the Khmer Empire, based largely on its Indian, Hindu and Sri Lankan Buddhist origins, were an elaborate and comparatively highly developed combination to which distinctly local elements were added during the centuries which have passed. The surviving specimens of the Empire are mainly of stone and bronze which display highly stylistic and ornate techniques. The modern Cambodians, prior to the devastating conflict and the years of Pol Pot, were conscious and proud of the fact that they are heirs of the once–mighty Khmer Empire.

The culture and livelihood of the peasants have remained relatively unchanged until recently; the French made no major effort to modernize them. A unique mixture of Buddhism and Hinduism has persisted until the past few years; the Buddhism of the Hinayana sect, which spread from the island of Sri Lanka (Ceylon), predominated in religious life. The Khmer (Cambodian) language was spoken prior to the arrival of Indian influence and is now written in a script derived from India. Among the few remaining educated citizens, French is still spoken. Women are the majority of the population and the largest percentage of the work force in most sectors, from agriculture to business, industry and service sectors.

They do not however hold significant numbers of positions of influence or management. Men continue to dominate decision–making in the economy.

The country's new constitution very explicitly contains language offering women equal rights but in practice these are not normally carried out. Cultural traditions which emphasize male authority are still strong.

There are, however, many non–governmental organizations which are quite active and emphasize improving the lives of women. As with other Southeast Asian countries, stories of the trafficking in women are very frequently reported.

Economy

A major challenge for the new government is to establish a national economy. Two decades of conflict and revolution have destroyed much of the country's industry. The presence of UNTAC, the United Nations force, caused distortion in the economy. In 1993, prices for housing went out of control. Some government officials actually sold state property. The local currency, the riel, lost almost 50% of its value against the U.S. dollar. The price of rice more than quadrupled. At one point UNTAC imported rice to feed the poor. Cambodia continues to have severe problems with deforestation although raw log exports were banned in 1992. Both Thai and Japanese entrepreneurs were still operating in 1993. Additional contracts were signed in 1995, in spite of the ban. Cambodia's national budget was approximately $330 million for 1995. About half of the country's operating budget comes from foreign aid. And, as might be expected, the military commands about 20% of the entire budget. The country continued to receive substantial amounts of aid and loans from individual donor countries, the International Monetary Fund (IMF), World Bank, and the Asian Development Bank (ADB) in spite of the deteriorating political conditions. One bright spot for the Cambodian economy in 1995 was the

jump in foreign investment to about $2.5 billion which included several major hotel chains. Other growing enterprises included smuggling and money laundering which will not be internationally tolerated indefinitely.

The Future

Cambodia's economy is still being kept afloat by foreign donors. The government is in danger of coming apart at the seams even though the *Khmer Rouge* is in retreat and losing support. Sadly, Cambodia is

rapidly earning a reputation as Asia's newest "narco–state." In early 1996, Washington placed Cambodia on its "watch list" of trafficker states.

Ambassador Charles Twining has charged that the country's richest businessman is a major drug trafficker who also happens to be underwriting the government. The odds for a peaceful transition to a stable democratic government are questionable. The government, in its present form, will be lucky if it lasts until the 1998 national elections.

A young Buddhist monk

The Republic of Indonesia

Tea pickers have their daily bundles weighed

Area: 741,040 sq. mi. (1,906,240 sq. km., covering an expanse equal to the width of the U.S. coast–to–coast.)

Population: 190 million (estimated).

Capital City: Jakarta (Pop. 7.2 million, estimated).

Climate: Tropical, with a monsoon season from November to March.

Neighboring Countries: Malaysia and the Philippine Republic (North); Australia (South); Papua New Guinea (East).

Official Language: Bahasa Indonesia (a formal version of the Malay language).

Other Principal Tongues: Malay, Common Malay (a dialect), and about 250 other Malayo–Polynesian languages and dialects, such as Sundanese and Madurese, Japanese, Dutch, Chinese.

Ethnic Background: Malayo–Polynesian (a mixture of Polynesian, Mongolian, Indian and Caucasian many centuries old, about 95%); Chinese (about 3%); other (including European, about 2%).

Principal Religion: Overwhelmingly Muslim, with small groups of Christians, Hindus and Buddhists.

Main Exports (to Japan, Federal Republic of Germany and other European nations): Petroleum, liquefied natural gas, carpets, fruits, nuts and coffee.

Main Imports (From U.S.): Aircraft and equipment, cotton textile fibers, engines, civil engineering equipment, pulp and waste paper.

Currency: Rupiah.

Former Colonial Status: Dutch Colony from about 1625 to 1949.

Independence Day: December 27, 1949. (August 17th, the anniversary of the 1945 date when revolutionaries proclaimed the Republic of Indonesia.)

Chief of State: President Suharto (since 1967).

Vice President: Tri Sutrisno.

National Flag: Two horizontal bands; the top is maroon and the bottom is white.

Per Capita GDP Annual Income: U.S. $3,705.

Stretched along the Equator between Australia and the Asian mainland for a horizontal distance of about 3,000 miles, Indonesia consists of some 3,000 individual islands. The largest are Sumatra and Java; Kalimantan occupies the southern portion of the island of Borneo, and Irian Jaya is the western portion of the island of New Guinea. About one–fourth of the land is covered with inland waters.

If Indonesia did not have a great variation in elevation, its climate would be uniformly oppressive because of its equatorial location. The heat and humidity of the coastal areas give way to more moderate temperatures as the altitude rises to breathtaking heights. Although Irian Jaya is predominantly low and swampy, as is Kalimantan, there are mountains that are snow–covered throughout the year on New Guinea.

This is an area of volcanic peaks—some dormant and some active—which have enriched the soil greatly during their centuries of destructively explosive activity. Krakatoa, located on a tiny island between Java and Sumatra, exploded with such force in 1883 that it produced a tidal wave which was felt around the world, and which inundated parts of nearby seacoasts. In other areas of the world, torrential rainfall such as occurs during the monsoon season is the enemy that washes valuable topsoil to the sea, exposing infertile land to the sun. In Java, the downpours are welcome—they wash away old soil and expose even richer volcanic ash and dirt which is fertile almost beyond belief.

The wildlife of Indonesia is more interesting and varied than almost any other country of the world. The Komodo dragon, ten feet long and a remnant of prehistoric times, inhabits the island of Komodo east of Java. The Javanese rhinoceros makes increasingly rare appearances in the Udjung Kulon ("western tip") preserve on the end of Java, where successive governments have tried to maintain the natural setting of plants and animals. The gibbon, most agile among the primates, swings overhead in the tall trees that provide thick shade for the banteng, a native ox with white legs that resembles an ordinary dairy cow. Although crowded by a multitude of species adapted to its character, this area, as well as most of the interior of the Indonesian islands, is extremely inhospitable to modern man.

History

Fossils and other prehistoric remnants of human skeletons indicate that Indonesia was the scene of one of the earlier areas of the world to be inhabited by man. The present population of the area acquired its somewhat uniform appearance about the second millennium B.C., a time when there was gradual intermarriage and mixture between native Polynesians and people from the Asian mainland. This combination, relatively stable since that time, is now referred to as Malayo–Polynesian.

Early Indonesian history is best seen as a regional history of diverse communities rather than as a unified early state directly tied through time to modern Indonesia. In fact many different communities existed though there were several commonalities among them, especially the presence of Hinduism and Buddhism, and their role in early international trade.

The arrival of Indian cultural, religious and commercial influences about the first century A.D. greatly influenced the people. Hinduism and Buddhism mingled with the ancient animist background of the Indonesians and produced an extremely complex, varied and unique culture, especially on Java and nearby Bali. The advances brought by the Indians and the availability of good harbors in the Malacca and Sunda Straits were the basis for the rise of two powerful commercial and naval empires at the beginning of the 7th century, A.D. Srivijaya was based on the island of Sumatra; Sailendra arose on neighboring Java. The empires thrived on a lively trade centered on the production of spices treasured throughout the rest of the world, though available only here. Especially important was these islands' control of the trade routes between India and China and, in Srivijaya's case, its ties to imperial China. Taxes were imposed on passing ships based on the number of passengers and the cargo carried.

But if Hinduism and Buddhism were prevalent in the early traditions of these island kingdoms, their modern heritage lies elsewhere. Indian merchants also brought Islam to the islands at the beginning of the 11th century, but it did not have much influence at first. The development of the Indonesian empires was briefly disrupted in the 13th century by a naval expedition sent by the powerful Mongol emperor of China, Khubilai Khan. Shortly afterward, a new empire, known as Majapahit, became dominant, and seized control of the valuable spice trade. Majapahit was the last major Indonesian kingdom headed by a Hindu.

After their departure from the scene, Islam became more and more common. It had long been spreading, and by the end of the 16th century the vast majority of the people had become Muslims. In a sense the early South Asian influence continued, but now in its Islamic, rather than Hindu form. Today only Bali, the famous tourist attraction within Indonesia, remains deeply committed to its traditional Hindu heritage.

The Colonial Period

Though Europeans had longed for the spices of the East for centuries (they were terribly limited—salt, garlic and vinegar), the profits from those valuable commodities were largely in the hands of Islamic middlemen during the pre–modern era. What the Europeans wanted was to gain access to those profits themselves. This explains the push in the 15th century to find new routes to the East. These images of fantastic wealth to be earned in the spice trade first brought Europeans to the East Indies, or Dutch East Indies as the islands were later called. The spices were, and now are, grown principally in the Moluccas (Spice Islands) and on Java.

There was keen interest in the area on the part of Portugal and Great Britain, but it was the Dutch who were ultimately successful in dominating Indonesia, controlling the area through a commercial organization, the Dutch East India Company.

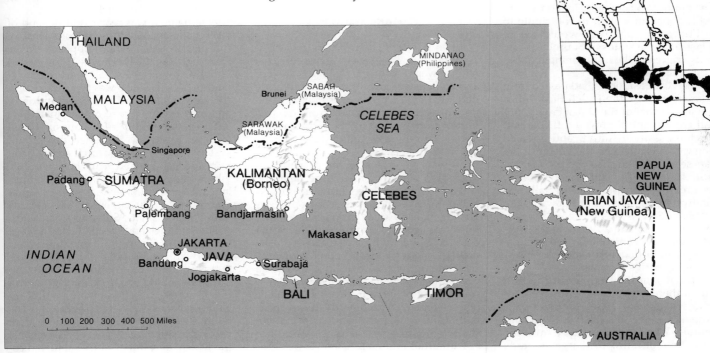

Indonesia

By then the Majapahit Empire was already in decline leaving the island of Java as a relatively easy conquest. It was quickly identified as the most strategic and fertile of the islands and one which could produce coffee, indigo and some spices. The local leaders were either militarily defeated or scared into surrender by the Dutch, who compelled them to deliver produce to the Company.

The colonial experience of the East Indies, as Indonesia was then known, was much the same as in other parts of the colonized world: centered around the process of extracting wealth from the colony. As was so common during colonialism, this was often carried out with extreme disinterest in the concerns of the indigenous peoples themselves. Thus for example, in an effort to drive up prices, the Dutch actually destroyed some island communities' ability to produce spices, devastating their economies and people in the process.

With the wealth gained, Holland emerged as one of the most powerful European countries of the early modern period and one which supported an impressive navy. But as would be the case in the 20th century their control over the East Indies was temporarily interrupted in the nineteenth century due to developments back in Europe.

The Napoleonic Wars in Europe resulted in a brief period of British occupation of Java from 1811 to 1816. But once the Napoleonic war was over the Dutch were able to reestablish their control partly because the British themselves, wanting to maintain a balance of power on the European continent, knew that Holland would need Indonesian wealth to contribute to that European stability. It would not be the last time the states of Southeast Asia were sacrificed to the needs of internal European politics.

By then the East Indies had passed from administration by the Dutch East Indies Company to that of the Dutch crown. But direct crown control proved difficult as it undertook administrative and judicial changes that challenged the power of the Javanese aristocratic class and provoked a war in the 1820s. The Dutch won but only after great loss of life. An especially exploitative economic system known as the *Cultivation System* was designed to gain maximum economic advantage for Holland from their control over the islands. This system added further to the hardships of the native Indonesians.

Eventually, in the last part of the 19th century there was a return to free economic development based on private investment. During this era there was considerable Western investment and the introduction of railroads. Large amounts of new land were put under cultivation. Indonesia emerged in this era as the world's largest producer of tin and rubber. The islands became so associated with the production of products such as coffee that the term "java" became synonymous with the drink itself.

By the late nineteenth century, feelings against Dutch control were growing in both Indonesia and the Netherlands itself. Responding to these new sentiments, the colonial government adopted the "Ethical Policy," under which strenuous efforts were made to promote the welfare of the Indonesians through public works and health measures. The government even announced that it would no longer take any surplus revenues generated by Indonesia and canceled the colony's debts.

Nevertheless, direct control over the East Indies grew during the early twentieth century even as new transportation methods allowed the Dutch themselves to become increasingly more remote from Indonesian society. They could, after all, send their children to schools in Europe and develop their own society more distant from that of the Indonesians they ruled. The phenomenon was a common one throughout much of the colonial world.

Not surprisingly local education was neglected and little serious effort toward preparation for self–government occurred despite the more general calls in the post World War I era for national self–determination. There was thus a rapid growth of both nationalism and communism in the interwar period in spite of increasingly harsh Dutch police measures.

World War II

When the Pacific War began in December 1941 Indonesia was, due to its great natural wealth, a prime target for the Japanese offensive in Southeast Asia. Weakly defended by a Dutch government–in–exile which had been driven from its own European homeland by the Germans, the islands rapidly came under Japanese control in early 1942.

As was the case elsewhere, many Indonesians warmly greeted the Japanese and sincerely believed Japanese claims that they had come to free Asia from Western colonialism. Many Indonesians, either for convenience or commitment, made the decision to work with the Japanese. Sukarno, the long term Indonesian nationalist, was among those who decided to use the occupation as a tool to help realize Indonesia's goal of national freedom. Eventually, he even managed to convince the Japanese authorities to help arm and train Indonesians in the struggle against the West.

The initial enthusiasm not withstanding, the Japanese administration soon convinced many Indonesians, as was to occur elsewhere in Asia, that they were hardly liberators, but merely new conquerors come to exploit the resources of Indonesia as the Dutch had before them. But if the Japanese hoped to build a new colonial base in Indonesia, their real impact was rather in fundamentally destroying the old colonial mentality rather than building a new one.

Moreover, although they were foreign conquerors, the Japanese not only destroyed the prestige of the Dutch in the eyes of the Indonesians, but in addition gave the latter valuable experience in political activity and public administration.

A New Nation

As soon as the war was over, Sukarno and fellow nationalist leader Mohammed Hatta, immediately proclaimed the independent Republic of Indonesia. This move had widespread support of other leaders and among the population of the outlying islands. And of course, it paralleled similar anti–colonialist developments elsewhere such as those of Ho Chi Minh in Vietnam. But declaring independence and actually winning it were not the same thing.

British forces soon arrived and used their power to help the Dutch reestablish themselves, though not before a massive public outbreak of anti–Dutch feelings and considerable violence. For the moment the Dutch would be able to reestablish themselves, but over the next four years a major independence struggle took place, which eventually saw the Dutch withdraw.

A settlement was reached at the end of 1949 that recognized the independence of Indonesia, which was supposed to be linked to the Netherlands through the Dutch Crown. West Irian, part of the island of New Guinea, was not included in the agreement; Dutch–owned industry and investment were to remain intact.

The new Republic of Indonesia, based on Java, promptly abolished the federal system created by the Dutch administration and established a unitary republic which later cut all ties with the Netherlands. Over the first several years it would operate as a parliamentary democracy with the charismatic Sukarno at its head.

The Indonesians faced independence under almost insurmountable difficulties. There were geographic and cultural differences, poor communications between the islands, and the dominant power of the Javanese, resented in the other islands—referred to as "Outer Islands." The political turmoil left by the years of Japanese occupation followed by battle against the Dutch, and the primitive state of eco-

Indesia

der the leadership of General Suharto, emerged in power. Suharto then crushed the rebellion. Resentment against the *PKI*, which had been smoldering in the islands for years, erupted into a massive slaughter that resulted in the death of hundreds of thousands of people suspected of being communists or their sympathizers. While the army itself was directly involved, a large percentage of the deaths seem to have actually been carried out by civilians with the military's encouragement. The total number killed remains unclear. The *PKI* was almost annihilated and was outlawed as a political party. The army soon stripped Sukarno of all power. He died in 1970.

Suharto

If Sukarno had led an authoritarian government with leftist leaning nationalist sentiments, Suharto would now offer his own version of authoritarianism but one that was more open to the West and based on the military. Ideologically it has been built around the idea of *Pancasila*. This state ideology incorporates the five principles of nationalism, democracy, internationalism, social justice, and belief in one God. All political parties are required to accept them and the armed forces have been given a legitimate role in the political process through the official government party, *GOLKAR*.

After the 1965 coup, the appointed *Pro-*

Presidents Sukarno and Eisenhower enter the White House, May 1956

nomic and political development, were adverse influences. In addition to these liabilities, there was the leadership role of Sukarno himself.

The Sukarno Years

Flamboyant, popular, unpredictable, self–indulgent, articulate, dictatorial and lovable are all adjectives that have been used to describe Sukarno. During the years of his control he moved Indonesia from a parliamentary system to a more authoritarian one called "Guided Democracy." Denouncing Western democratic traditions, he practiced a political leadership that stressed Indonesian nationalism above regionalism and non–alignment in the Cold War between Washington and Moscow. Although not a communist, he frequently worked closely with the *PKI*, the *Indonesian Communist Party*. The U.S., alarmed by this, arranged a tryst for Sukarno with a beautiful woman at his hotel in New York while he was appearing at the UN. Cameras recorded the whole event in detail. When confronted with it, accompanied by threats of being disgraced, he was delighted. He asked for a copy to play publicly in Indonesia to visually demonstrate his sexual prowess!

Politics in those years became a complicated mixture of *PKI* communists led by the young and energetic Aidit, the army and Sukarno. The charismatic Sukarno was usually able to command the support of both the communists and the army. But his economic policies weakened the country. Promises had been given to leave foreign investment intact, but these were not kept. Dutch assets were seized in 1957.

Some Chinese investment was nationalized in the following years. Most American assets were confiscated in 1963–1964.

Supported by Soviet diplomacy, Sukarno, in 1962, threatened West Irian, today known as Irian Jaya, with a substantial Soviet equipped military force. Under American pressure and mediation, the Dutch finally surrendered that western portion of New Guinea which they had until then continued to hold.

Sukarno then turned his attention toward Malaysia. This area of Southeast Asia was formed by the British when they united Malaya, Singapore and North Borneo (Sabah and Sarawak) into a single, independent nation in 1963. The British, unlike the Dutch in West Irian, were willing to fight to protect Malaysia.

The confrontation with Malaysia, launched in 1963 by Sukarno, led the *PKI*, which already had achieved considerable power, to demand the arming of communist–led "workers and peasants." This demand was resisted by the army, but endorsed by China and given an increasingly enthusiastic reception by Sukarno in 1965.

The events that followed remain unclear to this day though their impact transformed the country. What we do know is that a group of dissident military officers plotted to overthrow their more senior commanders. The exact relationship between the *PKI*, Sukarno himself, and the plotters remains uncertain. The results though are not.

As dramatized in the famous film, "A Year of Living Dangerously", events moved quickly during the fall of 1965. The coup attempt failed and the army, un-

President Suharto

Indonesia

visional People's Consultative Congress (MPRS) was purged of pro–communist elements. Later in March of 1967 it proclaimed Suharto president for five years.

Having achieved effective control of Indonesia, Suharto and the army ended the "confrontation" with Malaysia and began to tackle Indonesia's massive economic problems. Steps were taken to rejoin the UN, from which Sukarno's government had withdrawn in 1965. An interest was shown in resuming normal economic relations with the non–communist world, including the Netherlands and the United States.

Communist China, in contrast, denounced the new military regime as a gang of fascists, particularly after there was some anti–Chinese violence following the military seizure of power. The Soviet Union had more mixed feelings; it did not wish for communists to be slaughtered, but since the *PKI* had adopted the Chinese side of the disputes in international communism, the Soviets undoubtedly were gratified by the example of its failure—an example to other communist movements of the world which had sided with Beijing.

Unlike his rejection of Sukarno's anti–Malaysian foreign policy, Suharto's regime continued the latter's interest in West Irian. When the Dutch withdrew from West Irian in 1962, the UN promised that a popular vote would be taken to determine the will of the people. The alternatives were independence or union with Indonesia. However, Indonesian military officers present in West Irian in 1969 rigged a unanimous vote for union with Indonesia. Thus the region, known today as Irian Jaya, came to be part of Indonesia though even through the 1990s problems of anti–Jakarta regionalism have continued.

After the failure of the 1965 coup in Indonesia and the end of the "confrontation" with Malaysia, Indonesia joined with Malaysia, Singapore, Thailand and the Philippines to form the Association of Southeast Asian Nations (ASEAN). Brunei joined in 1984. The original purpose of this organization was to help stabilize regional power, develop the area economically and support the American struggle in Vietnam.

Its main visible functions were to maintain easy access for its members' raw materials to the markets of the developed countries, and to cooperate to a limited extent against communist insurgency. After the Vietnamese invasion of Cambodia at the end of 1978, ASEAN, with Thailand as the "frontline" state, began to play an important role in trying to negotiate an end to the struggle on terms that would include a Vietnamese military withdrawal.

It was announced in late 1969 that general elections would be held in mid–1971 in Indonesia. The result was an overwhelming victory for the government party, the Sekber *GOLKAR*, a federation of about 260 trade, professional and regional groups which enjoyed an overwhelming advantage over the other legal parties.

Nevertheless, widespread discontent over the lack of political freedom and social justice erupted in serious riots in early 1974. Most of the anger was nurtured by inflation, commodity shortages and was mainly aimed against the government. Other elements included dissatisfaction with the growing economic influence of Japan, and the commercial influence of local Indonesian Chinese whose preeminent role in the economy has often led to outbursts of anti–Chinese sentiment.

In the wake of the riots, President Suharto made some personnel changes that had the effect of strengthening the po-

Children at play in a poorer part of Jakarta . . .

. . . while the capital's business district plays the stock market.

sition of his principal assistant, Ali Murtopo. But government corruption, food shortages, an inferior educational system, tensions between the Indonesian majority and the important Chinese minority, continued to dog the country. In 1975, *Pertamina*, the government oil monopoly, nearly went bankrupt as a result of over–borrowing and poor administration.

In Indonesia's third general election in 1977, *GOLKAR* won 230 out of 360 seats in the House of Representatives. The *Development Unity Party (PPP)*, a coalition of Muslim parties, won 108 seats and the *Democratic Party* (PDI) won 22 seats. Neither though was in a position to really challenge *GOLKAR*. A few years later, in 1982 *GOLKAR* was again victorious, winning approximately 75% of the popular vote. Another body, the *People's Consultative Assembly*, elected Suharto to another 5–year term as President both in 1978 and 1983 and every five years since then.

Despite the authoritarian, military nature of the regime, Suharto's period in office has through the present made considerable economic progress. In fact, the government has defended the lack of political progress in recent years on the ground of economic development—whereas Sukarno used to justify the lack of progress under his rule by displays of political dynamism.

On the positive side, both the Sukarno and Suharto governments have dramatically raised the educational level of the In-

donesian people. Demanding a high degree of conformity, they have both tried to assimilate the Chinese community, which has complied to some extent; the government, however, does not want to pressure them to the point where they can no longer make an important contribution to the national economy.

Suharto's regime was committed to integrating Indonesia into the world economy and did so successfully. Over the following years Indonesia was able to offer its services as an assembly area for products produced in the dynamic Asian economies ranging from South Korea and Taiwan to Singapore and Hong Kong. And these efforts have substantially improved living conditions, raised living standards and added years to average people's lives. But the domination of Suharto's family and friends in the slowly but successfully growing Indonesian economy aroused tensions that continued through the 1990s.

Suharto's rather heavy–handed rule has naturally aroused opposition. Against him are ranged some of the most prestigious names in the country. In addition, there are two small legal opposition parties: the *Indonesian Democratic Party* and the *United Development Party* (the latter is Muslim–based). The opposition groups have often objected to what they believe is support for *GOLKAR* by powerful Americans.

In preparation for a parliamentary election scheduled for April 1987, the government screened all candidates, as usual, for

"security." *GOLKAR*, the government party, was allegedly "rejuvenating" itself through the appointment of younger people to important positions; in many cases, however, these were the children of the previous generation of leaders. Unrest continued in Irian Jaya (taken over from the Dutch in 1962) and East Timor (seized from Portugal in 1975).

The April 1987 elections resulted in a predictable victory for *GOLKAR* over the *Indonesian Democratic Party* and the (Muslim) *United Democratic Party*. It won 73% of the popular vote. But, perhaps under the impact of democratic developments in the Philippines and South Korea there has, in the last decade, been some liberalization of Suharto's authoritarian political system. One form this has taken is the revival of unofficial, as well as official, interest in the personality and career of the late President Sukarno. This has played a role in the recent prominence his daughter.

Suharto's own family also continues to be widely criticized for corrupt business activities. In an unusual display of disagreement, the army even put forward its own candidate for vice president, but Suharto's candidate was elected instead.

In the most recent presidential election of 1993 the *People's Consultative Assembly* again elected the 71 year–old Suharto to yet another term as president. The Assembly that elected him consists of 1000 members. Five hundred come from the *GOLKAR*–dominated House of Represen-

Indonesia

tatives and 500 are presidential appointees. The new vice president was Tri Sutrisno, a former presidential military aide and retired commander of the armed forces.

Meanwhile, Indonesia celebrated its 50th anniversary on August 17, 1995. Suharto used the occasion to improve the country's human rights image by freeing 81–year old former Deputy Prime Minister Subandrio, 77–year old retired air force commander Omar Dhani, and 77–year old police Brig. Soetarto, all of whom had been sentenced to death for their alleged role in an earlier *coup* attempt.

The government has maintained pressure on the media. In 1994 it arrested three members of the Alliance of Independent Journalists for slandering the government through their publication *Independent*. The government has even set up an Association of Indonesian Journalists to which all reporters must belong. But things have not always gone as smoothly as *GOLKAR*'s leaders might want. In a surprise move, devastating to the government, Information Minister Harmoko had a State Administrative Court rule that he had acted unlawfully in closing the popular publication *Tempo* in 1994.

A Challenge to the Regime?

Indonesian politics, since the blood bath of 1965, has remained relatively calm. The military and its partner *GOLKAR* allowed the impression of political plurality while maintaining a tight grip on political power. But 1996 showed their long term prospects may be less certain than otherwise thought. Certainly the military's long–term domination of the country, the growing disparity between rich and poor, despite the overall economic progress, the economic domination of Suharto's family and more general frustrations with the levels of corruption, all played a role in developing tensions. But the more immediate cause was the entrance into Indonesian politics of the daughter of Indonesian nationalist hero Sukarno.

Until 1987 Megawati Sukarnoputra, the former president's daughter, was not involved in politics. Only in the late 1980s was she elected to parliament and somewhat later, in 1993, did she emerge as the leader of the *Democratic Party of Indonesia* (*PDI*), one of the two non–governmental parties *GOLKAR* allowed to exist. But while many had dismissed this college educated former housewife, President Suharto did not. Over the last year he has moved to weaken the political base of this cautious leader who carries with her the inheritance of a powerful name in Indonesia's national memory.

Not content to harass her, Suharto's

Balinese vendor

government engineered her ouster as leader of the *PDI* by pro–government supporters within the party. No doubt the hope had been to remove Megawati Sukarnoputra's official base, but doing so appeared to backfire last summer when government–backed toughs attempted to force her supporters from the *PDI* headquarters. Rather than go quietly her supporters quickly gathered and a confrontation ensued which eventually saw several deaths and hundreds wounded. The government's strong–arm tactics had done no more than solidify her leadership before her followers, and raise the international prestige of her movement. By late fall she was being coupled in the public mind with other Southeast Asian women who have challenged the governments of dictators, women ranging from Corazon

Aquino of the Philippines to Aung San Suu Kyi of Burma.

But if Sukarno's daughter had shaken up the Indonesian military establishment, their domination still is assured for the immediate future. Perhaps more important than the question of the military's ability to dominate the political future of Indonesia is its own ability to maintain a level of unity within itself. As things stood in early 1997 President Suharto seems ready to run for president again in 1998. But given his age, (he is now seventy–five) jockeying behind the scenes among both military and civilian supporters has already begun.

Research and Technology Minister B.J. Habibie appears interested in running for vice–president next year and may hope to use that position to gain the presidency.

But knowledgeable observers consider it unlikely that the military, assuming it maintains its unity, will allow someone not from their own ranks to really emerge in power. In fact so confident of victory was *GOLKAR* that it announced weeks in advance of the spring 1997 elections the exact voting percentage they were going to win.

East Timor

When studying the modern history of communities like Indonesia it is important to remember that they were not single ethnic/linguistic/political communities before the colonial era. Rather, it was often the colonial experience itself that helped create the generation of nationalists like Sukarno or Hatta who led the struggle for independence. But like nations throughout the world, whose political borders were shaped by outside colonial powers, it has often been difficult to keep focused on their identities as Indonesians in the face of strong regional and ethnic ties. Even today, while Indonesia is much more cohesive as a country than it was even thirty years ago, separatist sentiments continue in regions from Aceh, near Malaysia, to Irian Jaya far to the east.

No Indonesian region though has experienced as much international attention for the level of its struggle and suffering as East Timor. Unlike much of the rest of Indonesia, which had been administered as the Dutch East Indies, East Timor was a Portuguese colony, a remnant of the Portuguese efforts during the early colonial era. Rather like Portuguese Goa in India or Macau near Hong Kong it was a small reminder of the once energetic Portuguese role in colonization.

But just as India's government had moved into Goa in the early 1960s, and China now prepares to take back Macau in 1999, Indonesia decided to absorb East Timor in 1975. The logic of Indonesian nationalism might have made the move seem appropriate, but culturally Indonesians and the East Timorese are very different. As we have seen, Indonesia is the largest Muslim country in the world while East Timor, by grace of its centuries as Portuguese colony, is Catholic. The Indonesian move was resisted by a leftist and nationalist movement called *Fretilin*, the *Revolutionary Front for an Independent East Timor,* and widely condemned internationally. Even today only Australia officially recognizes Jakarta's claim to the region.

In the years since, thousands have died in the many clashes between the East Timorese and the forces of Jakarta. As recently as November 1991, a pro–independence demonstration in East Timor was violently suppressed by the army. The government's statement after the massacre, although promising some improvement of conditions in the area, amounted to a whitewash.

Through the 1990s reports of human rights violations continued to be a problem for the Suharto government. Again in 1994, demonstrations erupted after the Indonesian military was involved in a scuffle with locals. Later that year, a second incident arose when several hundred Timorese attempted to protest the apparent insulting of two Catholic nuns. The military used force to restrain the demonstrators. In another incident, a prominent activist, Nuku Soleiman, was sentenced to four years in prison for insulting Suharto. When the case was appealed, an additional year was tacked on to the sentence.

Coffee pickers off to the fields

Indonesia

Men on the way to work

The Indonesian government currently has six battalions stationed in East Timor in an attempt to suppress *Fretilin*. Since September 1995, some fifty Timorese have sought asylum in various foreign embassies in Jakarta. According to a Timorese exile in the United States, thousands of people have been killed on the island by Indonesian military.

East Timorese nationalists got a much needed boost in 1996 when two of their most prominent members were awarded the Nobel Peace Prize for their efforts. Bishop Carlos Felipe Ximenese Belo, who continues to live in East Timor and Jose Ramos–Horta a militant leader of the movement in exile, shared the award which gave the struggle of East Timor much more international recognition than it had heretofore received. How much this publicity will really help its cause is, of course, uncertain.

Foreign Relations

As the fourth largest country in the world, Indonesia has always considered itself to be number one among equals within the Association of Southeast Asian Nations (ASEAN), composed of Brunei, Indonesia, Malaysia, the Philippines, Singapore and Thailand. And it is fair to say that the other ASEAN states usually have accepted the "big brother" role of Indonesia. The ASEAN headquarters is located in Jakarta. For its part, Indonesia has worked within the context of ASEAN, although Jakarta has often been less enthu-

siastic about the rapid elimination of trade barriers since it is the least developed of the member states.

Indonesia also prides itself on being an arbiter of disputes and a conciliator. Indonesia played an important role early on in the settlement of the dispute in Cambodia by hosting a series of informal "cocktail" parties to which the competing sides were invited. More recently, Indonesia has sponsored several seminars on the conflicting territorial claims in the South China Sea and especially the Spratley Islands. Six countries claim all or part of the sea.

Indonesia was a key player at the beginning of the non–alignment movement which traces its beginnings back to the Bandung (Indonesia) conference of 1955. In 1994, President Suharto was serving as the group's head. Over the years Indonesia has followed a non–aligned foreign policy. Under former President Sukarno, the policy definitely leaned left. Sukarno tried to organize the New Emerging Forces which linked Indonesia to such countries as China, North Korea and Vietnam. After his fall, President Suharto placed the country on a much more centrist path. The non–aligned nature of the policy is evidenced for example in the fact that the country does not have defense treaties with any major outside power or group of powers. This sets Indonesia apart from her ASEAN neighbors, excluding Brunei.

In November 1994, Indonesia was the host of the second Asia–Pacific Economic Cooperation meeting, the first of which

was held in Seattle, Washington, in 1993. President Suharto met with all of the Asian leaders, excluding President Lee of Taiwan, who was not invited, and issued the "Bogor Declaration" at the conclusion of the leaders' summit. The declaration states that the developed APEC states will strive for free trade by the year 2010 and that the less developed states, including Indonesia, will reach this target by 2020. Within the UN, Indonesia also replaced Pakistan in a two year non–permanent seat on the Security Council. This will elevate the visibility of the country worldwide.

The country's territorial waters expanded geometrically when the UN Law of the Sea Convention went into effect. Under the convention, all of the waters between the country's 3,000 islands now become Indonesian territorial waters.

In 1995, Indonesia enjoyed both successes and embarrassment in its foreign relations. Jakarta could be proud of its role in helping to secure a degree of freedom for the Burmese opposition leader, Aung San Suu Kyi, because of the good communications between the military regimes in Rangoon and Jakarta. The foreign minister, Ali Alatas, was also pleased that the Chinese publicly proclaimed their non–interest in the territory around Natuna island in the South China Sea, with its significant gas fields.

Relations with Australia however deteriorated to an almost dangerous level at mid–year when Canberra embarrassed Jakarta by raising questions about Indonesia's designated Ambassador. Canberra waited a very long time before asking questions concerning Lt. General Mentiri's comments about 1991 military actions in East Timor. He apparently expressed no regret over the violence which had taken place. By December 1996, the two countries concluded an agreement designed to bury the hatchet over past difficulties. This should ease Australian criticism of Jakarta, particularly in the area of human rights, and also improve Indonesia's regional standing.

Culture

Indonesia is a country of great cultural diversity. More than three hundred distinct groups are recognized, and over 250 different languages are spoken (although the Javanese constitute about 50% of the population). The largest non–native community is the ethnic Chinese who, while constituting only around 3% of the population, are especially dominant in private economy.

Indonesia is a nation of islands which traditionally had mainly indirect contact with each other—a nation ruled in effect by a cultural segment located on the island of Java. The vast majority of Indonesians are Muslims, though other important groups of Christians and Chinese Buddhists are also present. Animism, a common tradition throughout Southeast Asia, is also found among some of the more isolated communities. Bali, the island fabled in story and song in the western world, is the one significant part of Indonesia that still practices Hinduism, the tradition that once dominated the entire region.

Non–violence and courteous agreement are a tradition in Javanese culture. Open disagreement is avoided—differences are buried in an atmosphere of agreement, no matter how unreal. But, once it becomes apparent that differences cannot be hidden, violence becomes painfully real, as it has at several points in Indonesian history. In recent memory, Indonesian society has been disrupted by assaults against both Chinese and Christian citizens.

As is the case in many countries throughout the world, Indonesian women have many disadvantages when compared to men. Officially, they have the same rights as men but reality is often quite different. Those that work in industry usually get lower pay than men and often without the benefits men receive. Traditional Islamic family law prevails, making it legal for men to have more than one wife (although President Suharto, to make an example, has forbidden senior level officials and officers from actually doing so). At the lower levels of the civil service it is allowed, but men wishing to take on another wife are required to get the permission of the supervisor as well as the first wife.

Women's lower status is especially evident in the laws of citizenship. Women are not allowed to pass on their citizenship to their children. Thus a woman who becomes pregnant by a non–Indonesian citizen takes the risk of seeing her own children deported!

But real improvements have also been gained in recent years. The number of young women graduating from high school has gone up enormously in the last generation and a number of women's organizations have appeared to help improve the lives of Indonesian females. Moreover, at the upper more educated levels, the gap between women and men's salaries is lessening and many women now work at important mid–level positions in both government and the private sector.

The industrial accomplishments of the Suharto regime have brought into being a new middle class which enjoys many of the material comforts such groups have elsewhere. Unlike some elements in other parts of East and Southeast Asia they have not yet become particularly politicized, and do not appear likely to challenge the regime's authority in the near future.

Economy

Indonesia has a diversifying economy. Economic growth in GDP (Gross Domestic Product) has averaged about 7% annually since the 1970s. Foreign investment from 1988 through 1991 totaled $26 billion, more than twice the amount approved in the previous twenty years, aided by a less restrictive banking system. Indonesia's participation in the "growth triangle" with Singapore and Johor state in West Malaysia, are proving the merits of capitalism in the development process. Corruption continues to be a severe problem, although it is not as bad as in the Philippines, the leader of the ASEAN states in this respect.

In 1995, exports grew 13%, against a 29.7% increase in imports, shrinking the trade surplus to $3.7 billion. Inflation slowed to 8.6% (the government wants a 5% rate). In order to keep inflation from taking off, banks must now keep a reserve of 5.5% of commercial deposits. One–year loan rates are an astonishing 21%. But Indonesia's efforts to continue its integration into the world economy proceed. It has moved to reduce tariffs on over 400 capital goods items to help local producers. All of this means that GDP growth for 1997 should fall to a little above 7%.

A basic fact about Indonesia is the high cost of doing business. A case in point occurred in January 1996 when beer brewers cut off supplies to Bali, the tourist mecca of Indonesia, as a protest to the 400 rupiah (17 cents) levy applied to each bottle of beer by a company controlled by President Suharto's grandson. The President intervened and the levy was rescinded. This is one of many levies which have been revoked in an effort to convince businessmen that corruption is declining.

Another major problem for the economy is that Indonesia's foreign debt is not being handled correctly. This could cause the rupiah to devalue by as much as 5% against the dollar. Debt is being driven up by the fact that Japan is Indonesia's biggest lender—the rise in the value of the yen thus has artificially expanded what was already a significant debt. Government officials fear that investors will now begin to shy away from the country as a possible investment location.

Economically, although real growth has been generally steady, 26 million of the country's 190 million still live in poverty as defined by the World Bank and only about 22% have access to sanitation facilities. Even as the middle class continues to grow so do the shantytowns around the big cities.

The Future

Indonesia has come a long way since the days of Sukarno. Continued growth should put Indonesia firmly into the mid–level developed nations category by the end of the century. As economic progress continues, Indonesia can be expected to play an increasingly important role as the regional political leader. As the fourth largest country in the world, with over 190 million people, such a role is not inconceivable. But as the end of the Suharto era draws closer, uncertainties over who will take over will have to be dealt with effectively.

A Balinese song–and–dance drama

The Lao People's Democratic Republic

Area: 91,400 sq. mi. (234,804 sq. km., somewhat smaller than Oregon).

Population: 4,600,000 (est. 1993).

Capital City: Vientiane (Pop. 230,000, estimated).

Climate: Tropical, with a rainy monsoon from May–October and a dry season from November–April.

Neighboring Countries: China (North); Vietnam (East); Burma (Northwest); Thailand (West); Cambodia (South).

Official Language: Lao

Other Principal Tongue: French.

Ethnic Background: The majority of the people, living in the Mekong Valley, are the Lao, of Thai ancestry. There are a number of tribes, including the Meo, Yao, Kha and Lu, some of which are Thai, but most of which are Malay, Chinese and Vietnamese ancestry.

Principal Religion: Buddhism; animism is predominant among the tribes.

Major Exports: Electric power (to Thailand), timber and textiles.

Main Import (from Thailand, Russia, Japan, France, China, Vietnam): Rice, petroleum products, machinery.

Currency: Kip.

Former Colonial Status: French protectorate (1893–1949); member of the French Union (1949–1954).

National Day: December 24, 1954.

A Laotian newspaper

Chief of State: Nouhak Phoumsavan, President.
Head of Government: Khamtai Siphandon, Prime Minister.
National Flag: Two red stripes (top and bottom), a wide blue stripe between them upon which is centered a white circle.
Per Capita Income: U.S. $380.

Laos is a landlocked, tropical country largely covered with mountains and tropical forests interrupted by patches of low scrub vegetation in the areas where the soil is poor. From one point of view it is an extremely backward country with almost no roads, but from another point of view it is an area of the world where the natural beauty has not been greatly altered by the presence of man.

Most of the fertile land lies along the valley of the Mekong River, where it is eroded and flows as silt to the rice paddies in the Mekong Delta in southern Vietnam. The land receives ample rainfall, but the sandstone soils have little capacity to retain the moisture. In the last part of the dry season from November to May, the air becomes oppressively hot and very dry—this is the time when the tribesmen living in the mountain forests burn the trees to clear the land. This practice, coupled with natural forest fires, robs the land of much of its fertility; when the farmer ceases to cultivate the land it becomes choked with a primitive, ugly scrub vegetation.

History

The Lao people moved into northern Laos from the southwestern Chinese province of Yunnan beginning in the 11th century A.D. During the succeeding centuries they slowly expanded toward the south, founding two communities in central and southern Laos. In their efforts to settle these additional lands they came into frequent conflict with the Burmese and Thai who were also active in this part of Southeast Asia.

The French established their colonial authority over neighboring Vietnam by 1893. When there was a dispute between Thailand and Laos over demarcation of the border, the French proclaimed a protectorate over Laos in 1893, making it a dependency within the French Indochinese Empire. Because of its remoteness and lack of natural resources, the French did almost nothing to develop Laos; they did succeed in ending the payment of tribute to the kings of Thailand, however.

When the waves of Japanese soldiers inundated Southeast Asia in 1942, they supported their Thai ally in taking some border territory from Laos. A nationalist movement, known as the *Lao Issara* and directed mainly against the Japanese occupation forces, arose during World War II. When the French re–entered after the defeat of the Japanese, Thailand was forced by Britain and the U.S. to return the territory it had acquired while allied with the enemy. The *Lao Issara* promptly started anti–French activity from bases in Thailand. Preoccupied with resistance movements in Vietnam, the French granted Laos internal self–government within the French Union in 1949; this split the resistance movement. The non-communist majority took a leading role in the new government, but the communist and pro–communist minority formed itself into a party known as the *Pathet Lao*.

This communist movement opposed the new government and came increasingly under the influence of Ho Chi Minh's communist movement in Northern Vietnam. Following invasions of northern Laos by communist Vietnamese in 1953 and 1954, the *Pathet Lao* completely controlled the provinces of Phong Saly and Sam Neua on the Vietnamese border. Under the terms of an agreement reached in Geneva in 1954, it was allotted these provinces for "regrouping."

After prolonged haggling, the government, which had achieved full independence from France in late 1954, and the *Pathet Lao* agreed on political and military unification in 1957. The strong showing of the *Pathet Lao* in 1958 elections alarmed the Laotian government, and also the U.S., leading to a breakdown of the 1957 agreement. The situation became critical when the government tried in 1959 to integrate two battalions of the *Pathet Lao* forces into the army and to demobilize the remainder of the communist–oriented forces. The result was a confused, small–scale civil war in which the North Vietnamese seized the opportunity to give increasing aid in personnel and equipment to the *Pathet Lao*.

President Nouhak Phoumsavan

Prime Minister Khamtai Siphandon

The U.S. increased its assistance to the government to meet the threat.

A military *coup* replaced the rightwing government with a neutralist regime under Prince Souvanna Phouma in 1960. Diplomatic relations were promptly established with the Soviet Union; when the Prince was driven from Vientiane by right–wing forces in December 1960 he appealed for Soviet military aid. Russia promptly airlifted arms to the neutralist forces, but also sent an even larger shipment to the *Pathet Lao*, with whom Souvanna Phouma was cooperating. North Vietnam compounded the problem by sending its own forces into the mountains of eastern Laos at the beginning of 1961 in order to improve its access to South Vietnam via the "Ho Chi Minh Trail;" this was to assist in stepping up the revolutionary war against South Vietnam which was then in full bloom. It also increased aid to the *Pathet Lao*.

Evidently realizing that a war could not serve the aims of either side, U.S. President Kennedy and Soviet Premier Khrushchev agreed in 1961 that Laos should be neutralized. In spite of this, following intense jockeying for position, the *Pathet Lao* withdrew from the coalition government which had just been set up. The result was continuation of a highly complex and somewhat obscure, undeclared civil war. It included Thai volunteers and operations managed by the U.S. Central Intelligence Agency.

During the following years until 1971, military activity was related directly to the Ho Chi Minh Trail, vital to the North Vietnamese war effort in South Vietnam. The communists sought to keep it open, while the South Vietnamese, assisted by the U.S., sought periodically to close it, without success. As part of the accord suppos-

Laos

Lane Xang Hotel, Vientiane

edly settling the Vietnamese conflict reached in Paris, a form of agreement was reached in 1973 regarding Laos. It included many of the *Pathet Lao* demands and tended to lessen the influence of the right wing in the central government. Fighting practically stopped and all foreign troops were to leave the country within 60 days.

A coalition government was not installed until April 1974; it then became a means whereby the *Pathet Lao* greatly strengthened its political influence. Prince Souvanna Phouma's age and ill health reduced his role, and Prince Souphanouvong, the leading *Pathet Lao* in the coalition government, assumed the chairmanship of the Political Council. He in effect made it, rather than the National Assembly, the real legislative body. Although the *Pathet Lao* military located themselves in the government areas, non–communists were not allowed to function politically in or even to enter areas held by them. North Vietnamese troops remained in the highlands after the coalition government was formed.

A heart attack suffered by Premier Souvanna Phouma in mid–1974 made things easier for the *Pathet Lao*. Following more maneuvering for position, the early months of 1975 saw demonstrations by pro–communist elements (students, etc.) in some towns, as well as fighting in remote areas. The fall of South Vietnam and Cambodia in the spring of 1975 made a *Pathet Lao* takeover inevitable; the right–wing members of the government resigned in May. Soon there was a shift in favor of "hardline" communism—the monarchy was abolished and a new government was created with Souphanouvong as President. The ex–King was arrested in 1977.

In 1976, political "education" of the people was widespread, involving several thousand "advisors." A sizable Soviet aid program, including the building of an airfield on the Plain of Jars, was made available. Vietnamese influence was very great, and in fact, dominant. There were still Vietnamese troops on Laotian soil. Using "yellow rain" (Soviet-made natural poisons) for a time they fought Lao insurgents, some of whom are supported by China.

At a congress of the ruling *Lao People's Revolutionary Party* held in November 1986, there were some leadership changes with a tendency toward younger and perhaps better trained men rising to the top. The party, in line with recent Russian and Vietnamese moves and clearly troubled by the bad condition of the Laotian economy, called for better relations with China, Thailand and the U.S., as one means of improving the country's general situation.

Politics and Government

Under the 1991 Constitution, the *Lao People's Democratic Republic (LPDR)* continues to have a Marxist–Leninist style government. Political power rests with the Pasason, the central organ of the Lao *People's Revolutionary Party* (LPRP). The party Chairman is 69–year–old Khamtai Siphandon.

The National Assembly held its first meeting in February 1993. The unicameral Assembly, with 85 members, operates under the principle of democratic centralism, which allows the leadership of the LPRP to control the legislative process

Nouhak Phoumsavan is the *LPDR* President and Khamtai Siphandon, party chairman, is the Prime Minister. Last year concerned about the weakening health of the president, who is now 82, the Lao National Assembly created a new position of Vice President to help the president in his duties. The agriculture minister, Sisavath Keobounphanh was given the post.

The *LPRP* also controls the electoral process—candidates for the National Assembly are approved by the *LPRP* and in some cases picked by government departments. Assembly members also receive political training before assuming their responsibilities.

As has been the case in communist countries elsewhere, the *LPRP* continues to move the country toward a market economy and away from socialism. Like their Vietnamese and Chinese neighbors, the Laotian leadership apparently wants economic reform while seeking to hold on to political power. Nevertheless Laos, like so many of the East Asian political systems, may be moving toward an internal confrontation between the demands of an emerging developing economy and the wishes of an outmoded political leadership.

In 1997, the *LPRP* maintained firm control—there is no real political opposition in the country. The National Assembly has been trained to avoid politics and tend to other matters, including economic development. A second development within the government is the rise to power of various generals, who have taken over many of the cabinet portfolios and other key positions.

The paramount goal of the *LPRP* remains attainment of a market economy while maintaining control. The term for this is *chintanakan mai* ("new thinking"). Much of the real progress in changing the country can be traced to the Committee for Planning and Cooperation which has equal status with government ministries and has become quite powerful. This committee is staffed by young, better educated technocrats who are rising to the top quickly. The Deputy Prime Minister, Champhoui Keoboualapha heads the committee.

Recently the political landscape began to change with the passing of 86-year-old Souphanouvong (known as the "Red Prince") and Phoumi Vongvichit, a leader of the *Pathet Lao,* who died in 1994. Virtually all of the founding members of the *LPRP* have now either died or retired.

The Sixth Party Congress took place in April of 1996; it was in that meeting that the decision was made to add a vice president to the governing structure to aid the president, Nouhak Phoumsavan, in his work. Previous to the Congress some had

speculated that the 82 year old president would step down. For the moment that appears not to be the case. Nevertheless, his term of office is up soon. His successor would most likely be the Prime Minister, Khamtai Siphandon. Who then, would become Prime Minister?

The likely choices seemed to be Khamphoui Keoboualapha, Deputy Prime Minister and Head of the State Committee for Planning and Cooperation, or Minister of Defense Lt. General Choummaly Sayasone. The former is perceived to be more oriented toward reform, while the latter was more associated with maintaining state control and a slower approach to reform. It is worth noting, however, that the general has presided over the expansion of the military's role in the economy of Laos. Thus, when speculating about the political future of Laos, one should not discount Burma and Indonesia as possible alternative models. The military could be

the only social organization with the skills to administer the process of economic modernization. And their military cousins in Bangkok may be more than willing to help with the finer points.

In keeping with the National Assembly's emphasis on economic rather than political issues, the principal concern at the congress itself was how to deal with the growing gap between rich and poor which has emerged in recent years as a result of the new more open economic policies now in place.

Foreign Relations

LPDR foreign policy had a decided "look East" orientation for years. The country has had a long standing relationship with Vietnam. In 1977 the two countries signed the Treaty of Friendship and Cooperation. The agreement gives the Vietnamese, among other things, the au-

Lane Xang Avenue in Vientiane

Laos

Lao Buddhas

thority to enter Laos whenever it is deemed necessary. Vietnamese troops withdrew from Laos in 1989. Vietnam, however, no longer dominates the concerns of the Laotian foreign ministry.

Laos is also increasingly involved with its neighbor to the West, Thailand, which is already a major investor in the emerging Lao market economy. The recently opened Mitraphap bridge spans the Mekong River, and links Vientiane, the capital of Laos, to Nongkhai, Thailand. As the economic significance of this new link increases, the political influence of Bangkok will become stronger in the *LPDR*. Given Laos' interest in selling the energy products of their hydroelectric industry to Thailand, these ties are likely to

become even more important over the years.

Relations with the United States have been good in recent years. The two countries have worked together successfully in the areas of refugee repatriation and curbing the production of opium for export. Washington and Vientiane have also worked to resolve the status of Americans missing in action since the Vietnam War. Initial talks were held in 1987. Today, however, reasons for cooperation are obvious as Laos struggles with decisions about opening the country more and attracting outside investment. Laos has also signed an agreement for foreign assistance with North Korea. However, in recent years it seems Laos, despite all its problems, is in a

better position to give assistance then receive it from that beleaguered state.

The most obvious sign of Lao's emergence from the isolation it long held itself in is its upcoming move to join the Association of Southeast Asian Nations which is scheduled for next year.

Culture

In physical appearance and culture, the Lao are generally and accurately regarded as cousins of the Thai. They are an extremely easygoing and lighthearted people; their country was relatively peaceful in modern times until the turmoil brought about by the Vietnamese revolutionary struggle nearby.

Religious festivals, derived from very old traditions of southern Buddhism which had migrated from the island of Sri Lanka, are frequent, colorful and very similar to those of Thailand.

Although the government abandoned formal communist economic controls for a more open economic system after 1986, real changes in people's living standards are only just now beginning to be felt. Some wealthy urban dwellers now have the money for cars and TV's, and electricity now reaches 15% of the population. The capital, Vientiane, has itself seen important changes. For example, foreign newspapers are now available along with a new local paper *Vientiane Times*.

Unfortunately this new growth is uneven and half of the people remain at below the World Bank's poverty line. Illiteracy is still very high, and malnutrition is common among children. The new constitution provides equal rights for women though the traditional culture still favors males. Today women occupy positions of responsibility in business and government. The government, working through women's organizations, has also moved to educate young women about the dangers of labor recruiters who lure women and girls to the sweatshops and brothels of Thailand. As is frequently the case, the more educated urban women have more opportunities than the majority of the women who live in the countryside where many remain illiterate.

Economy

From the standpoint of economic geography, Laos falls into two clearly divided areas. In the Mekong Valley, productive agriculture centered on rice prevails. In the hills, the remote tribesmen sporadically cultivate the poor soils in a migratory fashion. Like the adjacent highlands of Burma, Thailand and China, the Laotian mountains are among the main opium producing regions of Asia. Most of this narcotic substance is smuggled out by air.

Communications are poorly developed and roads are almost nonexistent. The few that have been constructed are regularly washed out during the monsoon season. The *Lao People's Democratic Republic (LPDR)* launched the New Economic Mechanism (NEM) in 1986, in an attempt to modernize the country's economy. Since 1990, reforms include the introduction of a new accounting system for production and domestic trade, assigning a permanent staff to monitor budgetary revenue, creation of central banking laws, and the integration of official and parallel exchange rates.

Foreign investment regulations were also liberalized in 1989 and again in 1994.

In fact, Laos now has one of the most liberal environments for foreign investment in Asia. In 1994–1995, the country attracted significant foreign investment for the development of hydroelectric power. The second largest sector for investment is tourism, followed by mining and manufacturing, including clothing. One of the hydroelectric projects will be built by an Australian concern and will be the world's second highest concrete–faced, rock-filled dam. The government plans to sell much of the newly generated power to Thailand which needs an expanded supply for its development needs. Overall, Laos by the mid–1990s had been especially successful in attracting foreign investment. During the early 1990s it attracted more than a billion dollars in investment from over 30 countries. Nevertheless, the war years at times still hold Laos back. A Thai company recently canceled a project for fear of exposing its construction crews to the huge number of unexploded bombs that still litter the Laotian countryside!

Between 1990 and 1996, the economy averaged 6.5% growth. Unfortunately, growth has been uneven with poorer production in the agricultural sector. Inflation has been high in relation to growth rates of recent years. And, in spite of impressive growth figures, Laos is still among the poorest countries in the world with a per capita income well under $400.00 (GDP income $1,670) and a life expectancy of only fifty years.

The Future

Though Laos faces many challenges, the future is bright. Relations with Thailand have improved with the signing of a Treaty of Amity and Cooperation in early 1992. Laos is also looking to becoming a member of ASEAN. Laos is also attempting to broaden its relations by strengthening links with countries such as China and the United States.

Transplanting rice, Laos

Malaysia

The modern skyline of Kuala Lumpur   Courtesy: Embassy of Malaysia

Area: 128,775 square miles.

Population: 20.6. million (estimated).

Capital City: Kuala Lumpur (Pop. 1.2 million, estimated).

Climate: Tropically hot and humid.

Neighboring Countries: Thailand (North); Singapore (South); Indonesia (South and Southwest).

Official Languages: Malay and English.

Other Principal Tongues: Chinese, Tamil.

Ethnic Background: Malay (about 48%); Chinese (about 36%); Indian (9%) plus others, including indigenous people's languages.

Principal Religions: Islam, Buddhism, Hinduism, Christianity.

Main Exports (to Japan, Singapore, U.S.): Natural rubber, palm oil, tin, timber, petroleum.

Main Imports (from Japan, U.S.): Machinery and transportation equipment.

Currency: Ringgit.

Former Colonial Status: British commercial interests acquired the islands of Penang in 1786 and Malacca in 1824. The various states of Malaya entered into protectorate status from 1874–1895; they remained British colonies or protectorates until 1957 with the exception of the Japanese occupation from 1942 to 1945. Sabah was administered by the British North Borneo Company from 1881 to 1941, occupied by the Japanese from 1942 until 1945 and was a British Colony from 1946 to 1963. Sarawak was granted to Sir James Brooke by the Sultan of Brunei in 1841; it became a Brit-ish protectorate in 1888; after the Japanese were expelled in 1945, Sir Charles Vyner Brooke, the ruling Raja, agreed to administration as a British Crown Colony, which lasted until 1963.

National Day: August 31st.

Chief of State: His Majesty Tuanku Ja'afar Ibni Al–Marhum Tuanku Abdul Rahman (Yang di–Pertuan Besar of Negeri Sembilan), Yang di–Pertuan Agong, meaning King, or Supreme Head of Malaysia.

Head of Government: Dato' Seri Dr. Mahathir Mohamed, Prime Minister.

National Flag: Fourteen horizontal stripes of red and white with a dark blue rectangle in the upper left corner containing a yellow crescent and a 14–pointed star.

Per Capita GDP Annual Income: U.S. $9,470.

Located at the southern end of the Malay Peninsula, the mainland portion of Malaysia consists of a broad central belt of forested mountains. In the areas of Malaya where the mountains give way to lower altitudes, the vegetation turns into a thick green jungle situated on swampy plains, particularly in the coastal area. The climate is uniform during the year because of the closeness to the equator—hot and humid.

The Borneo states, also known as East Malaysia, contain wide coastal lowlands which have basically poor soil and are interrupted by frequent rivers. The altitude rises in the South as the border with Indonesia is approached. The division between the two occupants of the island straddles a scenic range of rugged mountains the highest of which is Mt. Kinabalu, towering majestically to a height of 13,000 feet. Few people of the western world have penetrated Borneo to view this remote area, which is inhabited by an indigenous people who have advanced little beyond Stone Age life. The people of Malaysia are quite similar to their Indonesian neighbors—a mixture of Polynesian, Mongol, Indian and Caucasian origins. There are also a large minority of Chinese who are descendants of laborers brought in by the colonial British.

History

The history of Malaysia, as a country, really begins during the colonial period, when the British started to establish their holdings in the area. Before that, the various regions that today are associated with Malaysia were part of several different political communities ranging from the mainland based Siamese kingdom to the north to the various commercial empires in what later became Indonesia.

The early Malay people themselves though were prominent enough in the region's early life to have had their language dominate commercial activities in the early modern era. In fact, throughout the region, regardless of a person's ethnicity, a knowledge of Malay was absolutely necessary to take part in the international trade of the region.

Malaya would probably have been colonized sooner than it was if the Dutch had not focused their attention on the fabled riches of Indonesia. The colonial history of both nations is very similar. The absence of Dutch control permitted the British to enter the area without opposition. In order to promote an orderly administration that would be a base for profitable trade, the British compelled the rulers of the small individual states of Malaya to accept "protection." This included the presence of a British advisor at each Malay court to insure that British goals were achieved. Four outlying, impoverished states of Siam (Thailand) in the North, were added to Malaya in 1909.

The rubber tree was brought from Brazil and planted in the rich soil to grow in an almost ideal climate. Drawn by the natural resources and the stability of the area, British capital poured in. There was also a mass influx of Chinese and Indian laborers to work the rubber plantations and the tin mines. In many cases these Chinese soon entered commerce and some became extremely wealthy and influential.

The arrival of immigrants from China and India set the stage for the most fundamental feature of modern Malaysian social and political life, the tripartite division of the population between native Malays who constitute around half the population and the Chinese and Indian communities who make up very significant minorities. In fact the Chinese, in contrast to their numbers which usually average around 10% throughout the region, make up closer to 40% in Malaysia.

During the British rule the later "division of labor" also began to appear as Chinese moved into the economy with the

**His Majesty
The Yang di-Pertuan Agong**

**Her Majesty
The Raja Permaisuri Agong**

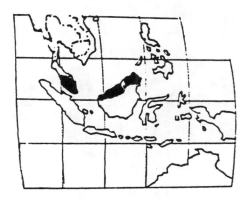

Malays largely remaining less urbanized or in some cases becoming part of the British civil administration of the area. The British often favored the Malays, often at the expense of the Chinese, a preference that more recent Malaysian governments have also followed. More importantly, British rule not only saw the evolution of the region from one that was relatively homogeneous to the more multi–ethnic society of modern Malaysia. As elsewhere British policy was to retain their authority by "divide and rule" processes which have certainly contributed to the prob-

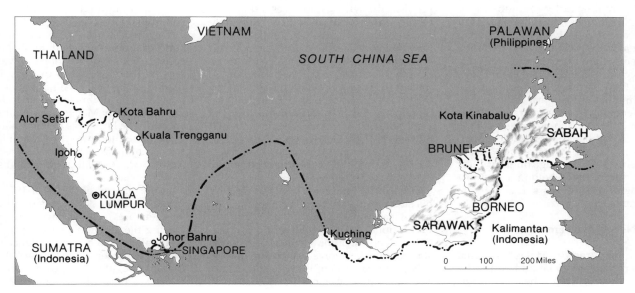

Malaysia

lems which have affected Malaysia in later years.

World War II

When the Japanese arrived in 1942, they treated the Chinese with much greater brutality than they did the Malays. In reaction, the local Chinese themselves, whose own politics were more tied to developments within China itself, developed an anti–Japanese guerrilla force of Chinese, most of them communists, which operated from bases deep within the thick jungles. Receiving weapons smuggled in by the British, the guerrillas fought their non–communist rivals as well as the Japanese. In contrast to the Chinese community, there was some sympathy among Malaysians for the Japanese activities. That is not very surprising considering that many people in Southeast Asia had been attracted to the Japanese calls to free the region from Western colonialism. That the Chinese themselves, well aware of the atrocities the Japanese had committed in China, did not view Japan's forces so positively is hardly surprising!

After the war, the British moved to unify the various regions which would later come to form modern Malaysia. A major problem though was the indigenous Malay concerns about maintaining their own dominance in a future independent Malay state. The eventual compromise offered freedom within a constitutional structure which included clear support for the traditional Malay leaders, the recognition of Malay and Islam as the official language and religion respectively and an overall structure that clearly favored the Malay over non–Malay peoples.

The arrangement as it was called included an understanding that while the Malays would dominate politics, the economy would be dominated by the non–Malay citizens. Nevertheless, not all members of the Chinese community were happy with the agreement and for the next decade a major insurrection developed led by local Chinese communists who had earlier been active in the resistance against the Japanese. While the entire period, known as "The Emergency," was very traumatic for the region, the rebellion was never able to draw much popular support and especially not from the Malay community itself. The British mounted a huge military effort which reduced the rebellion to almost nothing within a few years. It eventually ended years later.

A New Nation Emerges: 1957

The British granted Malaya internal self–government in 1955, and full independence in 1957. Under the able leadership of Prime Minister Tunku Abdul Rahman, head of the dominant *Alliance Party*, (now known as *the National Front*) which included then and now, a dominant Malay party known as the *United Malay National Organization (UMNO)* as well as other parties representing the Chinese and Indian communities. *UMNO*, which has dominated Malayian political life ever since, originally emerged as a reaction to British efforts to grant more rights to non–Malays. The party has not, in the years since, lessened its commitment to strengthening the position of Malay peoples within modern Malaysia. As we will see below, *UMNO* has dramatically improved the social and economic standing of the average Malay citizens but tensions over such favoritism continue to plague the country.

**The Prime Minister
Dato Seri Dr. Mahathir Mohamed**

By the early 1960s Malaysia's chief problem though was not over indigenous ethnic tensions but with their immediate neighbors, especially with Sukarno, the fiery nationalist leader of Indonesia. Faced with Sukarno's increased interest in dominating the region, and a marked swing to the left in Singapore politics, Rahman and the British devised a plan to unite Malaya, Singapore, Sabah and Sarawak into the Federation of Malaysia. (The tiny, oil–rich Sultanate of Brunei was also invited to join, but declined.) After many complicated negotiations the federation came into existence in September 1963.

Sukarno in Indonesia, encouraged by his success in acquiring West Irian, (now Irian Jaya) from the Dutch without a fight, was furious about the federation's formation. A "confrontation" with Malaysia was started, which involved sporadic fighting in the remote parts of Borneo, and unsuccessful attempts to land Indonesian guerrillas in Malaya. The "confrontation" was quietly discontinued in the mid–1960s after General Suharto seized power from Sukarno. (Indonesians usually have only one name.)

But the new Malaysian Federation faced significant domestic problems as well. There was continuing tension between the Chinese and Malays, especially over the role of Singapore, whose population is overwhelmingly Chinese, and which resented Malay domination of the central government. When Prime Minister Lee Kuan Yew of Singapore engaged in efforts to increase his party's influence and power beyond Singapore and within the Malaysian Federation at large, a crisis erupted which led to the expulsion of Singapore from Malaysia in August 1965.

A Challenge to the System

But if Singapore's expulsion from the federation only two years after its formation had lessened tensions between Kuala Lumpur and Singapore, the core issues of Malay, non–Malay relations continued. As will be recalled, the compromise of the late 1940s has seen emerge a political system which favored ethnic Malays while allowing the non–Malays to dominate the economy. But the elections of 1969 challenged that arrangement.

In the years leading up to 1969 the Malay political leadership had been able to successfully dominate the country's political system. But the elections of 1969 challenged the political and economic compromise which had been at the root of the new nation's stability. In the elections non–Malay parties won more votes than those of the Malay allies. While no dramatic change in government direction was immediately in the offing, it clearly aroused the concerns of the Malay population and hundreds died in the resulting communal violence.

This led the government to proclaim a state of emergency and to suspend the constitution; parliamentary government was, however, restored in early 1971. In the following years the government committed itself to a major effort to improving the status of Malays, economically and socially. The hope was that if Malays were more integrated into the economic life of the community there would be less cause for the sort of social tensions that so commonly existed.

In the general elections of 1974 *the National Front* (the *Alliance Party* plus some smaller ones) won a sweeping victory. During the elections, strong precautions were taken to avoid the violence of 1969. In fact, to preserve social peace it became literally illegal to even discuss the issues which separated the different ethnic com-

A Hindu wedding in Kuala Lumpur

Photo by Jon Markham Morrow

munities or the various programs designed to promote the economic life of the Malays.

A New Voice for Asia

Razak died in 1976, and was eventually followed by the leader who would dominate Malaysian politics over the next generation. First chosen as Prime Minister in 1981 Dr. Mahathir Mohamad, a physician by training, was the first non–aristocrat to become first minister and a man whose political views have led him, along with Singapore's Lee Kuan Yew, to be seen as one of the most articulate spokesmen for an "Asian Voice" in world affairs.

In the years after his arrival to power Mahathir managed to grow increasingly influential. He has consistently prevailed over his opponents within his own party, *UMNO*, and over other centers of power within Malaysia.

Mahathir originally gained public attention with a series of articles and then a book dealing with what he called the *Malay Dilemma*, which dealt with what he described as the second class status of Malays. A fervent nationalist, who wrote in English and even addressed such controversial subjects as the emancipation of women, his work was banned by the authorities when it came out in 1970. For a time he even had to go into hiding from the authorities for his outspoken comments against the leadership.

But given his support among younger Malays he was eventually invited back into *UMNO* and by the mid 1970s began his assent toward the premiership. In the years since, Dr. Mahathir has become one of the most outspoken leaders of his generation and a frequent and regular critic of the West even as he has successfully worked to integrate Malaysia itself into the modern industrialized world economy. In fact, Mahathir, along with Vice President Gore of the United States, are probably among the most committed and involved world leaders in the use of the Internet. He even has his own web site!

The Mahathir government has even over the years tried to curb the constitutional powers of the various Malay Sultans. In January 1984 it was successful in abolishing the Yang di–Pertuan Agong's power to veto legislation.

Several political problems of fairly serious proportions appeared in the last decade. One was leadership struggles within both the main components of the ruling coalition which governs the country: the dominant *United Malay National Organization (UMNO),* and the less powerful *Malayan Chinese Association (MCA).* The second was a rise in the activity of militant Islam, especially among the 20,000 Malaysian students in the United States and in Sabah (North Borneo), where there were violent Muslim demonstrations early in 1986 against the state government.

There were serious tensions within *UMNO* in 1987, reflecting a leadership struggle, a generational gap and a growing feeling that the party was strong enough to govern without the inconvenience of a coalition with other parties representing different races. Prime Minister Mahathir won a close vote for the party leadership in April and then purged some of his rivals. The relatively passive *Malayan Chinese Association* was troubled not only by a leadership problem, but also by a challenge from outside the National Front by the *Democratic Action Party (DAP),* a younger and more vigorous party.

The government cracked down on opponents of several types in October 1987, some of them *UMNO* members, but more of them belonging to the *DAP,* in a series of sudden arrests which were strongly criticized within and outside the country.

In a shocking ruling a judge held in February 1988 that because of structural problems at the regional level, *UMNO* was an illegal organization. This was a bizarre conclusion that had the main effect of intensifying the power struggle within the party. Mahathir responding quickly reorganized *UMNO* on a "legal" basis and strengthened his hold on it, and on the country.

Prime Minister Mahathir admires the economic dynamism of Japan and South Korea and would like to use them as models for Malaysia. He would also like to see an economic organization (the East Asian Economic Grouping) that would include the ASEAN states, China, South Korea, Taiwan, Hong Kong, and Japan, but would exclude everyone else, especially the United States. Not surprisingly Dr. Mahathir's ideas have not been well received in either the United States or Australia (or even among his Asian economic partners). Nevertheless, he, himself, has

PENINSULAR MALAYSIA
The nine states with hereditary rulers, and Penang and Malacca

Malaysia

Parliament House, Kuala Lumpur

become increasingly admired well beyond Malaysia itself.

Malaysian Politics

Malaysia, a member of the British Commonwealth, is a parliamentary democracy with a bicameral legislature composed of the Senate, *Dewan Negara,* and House of Representatives, *Dewan Ra'ayat.* The *Dewan Negara* has 58 members who serve six year terms. The *Dewan Ra'ayat* has 177 representatives. The parliament in Malaysia is not an effective institution for the discussion of public policy. The opposition has limited time to speak and often receives bills for consideration the same day that they are to be voted on. The "Standing Order of Parliament" prohibits treasonable or seditious words; the interpretation of those terms is left up to the Speaker of the *Dewan Ra'ayat* who is appointed by the government (Prime Minister).

Certain topics such as the special rights of Malays are not subject to discussion. Tough questioning by the opposition is rare and would not be widely reported in the media in any case since it is either owned or licensed by the government. The country has a very unusual system for selecting the Yang di–Pertuan Agong (King). He serves for five years and is selected on a rotational basis from among the hereditary rulers from nine of Malaysia's 13 states: the Sultans of Kelantan, Pahang, Johor, Kedah, Perak, Selangor, and Trengganu, the Rajah of Perlis, and the Yang di–Pertuan Besar (he who has been elevated to the highest position) of Negeri Sembilan. The states of Malacca, Penang, Sarawak and Sabah have governors, Yang di–Pertuan Negeri, appointed by the king. The latter two states compose East Malaysia on the island of Borneo while the former are part of West Malaysia.

Elections in Malaysia have generally

been clean, unlike those in many other developing countries. The single–member district formula benefits the government as does the fact that districts are often gerrymandered to favor the Malay voter. Malaysian politics continues to be controlled by the Malay–dominated *United Malay National Organization (UMNO.)* It heads the fourteen party *Barisan Nasional (BN)* coalition which governs the country. Opposition comes primarily from the *Pan–Malaysian Islamic Party (PAS),* the *Democratic Action Party (DAP),* and *Semangat '46'* ("Spirit of '46 Malay Party"). The latter's leader though recently rejoined *UMNO.* In practical terms, really significant political issues and the fate of individual governmental leaders are determined more within the political struggles of *UMNO* itself rather than between *UMNO* and the smaller parties.

The pivotal political event for 1993 was the November 4 election for the *UMNO* deputy president. This post within Malaysia's dominant political party is tantamount to a guarantee for gaining the post of deputy prime minister, which eventually leads to the prime ministership. The contest involved the Minister of Finance, Anwar Ibrahim, and the then current Deputy Prime Minister, Ghafar Baba. The Prime Minister, Mahathir Mohamad, seemed early on not to prefer a change of the old guard, but Anwar won a decisive victory. Ghafar Baba withdrew from the race and resigned from the cabinet, leaving the way open for the new *UMNO* deputy president. On December 1, the prime minister appointed Anwar as deputy prime minister.

Anwar's supporters from his *pasukan wawasan* (vision team) also won control of several *UMNO* party posts. However, the new team was split between Islamic and economic factions. A second splintering factor was that many votes for Anwar came from Sabah, the independent–minded East Malaysia state separated from West Malaysia by some 400 miles of South China Sea.

In 1994, and early 1995, the *BN* (National Front) coalition strengthened its overall position and Prime Minister Mahathir demonstrated that he was not yet ready to stand aside for Anwar Ibrahim. The *BN* had barely lost an important 1994 election in the East Malaysia state of Sabah, 23 seats to 25 seats, to the *Parti Bersatu Sabah (PBS)*. However, a month later the *PBS* splintered and the *BN* wound up in control of the state. National elections and elections for all other Malaysian states excluding Sabah and Sarawak were held at the end of April 1995. The *BN* won control of all states except Kelantan, which was won by the opposition coalition of *PAS* (24 seats), and *Semangat '46* (13 seats).

In early May 1995, Prime Minister Mahathir announced his new cabinet. The supporters of Anwar Ibrahim, Minister of Finance and heir apparent to the prime ministership, were held back. The group posed a genuine threat to the multi–ethnic fabric of Malaysia.

The BN victory in the national elections came in spite of several problems in 1994. In August, the Chief Minister of the state of Malacca and head of the *UMNO* youth organization, Abdul Rahim Tamby Chik, was hit with sexual harassment charges. This threatened Chik's career and also cast a negative light on the *UMNO* youth group. *UMNO* received additional bad publicity when Chik was not prosecuted. In September a bill was introduced in parliament to disband the Johor Military Force which is the private palace guard for the Sultan of Johor. It was accused of overstepping its authority in the area of local law enforcement. *UMNO* backed

down in the face of opposition which was feared could hurt the party's election chances in the upcoming national elections.

The coming to power of the Anwar faction can be expected to produce even more emphasis on economic development. There was some worry that it also signaled the beginning of "big money" politics in the country. The changes at and near the top may also signal the beginning of a winding down of the Mahathir era (though even by mid 1997 Mahathir did not appear to be planning to retire anytime soon). Nevertheless, Anwar and his followers have their own agenda.

The biggest challenge for the government in recent years came from the radical Islamic group, *Al–Arqam*. The sect was finally banned by the government. Sect leader Ashaari Muhammad was suspected of keeping an armed death squad of some 300 men in Thailand. The government became fearful when it learned that the *Al–Arqam* was successfully recruiting among the Malay middle class. As many as 7,000 civil servants may have joined the movement. *Al–Arqam* operated 257 schools and many businesses throughout the country. Total membership in Malaysia may have numbered up to 100,000.

A significant debate about the future of the Chinese parties within the *BN* governing coalition occurred in 1995. The *Malaysian Chinese Association (MCA)* and the *Gerakan* are both members of the *BN*. The leading opposition party, the *Democratic Action Party (DAP)*, is the third majority Chinese party in the country. While *UMNO* has done a good job in trying to be fair with its Chinese component parties, and with the 36% Chinese citizens of Malaysia, it has become clear in recent years that major policy decisions within the coalition are made largely without *MCA* and *Gerakan* input. In fact, both parties must rely heavily on Malay votes to defeat the opposition *DAP*.

There also appears to be a growing sentiment in the Chinese Malaysian community that the *MCA* and *Gerakan* are not assertive enough within the coalition. At some point, Chinese voters could reason that their only real voice is with the opposition, but sustained economic growth for everyone has dampened such arguments. Nevertheless, defection of even a moderate number of Chinese voters from the *BN* coalition would seriously threaten the fragile, multi–ethnic arrangement which the *UMNO* leadership has worked so diligently to build in Malaysian society. Prior to the 1969 riots, the *MCA* did share real power with *UMNO*. Perhaps with new leadership, *UMNO* may see some utility in returning at least partially to this governing formula. Tensions between the Chi-

nese community and the government were not likely to have been improved either when in late 1996 the government refused the Chinese community's request to establish its own institute of higher learning.

After the 1995 elections, Prime Minister Mahathir and the *BN* sailed through the remainder of the year. However, in March 1996, an unheard of event occurred. An *UMNO* insider and former Minister of Finance, Daim Zainuddin, publicly criticized the Prime Minister in *Utrusan Malaysia*, the country's leading Malay language paper. Daim charged that debate on controversial issues within the Malay leadership was often suppressed. He went on to say that there was no debate among the Malays, and that any questioning of policy, such as the commitment to rapid economic development, meant that you were anti–Malay.

Nevertheless the fall of 1996 brought yet another renewal of Prime Minister's Mahathir's power. Though the *UMNO* itself can not be realistically challenged by other Malaysian political parties, maintaining control within *UMNO* can be quite another thing entirely. In October, the coalition's convention saw very real competition between followers of the Prime Minister himself and his deputy and heir apparent, Anwar Ibrahim. For a time it even looked like Anwar's supporters were pulling ahead of those of Mahathir but that was only temporary. By the time the polling was completed a balance had been maintained between the two groups, and Mahathir's power to sway his party's loyalists was again confirmed.

Foreign Relations

Malaysia has been an effective actor in international politics for some time. In fact, Malaysia has increasingly taken the liberty of speaking for the developing countries in the world community and particularly in international forums like APEC and the WTO. In some ways, Malaysia and Singapore have emerged as the most effective representatives of an Asian vision for the future and one which is backed up by the economic accomplishments of both regimes over the last generation.

Malaysia also recently completed a two year term as a non–permanent member of the UN Security Council and it looks like it has a very good chance to become a base for United Nations regional peacekeeping forces. Malaysian troops have taken part in many United Nations efforts and the government is very interested in having the proposed base located within Malaysia.

Malaysia also maintains strong ties with the Islamic countries of the Middle East but also has at least officially attempted to

Malaysia

improve relations with Israel on a more practical level that has not always been easy. A visiting Israeli cricket team was greeted with major protests during its spring 1997 visit to this heavily Muslim country. Malaysia may be too small in population to evolve into a regional leadership position, but it continues to be a strong participant in ASEAN (Association of Southeast Asian Nations).

As elsewhere in the region, disputes continue over the many islands that dot the area. The disagreement with Indonesia over Sipadan and Ligitan islands off the coast of Sabah, East Malaysia, remained unsettled in 1997. The dispute over Pulau Batu Putih ("White Rock Island") with Singapore was referred to The Hague by mutual agreement. The claims and counter-claims continue throughout the region. For example, China, Malaysia and four other countries claim all or part of the South China Sea and the Spratley Islands.

Malaysia has agreed to purchase 18 Russian MIG19's for $500 million thus becoming the first non-communist state in Southeast Asia to operate Russian military equipment. India will train Malaysian pilots and technicians as part of the deal and Russia will set up a technical service center in Malaysia. Moscow also agreed to purchase $150 million in palm oil from Malaysia. Malaysia previously agreed to purchase F18's from the United States. Analysts wonder about the wisdom of purchasing two totally different fighter aircraft for a relatively small defense force.

Further, the problem of obtaining spare parts from Russia looms on the near horizon.

In general, the last few years have been successful for Malaysian foreign relations especially with respect to ASEAN dealings with neighboring states. Singapore and Malaysia came to a permanent agreement on their territorial waters boundary. They also reached agreement over Malaysian restrictions of the importation of Singaporean petro-chemicals. Relations with the Philippines and Thailand also improved somewhat. The promising idea of a Malaysia–Indonesia–Thailand northern growth triangle was still on track (Singapore, Malaysia and Indonesia have been highly successful with the "first triangle" which encourages free trade and makes special concessions to attract foreign businesses).

Culture

Malaysia's population is very young—about 45% are under the age of 15! A high percentage of the people are literate; primary and secondary school education is provided for all, and there are a number of colleges and 5 universities. Although Islam is the State religion and Muslims enjoy certain special privileges by law, there is complete freedom of worship for other faiths.

The most intricate handiwork is produced in wood, silver and pewter, both in traditional forms and in highly modern pieces. Kuching, the capital of the East Malaysian state of Sarawak has one of the finest museums in Southeast Asia, and the nation's graceful, rhythmic dances are legendary.

Malaysians are great sports enthusiasts, and although more traditional ball game forms have dominated in the past, soccer is now the nation's most popular pastime. There is also tremendous interest in horse–racing as seen by the country's five first–rate turf clubs.

The majority of the Malay community used to live in a fairly traditional manner, principally engaged in farming and fishing, but today Malays are increasingly entering the trading, professional and other sectors of the modern economy. Except for Singapore, Malaysia has the highest percentage of Chinese found in Southeast Asia. Divided into several linguistic groups which reflect the origins of their ancestors who migrated from China, they tend to remain apart except in economic activity—they dominate in the business community. Many educated Chinese, particularly among the younger generation, learn English and Malay. The more educated Malays usually speak English.

In Malaysia Muslim women are subject to Islamic legal codes. In contrast, non–Muslim women are subject to the more secular civil code. For Muslim women that means that practices such as polygamy are allowed. On a practical basis of course the situation is more complicated. While at least one Malay state has made it somewhat easier for a man to meet the requirements to take more than one wife (not, for example, having to gain the first wife's permission), Prime Minister Mahathir has made it clear he disapproves of the practice as have other national leaders elsewhere in the region. Mrs. Mahathir won't even welcome second wives into her home!

Islamic domestic law favors males in matters of inheritance but its application in Malaysia has varied from that practiced elsewhere. In fact, in 1989 the Islamic Family Law was revised to give Muslim Malaysian women more rights in such personal matters as divorce. Nevertheless, in some regions, where Islamic parties have been influential, in Kelantan, for example, their rights have been lessening lately.

Looking at today's Malaysia, women are still under–represented in decision–making positions and their role in the professions is only recently growing. Happily, as has been the case so often elsewhere, the next generation of Malaysian women seems well situated to gain more control over their lives than women of earlier generations. Today's civil law gives them equal rights in work and education, and today they are well represented among

Rural life, Penang

university student ranks. Two women now serve in cabinet–level positions.

Economy

Malaysia has one of the strongest and fastest growing economies in the Asia–Pacific region. Many expect Malaysia to become the "fifth tiger," joining Hong Kong, Singapore, South Korea, and Taiwan, in the developed country ranks. Malaysia's current national development plan, Vision 20/20, calls for the country to achieve full developed status by that date. Under the former New Economic Policy, the government was able to substantially raise the level of Malay participation in the non–agricultural sectors of the economy. Although the precise goals were not achieved by the target date, the success of the NEP was such that Prime Minister Mahathir was able to announce that there was no longer a need to stress the fulfillment of targets or quotas for specific ethnic groups.

Today, Malaysia has a significant and growing Malay middle and upper–middle class. There are also a significant number of very wealthy Malays, some of whom have made fortunes by having access to lucrative government contracts. The Chinese community remains very well represented in business and commerce.

The impact of sustained economic growth has been very visible. Longer life, improved health care, a significant increase in the number of people owning telephones, and an expanding national highway system, were all indicators of the country's economic success over the last decade. Malaysia's third car, a van, will be produced by a Japanese–Malaysian consortium. In 1995, Malaysia's first automobile, the Proton Saga, sold over 25,000 units in Europe. A second Malaysian–Japanese partnership has agreed to produce the country's first motorcycle.

But some problems have also surfaced. Over the last year more than thirty Taiwan firms have pulled out of Malaysia. It is not clear whether these were simply business decisions motivated by the rise of local labor costs or connected to displeasure regarding the lack of Malaysian support in Taiwan's continuing struggle with Beijing. Neither possible answer bodes well for the future. Other problems persist as well. The Science, Technology and Environment Ministry reported in late 1995 that two out of three rivers in Malaysia were polluted and that those unpolluted (28%) were deteriorating fast as a consequence of industrial waste. In March, it was estimated that 7 million fish died off the coast of Perak state from exposure to potassium cyanide. Malaysia will not have a treatment plant capable of handling toxic waste in operation until 1998. A shocking

Early morning fishing

estimate is that by 2005, the rain forest in the East Malaysia state of Sabah will have no marketable timber left. Native peoples are loosing their lands to greedy state politicians and Japanese plywood manufacturers.

Malaysia's gross domestic product (GDP) grew by 8% in 1996—down from over 9% in 1995, but still quite healthy, and inflation was only 3.2%. Job creation outpaced the labor pool. This shortage is causing problems for the government in the immigration area. There are currently some 500,000 legal and illegal immigrants working in the country. Most are Indonesian and thus easier to absorb than peoples from other states. However, there is growing concern on this issue.

The Future

As Malaysia continues to enjoy the benefits of rapid economic development, the old tensions generated by ethnic differences between Malays, Chinese and Indians will continue to fade. While the country was almost torn apart in 1969 by ethnically based violence, such events to-

day would be unthinkable. The country has come too far. As part of the Malay community has moved ahead to join the Chinese and Indian communities in business and commerce, some tensions have appeared between the old Malay community and this new group. In order to maintain its dominant political position, *UMNO* will have to pay close attention to mending fences within the Malay community.

It will also have to continue to make progress on the economic front. One third of Kuala Lumpur's people still live in slums, and the country is graduating too few technically trained college graduates to keep up with the demands of the growing economy.

The Islamic and militant *Al–Arqam* movement has also been especially worrisome because it has drawn support from the entire Malay community. Even well–educated middle class Malays were attracted to the sect. The ban on *Al–Arqam* was necessary and took courage on the part of the Mahathir government. For a society as multi–cultural as Malaysia, an overly strong emphasis on any one religious perspective could be a disaster.

Papua New Guinea

Shipping at Port Mosesby

Area: 178,260 sq. mi. (475,369 sq. km., somewhat larger than California).

Population: 4.3 million (estimated).

Capital City: Port Moresby (Pop. 130,000, estimated).

Climate: Tropical.

Neighboring Countries: Australia (South); Indonesia (West).

Official Language: English.

Other Principal Tongues: There are over 700 indigenous languages, and a pidgin English is spoken in much of the country.

Ethnic Background: Mostly Melanesian and Papuan, with a small minority of Australians and Europeans.

Principal Religion: Traditional tribal beliefs, with an overlay of Christianity.

Main Exports (to Japan, Germany, Australia): Copper, gold, timber, coffee, rubber and other tropical products.

Main Imports (from Australia, Japan, Singapore): Machinery, consumer goods.

Currency: Kina.

Former Colonial Status: Until 1975, a United Nations trusteeship administered by Australia.

National Day: September 16, 1975.

Chief of State: Her Majesty Queen Elizabeth II, represented by Governor–General Sir Wiwa Korowi.

Head of Government: Sir Julius Chan, Prime Minister.

National Flag: Divided diagonally from top left to bottom right, the top a red field upon which is centered a yellow bird of paradise, the bottom a black field showing five white stars in the Southern Cross.

Per Capita Annual GDP: US$2,470.

Occupying the eastern half of the large island of New Guinea, the western portion—*Irian Jaya*—being part of Indonesia, the nation was formed from Papua, the southeastern quarter of the island and the Territory of New Guinea, the northeastern quarter plus the nearby Admiralty, northern Solomon and Bismarck island groups.

The terrain is covered largely with very high mountains, swamps and jungles. The climate is uniformly tropical except in the more temperate altitudes of the mountains. There is an extremely small European minority; the indigenous inhabitants belong either to the Papuan group (on New Guinea) or to the Melanesian people (on the islands).

History

Prior to the late 19th century, apart from missionaries, New Guinea attracted two main types of Europeans: explorers and investors, lured by its supposedly substantial mineral resources. Dutch influence based on Indonesia became dominant in western New Guinea. The northeastern part of the big island and the smaller islands to the east were annexed by Germany in 1884. The southeastern part of the island known as Papua was placed under British protection in the same year, during the greedy scramble for colonial possessions that was then underway worldwide. Britain soon changed its policy toward Papua to a less possessive one and later transferred the area to Australia.

The German holdings in northeastern New Guinea and the nearby islands were seized by Australia during World War I and then were awarded to it under a League of Nations mandate which after World War II became a United Nations trusteeship.

In reality, Australia administered the entire dependency until 1974 from Port Moresby without regard to the legal distinction between the status of Papua, a di-

Papua New Guinea

rect Australian dependency, and New Guinea, the trusteeship.

In 1942 the Japanese conquered the islands east of New Guinea and invaded parts of the large island itself, including both of the eastern regions. Some of the bitterest fighting of the Pacific war occurred during the next two years as Australian and American forces drove the Japanese out of all but a few strongholds. Following the end of the war, Australian civil administration was restored. In response to growing UN criticism and a growing demand for self–government, an elected assembly was established in 1968.

In elections in 1972 to the House of Assembly (the parliament), the *National Coalition*, led by Michael Somare was victorious. His program, which called for full self–government in 1973, was accepted by Australia soon afterward, even though it was opposed by many of the European and indigenous inhabitants.

Politics and Government

Little has been accomplished in terms of the daily living standards of PNG citizens in the two decades since full independence. The vast majority of the population still lives at a subsistence level in isolated villages. Little headway has been made in developing the more industrial sectors of the economy or even helping the villagers compete in the world agricultural market.

These failures have led to severe financial problems, and most recently, a seven-year war on the island of Bougainville, rich in copper and desirous of independence. In fact the ongoing struggle there led to the most recent crises in PNG's governing system. In addition to the continuing revolt on Bougainville Island, the government has been dealing with independence demands from other New Guinea islands.

A major governmental reform was recently undertaken which resulted in the elimination of the country's 19 provincial parliaments. Non-paid local government officials along with the national parliamentary representatives formed local assemblies. They took the place of some 600 paid politicians who composed the provincial parliaments. The MP's in the new assemblies with the largest representation became Governors. They are to be the primary link between the local assemblies and the capital. The move may also have some impact on the unstable political party system, where new parties appear frequently, and where members shift from one party to another regularly.

In spite of the severe economic crisis and demands by the World Bank for reform, Prime Minister Chan, who came into power in 1994, was able to keep as a

part of the national budget $250,000 for the country's 109 members of parliament which they could spend as they pleased for their constituents. Prime Minister Chan appeared to be in firm control of the government at the end of 1996 but quickly lost support during 1997 for having made a questionable decision regarding the insurrection in Bougainville.

Hoping to end the revolt once and for all, Prime Minister Chan in early 1997 arranged for the hiring of a foreign mercenaries contingent to deal with the rebels at a cost of $36 million. But his own military refused to go along citing urgent needs for the PNG Defense Force. Led by Brigadier General Jerry Singirok, the military demanded the termination of the mercenaries' contract and forced the Prime Minister from office pending an investigation. When the final report came in, Chan immediately resumed office declaring that he had been absolved. Meanwhile, national elections are scheduled for June 14–28, 1997.

Foreign Policy

Prime Minister Chan has altered PNG foreign policy from a "look North" (toward Asia) to a "look everywhere" approach. The decision to employ the mercenary contingent was roundly condemned by the government's neighbors. But specifics of PNG's future policy will probably be much affected by the outcome of the elections.

Culture

The vast majority of the peoples of Papua New Guinea live in the rural areas and practice a traditional form of agriculture with many living at a purely subsistence level. Most of them practice some sort of Protestant Christianity; the majority are Lutherans. About one third are Roman Catholic. Traditional religious traditions are also an important part of the religious environment of the people. Western missionaries, many of them American, are quite active in the area.

A small portion of the indigenous inhabitants still live at an Old Stone Age level, hunting and gathering for a living. Unfortunately for PNG, the general impression that all of its citizens live under such traditional circumstances has at times made it difficult to attract foreign investment. The traditional social system is based on clans and tribes. Fighting and head–hunting among different tribes, once common, were suppressed by the Australian administration during the 1930's.

Although government legislation gives women extensive rights, they are in practice still discriminated against and some of the traditional cultural values which once offered women some protections have broken down in recent years. Polygynous marriages are allowed and often

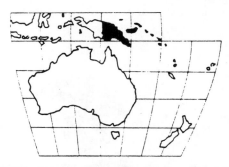

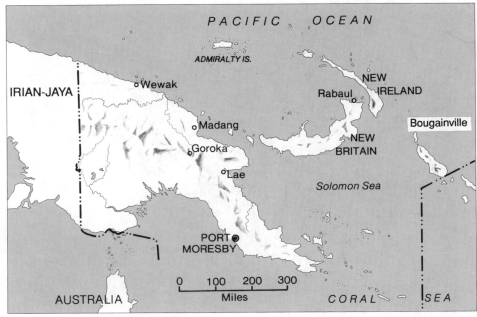

133

Papua New Guinea

are at the root of domestic violence. Traditional practices still tend to treat women as property which adds to the perception of them as second class citizens or even less. Only 40% of PNG women are literate and a third do not attend primary school.

Economy

The economies of the two areas, Papua (in the south) and New Guinea (in the north) are basically similar, except that most of the mineral deposits (copper, gold and silver) so far discovered are located in New Guinea. The external trade of Papua New Guinea is largely with Australia, the United States and Germany.

Almost 70% of PNG's exports come from mining; the country is now the world's sixth largest producer of gold. There are also substantial oil and gas deposits. Production was disrupted at several sites throughout the country by bandits and local armed gangs backed by land owners who want an increased share of the benefits from the country's resources. At the end of 1996 the World Bank and other international observers were concerned over how the country's budget was being handled. A new Investment Promotion Authority was initiated

Prime Minister Sir Julius Chan

with the power to allow increased foreign equity in designated national industries. Giving foreign investors a greater share of ownership is a common mechanism to induce increased foreign investment.

In spite of the country's political difficulties, economic growth was extraordinary in the early 1990s. It has not though been doing well in recent years and has in

fact declined sharply. In 1995, the country narrowly avoided financial collapse. In mid-year the government was forced to accept a World Bank–IMF structural adjustment package involving some $350 million. The package forces certain reforms on the government and its economic policies and included such items as: (1) reduced restrictions on foreign investors, (2) removal of price controls, (3) halting tax concessions and (4) the granting of monopolies. Further, there is to be an introduction of plans to maintain a sustainable timber industry, and the opening of books on national debt.

At the end of the year, the economy was in better shape. The government had initiated two freeway construction projects in Port Moresby and had taken other steps to put national finances in order.

The Future

PNG's biggest problems are internal. The government must work to establish stability in the political system and to eliminate the budget deficit. The strife on Bougainville is wasteful. More sophisticated use of the nation's vast resources would be of great benefit.

An alert "cowboy" in Papua New Guinea

Mekeo Tribesmen in ceremonial dress

The Republic of the Philippines

Majestic Mayon volcano, the most symmetrical mountain on earth, looms mistily over Legaspi City at the southern tip of Luzon. Still active, a curlicue of smoke issues from its summit.

Area: 115,700 sq. mi. (300,440 sq. km., occupying an area somewhat smaller than New Mexico).

Population: 66 million (estimated).

Capital City: Manila (Pop. 7.5 million, estimated).

Climate: Tropically warm with rainy monsoons in the summer.

Neighboring Countries: The Philippines' closest neighbors are Nationalist China on the island of Taiwan (North) and Malaysia (Southwest).

Official Languages: Filipino (a formal version of Tagalog) and English.

Other Principal Tongues: Tagalog and tribal dialects of principally Malay origin, including Visayan, Ilocano and Bicol.

Ethnic Background: Malayo–Polynesian (about 93%) Chinese, Negritos, mixed and European (about 7%).

Principal Religion: Christianity, predominantly Roman Catholic (about 91.5%), Islam (about 2.5%), animist and other (about 7%).

Main Exports (to the U.S. and Japan): A variety of coconut products—copra, oil and fibers, abaca—Manila hemp used in rope making, timber—Philippine mahogany, sugar, iron ore.

Main Imports (same trading partners plus Saudi Arabia): Industrial equipment, wheat, petroleum.

Currency: Philippine Peso.

Former Colonial Status: Spanish colony (circa 1570–1898); U.S. dependency (1898–1946); occupied by the Japanese (1941–1945).

National Day: July 4, 1946. (June 12, the anniversary of the proclamation of independence from Spain in 1898, is a national holiday).

Chief of State: Fidel Ramos, President (sworn into office June 30, 1992).

National Flag: The left edge is the base of a white equilateral triangle containing a yellow sun and three yellow stars; the rest of the flag is divided into two horizontal stripes with blue on the top, red on the bottom.

Per Capita Income: US$700.

The land which makes up the territory occupied by the Republic of the Philippines consists of a portion of a mountain chain running from northern Siberia in Russia through the China Sea to Borneo and New Guinea and the small islands of eastern Indonesia, and then southward through eastern Australia. Countless ages ago the sea invaded the lower part of these mountains—the Philippines are a small portion of the top of this mountain range that has sufficient height to rise above the surface of the tropical waters of the Southwest Pacific.

Philippines

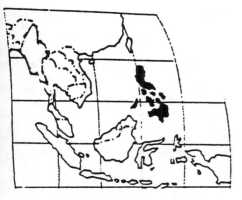

This nation includes eleven larger islands with more than 1,200 square miles of land on each island: Luzon, Mindanao, Samar, Negros, Palawan, Panay, Mindoro, Leyte, Cebu, Bohol and Masbate. More than 95% of the nation's land and people are located on these islands.

The remaining 7,072 (every time they are counted the total is different) islands are desolate, jungle–infested and mostly uninhabited tiny areas of remoteness. Few have an area of more than one square mile, and about 4,631 exist as land masses in the 20th century only because it is impossible to sail across them—they are dots on navigation charts not even possessing the dignity of a name.

The temperature is consistently warm. The altitude of the terrain, most of which lies above an altitude of 1,600 feet, modifies the oppressiveness of what might otherwise be an intolerable climate. Almost all of the islands are mountainous, containing a multitude of dead and active volcanoes. The eastern slopes receive ample rainfall during all months of the year. The westward–facing parts are moistened by the southwest monsoon from May to October. All areas of the islands have periodic, often devastating, visits from typhoons of the region, which bring torrential rains.

The land is covered with vast expanses of thick jungle which grows with incredible rapidity and contains among its taller trees the timber from which Philippine mahogany is marketed to the world. The part that has been tamed by the population varies from a thick growth of poor grass which supports grazing to plantation production of coconut, rubber, pineapple and other tropical crops.

History: About two centuries before the Christian era a fairly advanced people from what is now northern Vietnam and southern mainland China migrated to the large islands of the Philippines. They practiced a system of communal agriculture based on irrigation. Many of their descendants live in the islands today as small non–Christian communities. The larger group of Filipinos of Malayo–Polynesian origin arrived in the isles from the 8th to the 15th centuries from Java and the Malay peninsula. Their migrations occurred principally during the period of the strong *Srivijaya* kingdom in the Indonesia–Malaya area and during the *Majapahit* kingdom on Java, which dominated a large area up to the beginning of the 13th century A.D.

Muslim traders and pirates arrived during the 14th century, and there was a small Chinese community. Magellan was killed in the islands in 1521 during his famous

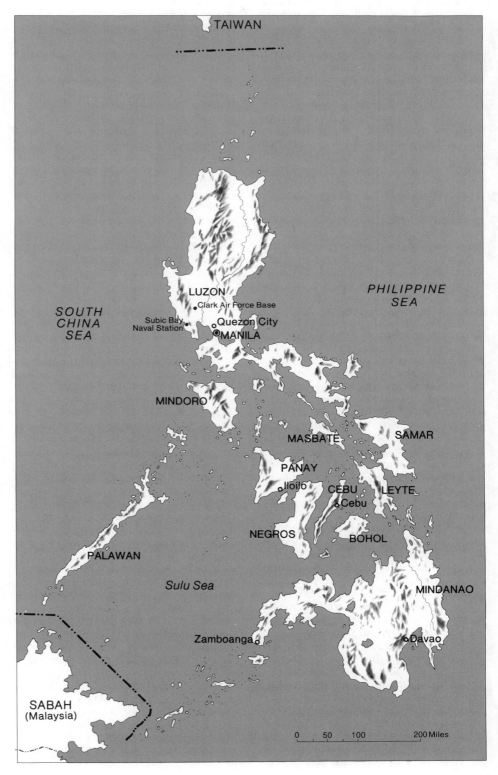

Philippines

voyage around the world, but there was no serious attempt by the Spanish to establish a colony until fifty years later. The Spanish occupation forces were dispatched and controlled by the authorities in the colony of Mexico. The initial settlement was small, and had as its only contact with the European world the annual visit of the "Manila Galleon" sent to Mexico once a year.

As they had done in Central and South America, the Spanish gave large tracts of fertile land to prominent Spaniards who had almost complete authority over their domains, and exploited the native inhabitants without interference. Many of the Filipinos who were driven from their lands by the Spanish went to the more hilly and mountainous areas of the islands and developed farms based on intricate stone terracing of the steep sides to enable their crops to grow on level land. The best friends that the Filipinos had among the Spanish were the monks living in the monasteries which grew rapidly in number and in wealth based on land ownership. Many of the natives were converted to Roman Catholicism and also were provided with some educational and other social services by the religious institutions, which had a limited success in protecting them from the demands of government officials and the local Spanish land–owning aristocracy.

When Spain lost its colonies in Central and South America during the first part of the 19th century, the Philippines assumed an even more important position. Efforts to develop the economy to serve the Spanish were largely unsuccessful, as were the efforts to subdue the warlike *Moros* (Muslims) in the southern islands, who had lived there for many decades without interference. The slow growth of education, the spread of European cultural and political ideas, and unrest caused by oppressive economic polices of the Spaniards, gave rise to a small group of educated Filipinos who demanded independence from Spain. Its most prominent member was the brilliant José Rizal, executed by the Spaniards in 1896, at a time when an open revolt against Spain had broken out.

Taking advantage of the preoccupation of the Spanish with the war being fought in Cuba against the United States, local leaders proclaimed an independent Republic of the Philippines early in 1898 and quickly adopted a European–type constitution. The Filipino leaders believed that the United States supported them in this independence move, and joined in a combined effort against the remaining Spanish forces in the islands. The U.S., partly out of fear that some other power, probably Germany, would seize the Philippines, forced the Spanish to cede them to the

U.S. as part of the terms of the Spanish surrender in 1898.

Rebel forces led by General Emilio Aguinaldo, immediately went into armed revolt against the United States, feeling that they had been betrayed by the Americans with whom they had fought against the Spanish for six months. It took a little more than three years before guerrilla activity against U.S. forces ceased; Aguinaldo had been captured earlier in 1901.

By 1916 the United States had committed itself to a goal of eventual independence for the islands and begun the creation of internally self–governing institutions. It purchased about 400,000 acres of land from the Catholic monasteries for distribution to the people—the colonial administration also made efforts in the fields of communication, public works and education. The economic policies of the administrators were not as helpful; the emphasis was on creating areas for profitable American investment and little was done to develop the economy as a whole for the benefit of the Filipinos. A foreign trade emerged that was almost totally linked to and dependent on the U.S. market. Feudal systems of sharecropping in the rural areas, which had arisen under the Spanish as a result of land grants, continued and became an even worse problem. The local elected governments permitted by the colonial administration drifted toward control by Filipino political machines and bosses who bore a remarkable resemblance to some of their contemporaries in Latin America.

In the 1930's, Manuel Quezon, who formed and led the *Nationalist Party,* emerged as the leading politician. Political idealism was one factor that prompted the United States to adopt legislation providing for an almost fully self–governing Commonwealth to be established in 1935. The other was pressure from U.S. sugar interests for protective tariffs against Philippine sugar, which were impossible unless it was independent. The first President of the the Philippine Commonwealth was Quezon. The growing threat of the Japanese in Asia in the late 1930's lessened the desire for total independence on the part of the more radical Filipinos, who saw the need for U.S. protection.

The islands were quickly overrun by a force of well–trained Japanese soldiers who inaugurated in 1942 the same cruel type of military rule over the people that was their policy in the other areas of Southeast Asia they conquered. This resulted in a limited guerrilla movement operating clandestinely in the rural areas to sabotage the military installations of the Japanese. Quezon and his government went into exile in the United States, where he died in 1944. His successor, Sergio Os-

meña, was soon able to return to the Philippines as a result of the progress of General Douglas MacArthur's forces in liberating the islands.

The economy had been devastated by the war, and it was necessary for the United States to pour in huge sums for relief and rehabilitation and to grant duty–free status to Philippine exports in the American market until 1954. Much of the aid, unfortunately, did not reach those who needed it. Osmeña died in 1946. For the next twenty years the Philippines were ruled, with one exception, by a succession of colorless, corrupt and inefficient leaders:

Manuel Roxas (pronounced *Ro*–has), 1946–1948. These years were marked by ineffective government, open corruption and black marketeering which made incoming aid of little benefit. Rural land tenancy problems remained unsolved. The armed guerrilla movement which had resisted the Japanese underwent a rapid and subtle transformation into a communist movement, usually known as the *Hukbalahap,* or "Huks," a name inherited from resistance movements dating back to Aguinaldo. In spite of these conditions, the U.S. proceeded with its plan for full independence on July 4, 1946.

Elpidio Quirino, 1948–1953. Dishonesty and scandal reached crisis proportions and the *Huks* went into open and initially successful revolt. An exceptionally able and energetic Secretary of Defense, Ramón Magsaysay, who would become the next president, enlisted American advice after his appointment in 1950; the guerrilla threat was greatly diminished. The army was transformed into an effective force forbidden to engage in its usual customs of looting and harassment. Amnesty and free land was granted to the *Huks,* who surrendered, almost totally eliminating them as a threat to stability.

Ramón Magsaysay, 1953–1957. He maintained a consistently pro–U.S. policy and took the Philippines into the Southeast Asia Collective Defensive Organization (SEATO) in 1954. In spite of his strenuous efforts the power of the small group of families who dominated agriculture, industry and trade—the descendants of the Spanish aristocratic class, continued. Magsaysay was killed in an airplane accident and was succeeded by his inept vice president.

Carlos García, 1957–1961.

Diosdado Macapagal, 1961–1965. The country remained stagnant under these two leaders, the latter of whom dabbled in an active, anti–U.S. foreign policy intended to make the Philippines more popular, powerful and acceptable in the Asian community.

Ferdinand Marcos of the *Nationalist Party,* defeated Macapagal in 1965 amid a general sense of urgent need of change among the people—change toward better performance by their rulers. Marcos embarked upon a reform platform similar to that of Magsaysay, but met the same intractable obstacles as his predecessor. Corruption remained a virtual custom among minor government officials and employees for the next twenty years. The *Communist Party* (PKP) abetted by discontent among the poverty–stricken rural people, resumed its guerrilla activity against the state, although they became divided among themselves. Traditional rivalry between the *Nationalist Party* and the *Liberal Party* continued.

President Marcos was reelected in 1969 over a *Liberal Party* opponent by a large majority and became the first Philippine President to win a second term. *Nationalist* majorities in both houses of the Assembly were sizable. But student and labor demonstrations in Manila which occurred in 1970 were symptoms of the country's malaise; some of the dissent had an openly anti–U.S. tone. The popular discontent was diverted to the business of revising the constitution through holding a national convention. Probably for reasons of domestic politics, Marcos revived an old Philippine claim to Sabah, a part of Malaysia closest to the Republic. The predictable result was a serious crisis with Malaysia, punctuated by a barrage of bitter charges and counter–charges. The dispute fizzled out within two years and the claim was formally dropped at the end of 1987.

Serious floods and growing insurgency on the part of communist elements in Luzon created a crisis atmosphere. Marcos proclaimed martial law in 1972. In the ensuing years he had some success in improving the state of law and order except in Mindanao, where an ongoing Muslim revolt has been in progress. Of greatest importance, however, he received approval by referendum of a new constitution under which he had virtual dictatorial powers for an unlimited period. There was another such referendum in 1975.

Principal opposition to the Marcos regime came from the Catholic Church and insurgent Muslims in the southern islands. The latter received (and still receives) support from other Muslim countries, principally Libya and Sabah. Some Arab countries tried unsuccessfully in 1975 to mediate the conflict. Fearing the consequences of endangering needed oil imports, Marcos did not press the war and announced that a truce had been concluded; in reality the war continued in spite of additional negotiations in 1976 and 1977.

Martial law delegated great political power to the armed forces, which became repressive and corrupt, although providing a semblance of order.

Mindanao's Maria Cristina Falls pounds out its dramatic message

Philippines

Ferdinand and Imelda Marcos at their zenith in 1972

Imelda Marcos, the attractive wife of the president, became Governor of Manila and announced ambitious plans for its redevelopment; although she set up a semblance of a power base, she remained loyal to her husband, although her plans to succeed him became widely known.

Marcos created a *National People's Council* in 1976 to advise him on legislative matters. Elections were postponed indefinitely, however. He apparently planned to revive the political system in such a manner that he would pick the candidates from panels chosen by various public bodies. An election for an interim parliament with limited powers held in 1978 resulted in a sweeping victory for pro–Marcos candidates.

As might be expected, the militant wings of the opposition groups began to resort to terrorist bombings in 1980. In an effort to save his son, who was targeted for elimination, Marcos made a secret deal which he fulfilled only in part by lifting martial law in 1981, but the bombings continued. Insurgency, particularly Muslim and communist, became a continuing problem. Despite the lifting of martial law, there was little improvement in the political situation. The country continued to be run by an alliance led by an aging and somewhat ill Marcos, his wife, the armed forces, the ruling *New Society Party* and rich and powerful men close to the president who operated for their own benefit in an economic system known locally and informally as "crony capitalism."

Marcos had talked of forcing the U.S. out of its huge air and naval bases in the Philippines, but this was almost certainly to divert popular attention from his domestic policies as well as to get greater concessions from the United States, including higher rents. In addition, he was determined to appear at home and abroad as entirely independent of the United States and as the leader of a truly Asian nation. Partly for this purpose, he visited and granted diplomatic recognition to the People's Republic of China in June 1975; another consideration was that he wanted, and apparently thought that he got, a pledge from Beijing not to support the small Philippine communist insurgent movement, the *New People's Army*. The Chinese urged Marcos not to squeeze the U.S. out of its bases, since China feared that an American military withdrawal from the region might create a vacuum that could be filled or exploited by the Soviet Union. Relations with the United States were reasonably good; President Ford visited in late 1975. Marcos established diplomatic relations with the Soviet Union in 1976. An agreement concerning lease of military bases was finally concluded with the United States in 1978 and a second in late 1983.

Opposition leader Benigno Aquino, probably encouraged by false reports that Marcos was about to undergo surgery in August 1983, decided to return to Manila from Malaysia where he had been living in exile. He was summarily gunned down at the airport upon the landing of his plane. The opposition blamed the government, and more specifically, the armed forces, for the murder. Immense demonstrations occurred in the cities against Marcos and in protest at the sham official investigation of the assassination. The confusion led to a cancellation of a visit to Manila by President Reagan scheduled for late 1983.

The opposition *United Nationalist Democratic Organization (UNIDO)* succeeded in early 1984 in getting the constitution amended by referendum so as to restore the office of vice president, the purpose being to reduce the chances that the widely–disliked Mrs. Marcos might succeed her husband to the presidency. The document permitted the election of a vice president from a different political party than that of the president.

The opposition was divided, however, on whether to take part in National Assembly elections scheduled for May 1984. Marcos' *New Society Movement* won the elections, but the opposition did well— Mrs. Marcos' candidates for seats representing metropolitan Manila were all defeated. Twelve opposition leaders announced an anti–Marcos "unity" platform in late 1984, but events in 1985–1986 showed anything but unity.

After an unnecessarily lengthy inquiry, armed forces Chief of Staff General Fabian Ver and 25 others were indicted in January 1985 for complicity in the Aquino assassination; the trial began in February and continued for months. When all the evidence was in and the jury had retired to deliberate, the Philippine Supreme Court took the unheard of step of dismissing the charges on the ground that there was insufficient evidence. Ver had been replaced on an acting basis by the moderate and popular General Fidel Ramos.

By the fall of 1985 it became clear that the defendants in the Aquino case would be acquitted (as they were in December), and political tensions rose. Under American pressure, in early November Marcos called a presidential election for February 7, 1986. An opposition candidate, Mrs. Corazon Aquino, widow of the slain Benigno Aquino, soon attracted widespread support, especially in the cities. The communists boycotted the campaign and the elections.

Although Marcos was officially declared to have won the election, which had been monitored by large numbers of official and unofficial observers, mainly American, it soon became obvious that his supporters had been guilty of massive fraud, and Mrs. Aquino had actually won. Accordingly, the United States government switched its support from Marcos to Mrs. Aquino after mid–February. A group of army officers belonging to a military reform movement usually known by its acronym RAM then began to plan a *coup* against Marcos.

Getting wind of it, he concluded that it was the work of Defense Minister Enrile and Vice Chief of Staff Ramos and began to move against them. They and their supporters promptly came out in support of Mrs. Aquino. Jaime Cardinal Sin, Archbishop of Manila, who favored Mrs. Aquino, urged the faithful to block the streets of Manila to the passage of troops loyal to Marcos. This move was effective, and with an offer of asylum from the United States, provided he did not use force against his own people, Marcos left for Hawaii as the month ended. Mrs. Aquino was then inaugurated President.

President Aquino repealed Marcos' repressive regulations and released his political prisoners. She initiated steps to recover the enormous wealth he had stashed abroad, mainly in the United States and Switzerland. President Aquino and her middle class cabinet, faced with a pro–Marcos majority in the Assembly and the Supreme Court, then declared a "revolutionary" government in order to be better able to eliminate the legacy of Marcos' rule.

About six months after her election, President Aquino began to move against her major problems. She visited the U.S. in September, and Congress voted an extra $200 million in aid for the Philippines. She began work on an ambitious and difficult land reform program, which was badly needed. In late November she fired Defense Minister Juan Ponce Enrile, who had been seemingly threatening a military *coup* against her. At that time, Chief of Staff Fidel Ramos ensured that the armed forces remained loyal to President Aquino rather than supporting Enrile, while quietly pressing her at the same time to get rid of some other inefffective cabinet members and take a stronger line against the communists and their *New People's Army (NPA).*

After long negotiations, the communists agreed to a 60–day truce, beginning December 10, 1986. The *PKP* used its interlude of legality to make energetic propaganda in the cities, but it ended by probably alienating more people than it impressed. Accordingly, it refused to renew the ceasefire and resumed its offensive. President Aquino countered with an offer of amnesty to any insurgent who surrendered. In January 1987 another dissident movement, the (Muslim) *Moro National Liberation Front* (based in Mindinao), signed a peace agreement with the government; it had been negotiated in Saudi Arabia.

There were some serious disorders, partly stirred up by exiled ex–President Marcos in late January, just before a referendum was to be held on a new constitution, but they were suppressed.

President Aquino's constitution got an unexpectedly high vote (about 75% of those casting ballots). It limited the president to one six-year term, created a bicameral legislature, granted the courts the power of judicial review of laws and provided that the U.S. bases must be non–nuclear and could be continued after 1991 only on the basis of a treaty approved by at least two thirds of the Philippine Senate.

President Aquino's supporters won a sweeping victory in elections for the Senate and House of Representatives held in May 1987.

But in August of the same year, in the most serious of several attempts made up to that time to overthrow President Aquino, a colorful paratrooper, Colonel Gregorio (Rambo) Honasan, led an attempted *coup* against her. It failed due to energetic action by loyal forces under Chief of Staff Ramos (made Defense Secretary in January 1988). For a time it appeared that President Aquino's position might be untenable, and in the fall her main political opponents, especially Vice President Salvador Laurel and former Defense Secretary Juan Ponce Enrile, seemed to be moving to form a coalition against her.

The president, however, staged an impressive rally. In September 1987 she curbed the influence of two important advisers, Joker Arroyo and Teodoro Locsin, who were widely regarded as leftist. Laurel resigned as Foreign Minister and was replaced by Raul Manglapus. Regrettably, President Aquino removed an able Finance Secretary, Jaime Ongpin, who committed suicide in December. She raised military pay and met some of the other demands of the armed forces; these changes signaled a tougher, more conservative line intended to be more acceptable to the military and to the business community.

Other trends were not so favorable. Land reform was making only slow progress against entrenched rural interests.

Hon. Corazon Aquino

Communist insurgency continued to grow to the point where President Aquino was apparently considering proclaiming a state of emergency. Frequently brutal anti–communist vigilantes emerged in many areas.

President Aquino's candidates did well in local elections held in December 1987–January 1988, albeit not overwhelmingly so.

Philippine political life continued to be riddled with corruption on the part of elected and appointed officials. There was also intense partisanship. The lower house of Congress was subservient to the popular President Aquino, whereas the Senate, whose members are elected by the national electorate rather than from local constituencies, was highly independent. Vice President Salvador Laurel evidently want-

ed to succeed, or even unseat, President Aquino. Former President Marcos, seriously ill in Hawaii, wanted to return to the Philippines but had not been allowed to do so. He died in September 1989.

Imelda Marcos was acquitted by a jury in New York City principally because the alleged wrongdoing, if any, took place in the Philippines. The latest report on her is that she is interested in buying some sort of estate in a very wealthy section of Virginia.

In June 1988, Congress voted a moderate land reform program that managed to please neither the landlords nor the tenants. Social unrest and Communist insurgency continue. The latter has changed its shape somewhat in recent years in a more military direction, with numerous local victories. The *New People's Army* is supported by the large and influential *National Democratic Front,* which has a following not only in the cities but abroad. The government has found no real answer to the *NDF.* To cope with communist insurgency in the rural areas, it has developed a so–called triad strategy: military pressure, intelligence activity and civic action (public works, etc.). Overall, and despite continuing human rights violations by the military and by right wing vigilante groups, the counter-insurgency campaign seems to be progressing better than in earlier years. Local elections have been held, and defections from the Communist forces and captures of their leaders have increased.

There were two major issues in current relations with the U.S. One was the Multilateral Assistance Initiative" (MAI), a program of up to $10 billion in economic aid that the U.S. was trying to organize with American, Japanese and other funding. Some of the prospective contributors were not very enthusiastic, since the Philippine government was already sitting on some $3 billion in unused aid money and has been unable to recover any significant part of the huge fortune acquired by former President Marcos, who had been indicted in the U.S. on charges of racketeering. Secondly, the U.S. bases were highly controversial in the eyes of the Philippine political elite and intellectuals, although most of the public, the non–communist Asian governments, and even China favored them. After difficult negotiations, an agreement was reached in October 1988 under which the U.S. was to give $481 million in economic aid (one third of what the Philippine side had been demanding) in 1990 and again in 1991, when the current base agreement expired. Any new agreement would have to be ratified by the Philippine Senate, and perhaps by a popular referendum. In May 1988, the Senate voted a ban on storage of nuclear weapons on

Philippines

the bases, but it appeared that in practice they could still be taken through in transit. No one, Philippine or American, showed any interest in a vague proposal by General Secretary Mikhail Gorbachëv that the U.S. give up its Philippine bases in exchange for a Soviet withdrawal from Camranh Bay, Vietnam.

A series of developments in late 1989 and early 1990 heightened the general impression that under President Aquino's indecisive leadership, the country was drifting or even regressing. In early December the sixth and most serious attempted military *coup* against her was quelled, but mainly because U.S. combat aircraft unprecedentedly flew over the rebel positions. Talks with the United States on the future of the bases and on economic issues began at about the same time. They promised to be long and difficult. The American side wanted continued access even after the bases passed to Philippine control. Manila wanted to get as much money as possible out of the entire transaction. Filipinos employed at the bases were concerned about their continued employment at superior wages.

Political unrest and attempted military *coups* continued to be a serious problem. As the end of President Aquino's term approached, various political figures began to jockey for succession.

One of these figures, surprisingly, was Imelda Marcos, the widow of Ferdinand Marcos. She returned from exile in November 1991 and got the government's permission to bury her husband in his native province, Ilocos Norte, although not in Manila as she preferred. Although facing criminal proceedings on charges of corruption, she soon began to campaign as the champion of the poor, notwithstanding her vast fortune.

The *Communist Party*, whose insurgency had not been doing well in recent years, announced in May 1991 that it would agree to a ceasefire if the government refused to extend the lease on the U.S. bases beyond September, when the agreement covering them was to expire. Early in 1992, however, after American forces actually had begun to leave the bases, the PCP intensified its military operations.

In 1991 the Philippines suffered a series of natural disasters, such as a storm that struck the central islands in November and caused unusually heavy damage (runoff and mudslides) because of heavy illegal logging in the area. The most important disaster was a massive eruption of Mt. Pinatubo, a volcano about 55 miles north of Manila and only 10 miles from U.S.–controlled Clark Air Force Base, in June, because it largely determined the outcome of the long and complex negotiations between Manila and Washington

on the future of the U.S. bases in the Philippines, especialy Clark and the large naval base at Subic Bay.

Before the eruption, Manila had been demanding $825 million per year for seven years in aid, in exchange for continuation of the base agreement. Congress was unwilling to appropriate that much, and Washington had been offering $520 million per year over 10–12 years. The bases were very valuable for repair and refueling of ships and aircraft and for training of personnel; Filipino labor was plentiful, cheap, and skilled. The U.S. side was concerned more with continued access to the bases than with control of them.

As someone said, the volcano had its own agenda, and it was clearly not the same as that of the negotiators. The eruption, apparently the most powerful anywhere in the twentieth century, not only heavily damaged the town of Angeles, near Clark, but covered the base with about a foot of ash, rendering it virtually useless; Subic and its environs also suffered some damage.

After the eruption, some haggling continued between the two sides, but the negotiations were basically over. The bases seemed much less important to U.S. strategic interests since the collapse of the Soviet Union, the main regional threat. In September, the Philippine Senate, in a nationalistic mood, voted not to ratify an agreement incorporating the U.S.'s final offer (Clark to be turned over, Subic to be kept for ten more years for $203 million per year), and American forces began to withdraw from both Clark and Subic. The units being withdrawn were to be separated into smaller packages and dispersed to Singapore, Hawaii, and Alaska. The irony was that, in the Philippine elections scheduled for May 1992, the new Senate might well have voted to keep the bases, assuming that option still existed.

Politics and Government: On paper, the Philippine political system resembles that of the United States. Prior to 1987, the Philippines was governed under the U.S.–modeled 1935 constitution. The constitution provided for a bill of rights, a bicameral legislature, an independent judiciary and a president with a four year term.

A new constitution was approved on February 2, 1987. The president is now limited to one 6 year term, and close relatives of the president cannot be appointed to public office.

Both the legislature and the judiciary may review the legal reasons for the imposition of martial law. The constitution also provides for civil liberties and is basically very democratic in form.

The country has a House of Representatives and a Senate. Under the constitu-

tion Congress has the power to declare war, restrict presidential emergency powers and control the appropriation of revenue. The Senate has twenty–four members with six year terms with a limit of two consecutive terms. The House can have up to 250 members elected from legislative districts apportioned by population. Twenty percent of the seats are filled through a party–list system.

The Philippines has historically been a two party system. The *Nacionalista* and *Liberal* parties traded control of the government between 1946 and 1972. Both parties tended to serve the interests of the political elites in the country and were vehicles for elites and their personal followings. During much of the Marcos era there was no effective political party opposition. Strong opposition began to emerge around 1980 with the formation of UNIDO which had the backing of anti–Marcos elites. Benigno Aquino Jr. established LABAN ("Fight"), as a vehicle for his political ideas. The political party landscape fragmented somewhat during the Aquino years. Politics continues to be highly personalized. Support is given to individuals, not platforms, programs or ideologies.

This situation continued under President Ramos. In 1993 and 94, weak party discipline prevented the Ramos party, *Lakas–National Union of Christian Democrats (NUCD)*, and the *United Muslim Democrats of the Philippines (UMDP)* from using its large majority effectively in the House. To strengthen support for the president, especially in the Senate, *Lakas–NUCD* formed a coalition with the major opposition *LDP* party, in August 1994. The two parties had to agree on the candidates for the 12 Senate seats open in the May 1995 elections. This coalition spurred the other opposition parties, the *National People's Coalition* and the *People's Reform Party* to combine forces. The situation with regard to political parties will remain fluid and will be affected if proposed electoral reforms are passed or if a parliamentary system of government is adopted.

Like many other communities in Asia and elsewhere, Philippine politics is much influenced by the presence of influential "patron–client relationships." Essentially, this means that political life centers on relationships that are personal and hierarchical. Political relationships are also built on the concept of *"utang na loob,"* obligations of indebtedness. Politics is therefore frequently dominated by personal loyalty to a hierarchical group. Patrons must provide resources to their clients to keep their loyalty. This is a major cause of corruption in the Philippines. The client in the relationship is concerned only with what the patron can deliver.

In this type of environment, institutions

President Fidel Ramos

like interest groups, and political parties and other organizations that could unite large segments of society, are less effective than they might be. A farmer is loyal to the elite above him in society who can provide benefits. He is not loyal to his group, farmers, which could unite in a common cause to better the group's position in society through political action. Thus, the institutions which have at times been so effective in countries from South Korea to the United States, are of less value in the personalized political culture of the Philippines. It will be extremely hard for any leader, no matter how dedicated, to bring about real change and resolution to major problems.

Fidel V. Ramos was elected president of the Philippines in May 1992. However, as one of seven candidates, Ramos, in winning, received only 23.4% of the vote. His closest challenger, Miriam Defensor Santiago, screamed fraud and did manage to have the Supreme Court consider the charge. Ramos, in short, did not start off with a lot of support, though Mrs. Aquino backed him strongly. Since his election, President Ramos and his government have faced several significant challenges: the need to establish law and order, opposition to the current political process by groups including the *National Democratic Front* (representing the communists), the *Muslim National Liberation Front, the Muslim Islamic Liberation Front*, the military officers' group *RAM–YOU* and the continuing entrenched position of the old political elite.

In early 1996, most of these challenges were still present but somewhat diminished. Yet In April, members of the *Muslim*

Islamic Liberation Front (MILF) under the leadership of Abu Sayaff attacked the town of Appall on Mindanao. Fifty–seven people were killed. The *MILF* was looking like a bigger threat than had been previously predicted. The year also witnessed an outbreak of bank robberies and kidnappings in Manila.But for the first time in a quarter of a century there was also reason for many Filipinos to rejoice. In September President Ramos and the *MNLF* leader, Nur Misuari, finally concluded an agreement that would hopefully bring to an end the generation–long struggle which had taken more than 120,000 lives. Overcoming the opposition of minority Christian communities in the south, Ramos and Misuari agreed to form a special presidential council headed by Misuari which would have responsibility over development issues in fourteen of the southern provinces. The deal, part of a larger plan that included the formation of a more autonomous Muslim dominated region after three years, marked a major breakthrough for efforts to reinforce Philippine stability.

Foreign Policy: Philippine foreign policy has long focused on strengthening its long–standing relationship with the United States. But that has been modified in recent years. Some now favor downgrading relations with the United States, and emphasizing stronger ties with such countries as Japan, South Korea and Taiwan. The Philippines is also seeking stronger ties with its ASEAN (Association of Southeast Asian Nations) neighbors. That has not always been easy.

President Ramos has visited Indonesia to discuss the possibility of links between Mindanao in the southern Philippines, and Indonesia. Problems have persisted though, especially around a recent Philippine–hosted human rights conference about East Timor, which continues to resist Indonesian rule. President Ramos himself had disavowed the conference, barred some foreign participants from attending the meeting, and reaffirmed that the Philippines continued to recognize Indonesia's right to rule in East Timor. Happily, the Indonesian government was still willing to offer important help to President Ramos in his own efforts to bring the confrontation with the *MNLF* Muslim leadership to resolution.

Manila experienced strained relations in 1995 with both Singapore and China. By far, China's occupation of Mischief Reef in the South China Sea constituted the most serious problem. In early 1995, Manila discovered that one of the small islands in the Spratley chain about 150 miles off the Philippine coast had been occupied by members of the Chinese navy. Mischief Reef is in Philippine territorial waters.

In May 1995 Philippine military officials tried to take a boatload of journalists to see the reef. A Chinese patrol boat blocked their path. The Philippine navy then detained a number of Chinese fishermen who were illegally in the country's territorial waters. At the August meeting of the ASEAN Regional Forum, ARF, the ASEAN states spoke with one voice in raising concern about the Chinese occupation. Beijing subsequently agreed to deal with the conflicting claims in the South China Sea multilaterally.

Minutes after an earthquake in northern Luzon, a huge boulder crashed down the mountainside to block the highway
Photo by Jon Markham Morrow

Philippines

Thus, Manila would have its fellow ASEAN member states as partners in negotiations over the Spratley Islands. This was far more preferable than going one–on–one with the PRC. Nevertheless, the problem of conflicting claims, among six different countries, remains a serious and difficult problem.

Relations with Singapore were also ruffled in February 1995, when the latter executed Flor Contemplacion, a Philippine overseas worker, for a double murder, over the appeal of President Ramos. Many Filipinos believe Flor was framed. Manila recalled its ambassador. The real casualty of the affair was Philippine Foreign Secretary Roberto Romulo, whom Ramos sacked in the aftermath. Many felt the government was being "soft on Singapore." By early 1996, though, Singapore and Manila had reestablished relations again.

Harvesting bananas in Cebu, Philippines   World Bank photo

**His Eminence
Jaime Cardinal Sin**

Culture And Society

Like so much of the developing world the contrasts in society are dramatic. Manila, a busy, modern city, has a sophisticated cultural atmosphere which can compare with most Western cities. In recent years, a building boom has made it look even more like some of its economically vibrant East and Southeast Asian neighbors. But many of the peasants live in poverty as extreme as anywhere in the world. The Philippines remain one of the most stratified countries in the world, a society where forty percent of the population can not meet their basic nutritional and other needs while the richest 10% hold 36% of all personal income.

The influence of the Catholic Church is very important. The church controls enormous holdings and Archbishop Jaime Cardinal Sin, who was instrumental in helping to end the Marcos dictatorship, is very influential. The church has played an important role in condemning corrupt political practices and campaigning for greater support for the poor. Not surprisingly the church's strong stand against birth control has made it very difficult for the Philippines to limit the country's soaring population.

Philippine women have not been influential in their country's politics and the careers of women such as Imelda Marcos or Corazon Aquino are more representative of the power of family connections than women's influence. In the work place their salaries are often one third that of men. Philippine women often travel abroad to find work to support themselves and their family. They go to places like Singapore and the Gulf States to serve as domestic servants and, as often in the United States, as nurses. Within the country domestic violence against women, as elsewhere, is common. Divorce is not an option within Philippine law.

The Filipino language, a refinement of the Tagalog spoken by the Philippine Malays, is the official language. Spanish is spoken by a dwindling number of descendants of the older aristocracy left by the Spaniards. Educated Filipinos cherish the English language as well as the esteem for formal education and academic degrees common to the United States—the economy has difficulty in absorbing all of those who have been trained to the fullest extent of their ability. For example, many Filipino medical doctors and nurses have settled in the United States.

Economy

The Philippine Republic is fairly rich in natural resources and, with the exception of the Manila plain, not overpopulated. The post–World War II economy was quite weak until recently when it started showing signs of the sort of economic vitality that many of its neighbors had demonstrated during the 1980s. There remain, of course real problems.

Much of the wealth still winds up in the hands of a small group of rich individuals and families. Corruption and inflation have been a continuing problem.

Under former President Marcos' *New Society*, a limited land reform program was in progress. Landlords, as part of the establishment, were well compensated by the government for what land they had lost, and this further inflated the economy. President Marcos sold highly profitable monopolies of such commodities as coconuts and sugar to his friends, a system known to the opposition as "croney capitalism." In addition, a number of properties and businesses were taken illegally by the president's family members and supporters from Philippine businessmen who were not pro–Marcos. After President Marcos was forced from office, some individuals were able to regain lost assets. For example, the Lopez family regained control of the *Manila Times*.

Philippines

Under President Aquino, a less stifling, but still harmful version of the "crony capitalism" that had flourished under Marcos emerged, and few of the benefits of reviving economic growth have been enjoyed by the poorer members of Philippine society. Today the estimated annual per capita national income is still only $1,184.

Happily her successor, the present President, Fidal (SP) Ramos, has been much more successful with economic reforms and has carried out a significant amount of land reform and other economic efforts. Called Philippines 2000, the government is striving to change its traditional agrarian–based, paternalistic economy to an industrial and market driven one. It has moved, for example to liberalize rules for investment, trade and banking among other economic activities.

Since 1994 the economy has been finally showing signs of strength. If the 5.1% growth figure of 1994 pales compared to double digit numbers of some of its neighbors, economic indicators are finally showing substantive growth.

The Philippines' economy had another good year in 1995 having posted a 5.8% growth rate for the year; 1996 came in at more than 7% with inflation dropping and the budget now in surplus for the third year in a row.

Many problems still exit. The economy of the Republic remains inadequate in relation to a rapidly rising population. The persistence of corruption and crime gives everyone cause for concern. The real problem with the Philippine economy is that the expansion is not benefitting the truly poor who live in the Patayas slum in Manila, or in the provinces. Construction is booming around Manila and Makati, but job creation is still small. Violent crime and kidnaping for ransom is common and tax evasion is a national sport. But for the first time in many years these developments are being balanced by significant accomplishments.

Despite earlier fears, the economy has also weathered well the departure of the Americans. The former American Clark Air Force Base is now operating as a civilian charter airport, and the former naval base at Subic Bay is serving as a successful tax free port and industrial base. The American–based FEDEX company has even made it its regional hub! Even tourists are starting to flock to the base to enjoy the amenities built for the departed servicemen. The new treaty with the Muslim community is likely to bring many economic benefits as well. By the time President Ramos hosted the APAC meeting in November 1996 he had plenty of reason to be pleased. And the facilities at the Subic Bay were ready to convince the arriving dignitaries that the Philippines, so long the laggard in the regime's economic spurt, was ready to make its own effort to become a new "Asian Tiger!"

The Future: The Ramos government has a chance to bring about significant change to the country. Unlike Mrs. Aquino, the president is not from the aristocracy. He can more easily deal with those who have been involved in the systematic looting of the country. It is encouraging to note that already the Ramos administration has turned over more land to the peasants than had been done in the previous 20 years. The treaty with the *MNLF* had also been accomplished. The turn–around in the Philippine economy bodes well for the country. If his new ally Nur Misuari of the Muslim community can bring the more radical of his own co–religionists along in the new agreements, there will be plenty of room for even greater optimism.

President Ramos has done a good job. He will serve his country well by not pushing for constitutional changes which would allow him to run for a second term in office although a substantial number of people favor this. As 1996 drew to a close, his opponents in the Philippine Senate were moving to make any such effort more difficult anyway.

A panoramic view of the Sierra Madre slopes.

The Republic of Singapore

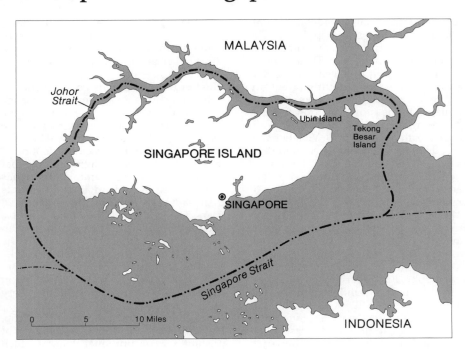

Area: 239 sq. mi. (618 sq. km., somewhat smaller than New York City).

Population: 3.4 million.

Capital City: Singapore (Pop. 2.79 million, estimated).

Climate: Tropically hot and humid.

Neighboring Countries: Malaysia (North); Indonesia (South).

Official Languages: Chinese (Mandarin dialect), Malay, Tamil, English.

Ethnic Background: Chinese (about 77%); Malay 14% Indian (about 7%).

Principal Religions: Buddhism, Hinduism, Islam, Christianity.

Main Exports (to Malaysia, U.S., Japan): Rubber, petroleum, tin, manufactured goods.

Main Imports (from Japan, U.S., Malaysia): Manufactured goods, petroleum.

Currency: Singapore Dollar.

Former Colonial Status: Possession of the British East India Company (1819–1867), British Crown Colony (1867–1958), occupied by the Japanese (1941–1945), internally self–governing (1958–1963).

National Day: August 9, 1965 (Independence Day).

Chief of State: Ong Teng Cheong, President (took office September 1993).

Head of Government: Goh Chok Tong, Prime Minister (1990).

Dominant Political Figure: Lee Kuan Yew, Senior Minister.

National Flag: Divided horizontally, with a white crescent moon and five white stars on a red field at the top and a white bottom.

Annual Per Capita GDP Income: U.S. $23,565.

The small island of Singapore is separated from Johor State at the southern tip of West Malaysia by a narrow strait of water; road and railway bridges provide access to the mainland. Although tropical, the island is highly urbanized. The city occupies the more agreeable part of the island on the southeast coast. Its harbor is naturally a good one, and it lies at the crossroads of Southeast Asia at one end of the Straits of Malacca. This is the best and shortest passage between the Indian Ocean and the South China Sea, and Singapore has been an important naval base and commercial port for 175 years.

History

Prior to the arrival of Europeans, Singapore was a small part of the Malay world, inhabited by people of Polynesian, Mongol, Indian and Caucasian mixed ancestry that blended smoothly into the civilizations of Malaya and Indonesia. The Dutch virtually ignored Singapore when they arrived in the 17th century because of their preoccupation with the then superior harbors at Malacca and Penang on the western coast of the Malay Peninsula.

Sir Thomas Stamford Raffles of the British East India Company occupied the island in 1819 after realizing the commercial possibilities of the harbor. It was made a Crown Colony in 1867. In spite of Dutch competition based on neighboring Java and Sumatra, the colony began to achieve the size of a major commercial port. The opening of the Suez Canal in 1869 attracted even heavier traffic from Europe to the Straits of Malacca. At the same time, the rubber and tin resources of Malaya were being developed and needed facilities to reach the world.

This commercial development also resulted in the migration of many Chinese to the island. They quickly became the majority ethnic group as they labored to process rubber and tin. Singapore became the principal British stronghold in the region. From their base there the British participated in the colonial rivalry underway in Southeast Asia in the late 19th and early 20th centuries.

Prime Minister Goh Chok Tong

Hon. Lee Kuan Yew

Singapore

Downtown Singapore

A large British naval base was constructed in the 1920's equipped with coastal defenses intended to protect it from attack by sea. But when World War II began their plans came to naught. Three days after the attack on Pearl Harbor in 1941, Japanese torpedo planes sank the Prince of Wales and the Repulse, two mammoth British warships which had been dispatched to Singapore. An invasion of Malaya was promptly undertaken by a large Japanese army highly trained in jungle warfare. It fell to the invaders within four weeks and the siege of Singapore began. The British held out for two weeks before the Japanese finally captured Singapore and 60,000 prisoners on February 15, 1942, in one of the worst military defeats ever suffered by Great Britain.

As elsewhere in Southeast Asia, the Japanese often mistreated those they had conquered, particularly those of Chinese origin. This behavior was ineffective; the Japanese were ultimately isolated from Singapore and other holdings in Southeast Asia by American sea and air action. The

Singapore

British peacefully returned to the island when Japan collapsed in 1945.

After the war Britain decided to continue to keep Singapore separate from Malaya to avoid upsetting the rather slim Malay majority on the mainland. Britain itself though began to slowly withdraw. It did retain its bases, but decreased their size as it embarked on a withdrawal. It maintained control over Singapore's external relations, but permitted increasing degrees of internal self–government. The government nurtured by the British was faced with serious civil strife in the mid–1950's which was promoted by labor unions and student organizations, both communist controlled, but it was able to maintain order.

After a new constitution was adopted, the leftist *People's Action Party*, the *PAP*, which had some communist members, came to power in an electoral landslide in 1959. The new Prime Minister, Lee Kuan Yew, though he had ties to the communist left quickly moved to lessen their potential influence. Sensing British and Malayan concerns over his election, he made strenuous efforts to create goodwill with them. But efforts to calm external concerns did not help in Lee's relations with his former communist allies.

A widespread and ambitious program of socialistic economic development and social welfare programs was instituted which caused the communists to redouble their efforts to seize control of the government—they feared a possible increase in popularity of the *People's Action Party*. During those early years of the new state the principal tensions were within the *People's Action Party*—between the moderate socialists who favored more ties with Malaysia and their more extremist communist allies. Eventually the *PAP*s principal leftists quit to form the *Barisan Sosialis Party*, which did well in local elections held in 1961.

The apparent strength of the left in Singapore was a major source of concern to Britain and Malaya. Prime Minister Tunku Abdul Rahman of Malaya immediately proposed that Malaya, Singapore and the Borneo territories of Sabah and Sarawak be joined into the Federation of Malaysia. His purpose was twofold: to protect the stability and progress of the entire region and to control the leftist trend in Singapore; his plan was vigorously supported by the British. Prime Minister Tunku had reason to be concerned for had Singapore become a communist state, Malaya would have suffered a serious economic blow because since the island processed and shipped the bulk of the rubber and tin which produced most of Malaya's foreign exchange. It would as well have posed a political threat.

In spite of opposition by the *Barisan Sosialis Party*, the *Malayan Communist Party*, and the vehement opposition of Indonesia's President Sukarno, the Federation of Malaysia came into existence in 1963. Sukarno immediately declared that Indonesia was in a state of "confrontation" (a sort of undeclared, irregular war) with Malaysia, severing all trade relations. Singapore suffered somewhat from this step, since Indonesia had been one of its most important trading partners, but Indonesia suffered equally, if not more. Actually, the economic needs of both gave rise to a widespread smuggling operation which helped to offset the effect of the official boycott.

The short–lived union of Singapore with the Federation of Malaysia came to an end in 1965. The Federation may have solved the immediate problems of a potential communist takeover, but it did not resolve the more basic antagonism between the Malays and Chinese which has long been the greatest internal problem within Malaysia. The Malay–dominated government of the Federation preferred to deal at arms–length with the Chinese–controlled regime on the island rather than add more Chinese to the Federation's population. Lee Kuan Yew's vision of a more multi–cultural Malaysian Federation was clearly threatening to the Malay leaders of Kuala Lumpur. When he energetically tried to extend the activities of the *People's Action Party* to mainland Malaya and to exert greater influence throughout the Federation, matters came to a head. Singapore was forced out of the Federation, left to survive on its own.

Birth of a New City

Although the separation of Singapore from the Federation of Malaysia was described as a matter of mutual consent, in reality Singapore was confronted with a demand to withdraw—it had no choice but to do so. Within Singapore leaders like Lee Kuan Yew had serious doubts that the newly independent country could survive on its own. There was little choice but to try.

Over the next years the immediate problem for Singapore was survival itself, but happily the new city–state had the advantages of excellent leadership under Lee Kuan Yew and a population committed to accomplishing that goal.

Over the next years, under the paternalistic leadership of Prime Minister Lee and *PAP*, Singapore did more than survive. It prospered and became one of the most successful economies of Southeast Asia with a major commitment to improving the living standards of its people. By late century its population enjoyed the highest standard of living in the region and was one of the safest societies. Some though have come to believe in recent years that Singapore's citizens have paid a high price in political freedoms for *PAP*'s economic successes.

Political developments during the early 1960s also complemented *PAP*'s ability to dominate the new nation's political life. In elections held in 1963, the *People's Action Party* elected 39 representatives to 23 from the *Barisan Sosialis Party*. But even then Prime Minister Lee Kuan Yew so dominated the political scene in Singapore that the members of the opposition party angrily stalked out of the Parliament in 1966.

Since then the *People's Action Party* has been almost completely in charge. A new leftist opposition party formed in April 1971 and was successful in electing one member in 1981. In 1984 it doubled its holding to two, but that has hardly been a dent on the *PAP*'s monopoly of political power.

In 1986, the debates in parliament began to be televised. This gave wide publicity to the speeches of one of the only two opposition members, an articulate ethnic Indian, J.B. Jeyaretnam, who in September of that year was expelled from the body for having allegedly defamed the impartiality of Singapore's judiciary.

Over the years, the government, which maintains a form of censorship, has tried to punish foreign publications which contain articles it does not like. These punishments have ranged from financial pressures to outright law suits.

Less than three years ago, in 1995, Christopher Lingle, an American academic teaching at the National University of Singapore (NUS), and four *International Herald Tribune* employees, were charged with criminal defamation for writing and printing an article in that influential daily newspaper which referred to intolerant Asian regimes and questioned the independence of their judiciaries. The *Herald* was eventually found guilty of libel and fined $674,000!

As concerns about Singapore's immediate survival have given way to economic success, Prime Minister Lee, who ran the country directly till 1990, began to concern himself with slowing the spread of what he believed were negative Western values. Distressed by the materialistic outlook of Singapore's "yuppies," he has tried to revive a modern version of Confucianism. He and other government officials have enthusiastically embraced Confucianism's more communal values and hierarchal perspective as more suitable for Singapore's predominantly Chinese population than Western individualism.

Nevertheless, while this emphasis on a Chinese approach to values has also encouraged the study of Mandarin Chinese in the schools of Singapore, the government has treated with considerable disdain and hostility those it perceives as pushing multi–cultural Singapore too far in the direction of being an exclusively Chinese nation.

Over the years Prime Minister Lee has viewed Singapore as fragile because of its ethnic diversity and vulnerable because of its small size as compared with its neighbors. Accordingly, he and his colleagues have done whatever they considered necessary for domestic and external security in the face of these threats. The armed forces are large for the size of the country and are impressively modern. The Internal Security Act, inherited from the British, is used by the political police, known as the Internal Security Department, to control dissent and the press.

Government and Politics

Lee Kuan Yew, in office since 1959, retired as Prime Minister in November 1990 in favor of his hand–picked successor, Deputy Prime Minister Goh Chok Tong.

The change though made little difference in the political realities of Singapore. Lee Kuan Yew remained in the government with the title of "Senior Minister." The Goh Chok Tong government has followed the path of the previous government.

By late 1993 Ong Teng Cheong assumed the revamped and enhanced position of president after receiving 58.7% of the vote in the August 29 election. The election was important because it made it clear that the "old guard" of the *People's Action Party* still had a firm hand on the affairs of state. Both the president–elect and his opponent, Accountant General Chua Kim Yeow, were establishment candidates. Ong was a former deputy prime minister and *PAP* member. Alternative candidates not approved by the government were not allowed to compete.

The elections of January 1996 saw Prime Minister Goh more genuinely emerge out from under Lee Kuan Yew's shadow. The Prime Minister was even said to appear much more in charge than after his earlier electoral effort in 1991. This time *PAP* even won a greater electorial victory than previously. In fact, they won not only 65% of

the votes (up from 61% in 1991) but 81 of the 83 possible seats in the parliament!

But the election was more than a triumph of Prime Minister's Goh's new authority. *PAP* and the government used all their powers to ensure a victory. They even announced that the government planned improvements in the city's housing infrastructure within which most of the city's citizens live and often own apartments. But the government warned that those districts that voted against *PAP* would be last on the waiting list for improvements!

The government's heavy hand and commitment to authoritarian rule is not the only thing that slows the growth of a more inclusive political system. *PAP* has been in power so long and has been so successful in improving living standards that few Singapore citizens actually trust the opposition. Well aware of that sentiment, the opposition parties have been careful not to field a full list of candidates during elections. For example, in the elections of early January 1997 the opposition only contested elections in 36 of the possible 83 electoral seats. The logic has been

Rush hour in Singapore

Singapore

A young boy in Singapore
WORLD BANK Photo

that if the voters know that *PAP* would win regardless of how they voted, the electorate would be more willing to allow an opposition to emerge within the parliament. But that apparently did not work well enough to make a difference. As mentioned previously only two opposition politicians made it into the parliament this year.

Foreign Policy

Singapore, as an independent mini–state, cannot hope to survive without friends. For years the government accepted the analogy of the poison shrimp which might be swallowed up but at great risk. In recent years, however, the strategy has been to make the country so valuable to the region that no one would wish its booming economy destroyed because of the repercussions which would be felt throughout the area. This strategy has succeeded. Singapore is one of the world's busiest ports and is the center of economic activity in Southeast Asia. It intends to keep its value high by always being the best.

In 1994, Singapore continued to champion free trade and greater economic co-operation throughout the ASEAN region. In October Singapore was the venue for the third Europe–East Asia summit the focus of which was to find ways to increase trade and investment between the two continents.

Singapore was also the site for the Five Power Defense Arrangement (FPDA) meeting in September. Members Singapore, Malaysia, Australia, New Zealand, and Great Britain, agreed on measures to improve defense capabilities for the FPDA. Singapore also hosted the FPDA annual naval exercise, "Star Fish."

Relations with Malaysia though can at times be complicated. Singapore has come to an agreement with Malaysia on their international sea boundary. A flap over a Malaysian tariff on Singapore petro–chemicals was recently put to rest also. Unfortunately though, more problems surfaced early in 1997 when Senior Minister Lee Kuan Yew made disparaging remarks about crime problems in one of the Malaysian cities closest to Singapore. The comments were not welcomed and Lee later apologized. Considering that Singapore gets most of its food and water from Malaysia, having a good relationship is especially important.

For more than a year, since the spring of 1995, relations were also strained with the Philippines over the hanging of a Philippine citizen, Flor Contemplacion, for the murder of another Filipino. The two countries disagreed over the facts surrounding the case. President Ramos and Prime Minister Goh agreed that bi–lateral relations should not be damaged; nevertheless, they were for a time. Ramos in particular was under some pressure to defend the national honor. He requested that the Singapore ambassador be recalled from Manila. Singapore, in the interest of good relations, agreed. Relations have finally been normalized again.

Perhaps the most profound aspect of Singapore's foreign relations is the influence it has had on the region as a model of economic and social growth under a non–communist but authoritarian regime. Despite Western preferences and claims that a free and vibrant economy can not exist without a politically open system, Lee Kuan Yew and the *PAP* seem to demonstrate that they *can*. It is an example that countries as close as Malaysia and as far as the People's Republic have watched closely.

Culture

Despite impressions held elsewhere, Singapore is a more multi–cultural city than many people realize. The vast majority of the population is certainly Chinese, but they immigrated from several parts of southern China and thus speak mutually unintelligible dialects, perhaps one of the reasons, aside from commercial, that learning "Mandarin" Chinese is encouraged. That is also one of the reasons English is used as the official language of instruction, business and in government. Moreover, the community includes a significant minority of Malays and South Asians as well. It is for that reason that the government has been so hostile against those who have encouraged a greater use of Chinese over other languages.

The central feature of society in Singapore today is that it is centered around the industry of a bustling port and its very urban citizens who enjoy the highest standard of living of the region. Rather than living in the countryside, they live in apartment blocks that the government built and that they have been encouraged to purchase.

An Engineered Society?

Singapore's leadership has made extraordinary improvements in the life of its citizens. It has done so at a price that many would find excessive. The government has intervened in almost every aspect of the life of its citizens, thus creating an astoundingly regulated society. There are rules for practically everything from gum–chewing to landscaping and cleanliness.

As a result of the government's almost puritanical attitude, Singapore is one of the safest and cleanest places in the world. Economic prosperity, however, has not been sufficient to keep the country's best and brightest at home. Significant numbers of highly educated young citizens have left the country in search of greater political freedom. While some have returned, the fact that prosperity alone is not sufficient should give the government cause to ponder how much authoritarianism is appropriate for a modern, well–educated society.

Education is highly admired in Singapore and the society is moving smoothly into the computer age. One third of the households have personal computers and a quarter of them are connected to the Internet. Unfortunately for the government, that has opened up yet another vehicle of potential disruption that the government would rather avoid.

Women in Singapore have the same civil rights as men and these were written into law in the early 1960s when the Women's Charter was enacted.

In contrast to some other parts of Asia the local minority population of Muslim women are covered by most of the provisions of the Charter though in matters of polygamy and divorce Islamic law prevails. The government has also mandated that women should get equal pay for equal work and no longer allows separate pay scales.

Inequalities do exist. For example, women do not have the same rights males do in passing on their citizenship automatically to their children. Moreover, medical benefits available to the families of male civil servants are denied to families of female employees.

Overall, the island has acquired a genuinely cosmopolitan atmosphere imported from the four corners of the earth because of its status as a major international port which lies at the crossroads of Asia. For a modern urban society Singapore is as well a very safe city whose crime rates have gone down every year for the last seven! That is an accomplishment many urban communities would like to boast of!

Economy

Singapore is heavily dependent on foreign trade and investment which it is doing its best to promote. There has been considerable industrial development, heavy as well as light, in recent years. Since the mid–1980s the economy has been growing at a rate of about 8% a year. In 1988, because of its high level of development and its various contributions to the U.S.'s trade imbalance, much to its annoyance, Singapore lost its preferential tariff status under the U.S.'s Generalized System of Preferences (GSP).

In the mid 1990s the growth rates have averaged around nine percent though they have been slowing down lately. Wages have increased but at least inflation has been relatively low. It has among the highest annual per capita GDP in the world at $23,565.

However, success can bring problems. A strong currency could weaken exports. The island currently has a glut of empty retail spaces and suffers from very high rents. Wages are high and rising because labor is chronically short. Prices are rising. Not surprisingly there has been a slump in retail sales within the city and some big retailers have pulled back on their operations.

Future

The success of Singapore may have less to do with the distinct values its leaders talk about than it does with the country's manageable size and optimum location. Some educated youth already find the tradeoff between economic prosperity and restricted political and social freedom difficult. This will probably only become intensified over time.

Two factors may well weaken *PAP*'s control over the long run. First, a weakening economy might make the population less willing to allow the government so much control and, second, the arrival to adulthood of a generation that takes the material advantages of life in Singapore for granted and thus does not fear to lose them, may soon demand greater political participation. Nevertheless, Singapore does indeed have many things which America, with all its social problems of recent years, has lost. However, a lighter touch at the helm of the ship of state will not destroy these advantages and may insure their survival.

Traffic system at rush hours to reduce congestion

WORLD BANK Photo

The Kingdom of Thailand (before 1935 known as Siam)

Bustling traffic in Chiang Mai

Area: 198,455 sq. mi. (514,820 sq. mi.,more than twice the size of Oregon).

Population: 60 million (estimated).

Capital City: Bangkok (Pop. 5 million, estimated).

Climate: Tropically hot with a wet monsoon season (May–October), dry and increasingly hot (November–April).

Neighboring Countries: Malaysia (South); Burma (Northwest); Laos (Northeast); Cambodia (Southeast).

Official Language: Thai (about 75%).

Other Principal Tongues: Chinese (about 14%); other (about 11%).

Ethnic Background: Thai (about 75%); Chinese (about 14%); Malay (about 4%); inland tribal groups (about 2%); Cambodian refugees (about 2%); other (about 3%).

Principal Religions: *Theravada* Buddhism, Islam.

Main Exports (to Japan, U.S., Singapore): Rice, sugar, corn, rubber, tin, timber.

Main Imports (from Japan, U.S., Saudi Arabia): Machinery and transport equipment, petroleum, chemicals, fertilizer.

Currency: Baht.

Former Political Status: Siam avoided becoming a European colony; it was a nominal ally of Japan during World War II.

National Day: December 10th (Constitution Day).

Chief of State: His Majesty King Bhumibol Adulyadej (b. 1927).

Head of Government: Chavalit Yongchaiyudh, Prime Minister (since Nov. 1996).

National Flag: Five horizontal stripes from top to bottom; red, white, blue (wider than the others),white and red.

Per Capita Income: GDP income $6,100.

The broad central plain of Thailand, through which flows the Chao Phraya River, is the most fertile and productive area of the country and contains the principal cities, including Bangkok. Viewed from the foothills which are found on the western edge of the plain, the land resembles an almost endless window with countless "panes of glass" when the precisely divided rice paddies are flooded with water.

The North and Northwest are more mountainous, and are covered with jungles containing timber and mineral resources. Valuable teakwood is still brought from the jungle on the tusks of the Asian elephant. The northeast region is dominated by the arid Korat Plateau. Ample rainfall occurs in the plateau, but it is not absorbed by the sandstone soil— it quickly collects into streams and rivers and runs to the sea instead of enriching the land. More people live here than can be supported by the limited agriculture that is possible.

The southern region consists of the narrow Kra Isthmus which is hot and oppressively humid, and the coastal belt, where quantities of rubber are produced by Thailand's Malay minority.

History

People of Thai origin today not only inhabit Thailand but also live in the adjacent regions of all of Thailand's neighbors with the exception of Malaysia. The original home of these people was in southwest China, where they were ruled by a highly organized kingdom in the 7th century A.D. The pressure of the Chinese and later the Mongols caused a migration of the Thais southward; they founded a state in what is now northern Thailand.

In sharp contrast to governmental traditions in China, the Thai kings ruled as autocratic divine beings. Although, they have not ruled directly for much of the 20th century, elements of this earlier tradition continue in the on–going reverence

the Thai people still hold for their monarchy.

During centuries of slow expansion they were eventually able to crush the Khmer Empire in neighboring Cambodia. In the 16th century, Siam, as it was then called, was conquered by the Burmese. Apart from sporadic contact by French merchants, the Europeans did not enter the area during the early centuries of exploration and colonization.

There was another Burmese invasion in 1767, but shortly thereafter Burma was invaded by the Manchu empire of China, enabling the Siamese to expel them. The present reigning dynasty came to power in 1782 and moved the capital city to the more secure location of Bangkok. Siam again emerged as a strong state. But though Siam's relations were already complicated, they were about to get much more so.

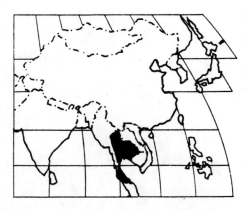

The Arrival of the West

Early in the 19th century, Siam began to have more extensive contacts, commercial and otherwise, with Westerners. Moreover, the British gradually established control over Burma and the French asserted their power over Vietnam. Laos and Cambodia had formerly been tributary states of Siam, but the French were ultimately able to combine them with Vietnam in their colony of Indochina. Thus, Siam was surrounded by the British on the west, the French on the east and the Manchu empire of China on the north.

Nevertheless Siam managed to avoid becoming a European colony by a lucky combination of factors, first, the advantages of having not one but two European colonial powers on their borders (who could then be played off against each other) and enlightened leadership which moved to strengthen the country through an increasing degree of modernization. It was a combination too few other non–Western states enjoyed.

In Siam's case, two important monarchs, during the critical late nineteenth and early 20th century, helped shield them from the worst of imperialism. The first was Mongkut, who reigned in the critical period of the mid–nineteenth century, and his son Chulalongkorn who followed him in power. It was Mongkut who was the monarch described in the book *Anna and the King of Siam* and in the musical *The King and I.*

Phra Maha Chulalongkorn, his son, was king from 1868 to 1910, and gained fame not only by abolishing Siam's feudal system, but by modernizing the government and army and introducing such conveniences as the telegraph and railroad. He also paid an extended visit to the European capitals.

Both monarchs, father and son, recognized the seriousness of the Western threat, took significant efforts to educate themselves in Western ways and to find ways to lessen the growth of Western power in Siam. Overall their policies were

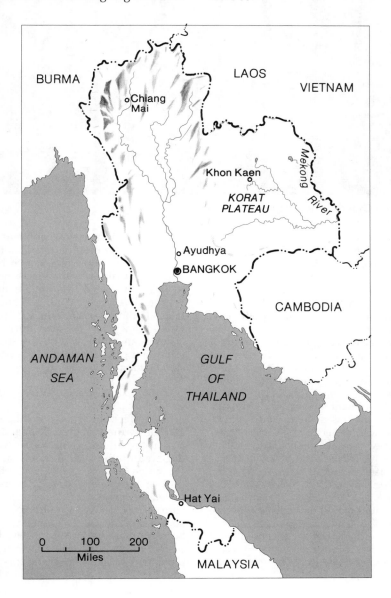

Thailand

The Grand Palace, Bangkok

a combination of tactical acceptance of various legal and territorial demands made by the Europeans while working overall to maintain the ultimate sovereignty of the Siamese state.

There were some later treaties in 1904–1907 which adjusted the borders with Laos and Cambodia. Under these treaties, regions were traded back and forth between France and Siam. In order to keep other colonial powers out of Siam, France and Britain established "spheres of influence"—the French east of the Chao Phraya River and the British west of the river.

As a result of its somewhat limited, but significant, modernization program, and the fact that it escaped being a colony of a European power, Thailand today lacks the sense of resentment toward the industrialized nations that many people feel in the countries of the former colonial world.

A New Political System

After World War I there was a period of extravagant spending by the royal gov-ernment, which was followed by a world–wide economic depression. This created tensions and discontent within Thailand and gave rise to intense political activity. The result was a bloodless overthrow of the autocratic monarchy in 1932 by a combination of civilian politicians and military leaders.

The two groups cooperated in the adoption of a constitution which limited the power of the king and established a parliamentary form of government. The first Prime Minister was a brilliant lawyer named Pridi Phanomyong. The king, dissatisfied with this system, abdicated in 1935, and was succeeded by his ten–year–old nephew and a regency council. This and other unsettling conditions, including the increased power of Japan in Asia, led to the overthrow of Pridi by Marshal Pibul Songgram. As World War II approached Marshal Pibul would prove to be especially nationalistic and pro–Japanese.

In theory the country continued to be governed by a coalition consisting of the Prime Minister, the military and Luang Pradit, the foreign minister. As the mili-tary acquired increasing political power, they displayed their nationalism by such means as legislation aimed at curbing the role of the Chinese commercial community and changing the nation's name from Siam to Thailand, meaning "Land of the Free." In the years since the 1932 coup the Thai military, like the later Burmese and Indonesian military, would insist on an important place for itself in national decision making.

The Pacific War

Three weeks after the bombing of Pearl Harbor by the Japanese, Thailand signed a treaty of alliance with Japan. War was declared on the United States and Great Britain on January 25, 1942. With the support of Japanese troops, Thailand compelled the French to cede some border territories in Laos and Cambodia. The four southern states of Thailand, which had been given to the British in Malaya at the turn of the century, were now returned to Thailand by the Japanese after they seized the British colony of Burma. Thailand

Thailand

probably had little choice in cooperating with the armies of imperial Japan. The Japanese certainly had the means to impose their will on Thailand and had demonstrated their strength in early clashes with the Thai forces.

As the war began to turn against Japan, the Thai government, which has a long history of protecting itself through power politics, began to change sides. An anti–Japanese guerrilla movement arose, and American military intelligence officers were able to operate almost openly in Bangkok during the last months of the war.

Pibul, the pro–Japanese premier, resigned in 1944 in favor of his rival Pridi, the former premier, who was more acceptable to the increasingly victorious Allies. At the end of the war, Britain took the position that Thailand was an enemy country and compelled payment of reparations in the form of rice, which was sent to Malaya. The U.S. however viewed Thailand as a more reluctant Japanese ally, and was able to persuade the British to adopt a similar policy.

The Postwar Years

Thailand's most immediate problem in the postwar years was to reintegrate itself into the world community after having been allied with Imperialist Japan and to establish a stable government. The former proved easier than the latter. The lands taken from France and Britain during the war were returned and Thailand was admitted to the UN in 1946.

Political stability however proved more difficult. The king, who had only recently been enthroned, was found dead of a gunshot wound in 1946. Premier Pridi, who was accused, apparently falsely, of having played some part in the slaying, was deposed. The army, still led by Pibul, again seized power. It was a pattern that was to continue through the 1990s.

The Cold War

Initially it appeared uncertain as to what position Thailand would take in the Korean war. Once it decided to support the American–backed UN troops, it began to receive U.S. military aid. This further strengthened the political position of the army in domestic affairs, making it more and more powerful within Thailand and, given the economic support of the wealthy Americans, helping to build the country's economic infrastructure.

The early 1950s saw many leaders like Nehru of India and Sukarno of Indonesia attempting to build a non–aligned movement during the height of the Cold War. Some governments accepted this position, but Thailand chose to align itself more directly with the Americans. Thailand became a founding member of the SEATO, the Southeast Asian Treaty Organization (designed to be an Asian equivalent of NATO) and supported the American war in Vietnam.

Premier Pibul did permit freer discussion of political issues and actually began to encourage a growth of neutralism. Concerned about potential Communist Chinese influence he also took steps against the local Chinese community that traditionally had been involved in the economy but refrained from taking part in politics.

Nevertheless, Communist gains in Laos between 1960 and 1962 created more uneasiness in Thailand, which was dispelled when the U.S. pledged direct assistance in the event SEATO failed to fully support Thailand.

Pibul was overthrown in 1958 by Marshal Sarit, who kept Thailand firmly in an anti–communist posture. The country had an orderly, stable and not terribly intrusive government, at least not very oppressive government compared to the records of some other regimes in the region. As was true in so many nations, the military leader was able to accumulate a vast private fortune through corruption.

Less effective military leadership continued after 1963 under subsequent leaders. Reliance was placed upon the ability of the popular royal family to maintain the unity of the Thai people, as well as on an increased degree of official respect shown for Buddhism and its various organizations. However, communist–inspired unrest in the poverty–stricken northeast region became more serious. The government treated this as a genuine threat, though perhaps partly to obtain additional American aid.

Once the United States fully committed to the struggle in Vietnam, Thailand permitted the Americans to use its air bases for attacks on North Vietnam and the Viet Cong. Thailand itself sent about 11,000 troops to fight in Vietnam and Laos. Having sided with the wealthy Americans, Thailand was able to gain enormous economic aid which helped in it own development and, as before, especially assisted the Thai military continue to assert itself.

The reaction from the communist side

Geese raised on a poultry farm south of Bangkok

155

Thailand

The Royal Family of Thailand

was predictable—as Thailand increased its assistance to the U.S. and South Vietnam, the communists stepped up their guerrilla activities within the country. The increased U.S. military buildup in Thailand was thus paralleled by a greater flow of U.S. aid to the Thai armed forces. But if Thailand's clear association with the anti–communist side was clear in these years its own domestic politics were less so.

The National Assembly was dissolved in 1968, and there was no representative body in Thailand. Eventually, a constitution was drafted by a Constituent Assembly and promulgated by the King in mid–1968. Elections of 1969 gave the *United Thai People's Party*, the government party, the victory. The Senate was then appointed by the government.

But, a powerful military, unhappy with developments, suspended the parliament and reshuffled the cabinet. In 1972 a new constitution was proclaimed under which 299 members of a National Assembly were all appointed by the government, i.e. the army.

A Democratic Experience, 1973–1976

But the next year, the army–dominated government was toppled by student demonstrations that had the support of the King and at least part of the Army itself. A civilian government was then ushered in, committed to greater freedom and reform. It was yet another step, such as in 1932, when the autocratic monarchy had ended, that gave Thailand the possibility of moving toward a more democratic form of government. And in this case, it was partially as a result of the intervention of the monarchy itself which had not played a political role since 1932. As the new government was formed in 1973 Thailand seemed on the verge of taking yet another step toward more inclusive political decision making.

But true parliamentary government was not to develop in Thailand at least not during those years. A combination of insecurity caused by the growing strength of Communism in the region—Vietnam had been unified under Hanoi and Cambodia taken over the *Khmer Rouge*—as well as unhappiness about the open political battles within the new democratic government moved the military to once again reassert itself and stage another coup in 1976. In October of that year, with the backing of the King, the government was overthrown and the democratic constitution suspended.

Over the next years Thailand's politics have been moved by several factors—the emerging democratic movement, which had had its first real chance to govern in the mid 1970s, the ever influential Thai military and the King who has continued to be revered and has demonstrated a willingness to intervene in the governing system when he deems it appropriate.

An informal power sharing arrangement between the army and civilian politicians and officials has been common over the last generation. Army leadership has divided between those willing to work with civilians and those who are not. Rule has shifted between civilian and military–dominated governments, with and without ex–generals in the premiership, and outright military rule. Corruption has been commonplace. One cannot detect any significant change in the most recent events but there have been signs in the 1990s that the military's domination of Thai politics is increasingly challenged by the growth of a more politically conscious middle class population.

Another civilian government was brought down because of corruption charges by the military in a 1991 coup. Rule then shifted to the military dominated National Peacekeeping Council. In

March 1992, a three party coalition favored by the Council won control of the government with 53% of the seats in the lower house of parliament. The NPC then appointed all 270 members of the upper house with most having military backgrounds or connections.

But when agreement could not be achieved on a new prime minister, the leader of the "junta," General Suchinda Kraprayoon, a key figure in the coup, and an individual especially unpopular with those who supported democracy, stepped into the post. Public demonstrations against Suchinda then led to severe repression by the Thai military. The level of violence against the civilian population was unparalleled in the constitutional period (since 1932).

The King stepped in to calm the crisis. On May 20, Suchinda appeared on national television kneeling before King Bhumibol. He was ordered to settle the crisis peacefully. After a short period of "caretaker" government, new elections were held on September 13, 1992. Chuan Leekpai was chosen as prime minister. The constitution now required that the prime minister be chosen from the lower house

of parliament. The new government was ruled by a five–party coalition. This made it difficult to proceed with the legislative agenda which centered on constitutional reform. Nevertheless, the army had been warned. It could no longer assume the civilian population would simply go along with anything it attempted.

In May 1995, Prime Minister Chuan Leekpai was forced to dissolve parliament when the *Palang Dharma* party pulled out of the ruling five party coalition. Elections took place on the following July which saw the Prime Minister's coalition lose. Thai voters then elected the *Chart Thai* party's Banharn Silpa–Archa as prime minister. The Banharn government was built around a seven party coalition led by his party, *Chart Thai*, and the *Palang Dharma* which defected from Chuan's coalition prior to the election. The coalition won 169 seats in the House of Representatives.

But the new government came under fire almost immediately for a kickback scheme involving the Prime Minister's party and a Swedish submarine manufacturer, and for protecting a minister involved in vote–buying.

Moreover, the military's recent reticence

to intervene seemed less sure when a military radio broadcast criticizing the government for its management of the economy raised concerns in Bangkok and abroad. A disagreement over military promotions between the Minister of Defense and the Army Commanding General, Wimol Wongwanich, also worsened civil–military relations. To make matters worse, the King criticized the government for the traffic chaos in Bangkok. By mid–1996 prospects were not looking bright for the Banharn government and by November new elections brought Chavalit Yongchaiyudh, the Defense Minister, from the previous government, to power.

As a former Armed Forces Chief, Chavalit has close ties not only to the military but to Burma's military junta as well. The new leader is now 65 and says he is committed to cleaning up corruption. That is probably a good idea since his own party, the *New Aspiration Party*, is said to have been the most involved in buying votes during the recent elections!

Unfortunately, political corruption and vote buying is a problem for more than merely the new prime minister's party. As

An informally dressed King Bhumibol speaks with villagers in northern Thailand

Thailand

Houses in the vicinity of Bangkok

has been the case in so many other countries, Thai electoral politics have been driven by money. In fact, enormous sums of money are spent to influence elections including even the purchase of votes in rural areas of the country.

Some have even called for a clean–up campaign of the sort that has taken hold in South Korea, though, given the tendency of such efforts to backfire on those who begin them, it is hard to believe that many would invite the sort of problems that have beset Seoul over the last year. Nevertheless, to address the problem a group of former parliamentary members and legal experts have been chosen to write a new constitution. For the moment, the question is how soon they will compete their work and how quickly the new prime minister will have to defend this government at the polls again.

Today, the Thai political system could be called semi–democratic. The military is still very influential but apparently somewhat less willing than in the past to intervene. As we have seen, Thailand has struggled to evolve a modern workable political system since 1932. The first four decades of the constitutional period were dominated largely by the military. Civilian–led governments though have become more common since 1970s. But they have not always been very stable. During

the last two and a half years Thailand has had three different Prime Ministers!

The Thai political system has also suffered from a lack of a legitimate means for dealing with the succession of power. This explains the large number of coups which have occurred. The military has often been unwilling to leave policy decisions to the civilian sector. In order for civilian government to work, several things must take place. First, corruption must be curtailed. As Thailand's educated middle class grows, this segment of society, like elements of the military, will no longer accept the old way of doing things. The political parties and the elites who run them must find another way to advance their agendas if they are to survive. Secondly, national politics must be expanded beyond Bangkok to all parts of the country. Mass political participation is essential to a well–run political system. Should the civilian politicians be unable to rise to the occasion, the military will, sooner or later, find a reason to intervene once more.

Foreign Policy

Thailand's foreign relations are driven by its geographic location and pragmatism. It has a fascinating history of keeping enemies at bay through diplomatic and other means which generally have not in-

volved the direct use of force. The country's location means that Bangkok in some ways pays more attention to Burma and the Indo–China states, Laos, Cambodia and Vietnam, than to its long–standing ASEAN partners. China too is important. Thai officials profess not to be worried about China's growing military might.

However, there is concern over the potential for large scale Chinese migration into the country and possible impact from a flood of inexpensive products from the north which could undercut sectors of the Thai economy. These concerns are long term and unpublicized but they are real.

Nevertheless, rather than shut China out, Thailand wants to see relations between the two countries expand. Because of its well integrated overseas Chinese community which dominates the business sector, Thai officials and businessmen feel they have an advantage over other Southeast Asian states in opening up new economic links with China, and that they can even provide a link for the other ASEAN states to the "middle kingdom." In contrast to many other Southeast nations, the local Chinese community also takes an active part in politics. In 1995, the huge explosion in the study of Mandarin was welcomed in Bangkok.

The defeat of the Karen rebels in Burma in January 1995, sent thousands of refugees across the Thai border and altered relations between the two countries. The Burmese believed the Thais were aiding the Karens. Bangkok was upset because of Burmese military raids on refugee camps inside Thai territory. In March, Burmese officials closed a major border crossing at Mae Sod which resulted in a significant economic loss for businesses on the Thai side of the line. Later, Thai fisherman killed six Burmese fisherman off the southern coast of Thailand. This resulted in another border closing. A visit to Rangoon by the Thai Defense minister in September may have eased tensions. However, additional fence–mending needs to take place.

High ranking Thai officials, civilian and military, deny that the country's policies have favored the *Khmer Rouge*. It is quite likely though that individual civilians and military officers have been involved in aiding the *Khmer Rouge* for monetary reward. Whether one accepts Bangkok's position or not, it should be understood that Thailand has legitimate security concerns regarding its eastern border. Bangkok does not believe that the dual government arrangement in Phnom Penh can last indefinitely. And, the stronger of Cambodia's two prime ministers, Hun Sen, is probably not a favorite in Bangkok. He was the head of the government during the Vietnamese occupation. Talks have begun though between Thai officials and their Cambodian counterparts through the vehicle of a Thai–Cambodian Joint Commission that first met in May of 1995.

Other tensions, including concerns over competing offshore territorial claims have also impacted in the region. In May 1995, Thai and Vietnamese navy patrols exchanged gunfire off the Thai coast. Thai fishing boats and crews were taken by the Vietnamese. It is worth noting that Burma and Malaysia have also seized Thai fishing boats. The Thai–Vietnamese event was played down owing to the fact that Vietnam was then in the process of moving toward "observer" status in ASEAN, the Association of Southeast Asian Nations, of which Thailand is a founding member. Thailand and Vietnam have been in negotiations over their disputed exclusive economic zones (EEZ). As resources become more scarce in the sea, expect such incidents to increase.

The general trend in Thailand's foreign relations in recent years has been toward improving relations with its neighbors including Cambodia, Vietnam and the People's Republic of China. There has been as well more enthusiasm for challenging the United States on its demands for more protection for intellectual copyrights. This later point is an example of the more typical trend of international relations in recent years to emphasize more economic issues than in the past.

Culture

Shortly after their arrival in Southeast Asia the Thai were converted to the *Theravada* school of Buddhism, which came from the island of Sri Lanka (Ceylon). The numerous colorful festivals and the participating monks almost completely dominate the traditions of the people. Thai architecture is unique and is as extremely colorful and elaborate as the clothing, dancing and sports typical in the Chao Phraya River Valley.

The customs and traditions of the larger cities and Bangkok have been modified somewhat by increased contacts with the West, particularly with Americans. This undoubtedly is true from the point of view of the people who cherish their individuality and distinctive culture. Certainly Thailand is among those developed countries with the greatest divergence between the very urbanized middle classes of Bangkok and the peasant farmers in much of the rest of the country.

Women

As elsewhere Thai women have grown up in a region that generally values boys more than girls Today, the situation of women in Thailand is especially complex

and combines both examples of considerable progress and proof of their continuing lack of control over their own lives.

For Thai women, though the military have allowed a few into their upper ranks, girls are still not allowed to attend the nation's military academies. Women have fewer rights than men in obtaining documents like passports, and domestic law favors husbands. Men for example have more rights under the divorce laws. Politically women are less than 10% of those appointed to the Thai senate. On the other hand young women have far more access to education today, and half of the college graduates are female.

Where the problem is especially acute is not among Thai women themselves but among the thousands of young women from Thailand's poorer neighbors, especially countries like Vietnam and Burma who are lured to Bangkok with offers of jobs and then find themselves in virtual debt slavery in the brothels of that huge city.

In early 1994 an ominous cloud appeared on the horizon. A report by an international organization revealed that Thailand now has the fastest growing AIDS population in all of Asia. In spite of a very successful birth control program a number of years ago, there has been little public education about AIDS until recently. Figures for young women especially in northern Thailand are very high. In Bangkok, perhaps 50% of the prostitute

community is infected. To make matters worse, a new more powerful strain of AIDS was discovered in Thailand in 1995.

The Thai government has attempted to move against the traffickers, and various international organizations have attempted to improve the situation of these young women, but the situation remains a very tragic one today.

Economy

In recent years the Thai economy has been among the fastest growing in the East Asia region. If the economy continues to grow at its present rate, the country could well become the "fifth Tiger," joining Taiwan, Hong Kong, Singapore and South Korea. In fact, according to the World Bank, Thailand's growth between 1985 and 1994 was a robust 8.2%, even better than South Korea in those years.

This last year the economy received an enormous boost when it enticed General Motors to sign a deal for a new car plant that is worth over $750 million dollars and promises 1500 new jobs for its people. And the Japanese are expected to raise their investments in Thailand by an additional 25% during 1997.

But the country does face serious problems with its natural resources and limited technological base. Because so much of the country's timber has been cut, erosion is rampant. The quality of the soil is being negatively effected, and flooding is com-

Sculptured topiary elephants on the grounds of the Royal Summer Palace.

Courtesy: Marilynn and Mark Swenson

Thailand

Carving teak furniture, one of Chiang Mai's cottage industries.

Courtesy: Marilynn and Mark Swenson

mon. Happily, while the environment remains a critical problem and will be for decades to come, there is now visible evidence of government efforts. One can now see miles of newly planted trees along major highways. Like other countries of the region, Thailand also faces shortages in the personnel needed to run a modern technological society. It clearly needs more college graduates with technical training.

In the first half of the 1990's, it appeared that the infrastructure of the country was simply unable to keep pace with the rapidly growing economy. Efforts are only now underway to put a mass transit system into place in the horrendously congested Bangkok area, but that is not expected to be completed until at least next year. For years visitors to the city have had to put up with some of the worst traffic in the world. Today the situation is improving. Parts of the Bangkok expressway are now open, and it is now possible to get from one part of the city to another without planning an all day excursion.

Progress in building up the country's infrastructure base in a logical way is clearly being made. New factories are being located outside the Bangkok area in industrial parks. Each is required to have its own waste water treatment plant. The water coming out of these plants today is far cleaner than the water taken in for use by the industries.

In addition to the environmental impact, there should also be an equally important impact on the distribution of income throughout the country as better paying jobs move out of the capital to different regions of the country. Sixty percent of the labor force is still in agriculture, while the sector only produces 12% of the national GDP. The need for new opportunities is evident.

Inflation has been floating in the 4–5.9–6% in recent years, not high by many standards but a cause for some concern. During late 1997 export figures were weakening as well, which adds strains on the new government. One major problem is that Thais are spending too much and saving too little. The savings rate of 34% of GDP looks very good but is sustained by corporations and the government. The savings rate for individuals for 1995 was 7.3% of GDP, compared with 15% back in 1989. The average citizen has gone on a buying spree which is running up imports, in-

creasing them by 28.4% to $675 billion in 1995. The merchandise deficit for 1995 was approximately $13.4 billion. The current account continues to look good but only because of foreign investment in the Thai stock market.

To boost tourism the government even has plans to rebuild the famous "railroad of death" whose construction during World War II brought the death of so many prisoners, and which was made famous later by the Hollywood film, "The Bridge Over the River Kwai."

The Future

A basic question which Thailand must decide is what is to be the role of the Thai military in the future of the country. Military interference in Thai politics has often been very heavy–handed and could be so again as well. Also important will be the ability of the monarchy to continue its respected status into the next generation. That is important because the current monarch, King Bhumibol Adulyadej (b. 1927), has often served as an important symbol of stability during various crises.

Boats on the Chao Phya River

The Socialist Republic of Vietnam

Secondary school students being instructed in computer techniques.

Area: 128,190 sq. mi. (329,707 sq. km., about 1/3 smaller than California).

Population: 71,800,000 (1993 est.).

Capital City: Hanoi (Pop. 2.5 million, estimated).

Climate: Subtropical, with cooler weather in the higher elevations. The Mekong Delta area is hot and humid.

Neighboring Countries: China (North); Laos and Cambodia (West).

Official Language: Vietnamese.

Other Principal Tongues: French, Chinese.

Ethnic Background: Vietnamese (about 85%); Thai, Cambodian, Lao, Chinese, tribesmen (about 15%).

Principal Religions: Buddhism, Taoism, Confucianism, subdivided into many sects; Roman Catholic Christianity is a strong element in the South; animism, Islam and Protestant Christianity.

Main Exports (to Japan, Hong Kong, Malaysia, Thailand, Singapore, and Indonesia, principally): Agricultural products, coal, minerals and oil.

Main Imports (Japan, Hong Kong, Indonesia, and Singapore): Steel products, railroad equipment, chemicals, medicines.

Currency: Dong.

Former Colonial Status: French colony (1883–1954); occupied by the Japanese (1942–1945); anti–French struggle (1945–1954); civil war (1954–1973).

National Day: July 21, 1954. The government recognizes September 2, 1945 when independence from the French was declared and the Democratic Republic of Vietnam was proclaimed.

Chief of State: Le Duc Anh, President (since October 1992). Pronounced Lay Duke An.

Head of Government: Vo Van Kiet, Prime Minister (Since August 1991). Pronounced Voh Van Key–yet.

Chairman, Communist Party: This post has been vacant since the death of Ho Chi Minh in 1969.

General Secretary, Communist Party: Do Muoi. Pronounced Doe Moy.

National Flag: A red field with a five pointed yellow star in the center.

Per Capita GDP Income: $1,310.

The map of Vietnam is shaped like a dumbbell. The northern "bell" is an area formerly known as Tonkin—it is quite mountainous, with peaks as high as 10,315 feet, close to the southern Chinese border. The mountains gradually diminish in height as they approach the plains and river deltas closest to the Gulf of Tonkin.

The Red River originates in the lofty plateaus of the Chinese province of Yunnan, some 8,000 feet above sea level, and forms the border with China for a distance of about thirty miles. When it enters northern Vietnam it is 260 feet above sea level, descending through a narrow gorge until it widens; after being joined with the River Claire it meanders 93 miles to the sea, flowing in a shifting, irregular course that is 140 miles of curving and twisting water.

The two principal cities of northern Vietnam, Hanoi and Haiphong, are situated on the river and flooded by its waters during the wet season each year—waters which are colored red by the silt washing to the sea from the highlands. It is in this river delta region that the food of northern Vietnam is produced by peasants laboring in the fields with limited tools used by their forebears.

The "bar" of the dumbbell is a thin, coastal plain, closely confined on the west by the Annam Cordillera, a north–south range of mountains forming a natural barrier between Vietnam and Laos to the west. This coastal belt is narrow and somewhat inhospitable. Its lands are not enriched by the silt of any large river, and the typhoons of the South China Sea frequently do much damage.

Vietnam

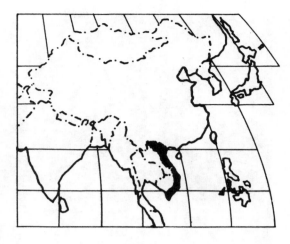

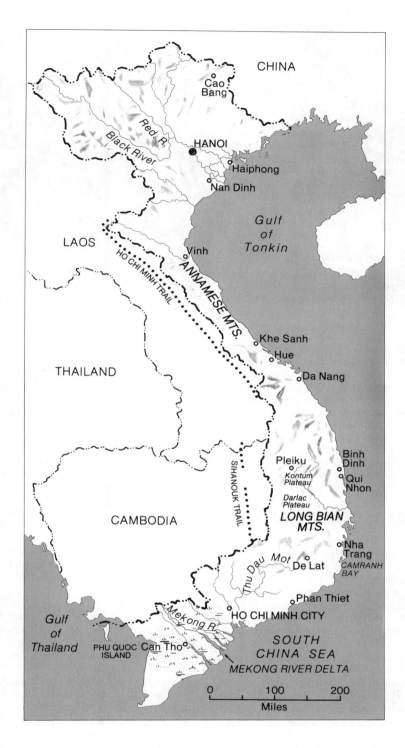

in the Mekong River Delta to produce large surpluses of food in the past and present. Traditionally, two harvests of wet paddy rice are possible each year—a feat possible in very few places of the world. In contrast, only dry field rice can be grown in parts of northern Vietnam.

History

Linguistically the Vietnamese speak a language similar to Chinese and in appearance most closely resemble other Asian peoples of mongoloid origin. They began to move southward from central and southern China in the last centuries B.C., entering what is now Vietnam shortly before the modern era. Conquered by the powerful Han dynasty of China about 100 B.C., they remained a part of the Chinese empire for the next millennium.

It was natural that during these many centuries the Vietnamese adopted much of the Chinese political system and cultural patterns, but they actually feel a combination of respect, dislike and fear toward the Chinese. Through history, the Vietnamese have tried to simultaneously be "better Chinese than the Chinese" while trying to define Vietnam in terms of what is not China.

After the collapse of the Tang dynasty in China in the early 10th century, the Vietnamese broke away from direct Chinese control. They avoided further conflict with China by acknowledging themselves to be a tributary state until conquered by the French in the late 19th century.

In the late 15th century, the Vietnamese conquered lands to the south occupied by the Chams, who spoke a language similar to that of Indonesia and had adopted many of India's cultural patterns, including Hinduism and Buddhism. By the 18th century they began to colonize the Mekong River Delta after seizing the kingdom of Funan, also an Indian type of state.

The lower "bell" starts with an area of central highland plateaus which are heavily forested and inhabited by more traditional peoples who till the limited available land after clearing it by burning. These highlands gradually give way to the Mekong Delta, where Ho Chi Minh City (formerly Saigon) is located.

The Mekong River starts in remote Tibet where snows gradually melt in the thin, icy air, gathering into small streams.

Before reaching Vietnam, the waters travel almost 3,000 miles through some of the most rugged country in the world. The river is yellow and sluggish by the time it enters the country—the tides of the sea are felt as far back as Phnom Penh in Cambodia during the dry season, and even further upriver during the wet months each year.

Intensive agriculture, dominated by rice production, has enabled the people living

Vietnam

Town on the Mekong River

French Colonialism

French interest in Indochina, the name given to the eastern portion of mainland Southeast Asia, began in the 18th century. Initially taking the form of commercial and missionary contacts, the French effort did not become serious until the mid–19th century. Forces of Napoleon III conquered Vietnam in a series of military campaigns, beginning in the South and working slowly northward. Initially, the French navy was far more interested in the region than the French government but over time the national commitment grew. The proclamation of a protectorate over the Annamese (Vietnamese) state in 1883 was followed by a short war with the Chinese to force the Manchu emperors to recognize the end of the tributary status of Annam.

The French divided their newly won possession into three segments: Tonkin in the North, Annam in the narrow middle belt and highland plateaus of the South and the colony of Cochin China in the Mekong Delta. These three areas were ruled by a governor general who also presided over Cambodia and Laos after 1887.

Actual administration of the colonies was by the French during the colonial period, although an imperial court was permitted to exist in Annam. The French introduced a narrow gauge railroad from Hanoi to Kunming in China which allowed them to extract mineral wealth from the North. In addition, intensive cultivation methods were introduced to produce large quantities of rubber.

During the early colonial period the French encouraged the migration of people from Tonkin in the North to the delta of Cochin China; immigrant Chinese were also permitted in the southern colony though at times the European businessmen there resented their competition.

Considerable effort was put into the promotion of French culture among the Vietnamese. As a result, an upper class of Vietnamese eventually emerged that was fluent in French, at home in French culture, and often Roman Catholic, but usually bitterly resentful of French political domination. It was a pattern that was followed frequently throughout the colonized world.

World Wars and Nationalist Struggles

Shortly after World War I, a nationalist group, composed of people supported by the French–speaking upper class emerged, competing with a communist movement led by a dedicated patriot and communist known as Ho Chi Minh. Both of these movements attempted unsuccessful armed uprisings against the French in 1930. The communists survived by going underground. Ho also strengthened his position by betraying some of his nationalist rivals to the French police. Once the Second World War had begun, the Japanese took French Indochina by default after Germany installed the puppet French Vichy government. Japan demanded the right to land forces in the area, which was granted by the French. Within three months the Japanese controlled all of northern Vietnam. In July 1941 they occupied the South as well.

In 1943 Ho Chi Minh was able to gain the support of Nationalist Chinese generals in southern China for what was supposed to be an anti–Japanese guerrilla movement. It turned out to really be an anti–French movement, since the Japanese nominally administered the country through the colonialists. This guerrilla movement had been formed by Ho in 1941 and was called the *Viet Minh*.

In 1945, the Japanese ousted the local French authorities whom they correctly suspected of being in contact with General de Gaulle and the Allies. Direct Japanese authority though was short–lived—surrender came within six months. At the Potsdam conference in 1945, the Allied powers decided to divide Vietnam at the 16th parallel for the purpose of disarming and evacuating the Japanese. The southern region was to be occupied by the British and the north to be occupied by the Nationalist Chinese. If this had not been done before the Japanese troops had gone home, it is probable that Ho Chi Minh would have seized control of all of Vietnam in 1945.

Ho, recognizing the moment he had been waiting for had finally come, hastily proclaimed the Democratic Republic of Vietnam at Hanoi on September 2, 1945—the same day that the surrender of the Japanese was signed on the U.S. Battleship Missouri in Tokyo Bay. Shortly thereafter the forces of the Chinese Nationalists moved into the northern region.

Ho expanded his power in the rural areas of the North, eliminating Vietnamese Nationalist rivals and managing to co–exist uneasily with the Chinese occupation forces which gave every indication of hoping to remain in Vietnam.

Meanwhile in the south, the British suppressed activity by the *Viet Minh* and quickly returned the area to the French. Seeking a withdrawal of the Chinese in the North, Ho and the French put pressure on them. Fortuitously, the outbreak of civil war in China helped instigate a Chinese withdrawal in early 1946.

Ho permitted the French to re–enter northern Vietnam, promising to keep the Democratic Republic of Vietnam within the French Union, so long as its autonomy was respected and providing it was allowed to control all of Vietnam. He certainly wanted French economic aid, but the chief reason for this attitude was very probably Stalin's desires at the time. The Russians wanted a French communist victory at the polls in France, and did not wish to alienate French voters by supporting a communist revolt in Vietnam.

An Anti–Colonial Struggle

The French colonial regime however refused to allow *Viet Minh* control of Cochin China. Moreover, some of its most important officials showed considerable bad faith in dealing with Ho. By the end of 1946, fighting erupted between the French and the *Viet Minh*, who retreated to the mountains above Hanoi to conduct a guerrilla war. In an effort to find a political cover for their desire to reestablish their former colony, the French selected Bao Dai, the hereditary Emperor of Annam and a descendant of the royal family which had once ruled from a massive palace at Hue. Bao Dai finally accepted the French offer in 1946. He became Provisional President and later permanent chief of state of a government obviously organized by the French to maintain their power in Indochina. The arrangement hardly pleased real nationalists like Ho, and the struggle continued.

The American attitude toward Vietnam in the immediate aftermath of World War II was ambivalent. On one hand America had had a long–term commitment to anti–colonialism, and FDR especially had long made it clear that he did not favor the simple resumption of European colonies in Asia after the war. These American attitudes were well known. In fact, as early as 1919 the young Ho Chi Minh had attempted unsuccessfully to meet President Wilson at the Paris Versailles conference to discuss Vietnam with the influential American president who was so associated with the idea of "national self–determination." A generation later, even as Ho proclaimed the independence of Vietnam after World War II, he chose phrases from the American Declaration of Independence and still hoped to gain U.S. support for his fledgling nation.

But in the years after World War II there was also an interest among the Americans in strengthening their erstwhile allies the French, and the French wanted to regain their hold over Indochina. As the tensions between East and West grew, American attitudes hardened. After the development of the Cold War, Ho's nationalist credentials loomed far less large in minds of American decision–makers than his equally strong commitment to communism. Once the Cold War had developed, Americans would develop a strong antipathy for Ho and his movement. However, it would be another generation before they would act directly on those attitudes.

In early 1950, the *Viet Minh* received diplomatic recognition from newly communist China. With Chinese military aid, they cleared French troops from the border areas of northern Vietnam later in that year. What had been an internal, colonial struggle now became in the minds of many Western decision–makers, the major theater of the Cold War in Asia, a fact which led to increased involvement of the United States and of the People's Republic.

France, which had initially had trouble convincing the Americans to support their efforts to reestablish their control over Vietnam now had little trouble convincing those same Americans that France was now fighting, as the U.S. was in Korea, on the front lines of the Cold War against communist expansion. Ho Chi Minh, a nationalist and communist, had not changed but the context in which he was viewed by the powerful Americans had.

Nevertheless, by the spring of 1953, the French prospects in Vietnam were bleak— the approaching end of the Korean war was expected to enable greater Chinese effort in Vietnam. In desperation, the French granted further political, economic, and military concessions to the non–communist Vietnamese state and substantially increased their own military efforts. Their purpose was not to defeat the *Viet Minh*, since such a goal was unrealistic, but rather to obtain a "face saving" political settlement. The U.S., the Soviet Union, Britain and France decided that a conference should be held in the spring of 1954 at Geneva, Switzerland, to deal with the questions of Indochina and Korea. But developments in the battlefield were moving faster than diplomacy.

Dienbienphu

The French had fortified a position at Dienbienphu in northwest Vietnam in response to a *Viet Minh* thrust into neighboring Laos. The *Viet Minh* then surrounded the French with artillery and mortars supplied by the Chinese and laid siege to the French camp. Although the decision to make Dienbienphu the central symbol of the struggle over Vietnam only grew slowly, the battle eventually grew into one that

Ho Chi Minh leaves the French Foreign Ministry, July 1946

Vietnam

Ho Chi Minh

symbolized the entire Franco–Vietnamese war. Overly confident, the French assumed their position within a valley surrounded by soldiers who held higher ground, would not be a problem. They were wrong. The *Viet Minh* quickly destroyed the air strip to prevent reinforcements and supplies from being sent in, and the siege began in earnest. Even as the battle raged, many within the American administration argued that as the symbolism of Dienbienphu grew, the United States should intervene. Though there was considerable opposition to doing so unilaterally, Washington did go so far as to approach London about a joint effort to save the French. But Winston Churchill, again the British Prime Minister, declined. The French were left to fight alone. The tiny base fell on May 7, 1954, the day before the matter of Indochina was to come before the Geneva conference.

There were few times in recent history when the fate of a small country so depended on world politics. The French wanted to get out of Indochina on any reasonable basis. The Soviet Union did not want to press France to the extent that it would join the European Defense Community, a multi–country army then being proposed. Russia desired even less a direct clash with the U.S., which had only recently completed a massive series of hydrogen bomb tests in the Pacific. The People's Republic of China also wished to avoid conflict with the U.S. and apparently did not want Ho Chi Minh to achieve too much power.

The Geneva Settlement

Ho Chi Minh's delegation to the conference arrived with a demand that the three nations of Indochina be treated in such a manner that would have produced a communist victory not only in Vietnam, but also in Cambodia and Laos. But the Chinese delegation conceded that a final settlement would treat the three countries separately. Ultimately, the final settlement contained some minor concessions to the communist movement in Laos, but none in Cambodia.

Vietnam was divided at the 17th parallel, considerably further to the north than had been demanded by Ho Chi Minh. Elections were scheduled for mid–1956, to be held in both regions. Military details of withdrawal, etc., were left to the French and Vietnamese. This was a defeat for Ho, who desired immediate elections before a non–communist government could solidify itself in the South. He was sure of victory in the North, since he was credited with expelling the French colonial government. In fact, it was generally agreed by most observers, including the Americans, that Ho Chi Minh, the long time leader of the Vietnamese struggle for independence, would easily win the scheduled elections. Ho appeared posed to win at the ballot box what he had largely won on the battlefield already.

In order to exclude American military forces from Indochina, the settlement enjoined any foreign power from maintaining forces in Vietnam. A general political agreement was included in the final version in which many things were left subject to interpretation. The U.S., unhappy with the settlement which appeared likely to bring a unified Vietnam under communist control into being, declined to sign the agreement. The Chinese, although angered by this refusal, agreed to accept an informal American promise not to "disturb" the agreement by force. The settlement was then "adopted" without actually being signed by the representative of any nation in July 1954.

Ho Chi Minh's regime promptly took over North Vietnam from the French. It began to build a strong and effective regime with large amounts of economic and military aid from the Soviet Union and China. Exhibiting revolutionary zeal, the new government embarked on an extremely brutal program of collectivization which soon cost the party considerable popularity. In fact, the program provoked a peasant revolt in Nghe An, the southernmost province, which had to be suppressed by government troops in 1956. Ho was forced to moderate his programs in order to regain his popular support.

The U.S. and South Vietnam

Nearly everyone at the Geneva conference had expected South Vietnam to collapse, or to go communist via the ballot box. Bao Dai had no real authority and was under the influence of corrupt military leaders. In mid–1954 however he appointed Ngo Dinh Diem, premier. Diem, an energetic Catholic and committed nationalist, had strong ties to the Americans. In fact he had only just recently returned from an extended stay in the United States. Having appointed the anti–communist Diem, Bao Dai then resumed his luxurious life in France. Diem later deposed him.

In October 1956 Diem proclaimed South Vietnam a republic and assumed the office of president. From the time of his appointment, Diem had enjoyed the support of prominent U.S. officials who hoped to strengthen his position enough to allow him to pose as a non–communist alternative to Ho Chi Minh.

Diem also received the support of the several hundred thousand Catholic refugees who flooded into the South in 1954. He also gained the allegiance of the traditionally corrupt army, and defeated the dissidents of the two main hostile religious sects.

Not surprisingly, the United States backed Diem's 1956 decision against holding the national elections called for in the Geneva Convention and in his efforts to establish South Vietnam as a separate country. In fact, seeing Diem's regime as a way to stop the unification of the country under Ho Chi Minh, which elections would have probably brought about, the U.S. offered massive amounts of military and economic aid. It had earlier supported the French effort against Ho; now that effort would grow larger and more direct.

As might have been expected, North Vietnam was furious and called for international action against Diem, but this received no support from the Soviets or the Chinese. Initially hoping that Diem's regime would literally collapse from its own weight of dishonesty and corruption, Ho discouraged the communist guerrillas, who had remained within South Vietnam after the Geneva division of the country, from taking action. But in 1957, calling themselves *Viet Cong*, the rebels undertook a terrorist campaign to force village support of their communist movement.

Diem and his conservatives responded as might be expected—a virtual police state was set up to smother all opposition, non–communist and communist. He was able to withstand a military revolt in 1960 and tried to promote the regime's power in rural areas by use of anti–*Viet Cong* measures.

This crackdown against the *Viet Cong* by Diem was successful enough to push them to adopt new, more militant tactics. Initial Southern success though turned into a virtual loss of control over much of the countryside as *Viet Cong* strength swelled and its military activities increased.

In contrast to the conservative American assumption of an unrelenting global conspiracy to spread communism throughout the world, there was no major direct support of the *Viet Cong* by North Vietnam until 1959 because of the reluctance of the Soviets and Chinese to provoke another crisis in the region. Moreover, because of serious economic difficulties in 1960, China sharply reduced its aid to North Vietnam. Nevertheless, despite the international situation Hanoi itself did begin to give substantial and active support to the *Viet Cong* in the South.

In response, the United States, during the first months of the Kennedy administration, increased its aid to the Diem government and raised the number of American military advisers to the South Vietnamese army. The Chinese, in return for Vietnamese support in their ideological disputes with the Soviet Union, also increased their support of Ho's effort to bolster the *Viet Cong.*

The dictatorial Diem government further alienated public opinion in South Vietnam, which resulted in growing support for the *Viet Cong.* Moreover, Diem, whose own background was among the minority Catholics, infuriated the Buddhist community by publicly allowing discrimination against their practices while supporting similar Catholic activities. By the spring of 1963, he had alienated the most influential segment of the public by his harsh measures.

Buddhist demonstrators, aroused by government attempts to ban public religious displays, were fired upon by government troops. Soon the international news was filled with images of Buddhist monks burning themselves to death to protest the actions of the American–backed Diem regime.

Predictably, the U.S. government was becoming increasingly embarrassed and disgusted with Diem. An army group, with American support, deposed him in late 1963, resulting in his violent death. Over the next year or so the government of South Vietnam was in uncertain hands. For a time, leadership was held by General Duong Van Minh, but he proved too independent for the Americans and was himself quickly deposed. Power was supposedly centered in Saigon, but local military leaders in the provinces were all but independent of the central government. The U.S., entering an election campaign in 1964, didn't want to disturb the shaky status quo.

But that uncertain period after Diem's death was interrupted in August when news reports indicated that North Viet-

namese torpedo boats had attacked a U.S. destroyer in the Tonkin Gulf. Public reports at the time suggested that on two different occasions North Vietnamese boats had threatened the American ships. More recent evidence suggests that though no one was hurt, the American ships operating off the coast of North Vietnam may have provoked one attack and that the second reported assault probably never occurred.

But at the time, given the fact that the United States government had been actively looking for an excuse to step up their efforts, the reports were not questioned. President Johnson manufactured a crisis out of the event and secured a vague resolution from Congress authorizing him to take military action in response. Eventually, the Tonkin Gulf vote would be viewed as the single most important element in U.S. congressional support of the war. In fact it became a *de facto* declaration of a war that never formally occurred.

Because of their opposition to Diem's harsh rule, a great many non–communists also supported the *Viet Cong* and its political arm, the *National Liberation Front.* When he was deposed, this ended. Feeling the need of greater support, and believing it more possible that military action would succeed after the downfall of Diem, the *Viet Cong* embarked on wider military efforts. They were joined by regular units of the North Vietnamese army for the first time at the end of 1964. There was a rapid increase in the area under communist control, particularly in the central highlands of South Vietnam. The Russians, sensing an imminent victory, sent their premier to Hanoi in early 1965 to give assurances of Russian participation (and, hopefully, influence), particularly in the form of defensive weapons against American air attacks on the North. At the same time, the *Viet Cong* launched a series of assaults on U.S. military installations in the South.

The U.S. in Vietnam

The result was U.S. air attacks on North Vietnam in early 1965 while Soviet Premier Kosygin was still in Hanoi. This was followed by large deployments of U.S. Marine and Army combat units. The days of the "advisors" were over. Now American troops under U.S. officers would fight the North Vietnamese and their supporters directly. South Vietnam finally had the formal direct support of their major superpower ally, the United States. Given the changing circumstances, Hanoi would need similar help, but developments within the communist world were getting more complicated.

Ideological differences had led to a

breakdown in Soviet–Chinese relations. The differences between these two communist giants now included disputes about what role each nation should play in aiding Ho Chi Minh's forces. After 1965, China's leadership resented the superior economic ability of the Russians to buy influence in Hanoi, and limited its own assistance to the maintenance of the Chinese–North Vietnamese rail line and the shipment of infantry weapons. Although there was an agreement to ship Soviet equipment through China to North Vietnam, the trains were often delayed and harassed by "Red Guards" active in Mao's *Great Cultural Revolution,* then in progress in China.

Meanwhile, in Saigon a dashing young Air Force general, Nguyen Cao Ky, emerged as a leading figure in the military establishment of South Vietnam. In mid–

Gen. Nguyen Cao Ky

1965; he became premier and retained that position for two years. This provided a welcome respite from the seemingly continuous change of rulers in the country. It became clear though that during his rule the armed forces exercised almost all political power—a fact that continued to arouse Buddhist opposition.

The cost to the U.S. rose to more than $30 billion a year, placing a serious strain on the American economy and on its political system. Within the U.S., opposition to the war began to grow more and more significant, especially among college–age students who did not share their leadership's obsession with anti–communism and who were more likely to view the

Vietnam

Black smoke covers areas of Saigon during the Tet offensive

struggle in South Vietnam as a civil war rather than as a part of a world–wide struggle between communism and capitalism. Moreover, the clearly undemocratic nature of the South Vietnamese regime made it hardly seem worthy of the sacrifices Americans were increasingly being asked to make. Recognizing that last issue, President Lyndon Johnson set out to improve Saigon's image.

Under pressure from Washington to offer at least the appearance of a democratic regime, some political progress took place in South Vietnam. A constitution was enacted and elections were held in 1967 for a new National Assembly. Military intrigue reduced General Ky to the candidacy for vice president and General Nguyen Van Thieu, a Catholic, was elected president though in a relatively poor showing that saw a considerable number of votes going to an anti–military "peace" candidate.

The new government had a broader base, but the habit of jailing political opponents persisted. The military situation, bolstered by a half million U.S. troops, improved. The South Vietnamese army alone could simply not hold its own against North Vietnam and *Viet Cong* units. The government did gain control of half the land area by the end of 1967, but in many cases this control was shaky.

TET: A Battle Won and Lost

As 1968 began, both sides found themselves involved in a bloody conflict that was terribly costly and had little hope for settlement. Yet little was being accomplished to seek resolution of the struggle. The U.S. was distracted by the 1968 elections in which President Johnson had declined to run, and the Soviets dared not appear to be less revolutionary than the Chinese. On Tet, the Lunar New Year holiday traditional to the Vietnamese, the communist forces started an unexpected all–out offensive. They invaded most of the provincial capitals, parts of Saigon and held a portion of the ancient imperial capital, Hue, for several days. U.S. encampments and installations were attacked, causing tremendous losses of material and manpower. Moreover monsoon rains prevented effective American defensive air strikes.

In the end the spectacular offensive was militarily unsuccessful. It had certainly revealed the weaknesses of the South Vietnamese and U.S. forces and driven them back temporarily. But the North's offensive was later dramatically defeated with great loss of life. The goal of generating a popular uprising was also a dismal failure. Nevertheless, the North had proven that, official American claims to the contrary, the war was not being won and that it was likely to go on for many years to come. For Hanoi, committed as it had been for generations to the unification of the country under its rule, that price was acceptable. For the United States, by now more interested in simply finding a way out of the costly but ultimately peripheral struggle, it was not.

Seeking "Peace with Honor"

A somewhat desperate U.S. President Lyndon Johnson suspended the bombing of North Vietnam (except the southern provinces) in 1968 and proposed talks between the combatants. Knowing he could probably not be re–elected, Johnson, as stated, declined to run again. At last, negotiations were begun but organizational issues, such as the status of the *Viet Cong* and seating arrangements at the conference table resulted in endless haggling and little progress. But events within the United States were moving faster than the negotiations themselves.

After a divisive campaign that saw the Democratic Party almost destroy itself over the war, Richard M. Nixon, the former Republican vice president, who had once advocated American intervention at Dienbienphu, was elected president of the U.S. During the campaign, Nixon had spoken somewhat vaguely about a "secret plan" to end the war. Once in power his plans became clearer.

The newly elected President was no longer primarily interested in South Vietnam but in ending the war in a fashion that would retain American influence in the postwar era. Simply pulling out, as many Americans advocated, would not have accomplished that. Rather, Nixon feared, it would send shock waves through the entire American alliance system. Thus, Nixon wanted a way to withdraw that would allow U.S. prestige to continue undiminished.

His method to accomplish these goals

came to be known as "Vietnaminization." What Nixon and his soon famous advisor Henry Kissinger had in mind was to transfer the bulk of the ground war to the Army of the Republic of South Vietnam. In their plan, the United States would withdraw to the relatively safer position of offering air support. The goal was to reduce the number of American casualties while building up South Vietnam's ability to defend itself. Certainly a good idea in theory, the plan nevertheless dangerously reduced American military force in Vietnam even as its prestige remained closely tied to events there.

U.S. troop withdrawals thus started in 1969. From Hanoi's perspective their chances of victory probably seemed closer than ever. In mid–1969 they proclaimed a "provisional government" for the South. Nevertheless, 1969 also saw the death of their long time leader Ho Chi Minh.

The Saigon government of President Thieu then turned to what it considered the most reliable elements for support: the armed forces and the Catholics. The economy, spurred by land reform in the South, improved. President Thieu was reelected (unopposed) in late 1971 in a contest his opponents charged was rigged. Although he made an attempt to build an effective government party, disruption came when the northern provinces of South Vietnam were struck by a massive North Vietnam invasion in March 1972.

President Nixon, facing a reelection contest, responded by ordering the mining of Haiphong Harbor. This precipitated yet another international "crisis" for a time. The military stalemate was acutely embarrassing to President Nixon as the fall elections approached. Yet, for a time it looked, as Henry Kissinger was publicly quoted "that peace was at hand." But no formal agreement was reached before Nixon's landslide reelection victory of 1972. Once he was reelected, Nixon ordered a resumption of the heavy bombing of North Vietnam in an attempt to persuade Hanoi to accept terms acceptable to the Saigon government.

The End

After the intense December 1972 bombing, the North Vietnamese verbally agreed to end the conflict. The formal agreement was signed on March 2, 1973. The U.S. had already given up its insistence on a North Vietnamese withdrawal from South Vietnam and continued its own withdrawal. In exchange, it got its prisoners back, although some insist to this day that many were held against their will in violation of the promise.

Hanoi accepted a political arrangement that did not guarantee the overthrow of the Thieu government as had been previously demanded. Neither North nor South Vietnam had any genuine interest in abiding by the political provisions of the January 1973 agreement, which called for a vaguely defined coalition government and general elections.

To strengthen its hand, Hanoi, with the help of military aid from the Soviet Union and China, then began to create a "third Vietnam" under the nominal control of the *Viet Cong* in the highlands of South Vietnam. This activity, much of which was in flagrant violation of the agreement, included road building, troop buildups, the stockpiling of weapons and other measures.

Meanwhile Saigon's principal supporter, the United States, was moving deeply into the Watergate scandal which eventually destroyed the Nixon administration. Deprived of American air support by Congressional prohibitions and unwilling to commit its own air force against communist–held areas in the highlands, South Vietnam made no genuine military effort to contain their long–time foe.

In the Saigon–controlled areas, which included nearly all the population until March 1975, the Thieu government continued its own repressive policies. Although Thieu fired a number of corrupt military and civilian officials, including some who had been close to him, there was no basic change in the style of the regime.

Anti–Thieu protest movements arose in 1974 among both the Buddhists, who stressed liberalization and peace, and the Roman Catholics, who emphasized opposition to corruption. Concessions were promised to both in late 1974, but little actually happened. By early 1975 five major opposition newspapers were closed down.

During 1974, North Vietnam emphasized the development of its economy through aid from other communist countries, principally the Soviet Union and China. The military strength of Hanoi was built up as was that of the *Viet Cong* in the highlands of South Vietnam. A strategy of "accelerated erosion" began through nibbling at Saigon's military positions in both the highlands and in the Mekong Delta. This approach was obviously inadequate to achieve Hanoi's two principal objectives: imposition of the political provisions of the January 1973 agreement and/or the downfall of Thieu. One reason for this cautious approach was probably the attitude of the Soviet Union and China, which did not want their "détente" with the United States to be endangered by a major resurgence of fighting in Vietnam.

Nevertheless, the North Vietnamese capture of two provincial capitals in early 1975 and another closer to Saigon was the beginning of the end. Shocked by the loss of these towns and unquestionably worried by the refusal of the U.S. Congress to vote further large–scale military aid, President Thieu simply abandoned the three provinces in March. What was perhaps meant as a retreat quickly turned into a rout as communist forces, taking advantage of the dry season and the government withdrawals, moved forward. By the end of March the two important coastal cities of Hue and Danang had fallen to the com-

South Vietnamese President Nguyen Van Thieu decorates soldiers

Vietnam

Harvesting salt in the Central Plain.

munists. Saigon fell at the end of April in a morass of confusion as people with close contacts with the Thieu administration or the Americans desperately tried to flee in overcrowded boats and planes.

The behavior of the leadership during 1975 in South Vietnam demonstrated that their concern was mainly for their personal safety rather than for the future of South Vietnam. Thieu issued military orders which were disastrous, changed daily, and lead nowhere. Many field officers deserted to seek safety for themselves and their families. Ultimately, several hundred thousand refugees fled, most ultimately to the U.S. Thieu went to Taiwan. Almost the entire leadership was able to depart with substantial wealth, in contrast to most of the refugees who had little more than the clothes they wore.

The reasons for the loss of the war were many, but certainly especially important was the weakness of the Southern regime. Despite its access to American support it never developed deep roots among the Vietnamese population, certainly nothing similar to what Hanoi was able to call upon from the populations under its control. When South Vietnam started to lose the support of even the Americans its ability to maintain itself became even more problematic.

A Unified Vietnam

If Hanoi's tenacity had allowed it to finally unify the country under its own control, actually ruling a united Vietnam would require very different skills. In the first decade, though, the party's efforts were not very impressive.

After its "liberation" from the Thieu regime, South Vietnam was run by men sent from Hanoi, the chief of whom was Pham Hung, who, although a southerner, was a member of the top leadership of the *Vietnam Workers Party*—the communist party. Imposition of communist controls on the South proceeded fairly slowly, and without the bloodbath that had been widely predicted.

Nevertheless there were some executions and a great deal of forced political "reindoctrination," of more than two million people. Former employees of the Thieu regime often found it difficult to find jobs and even food. There was some armed resistance in early 1976, mainly in the central highlands as well.

The new regime planned to reduce the population of Saigon, renamed Ho Chi Minh City, through forced resettlement in the countryside. The leadership also announced in late 1975 that there would be elections in 1976 for a single National Assembly for the entire country. They were held on schedule with only communists eligible to run for office. In spite of its slightly larger population, the South was allotted 243 seats, and as a token concession the voters were allowed to choose from among 281 candidates. In the North there were 249 candidates for 249 seats. The new Assembly met and adopted a new constitution. Unification of the country was officially proclaimed.

The ruling party held its Fourth Congress in late 1976, at which it renamed itself the *Vietnam Communist* (rather than "Workers") *Party*. The domination of the North over the South was clear. Soviet aid to and influence on the new regime was also substantial. Somewhat later the Soviets took over the huge naval base at Camranh Bay built by the U.S. Chinese influence in contrast was considerably less than that of the Soviets. Clearly Vietnam was tilting toward Moscow as the Sino–Soviet disputes continued.

Hanoi continued to hope for the $3.25 billion in reconstruction aid Nixon was said to have promised. But no aid was forthcoming as little progress was being made on the Missing In Action matter and Hanoi was widely disliked.

Nevertheless, having finally won its long independence and unification struggle, Hanoi then moved to impose a socialist economy on the south. That effort, though, was not well received by the southerners who passively resisted efforts to collectivize agriculture and redistribute land. When efforts to socialize the urban area brought an end to the free market system of the south, large numbers of indigenous Chinese, the backbone of the urban economy, fled the country creating yet another wave of "boat people" who had already filled refugee camps throughout Southeast Asia.

But more than internal economic errors weakened the newly unified Vietnam. The Americans continued to maintain their economic embargo and newly developing tensions with China over Vietnam's role in Cambodia were soon to complicate matters even more.

Vietnam's Cambodia Involvement

In the late 1970s Vietnam developed a border conflict with Cambodia which was then controlled by the murderous Pol Pot regime, a government supported by China. By 1978 Vietnam launched a full–scale invasion of Cambodia. In doing so Hanoi claimed they were responding to the long term border tensions and to end the Pol Pot regime's genocidal–like killing of so many of its own people. Not surprisingly many Cambodians initially viewed the invading Vietnamese and their supporters as liberators from the hated *Khmer Rouge*. Nevertheless, despite the general hatred of the Pol Pot regime, Vietnam's own invasion was also widely condemned. The Chinese, who had been especially supportive of the *Khmer Rouge*, were outraged and saw Hanoi's actions as an extension of their enemy, the Soviet Union's influence in Southeast Asia. From Beijing's perspective that was unacceptable.

In retaliation for this strike against its

ally, China began to pour troops over the Vietnamese border in early 1979, occupying, after heavy fighting, a portion of its northern territory. Beijing's efforts, though, were clearly less than they had expected. The Chinese troops had not fought in a generation and were hard pressed to deal with the Vietnamese military fresh from its generation–long struggle with the United States. China's efforts to teach Hanoi a direct lesson had clearly failed. After that Beijing directed itself more toward supporting the fallen *Khmer Rouge* and making life "difficult" for the Vietnamese in Cambodia.

Over the next decade, Vietnam's commitment to Cambodia and its allied government would grow to be a major burden on the regime. Predictably, as time went on, the Vietnamese who had initially been welcomed as liberators from the hated Pol Pot were themselves seen as aggressive occupiers. By the late 1980s Hanoi began its withdrawal from Cambodia after a decade which had seen the commitment there contribute to the weakening economic conditions in Vietnam itself and its international isolation.

A New Economic Path

Economically the first decade of independence was a disaster. The most productive citizens had been driven to flee the country and the socialist economic planning had alienated many others. Moreover the war in Cambodia had added to the economic strains.

The aging, largely North Vietnamese leadership, and its economic policies, had not seen the economy grow. The continuing isolation of the regime due to the American–led boycott had hardly helped. The efforts of many communist states from Eastern Europe to improve ties with Beijing meant less than enthusiasm for Vietnam. Hanoi's isolation was growing. Economically, for example, inflation, was running at around 700%!

By the mid 1980s it was clear that a new direction was required. Not surprisingly this new thinking emerged as China under Deng Xiaoping itself was several years into an economic reform program and even the Soviet Union, under its new leader Gorbachév, was talking of the importance of reform.

Happily, a change for the better became a possibility with the death in July 1986 of Le Duan, the longtime General Secretary of the *Communist Party* of Vietnam. He was succeeded by Truong Chinh, also elderly but more flexible and with a reputation for being pro–Chinese.

Accordingly, at a Party Congress held in December 1986, Truong Chinh, Le Duc Tho and Pham Van Dong "resigned" from

Shopping in Ho Chi Minh City (formerly Saigon)

the Politburo, although all continued to be "advisors." Chinh retained the presidency of the state and Dong the premiership of the government. A new General Secretary of the party, Nguyen Van Linh, a Southerner and an economic reformer, was elected. In February 1987 there were major personnel changes in the government, although Chinh and Dong remained in place; the newcomers were mostly southerners with some economic expertise. The new leadership group were clearly interested in moving more decisively away from central control of the economy.

Over the next several years agriculture was decollectivized and many financial reforms were put into place. State factory managers were given more authority, and a partial revival of private enterprise was permitted. By 1989 Vietnam had re-emerged as a major rice exporter. Private businesses such as restaurants and shops were opened and flourished as well.

Not surprisingly, these changes were inspired both by internal developments in Vietnam as well as the influence of the new Gorbachév leadership in the Soviet Union. These changes came to be known as *Doi Moi*, or "renovation" and if they are less well known than the famous *Glasnost* and *Perestroika* of Gorbachév, they were born of the same problems in the socialist world.

A similar relaxation of cultural controls occurred in Vietnam in the late 1980s, which also parallel developments in both the Soviet Union and the People's Republic of China. It became possible for greater press freedoms, the introduction of Western music videos and even greater religious freedoms for Vietnamese Catholics. Some 6,000 political prisoners were released in September 1987.

The idea of a "new Vietnam," eager for foreign contacts, was energetically promoted by an able Foreign Minister, Nguyen Co Thach. Hanoi expressed an in-

Vietnam

The crowded waterfront of a Mekong Delta town at market time.

Courtesy: William Garrett Stewart

the ruling party's monopoly of political power. Political opposition in Vietnam, given the history of repression, has been almost nonexistent. Accordingly, the regime had felt free to proceed along the same lines as in China: minimal political reform combined with some reasonably effective economic reform. But the events of the 1989–1991 era had clearly shown how easily reform efforts in the communist world could swirl out of control. And the Party had no desire to lose its mandate on power. The key appeared to at least make reasonable progress on economically improving peoples lives without loosening up on political controls. One requirement in that effort was the establishment of normal commercial relations with the industrial countries. The 1989 withdrawal from Cambodia helped this process, but Washington was still demanding a full accounting for MIAs.

Relations with the U.S. remained difficult. In 1986, Hanoi reneged on two pledges that it had apparently given: to resolve fully the issue of American personnel still considered missing in action during the Vietnam war (the MIA's) and to release to American custody several thousand Vietnamese prisoners being held for having collaborated with the U.S. during the war. In view of this behavior on the Vietnamese side—especially their role in Cambodia and internal U.S. politics, Washington continued to withhold diplomatic recognition and trade from Hanoi through the 1980s.

Thus Hanoi became increasingly cooperative on the MIA issue. By the end of 1991, the State Department began to authorize tour groups of Americans to visit Vietnam. The U.S. Presidential election prevented earlier action, but in late November of 1992 President Bush permitted U.S. companies to open offices in Vietnam and begin negotiations for future trade relations.

Throughout the early 1990s many signs pointed to the continued opening of Vietnam to the outside world. Vietnamese officials were being trained in contemporary diplomatic practice, a Fulbright program was begun, and American professors were in the country at several institutions teaching business and economic courses. Americans also visited Vietnamese military bases and government offices in search of additional information on American MIA's. Vietnamese were also being trained to aid them in the process of determining the fate of their own MIA's which far outnumber the Americans lost. By 1995 the Vietnamese government was working to establish a bureaucracy and legal system which foreigners' business could work with and trust. A new legal code was approved in October.

terest in joining ASEAN. In response to foreign concern over the state of human rights in Vietnam, some political prisoners were released and some boat people allowed to return. Even official anger at the Vatican's canonization in mid 1988 of 117 Vietnamese martyrs of the seventeenth and eighteenth centuries was not allowed to derail a policy of increased toleration of religion, including Catholicism.

But even as Vietnam modeled some of its internal policies on developments in the Soviet Union, relations with its patron, remained edgy. The Soviets retained major naval and air bases at and near Camranh Bay and clearly could not afford to alienate Hanoi, the host government. On the other hand, Moscow was unhappy with Vietnamese misuse of Soviet aid and was itself moving to improve its own relations with Hanoi's nemesis, China.

The Soviets applied cautious pressure on Hanoi to improve its relations with Beijing. Nevertheless, disagreements and

even tensions with the Soviet Union, probably including Soviet pressures for a Vietnamese withdrawal from Cambodia on the model of the Soviet withdrawal from Afghanistan, did not disrupt this important relationship.

The Effect of Communism's Collapse

The dramatic developments of 1989–91 in the Soviet Union and Eastern Europe had a considerable impact on the Vietnamese leadership. The basic reaction was one of alarm and of determination that the erosion of the ruling parties' power would not be repeated in Vietnam. On the other hand, Hanoi hoped to avoid the opposite extreme—a bloody crackdown in the Chinese manner—by means of very cautious political and economic reforms (*Doi Moi*). Particularly shocking was the late 1989 fall of the Ceaucescu regime in Romania.

In 1991 the divided leadership in Hanoi continued to work out a plan for improving the limping economy without diluting

Foreign Relations

In July 1993, President Clinton ended U.S. opposition to International Monetary Fund (IMF) loans to Vietnam. Somewhat later he announced that American companies could bid on infrastructure projects funded by the international lending agencies. The next year the 19–year U.S. trade embargo was finally ended. Full diplomatic relations were announced in July 1995, and fulfilled in May 1997.

Normalization of relations with the United States was clearly a major event in Hanoi's efforts to strengthen their economy. Nevertheless important matters still need to be resolved. Hanoi and Washington have not as yet concluded a trade treaty, which would cover among other things the important area of intellectual property rights. Vietnam also needs to gain "most favored nation" status as soon as possible. This is important because it allows foreign goods to enter the U.S. as cheaply as those from America's other trading partners. Despite the term "most favored nation" this designation merely means that goods can enter the United States on a parity with the world's other nations. But due to American legislative requirements, countries classified as "communist" must have special permission to be so treated. Hanoi has been so committed to improving its relations with the United States that it even, in the spring of 1997, announced it would assume the debts of the former government of South Vietnam!

Thus the ties continue to grow. United States firms have become the 6th largest investor in Vietnam, though some like Nike, have come under considerable public criticism for the work conditions they have established there. Happily, despite problems, relations with China, Vietnam's other long–term enemy, are also better. After more than eighteen years the border between them has opened for rail service. President Jiang Zemin of the People's Republic recently visited as well. The two communist parties find they now have more in common in the era after the collapse of so many other socialist states than they once did.

This is certainly an improvement over their earlier relationship. The two fought one conflict in the late 70's, and have come to blows over conflicting claims in the South China Sea several times. As recently as 1994, relations worsened. A Vietnamese patrol boat seized three Chinese fishing boats off Bach Long Vi, an island claimed by Hanoi half way between Vietnam and Hainan island (Chinese territory). A Chinese boat opened fire the next day on another patrol, wounding two Vietnamese.

Especially important is Vietnam's integration with its Southeast Asian neighbors. Vietnam is now the 7th member of ASEAN (Association of Southeast Asian Nations). This provides the country with significant economic and strategic benefits. Trade with the other ASEAN six (Brunei, Indonesia, Malaysia, Philippines, Singapore, and Thailand) will grow more rapidly. Also, being a member of ASEAN provides Vietnam with some cover in its relations with China. An important example of this occurred when the ASEAN states recently spoke out with one voice at the second ASEAN Regional (security) Forum in Brunei on the issue of conflicting claims in the South China Sea. China had insisted that these claims be addressed on a bilateral basis. Countries like Vietnam and the Philippines, who have had run–ins with the Chinese military in the Sea, much prefer the multilateral approach.

Vietnam also continued to talk with Cambodian officials about the treatment of ethnic Vietnamese located along the border just inside Cambodian territory. Relations though are not the best and they could deteriorate easily. In fact, last year saw considerable tensions between the two as Cambodia claimed that Vietnam had actually moved the border markers between the two countries!

Culture

The Vietnamese have been influenced by the culture of the Chinese to a greater extent than all other nations of Southeast Asia, except Singapore, where there is a Chinese majority. Chinese characters were used to write the Vietnamese language until the French replaced them with an alphabetical system. The Red River in North Vietnam is controlled with dikes of Chinese design.

Vietnam is religiously divided between *Mahayana* Buddhists with a variety of practices that are quite distinct and many Roman Catholics. Vietnamese Buddhism includes traditions ranging from animism and Taoism to Confucianism and Buddhism and is often simply called the Triple Religion or "Vietnamese Buddhism". Along with Korea and the Philippines, Vietnam has one of the highest percentages of Christians in Asia. There are also considerable numbers who follow minority traditions like the Cao Dai and Hoa Hao sects. Overall, though, society in recent years has become quite secular.

Most citizens are ethnically Vietnamese with a small percentage of Chinese and a

Prime Minister Vo Van Kiet

Do Muoi, General Secretary, Communist Party

Vietnam

block of some 60 different smaller groups that collectively are sometimes known as Montagnards. Unlike China which has committed itself to reducing the population growth, Vietnamese efforts have not been nearly as dedicated, and few restrictions exist to limit the number of children a family might want.

Other controls though still remain strong. The government controls how much free speech, or press freedoms, are allowed and outside sources of information ranging from telephones to e–mail (faxes are also controlled). Nevertheless, there have been enough improvements in recent years that many Vietnamese who earlier fled are returning home. That has been allowed though they are not permitted to take part in any public activities.

Most of the population remains poor and largely rural. The real economic changes made in recent years have been significant but they have also added to the gap between the rich and poor. In fact, half of all Vietnamese still live under the World Bank's standard of poverty. And burdens have become even more demanding in recent years as people are now required to pay for their own health care, something that was available without expense earlier. As mentioned in the background section of *East, Southeast Asia, and the Western Pacific*, Southeast Asian women have historically enjoyed more rights than their sisters in other parts of Asia. In modern Vietnam women often played important roles in the nationalist struggle, though the first female did not take her place in the party's all important politburo until the summer of 1996. Women have made strides in the economy as well. REE, the Refrigeration Electrical Engineering corporation, one of the more successful state companies, is run by a woman.

Economy

Vietnam has, for several years, appeared as if it was on the verge of becoming another "Asian Tiger." The term, refers to the rapidly growing economies of Asia: Singapore, Taiwan, South Korea and Hong Kong. Malaysia and Thailand are the new "cubs." In Ho Chi Minh City, fine restaurants, new high rise buildings, television, and lots of new cars are plentiful.

From 1987 to 1994, the country experienced a real boom. This was based on the *Communist Party's* policy of *Doi Moi*, or restructuring, which ushered in a series of market reforms. Many restrictions on the private sector were removed. One result is that Vietnam is currently the world's fourth largest exporter of rice, behind Thailand, the U.S., and India. Inflation was under 6% in 1993, and about 16% in 1994. Excess labor from closed state enterprises was absorbed by almost five million new jobs in the private sector. However, in 1995, per capita income was still only about $250, or using figures adjusted for living standards, around $1,310. Foreign trade continued to expand with only a small deficit.

Still committed to the state firms, how-

Market area, Hanoi

174

Ho Chi Minh City's bustling port

Courtesy: Caltex Petroleum Corporation

ever, Hanoi may be siphoning off resources needed by the private sector to help state enterprises. For example, textiles made in state concerns are given preference for export. These companies also benefit from better access to foreign currency loans. Foreign companies are even being forced to form joint ventures with local state owned businesses.

Growth for 1996 remains very impressive at over 9%. Visitors report a surging sense of change in the main cities with signs of investment and growth ever present. Even inflation has finally been brought under control. The government's goals are to join both the World Trade Organization and the Asian Pacific Economic Community.

But the government's basic ambivalence about these changes continues to hamper its ability to reassure foreign investors. Investment in Vietnam is still considered the most risky of any in the region, and the decision last spring to encourage the growth of communist cells in foreign firms is not likely to improve confidence. Vietnam has yet to develop a stock market as their giant neighbor to the north, China, did some

years ago. The state–run companies are still 43% of the GDP of the country. In contrast to China, which seems to want their importance diminished over time, Hanoi's leaders claim they hope to have these firms remain important.

This ambivalence toward these economic changes naturally contributes to contradictory regulations issued by government ministries which have soured some investors on the country. Foreigners complain about poor banking conditions which also hamper investment efforts.

Some progress was made in 1996 in dealing with the country's outstanding loans. A deal was worked out whereby Hanoi was able to have 50% of its debts forgiven. This should make it easier to obtain loans in the future.

The Future

The end of the U.S. embargo, full diplomatic relations, and the flood of foreign investment and personnel into the country, will of course hasten the pace of change. Not all of this will be good. The environment will suffer and many indi-

viduals will not benefit from the initial stages of economic growth and development. Vietnam is rapidly becoming the equivalent of an old West "boomtown," where fortunes will be made and government may ambivalently go along for the ride. But the *Communist Party* still runs the country, though Vietnam also has a new constitution and a National Assembly that has been given a greater voice in public affairs. There should be no mistake that the party will try to hold on to power as long as possible. The principal issue for the future is how long the ambivalence will remain within the leadership regarding the changes occurring in the country. Hanoi understands that bringing Vietnam more into the global economy is important for improving the lives of its citizens and avoiding the sort of confrontations that have occurred elsewhere. Nevertheless, these changes bring with them potential challenges to the leadership's authority. How much change the politburo is going to be comfortable with is likely to be a major factor in how well Vietnam will find a place for itself in the global economy of the future.

Nations of the Western Pacific

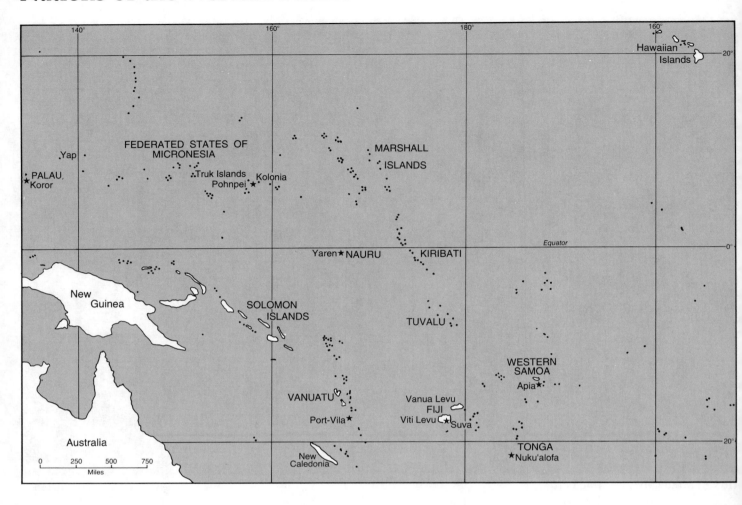

"... the seas bring us together, they do not separate us ..."

(From the preamble to the Constitution of the Federated State of Micronesia)

Scattered like brilliant pieces of jade across an area covering more than 3 million square miles of the Pacific Ocean lie a number of island states which have achieved independence or have become self–governing; they have been under British, French, U.S., Japanese, Australian or New Zealand administration either as colonies, protectorates, or UN trusteeships. They range in population from Fiji's 796,000 to Nauru's 10,000 inhabitants. Most islanders are ethnically Polynesian, Melanesian or Micronesian, although some Asian groups such as Indians, Chinese and Vietnamese have settled in the islands in the last century.

On the majority of the islands the terrain is generally low, sometimes only a few feet above sea level (of coral origin) or mountainous (of volcanic origin) covered by lush vegetation and bordered by legendary white beaches. Many, however, bear the ugly scars and rusted armaments

brought to them by the savage engagements waged throughout the region during World War II; gentle wavelets brush the bows of hulking battleships sunk during those years, while palm trees sway in the cooling breezes which moderate the tropical climate. World–renowned for their beauty, the islands are subject to fierce typhoons from June to December.

Long before the era of Christianity, Asian peoples migrated into the area. Spanish explorers plumbed the region for gold and spread Christianity among the people, a belief which was often blended with their traditional deities. Spain simultaneously laid claim to much of this area of scattered islands.

In the latter 1800's, Germany desired to compete with other European nations in colonization. Its control was eventually imposed over most of the Spanish–claimed region. After World War I, Japan, which had joined the victorious Allies, was rewarded with possession of the former German–held islands north of New Guinea, but during World War II an is-land–by–island struggle by Allied troops wrested the area from the Japanese, and the islands came under control of the

United States, Great Britain, France, Australia and New Zealand, with the Dutch reclaiming their former colony of the Dutch East Indies. Most of the latter forms Indonesia. Over the years the islands achieved independence (see individual nation entries).

Some exports of the islands are quite specific, as in the case of Nauru with its dependence on phosphate deposits, but others generally produce in varying quantities basic products of a tropical climate coconut and palm oil, fish, copra, fruits and—in the case of Fiji—sugar and some gold. Timber is also an important export for both Fiji and the Solomon Islands. Another prime source of income which all are successfully developing is tourism.

The Solomon Islands, Tonga, and Vanuatu are members of the (British) Commonwealth of Nations. Nauru and Tuvalu are special members, i.e., they may participate in all functional Commonwealth meetings and activities, but do not have the right to attend meetings of the Commonwealth Heads of Government.

The poor condition of the economies of most of these states (Nauru is the exception) have accentuated tensions with the

West and especially with the United States, whose tuna boats fish aggressively in the South Pacific. There are also tensions with France caused by its persistent testing of nuclear weapons in its part of the South Pacific and the delay in granting independence to New Caledonia.

The states of this region, including Australia and New Zealand, have formed an organization called the South Pacific Forum. In 1985 they signed a South Pacific Nuclear–Free Zone Treaty barring such weapons from the region's territories, but not banning transit through its waters by nuclear–armed or nuclear–powered ships.

Following World War II, the United Nations established a trusteeship over three primary archipelagos north of the equator: the Carolines, the Marshalls, and the Marianas (except for Guam, a U.S. possession since the end of the Spanish–American War in 1898.) The U.S. was the trustee, and the Department of the Interior took jurisdiction over these islands from the Navy in 1951.

In 1975 the Northern Marianas (again, except for Guam) was given separate status as a commonwealth. The rest of the territory was divided into the Marshall Islands (in the East), the Federated States of Micronesia (in the South), and the Republic of Palau (in the Southwest).

In 1986 the United States, having held the role of trustee, approved a Compact of Free Association for them; it consists of two agreements included in the same act of Congress—one between the U.S. and the Federated States of Micronesia and the other between the U.S. and the Marshall Islands. The Compact provides for extensive cooperation in numerous areas such as law enforcement, narcotics control, economic and technical assistance, resolution of nuclear–cleanup programs, health care, fishing rights, etc. With the enactment of the Compact, the Trust Territory of the Pacific Islands essentially ceased to exist. The FSM and the Marshall Islands are now independent republics and members of the United Nations.

The islands as a whole have considerable strategic importance, and there are a number of U.S. bases in the islands. The Eniwetok and Bikini atolls in the Marshalls were the site of H–bomb tests in the 1950's and are still considered contaminated. Not surprisingly there is considerable local discontent over the use of the region as a nuclear testing area.

The Republic of Palau is also a part of the Compact, but its dependence on the U.S. is far more pronounced. The Compact of Free Association is subject to many varying (and more often vague) interpretations. Palau, because of its nearness to important shipping routes linking the western Pacific and the South China Sea with the Indian Ocean, has been considered for development as a major port complex and military base; these are not welcome to the inhabitants.

Contrary to the wishes of many voters, who are anti–nuclear and suspect of the U.S. seeking bases in Palau as a possible replacement to those in the Philippines, the government of Palau managed to get a vote accepting a "compact of free association" with the U.S. in 1987. In effect, Palau receives economic aid from the U.S. in exchange for an American option on bases.

On October 2, 1994, Palau formally proclaimed its independence from the United States. But it continues to receive $500 million annually in assistance from Washington.

Tensions throughout the area rose considerably when in 1995 the French announced that they planned to resume nuclear testing in the region. The decision resulted in an effort, unsuccessful, by New Zealand to use the International Court of Justice to pressure Paris not to start testing again, as well as a worldwide protest that included governments, religious and anti–nuclear groups.

Happily, in early 1996, French President Jacques Chirac announced that having carried out six of the originally planned eight nuclear tests, the French would discontinue the program.

Typical island scene, this one in Micronesia

Australia

Aberdeen Angus cattle on the Hunter River, New South Wales

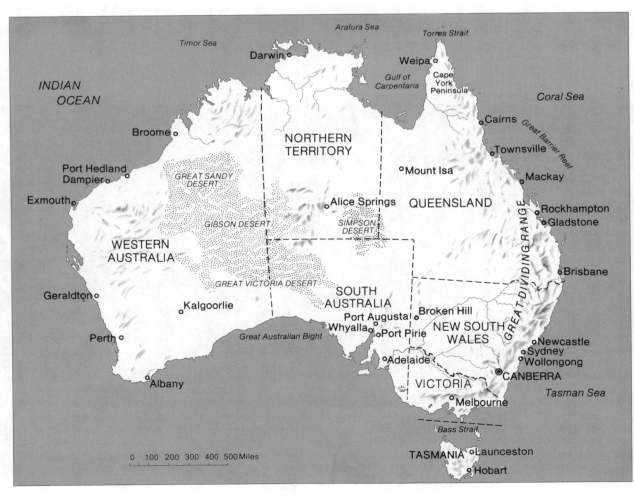

Australia

Area: 2,970,000 sq. mi. (7,692,300 sq. km.), slightly smaller than the continental U.S., the "lower 48" states.
Population: 18.3 million (estimated).
Capital City: Canberra (Pop. 265,000, estimated).
Climate: Tropical to subtropical in the north, temperate in the south; the interior is highly arid.
Neighboring Countries: Indonesia, Papua New Guinea lie to the north; New Zealand to the southeast.
Official Language: English.
Ethnic Background: British, other European, Asian, indigenous aborigines and aboriginal–European mixed ancestry.
Principal Religion: Christianity.
Main Exports: Coal, gold, wool, meat, iron ore and aluminium ore.
Main Imports: Automobiles, computers, petroleum and telecommunication equipment.
Currency: Australian Dollar.
Former Colonial Status: British dependency (1788–1900).
National Day: January 26 (anniversary of the first British settlement at Sydney in 1788).
Head of State: Her Majesty Queen Elizabeth II, represented by Sir William Deane, Governor General.
Head of Government: The Rt. Hon. John Howard, Prime Minister.
National Flag: A blue field with the Union Jack in the upper left quarter, a seven–pointed star in the lower left corner, and five stars at the right side.
Per Capita Annual GDP: US $19,960.

The enormous island called Australia is so immense that it is classified as a continent—at 2.97 million square miles it is almost the size of the continental United States. Its 12,000 miles of coastline is relatively smooth with few harbors, but in the northeast the sandy coast is in the lee of the Great Barrier Reef, a 1,200 mile chain of coral reefs and islands extending north almost to Papua New Guinea. With its vivid coral and a profusion of other marine life, the reef is one of the world's natural wonders and a magnet for scientists and tourists.

Australia is one of the oldest of the continents and also one of the flattest and driest. Its few mountains have been worn with the passage of time and the highest peak today is Mt. Kosciusko at only 7,300 feet. The largest chain of mountains is found in the east and is called the Great Dividing Range; in the southeast they are known as the Australian Alps. They divide the narrow crescent of land along the coastline from the vast interior. It is in the fertile eastern coastal area that the great majority of Australians live and their largest cities are located.

To the west are large lowlands and plateaus which begin the vast interior region known to Australians as the Outback. This is the region containing the two–thirds of Australia classified as desert (fewer than 10 inches of rain annually) or semi–desert (fewer than 15 inches). The region's "rivers" often are chains of waterholes and flow only following infrequent rains. Most never reach the sea, but instead widen into areas called lakes which most of the time are actually mud flats encrusted with salt. By drilling to great depths it is possible in some parts of this region to locate limited amounts of ground water, making possible the raising of livestock. However, large areas are needed to support even small numbers of animals—some Outback cattle ranches in Australia are larger than the smaller European countries. Apart from mining settlements, population is scattered and averages fewer than two persons per square mile.

Australians many years ago introduced the Royal Flying Doctor Service, utilizing two–way radio and light aircraft to bring medical services to those living in this isolated environment. Outback children also use the radio system as students of the School of the Air, working through their daily lessons with a teacher in a studio–classroom in the nearest township hundreds of miles away. Large parts of the region are not inhabited at all. An occasional thunderstorm moistens the thirsty land, and grasses and wildflowers rapidly spring up, flower, wither and die, dropping their seeds to the ground to await the many months before the next rainfall. To the southeast, in the regions of the Murray and Darling Rivers, the land becomes more moist, but the need for water is still so great that these rivers are dammed for irrigation.

Apart from its dry center, Australia has a widely varied climate. It covers more than 30 parallels of latitude and more than a third of the country is in the tropics. Normally snow falls only on the southeastern ranges during the winter as Australia's position surrounded by sea and the absence of marked physical features give a more temperate climate than other land in corresponding latitudes. Because of the low humidity in many places, the high summer temperatures are not as enervating. The North is subject to tropical cyclones (hurricanes), and the city of Darwin was almost completely destroyed by Cyclone Tracy in 1974.

Isolation from other countries by wide expanses of water has affected Australia in many ways from its plant and animal life to its contemporary culture. Australia has many wildflowers found nowhere else. The main native trees are 500 varieties of eucalyptus and 600 species of acacia (known to Australians as *wattle* and akin to the mimosa of North America). About half of Australia's native mammals are marsupials—animals which produce their young in embryo form which is a tiny fraction of the adult weight of the parent. The newborn offspring finds its way miraculously to the adult's pouch where it continues its development; the mammary glands on which it suckles are located within the pouch. Only when it is the equivalent of a three to five year old human does it leave the pouch, returning for nourishment as needed until even more mature. Marsupials include members of the kangaroo family, the koala, the wombat and possums. Australia is also the home of another of nature's oddities—the duck-billed platypus, a cross between bird and mammal. It lays eggs, but then nurses its young after they have hatched, yet its body is covered with fur and it lives in a water habitat. Australia's 800 bird species include the ostrich–like emu and many brightly colored parrots.

History

During the many centuries of development of the Western world, Australia was thinly populated by an estimated 300,000 Aborigines, a nomadic, tribal hunting and gathering society. (Strangely, they bear a striking resemblance to a similar people found in southern Africa.) About 160,000 Aborigines remain today, but many have embraced a largely Western life style; some later racially intermixed with the European settlers. They now are a disadvantaged and increasingly assertive minority.

The Rt. Hon. John Howard

Australia

This painting by Algernon Talmage shows the unfurling of the British flag at Sydney Cove. Captain Arthur Phillip and his men drink to the health of King George III.

Ships of the Dutch East India Company touched on the Australian coastline in the early 17th century; the Dutch explorer Tasman circumnavigated the continent in 1642–43. The first real penetration was by the British, led by Captain James Cook, who claimed the eastern portion of the island in 1770 in the name of the British Crown.

The principal interest of Britain in Australia was initially as a penal colony where its criminals could be exiled or held in prison. The first settlers, numbering 270 soldiers and sailors and 760 convicts, landed on the present site of the city of Sydney in 1758 to establish the colony of New South Wales under the royally appointed Governor, Captain Arthur Phillip.

The Crown later permitted non–convict settlers to emigrate from the British Isles to Australia. Most of them became interested in sheep raising, to which the island was ideally suited. A close social organi-

zation quickly emerged among these free settlers; they dominated the New South Wales Corps, which was a special military police force. They became very influential and struggled with a succession of royal governors, sometimes gaining the right to use the services of convict labor at a low wage, and to expand their sheep raising activities. They also sought control over internal and external trade.

The notorious Captain Bligh, the former commander of HMS *Bounty*, struggled with the New South Wales Corps when he was governor in 1805 and lost. The next governor, Macquarie, was much more respected and successful. He curbed the power of the police force, set limits on land grants and organized and permitted rapid economic development. No more convicts were sent to Australia after 1868.

The discovery of gold in 1851 gave a great boost to the Australian economy and was accompanied by disorders in the min-

ing camps, similar to those in the American West during the same period. In the succeeding decades, additional immigration of free settlers, exploration of the eastern and later the western parts of the continent, and with general economic development, took place at a steadily accelerating rate.

Six British crown colonies were successfully established in Australia from 1788 through the first half of the 19th century. All had been granted self–governing independence by the end of that century. In 1901, the colonies became the six States of an Australian Federation under the title Commonwealth of Australia. This status continues today.

Although an independent, self–governing nation, Australia, along with other countries of the British Commonwealth, recognizes the British sovereign as the head of state, symbolizing historical links with Britain. The Queen (or King) is represented in Australia by a Governor–General. Australia's chief executive is a Prime Minister elected by members of the majority party in the Federal Parliament. The Parliament consists of a Senate and a House of Representatives functioning under a written constitution which borrows from both British and American experience. There is no elected President. Cabinet officers must also be members of Parliament.

Australia sent volunteer units that fought bravely on the Allied side in the Middle East and on the Western Front during World War I. The demands of the British war effort benefited the Australian economy. During the period between the two World Wars, it continued to experience growth, as well as the emergence of a powerful labor movement pressing for benefits for workers. It was gripped by the worldwide depression, with a sharp drop in trade in 1931 and the following years.

Prior to World War II, the foreign policy of Australia was one of comparative isolation from the community of nations. In spite of this, Australia responded to the outbreak of World War II by coming to the aid of the British in the European War in 1939, and after 1941 joined the Allied war effort in the Pacific. For Australia, the war was made much more complicated and dangerous because of the closeness of Japan.

Japanese troops quickly conquered most of Southeast Asia by mid–1942. Australia became the base for the headquarters of General Douglas MacArthur after the fall of the Philippines. The main concern of the Australians was that they also might be invaded next. Darwin, the northern seaport, suffered heavy Japanese bombing raids. However, Allied victories in the Pacific and fighting by Australian troops in New Guinea prevented a Japanese invasion.

The *Labor Party*, led by Prime Minister John Curtin, had come to power in late 1941 and was responsible for major changes in Australian international thinking during World War II. After such close cooperation with the United States in achieving ultimate victory, Australian strategic thinking turned towards the United States after the war.

The end of World War II brought another period of growth and prosperity. Substantial immigration, encouraged by the government, resulted in a larger population, primarily Caucasian. Until 1966 Australian immigration policies discriminated against non–Europeans and in earlier years this had been known as the "white Australia" policy. Since 1966 successive governments have removed discriminatory restrictions. However, the overall rate of immigration was reduced

during the 1970's. Today, one in every three Australians was born overseas or is the son or daughter of an immigrant. The influx of newcomers has brought marked changes in Australian society, lifestyle and culture.

The country was governed by a coalition of the *Liberal Party* and the *Country Party* between 1949 and 1972, for 17 years under its leader, the colorful Sir Robert Menzies, then Harold Holt, John Gorton and William McMahan. All maintained steady support for U.S. policies and efforts in Southeast Asia. Australian troops took part in the war in Korea, the campaign against communist terrorists in Malaya (1948–1960) and the Vietnam war.

Elections in 1972 returned the *Labor Party* to power. The new Prime Minister, E. Gough Whitlam, a man of strong personality and intellect, recognized the People's Republic of China and established diplomatic relations with North Vietnam, North Korea and East Germany. He also withdrew the remaining Australian troops from South Vietnam and moved to establish closer economic relations with Japan. He then abolished the draft, lowered the defense budget, began fairer treatment of the Aborigines and introduced ambitious domestic social programs.

The world oil crisis of the early seventies though affected Australia as it did other communities. Both inflation and unemployment went up. Faced with these problems, Whitlam called an election in April 1974 that reduced his majority in the House of Representatives but did enable him to continue in office.

By late 1975, the continuously poor state of the economy and controversy over various *Labor Party* programs prompted the *Liberal* and *National Country* parties (the latter previously known as the *Country Party*) opposition to press for new elections. When Whitlam refused, the opposition took the unprecedented action of using its Senate majority to block the gov-

ernment's budget appropriation bills, leaving it without authority to pay its creditors, including Federal employees and recipients of social security and other benefits. As the government's reserves of money ran out, the constitutional crisis intensified. It is at this point that one of the more peculiar features of Australia's government became apparent.

The Governor–General, the representative of the British Crown, stepped in, dismissed the sitting Prime Minister and asked J. Malcolm Fraser to form a new *Liberal* government. The party, in a coalition with the *National Party*, won the next election. Thus, a representative of a foreign nation was able substantially to interfere in Australia's domestic political process!

Politics and Government

Australia is a parliamentary democracy whose political institutions and practices follow the Western democratic model, reflecting both the British and American experience. The Australian federation has a three–tier system of government: the national government consists of Parliament (House of Representatives with 148 seats and the Senate with 76 seats) and the Government—the party or parties with a majority in the lower house constitute the government, controlling all ministries); six state governments, the Capital Territory and Northern Territory (similar to states); and some 900 local governmental bodies at the city, town, municipal and shire level. Senators in the Federal Parliament serve six year terms (Senators for the two territories serve three year terms), and Representatives serve for three years.

Australia has a written constitution which came into force on January 1, 1901, when the colonies federated to form the Commonwealth of Australia. The constitution can be amended if a majority of voters in a majority of states plus an over-

Kangaroos cavort on a reserve near Melbourne   Australian Information Service

Australia

Barbecued chicken on Christmas Day at Sydney Harbor   Australian Information Service

all majority approve the change. Proposed changes must be passed by an absolute majority in both houses of Parliament. If an amendment is passed twice by one house but fails in the other, the Governor–General may submit the amendment to the electorate.

Australia pioneered the secret ballot in parliamentary elections and has used the system since 1879. Voting is compulsory at the national level. The franchise extends to everyone over 18 years of age except criminals and the mentally incompetent. The Australian system of law resembles the British system from which it was taken. Australian law places great importance on the rights of the individual. The law provides for *habeas corpus* (which prevents arbitrary arrest or imprisonment without a court hearing), bail, trial by judge and jury, the presumption of innocence until proven guilty, and prevention from double jeopardy.

The High Court resembles the American Supreme court and deals with federal and state matters. It has original jurisdiction in important areas, including interpretation of the Constitution, determination of legal disputes between the federal government and state governments, suits between state governments, and suits between citizens of different states. The Court has a Chief Justice and six other justices. The Federal Court is a specialized court dealing with matters such as copyrights, industrial law, trade practices, bankruptcy, and administrative law, appeals from territory supreme courts and tribunals administering federal laws. The other specialized court is the Family Court

which deals with divorce, custody of children, and associated matrimonial property disputes.

All states and territories have supreme courts and magistrates' courts, and several have intermediate district or county courts which deal mainly with state laws, federal criminal offenses and federal income tax. The supreme courts have the same role at the state level as the High Court does federally. Magistrates' courts deal summarily with most ordinary offenses and preliminary hearings to determine whether sufficient grounds exist in more serious offenses to be tried before a judge and jury. The capital territory and external territories of Norfolk Island, Christmas Island and the Cocos islands have court systems similar in general to the states. Australia has independent federal, state and territory police.

Political Issues

Today the two major political parties are the Australian *Labor Party* (ALP), and the conservative *Liberal Party*. The *ALP*, under the leadership of Prime Minister Robert Hawke controlled the government from 1983 to December 1991 when Paul Keating replaced him as head of the party and Prime Minister. Mr. Keating was returned to office in the March 1993 elections.

In addition to the two major parties, other parties represented in the parliament are the *National Party,* the *Australian Democrats,* the *Northern Territories Country Liberal Party*, and the *Western Australia Greens*. A new party, the *One Nation Party,*

appeared on the scene in 1997 but has yet to contest an election.

The *Liberal Party* selected its fifth leader since 1983, when 42–year–old Alexander Dower replaced John Hewson, who had taken the blame for 1993 election losses. *ALP* continued to rule with 80 of 147 seats in the House and 30 of 75 seats in the Senate. The *Liberal–National* opposition coalition controlled 49 and 16 seats and 30 and 5 seats respectively in the House and Senate.

Former Prime Minister Paul Keating, on the other hand, remained atop the *ALP* in spite of a scandal involving Roslyn Kelly, the only woman member of the cabinet, who allegedly doled out sports grants for political purposes prior to the 1993 elections. Brian Burke, former Western Australia *Labor* premier, was sentenced to prison for misuse of government and party funds. Internal squabbling in the *ALP* was also a problem in 1994. This was exacerbated by the release of the memoirs of former Prime Minister Robert Hawke.

There were other serious issues arising during the year including the question of the future role of women in the *ALP,* and declining support for the party among unions, which comprised only about 37% of the membership.

In March 1995 the declining fortunes of the *ALP* seemed to be changing when the party's Bob Carr narrowly defeated *Liberal Party* candidate John Faye for the premiership of New South Wales. However, the *Liberals* defeated the *ALP* in the Nappa Valley by–election with an 18% swing in the vote from the previous election, one of the worst defeats in a by–election in recent Australian history. A 2% rise in the interest rate was apparently a major issue. In July the *ALP* retained control of Queensland with a 16 vote margin.

But nationally, the *Liberal Party* was experiencing a resurgence. John Howard was selected as the new party leader and throughout the year he gained popularity, especially among older Australians. However, Howard did not appear to be a strong leader, having tried once before, in the late 1980s, to guide the *Liberal Party*. He did manage to moderate some of his views, for example, calling for a referendum on the question of whether the country should become a republic (he had earlier been a monarchist). In the end, however, the economy and the personality of the two contenders, Howard and Keating, proved decisive.

The conservative *Liberal–National* coalition won a landslide victory on March 2, 1996 in national elections which gave the new government a 40 seat margin in the lower house of Parliament. The victory ended 13 years of *ALP* rule. But the swing to the right seems to have gone beyond the move toward the conservatives in the country's political life.

A newly elected political independent, a former operator of a fish and chips shop named Pauline Hansen, rose in September 1996 to give her maiden speech in parliament. Once standing she proceeded to attack the Australian Asian and aboriginal community with considerable vehemence. Hansen claimed that Asian immigration was swamping Australia. Her attacks on Australia's non–white community were nothing new. Indeed, for much of Australian history a largely "whites only" policy had been the norm. But this was in late 1996, and after years of official attempts by the government and business community to improve their relationship with Asia. The storm of controversy she began has not yet let up. Indeed, political polls show that 10% of the population supports her racist comments and many showed support for the new political movement, the *One Nation Party*, which she launched during the spring of 1997.

Though pushed to do so for months, not until March of 1997 did the conservative Prime Minister, John Howard, launch an official effort to discredit the racism of her message. And given her new party's poll numbers, that may have been more of a political than a moral decision.

Foreign Relations

Several issues have dominated Australian foreign policy of late, the most important of which is the new government's interest in pulling back somewhat from the several–year effort to associate themselves more closely with Asia.

In early 1995, the former labor foreign minister, Gareth Evans, reemphasized the country's relations with Asia when he called for "full partnership" with the region. It was also stressed that Australia did not look toward the United States as a guarantor for the security of the area. In early 1996, however there were indications that the new government intended to reorient the country's foreign affairs position to emphasize that Australia still valued its relationships with the West despite the newer interest in Asia. The government appeared to be backing away from recent trends to integrate Australia more closely into the dynamic East Asian communities. President Clinton's November 1996 visit reinforced that effort, as have increased Australian–American military cooperation and the Australian offer (not accepted) to locate U.S. military equipment in Australia.

Not surprisingly, Beijing has been aroused by these developments which stirred the Australian Foreign Minister to deny that Australia has any interest in "containing" China. Nevertheless Australia also took a strong public stance against Chinese nuclear tests. Still, relations between Australia and the People's Republic have generally been good. Australia is looking to increase trade between the two countries.

Predictably, relations with southeast Asia have been strained of late not just due to the country's recent moves toward the West but by the more overt racism of the new *One Nation Party* and its leader, Pauline Hansen. Certainly these developments have reinforced those in the Asian community who have not welcomed Australia's recent attempts to associate itself more closely with Asia.

Aerial view of Canberra with Lake Burley Griffin in the background

Australian Information Service

Australia

Indonesia, because of its proximity, and status as the world's fourth largest country, is their top priority in the region. The two countries have had strained relations in the past over human rights issues and especially over the status of East Timor. Most recently these tensions have resulted in an unwillingness to accept the credential's of the countries' respective ambassadors.

In March 1995, relations with Cambodia were negatively affected when the Phnom Penh government granted amnesty to Khmer Rouge General Tuk Rin. The problem centered over the fact that the general may have had a part in the killing of an Australian, David Wilson, who was kidnaped while on vacation in Cambodia. Kellie Wilkinson, another Australian, was killed in Cambodia earlier in 1994. A Khmer Rouge field commander, Paet, is believed to be the one directly responsible for Wilson's death. The Australian government indicated that amnesty for the commander was not acceptable.

Former Prime Minister Keating spoke out strongly against French nuclear tests in the latter half of 1995, at one point charging that it "defied common sense." Australia has also called for new international controls on nuclear weapons production and stockpiling.

Culture

In the years after Europeans first began settling in Australia it quickly became a society largely dominated by Westerners whose culture resembled that of North America and England. The original aboriginal peoples, like Native Americans, increasingly lost their land to the aggressive Westerners, and immigration laws strongly discriminated against Asians. This "Whites Only" attitude of Australia was a feature of Australian society until fairly recently. Within those parameters, Australians built a society similar to many other Western societies.

Education is free and compulsory through the secondary school level. There are no tuition fees at the 18 government–funded universities and many colleges offering diplomas, degree and post–graduate studies.

Because of the climate, outdoor sports such as swimming, surfing, several types of football and tennis are very popular, and Australia has produced many Olympic champions. Horse racing is widely enjoyed, and betting on the horses is a consuming topic of interest among many.

Though it has vast spaces and relatively few people, Australia is highly urbanized, perhaps because most population growth and development has taken place only over the past 75 years. More than 80% of the population lives in urban centers and more than 60% are concentrated in five major state capitals. Two cities dominate urban life. Sydney faces the southeast coast and has a population of more than 3.5 million; Melbourne (2.8 million) faces the southern Bass Strait. All of the cultural entertainment and events common to Europe and America are abundant in both. Perth, with a population of 850,000 and lying on the southwestern coast, is caressed by a gentle climate similar to that found in the Mediterranean and Caribbean resorts of the western world.

Australia's Federal Capital is Canberra, a 20th century city, the basic plan for which was conceived by Chicago architect Walter Burley Griffin shortly before World War I. Today, it is a garden city of more than 265,000 people—with over 8 million trees planted in the last half century—and it occupies the site of a former sheep station (ranch) in the foothills of the Australian Alps.

The world of white Australia has usually not been shared equally with that of its aboriginal community whose lot is decidedly less attractive. Aborginal Australians can expect to live twenty years less than whites and a quarter of them are unemployed. Of late, new controversies have entered the public arena that have aroused even more tensions between the two communities. On one hand there is growing sentiment against the social welfare programs the government supplies for the aboriginal community, but on the other great anxiety about a number of recent court decisions that have authorized greater aboriginal rights to millions of acres of land now being used by Australian ranchers.

From the perspective of some aboriginal leaders, these new rights should allow their people to wean themselves from government welfare programs, something whites should theoretically welcome. But since aboriginal economic empowerment is, in the case of the land, tied to competing White claims, the problems are not likely to be resolved soon.

Economy

Australia's economy has changed much in the last fifty years from one which relied heavily on primary production to a mature, diverse one with nearly two–thirds of production in the service sector. World War II and post–war immigration spurred rapid expansion of secondary industry, diversification and overall economic growth. Large investments were made in mining and energy projects. Although the agricultural and mining sectors account for a small part of the country's production, they account for 75% of total exports. Australia leads the world in wool production and is a major supplier of wheat, meat and sugar. Australia is also a leading exporter of coal and a major supplier of iron ore, gold, bauxite, and alumina.

The export base was diversified in the 1980's, with the fastest growth in manufactured products and in services. Tourism has been strong though there is some concern of late that the new racial tensions make the country less attractive to Asian tourists. The country has had strong economic and employment growth over the past twenty years. In the 1980s, the Australian economy ranked fifth and employment was second in terms of growth among the OECD countries. These figures would, however, put Australia far behind its ASEAN neighbors.

At the end of 1995, complaints were being heard about the economy. Unemployment was high although jobs were being created at an expanding rate. The current account deficit for fiscal 1995–1996 was predicted to be about $16 billion, worrisome but considerably better than the $20 billion of the previous year.

In late 1996 two liquid natural gas (LNG) projects were announced for Western Australia; on completion an estimated nine million tons of LNG per year will be available for export which should improve the balance of trade considerably. Still, Gross Domestic Product (GDP) for 1996 was down and the government raised some eyebrows recently by selling off some national assets, including Quantas airlines.

The Future

Australia faces no immediate external threats. Its growing involvement with the countries of East Asia, particularly the ASEAN states of Southeast Asia, can only help to improve her regional economic position. But they will require a sophisticated handling of the recent resurgence of some white Australian racist sentiments. Growing trade with Japan, China, and Vietnam will also provide a boost to the lagging economy. Increasing tensions in the ASEAN region over the South China Sea and arms build–ups may require a greater military presence by Australia in the region, especially if the United States becomes less visible over the next few years. Australia has the resources and location to be a vital full partner with the countries of East Asia.

Koala kindergarten

The Republic of FIJI

Prime Minister Sitiveni Rabuka

Area: 7,055 sq. mi. (330 islands) of which about 97 are inhabited).
Population: 796,000 (estimated).
Capital City: Suva (Pop. 151,000 estimated).
Languages: English (official), Fijian, Hindi.
Principal Religion: Christianity.
Main Exports: Sugar, tobacco, textiles, chemicals.
Currency: Fiji dollar.
Annual GDP Per Capita: U.S. $ 2,600 (estimated).
Former Colonial Status: British Crown Colony.
Independence Date: October 10, 1970.
Chief of State: Ratu Sir Kamisese Mara, President.
Head of Government: Major General Sitiveni Rabuka, Prime Minister.

One of the best known of the many island nations of the South Pacific, Fiji attracts tourists from Australia, New Zealand and North America. Sadly, this former crown colony of the British has often experienced considerable ethnic tensions between the native Fijians who make up around 45% of the population and the many Fijians of South Asian and mixed heritage. The primary cause of the tensions has been the effort of the Fijian–dominated government to maintain their political control over the other ethnic communities.

Fiji is attempting to raise the level of its foreign relations with its neighbors. The country's central location, among the Pacific island states, places it in a geographically advantageous position. In 1994 a memorandum of understanding was completed on fisheries and handicrafts with Tuvalu. Fiji is a member of the Pacific Fo-

rum but has thus far declined membership in other, more sub–regional groupings such as the Melanesian Spearhead Group. It is broadening its horizons with a new "look North" policy which will focus more on Asia. The country already has well developed ties to the west with Australia and New Zealand.

The Republic of KIRIBATI
(pronounced Kiri–baas)

Beretitenti **(President) Teburoro Tito**

Area: 338 sq. mi. (33 small islands).
Population: 80,919 (estimated).
Capital City: Bairiki (on Tarawa).
Languages: English (official), Gilbertese.
Principal Religion: Roman Catholic Christianity (48%), Protestant Christianity 45% (Congregational).
Main Exports: Fish, copra.
Annual GDP per capita: U.S. $ 860. (estimated).
Currency: Australian dollar.
Former Colonial Status: British Colony as the Gilbert Islands.
Independence Date: July 12, 1979.
Chief of State: Teburoro Tito, President (pronounced See–Toe, since 1994).

One of the least developed nations of the world, Kiribati is made up of 33 islands whose population is overwhelmingly Micronesian in origin. Most families live by growing produce such as bananas, breadfruit and taro; in recent years the leading export has been copra. Among this small nation's leading resources is its control of fishing rights in its territories.

Politically the Republic of Kiribati is governed by a unicameral parliament which nominates candidates for the presidency. Candidates for president are then voted upon in elections with universal suffrage. A parliamentary vote of no confidence can bring down the government.

Marshall Islands

Area: 68 sq. mi. (31 small islands).
Population: 55,000 (estimated).
Capital City: Majuro.
Language: English.
Principal Religion: Christianity (mostly protestant).

The Republic of the MARSHALL ISLANDS

President Imata Kabua

Main Exports: Copra, copra oil, agricultural products, handicrafts.
Annual GDP Per Capita: U.S. $2,000 (1994).
Currency: U.S. dollar.
Former Political Status: Part of the UN Trust Territory of the Pacific under U.S. administration.
Independence Date: October 21, 1986.
Chief of State: Imata Kabua, President (since January 1997).

The inhabitants of the Marshall Islands have been among the peoples most affected by the nuclear arms race after the United States assumed their control from Japan following World War II. They were dubiously honored by being chosen as a nuclear test site. From 1946 to 1958 the atolls of Bikini and Eniwetok were used to test nuclear weapons; their people were removed to other islands. After attempts to clean up the toxic effects of the bombing were carried out, some former inhabitants of Bikini attempted to return home, but by the late 1970s they had to leave again. The area was found still to contaminated. The Kwajalein atoll is still used by the United States as a missile testing ground. Economically the island nation is dependant on the United States for 90% of its income.

The Republic now has embassies in China, Fiji, Japan, the U.S., and the United Nations; with consulates in California and Hong Kong. The Chinese are using the Marshall Islands to circumvent the limit on the amount of garments that it can export to the United States; China and the Marshall Islands agreed on a joint venture in December 1993 to build a garment factory. It will produce almost one million pieces a year and will employ Chinese workers initially. Marshallese will eventually take over all of the production jobs.

The Federated States of MICRONESIA

President Bailey Olter

Area: 271 sq. mi (about 600 islands, the largest of which are Pohnpei, Truk, Yap, and Kosrae).
Population: 128,000 (estimated).
Capital City: Kolonia (on Pohnpei).
Language: English; other indigenous languages are spoken.
Principal Religions: Mostly Roman Catholic and Protestant Christianity.
Main Export: Copra.
Currency: U.S. dollar.
Annual GDP per capita: U.S. $1,700 (estimated).
Former Political Status: Part of the UN Trust Territory of the Pacific under U.S. administration.
Independence Date: November 3, 1986.
Chief of State: Bailey Olter, President (since May 1991).

Over the years the islands that became the Federated States of Micronesia have been ruled successively by Spain, Germany, Japan and the United States. Micronesia is still dependent on the United States for financial grants. Other sources of income include fees from foreign ships fishing in national waters. Most people live by subsistence farming and fishing.

Under the terms of its relationship with the United States the latter continues to provide for the country's security and defense as well as financial aid which is expected to total $1.3 billion during the period 1986–2001.

The Republic of NAURU

Former President Bernard Dowiyogo

Area: 8.2 sq. mi.
Population: 10,273 (estimated).
Capital City: Most of the government offices are located in the Yaren District of the island.
Language: Nauruan (official); English is widely spoken and used in government and commerce.
Principal Religions: Protestant Christianity (65%), Roman Catholic Christianity (30%).
Main Export: Phosphates.
Currency: Australian dollar.
Annual GDP per capita: $10,000 (estimated).
Former Political Status: UN trusteeship under Australia, New Zealand, and the UK.
Independence Date: January 31, 1968.
Chief of State: Kinza Klodimar, President (since February 1997).

Unlike most of its Pacific neighbors, whose nations are often made up of hundreds of islands, Nauru consists of only a single island. But that single island is richly endowed with phosphate, a mineral essential in making fertilizer. Thus Nauru's small population enjoys one of the highest standards of living in the area. Education is free and there are two well-equipped hospitals.

New Zealand

Cosmopolitan Wellington at dusk

Area: 103,000 sq. mi. (268,276 sq. km., the land surface somewhat smaller than Colorado).

Population: 3.6 million.

Capital City: Wellington (Pop. 365,000, estimated).

Climate: Temperate, with ample rainfall; subtropical conditions at the northern tip of the North Island, with colder temperatures in the South Island.

Neighboring Countries: Australia, about 1,200 miles to the northwest.

Official Language: English.

Ethnic Background: European, mostly British (about 92%), Maori (about 8%).

Principal Religion: Protestant Christianity (82%).

Main Exports (to Australia, U.K., Japan, U.S.): Meat and dairy products, fish, wool.

Main Imports (same trading partners): Petroleum, cars, trucks, iron and steel.

Currency: New Zealand Dollar.

Former Colonial Status: British Colony (1839–1907).

National Day: February 6 is Waitangi Day, anniversary of the signing of the Treaty of Waitangi in 1840 between the British and the Maoris.

Chief of State: Her Majesty Queen Elizabeth II, represented by Governor General Dame Catherine Tizard (since Novembver 1990).

Head of Government: The Rt. Hon. Jim Bolger, Prime Minister (since July 1990).

National Flag: A purple field with the Union Jack in the upper left corner and four 5–pointed stars in the right half of the field.

Per Capita Income: U.S. $12,500.

The remote islands of New Zealand are about 1,200 miles from their nearest neighbor, Australia, and prior to the advent of air transportation it was one of the world's most isolated nations. The North Island is the more habitable of the two, and, though smaller than the South Island, it has more than half the country's population.

In the North Island there are volcanic and thermal areas dominated by three volcanic peaks, Ruapehu, Ngauruhoe and Tongariro, all active and given to occasional eruptions of steam and ash. In the central plateau area there is activity caused by the thermal pressure from deep within the earth in the form of geysers, hot springs, steam vents and foul–smelling deposits of sulphur. The average annual rainfall for the whole country is about 60 inches, which allows for quick growth of rich vegetation to feed the 60 million sheep that abound in New Zealand.

The South Island is much more rugged and contains the Southern Alps which equal their European namesake in beauty and wildness. In this mountainous region the climate can sometimes be subarctic. In contrast to the abundant growth of the North Island, the grasses of the South Island are more suited to rearing Merino sheep which have a fine coat to protect them from the chilly air. Most of the sheep of the North Island are crossbreeds, designed to produce both meat and wool.

In terms of the Northern Hemisphere,

188

New Zealand

New Zealand occupies a position in the Southern Hemisphere which would run from the mild climate of southern California northward to the much cooler central part of British Columbia, which has bitterly cold winters. The reversal of warm and cold zones and of summer and winter in the Southern Hemisphere make northern New Zealand the warm, subtropical area and the southern region the colder one.

History

At a time unrecorded in written history, the Maori people, vigorous and handsome Polynesians, migrated to New Zealand. Their South Pacific way of life had to change; there were no coconuts to harvest, dress had to be warmer and their overall diet had to be adjusted accordingly. Fresh water fishing in the rivers and sparkling lakes became an important new source of food.

The first European to make more than a quick visit to New Zealand was the famous British navigator, Captain James Cook, who made a landing in 1769. The growth of the whaling industry in the next decades attracted increasing British colonization and trade because of the closeness of the islands to the southwest Pacific whaling areas. Missionaries settled in 1814 and quickly began the task of converting the Maoris to Christianity.

After several thousands of Britishers had settled in New Zealand, Great Britain annexed the islands in 1839 with the signing of the Treaty of Waitangi. The Maori people resisted the colonizers. There was sporadic bitter fighting in the 1860–1870 period—the native population which had been about 150,000 at the beginning of the century was reduced to less than 50,000 by the 1870's.

The system of individual provinces that had been in existence until 1876 was abolished, and a centralized, more efficient, administration was established. The economy provided a bare support for the colonizers and their descendants until the turn of the 20th century, when faster ships and refrigeration boosted the export of New Zealand's agricultural products, which went mainly to Great Britain. The *Liberal Party* was in control from 1890 until 1912.

New Zealand was granted dominion status within the British Commonwealth in 1907 as a result of a new vigor imparted to the country's politics and administration by energetic *Liberal* leader Richard John Seddon, Prime Minister from 1893 to 1906. For all practical purposes it was independent from that time on.

At the same time the Maori population was undergoing a gradual transformation; they adopted Western dress, and among other things began to practice agriculture and animal husbandry in the manner of the Englishmen. The Maoris now number about 290,000, many of them of mixed Maori and European parentage.

As it entered World War I, New Zealand was governed by the *Reform Party,* and later by a coalition government. New Zealand fought on the allied side and took part as an independent state in the peace settlement at Versailles. It joined the League of Nations and was awarded a mandate over the islands of Western Samoa which had been captured from the Germans during the war.

Adverse economic conditions during the 1920–1940 period created an increase in labor organization and unrest. By the late 1930's, however, aided by an ambitious program of public works and social security under a succession of *Labour Party* governments, prosperity began to return. New Zealand took an active part in World War II, although it did not face the Japanese threat to the extent that Australia did. In the postwar period, New Zealand recognized the declining influence of Great Britain in Southeast Asia and the rise of U.S. power in the region; it entered into the ANZUS treaty with Australia and the U.S. to provide security against a possible revival of Japanese militarism, and later against the communist threat. It also joined the SEATO treaty with the United States, Australia, Britain, France, Thailand, Pakistan and the Philippines primarily to assure Thailand of Western support against communist subversion, and generally to meet the threat posed by the growth of communism in the region.

The *National Party* dominated the political system of New Zealand, modeled after the parliamentary system of England, until 1972. The *Labour Party* came to power in that year, winning 55 seats in Parliament on a platform of more welfare benefits. This was reversed in elections held in

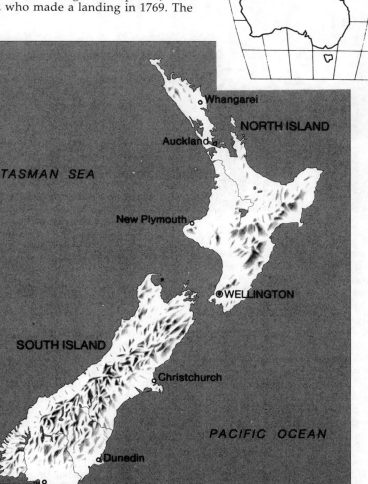

New Zealand

Late afternoon at Lake Hayes, South Island

Courtesy: New Zealand Information Service

late 1975 when the *Labour Party* was defeated because of its liberal domestic policies; the *National Party* won 55 seats. Its forceful, conservative leader, Robert Muldoon, became Prime Minister; the opposition was reduced to 32 seats and other smaller factions elected no representatives.

Because of the loss of a guaranteed market for its meat and dairy products when Britain joined the European Common Market, as well as because of its general ineptitude, the conservative Muldoon government lost support even among businessmen as New Zealand piled up an $11 billion foreign debt. Accordingly, *Labour* won by a fairly wide margin in the House of Representatives in mid–1984 (56 to 37).

The next Prime Minister, David Lange (pronounced *Lon*–jee), was much more favorable to private enterprise than are

many of his *Labour* colleagues. Therefore, in order to pacify the left wing of the party, Lange announced that no nuclear-armed U.S. naval vessels would be allowed to call at New Zealand ports—he had previously been a moderate on the nuclear issue. The left in New Zealand does not feel threatened by anyone, does not want to be defended by nuclear weapons against what it regards as a nonexistent enemy, and hopes to start a trend toward worldwide nuclear disarmament. Some leaders of other countries and territories in the South and Southwest Pacific feel the same way. Since the U.S. refuses on principle to say whether or not any particular vessel is nuclear-armed, this meant that *no* U.S. naval vessel could dock in New Zealand.

As the U.S. began to apply counter-pressures, including the withholding of some intelligence information and threats to cut

back on imports from New Zealand, the ANZUS alliance (Australia, New Zealand and the U.S.) began to come under serious strain. The U.S. was afraid that New Zealand's action might be imitated by other allies such as Australia and Japan.

Finally, in June 1986, at a meeting in Manila between Prime Minister Lange and Secretary of State George Shultz, the chain broke—at least temporarily. Good naturedly, Shultz admitted to the press that, "We part company on security matters as friends, but we part." Lange was equally gracious, but stood by his government's policy of not allowing port access to U.S. ships unless it was convinced that they carried no nuclear weaponry. In August the U.S. suspended its security arrangements with New Zealand under the ANZUS treaty until "adequate corrective measures" were taken.

Since the government of Prime Minister

190

Lange was determined to bar U.S. nuclear–armed and/or nuclear–powered naval vessels from its ports, and the U.S. would "neither confirm nor deny" that any given ship was nuclear, in 1986 the U.S. declared that since the alliance could not survive without such visits, New Zealand had in effect withdrawn from ANZUS and was no longer entitled to American protection. New Zealand maintains its defense ties with Australia, which stayed in ANZUS, however. The Lange government proposed in early 1987 a buildup of New Zealand's forces that would maintain its security by being able to operate in its general vicinity, but without the mission of capability of fighting in distant areas as its troops had sometimes done in the past.

In August 1987 the *Labour Party* won an election with a 15–seat majority in the 97–member parliament, the same as before. The Lange government's program of economic liberalization and privatization, which includes lower tax rates for the upper income brackets, has aroused considerable political opposition. Unemployment has doubled.

In 1989 the *Labour Party* government took a strong position against the U.S. over the issue of whether nuclear weapons were entering the country's territory aboard American naval vessels. Prime Minister Lange discussed withdrawal from the ANZUS defense treaty. The *National Party* took a more conciliatory position on the issue toward the United States. Prime Minister Lange resigned in August 1989, and Geoffrey Palmer took over the premiership. He also opposed visits by U.S. naval vessels carrying nuclear weapons. The *National Party* won the 1990 elections. Unemployment appeared to be more important than the nuclear issue.

Politics and Government

New Zealand is a member of the British Commonwealth with a parliamentary form of government. Differences with the British model include a unicameral House of Representatives with 99 seats, and a three year term for the Prime Minister. The political system is multi-party in nature with the major parties being the *National Party*, *Labour Party*, *Alliance*, and *New Zealand First*. The Queen of England is represented by a Governor General. Last year the electoral law was been changed to a mixed–member proportional representation system. This awards seats in a district based on the percentage of votes won by a party, tending to help smaller parties and encourage a multi–party system.

In elections of late 1996. the *National Party* under the leadership of Prime Minister James Bolger, which had been in

Prime Minister J. B. Bolger

power since November 1990, was returned to office. Last year, however, was one of realignment among the country's political parties. The *National Party* did maintain control of the government but its majority eroded.

Within the opposition there have been problems in recent years as well. The *Alliance Party* split with the Greens. Dissident Greens left to form the *Green Society*. This part of the political spectrum is not insignificant and has had an effect on national policy issues.

More significant was the growing strength of the *New Zealand First Party*. Led by Winston Peters, a Maori lawyer, it has lashed out against Asian immigration which its supporters claim has swamped the country with people who lack a commitment to the nation. As we have seen in Australia, the anti–immigration campaign has attracted not only considerable attention and controversy but political support as well. In fact *New Zealand First* did quite well in the fall 1996 elections.

As had been expected the elections led to the formation of a coalition government again headed by the *National Party*'s Jim Bolger. But this time Winston Peters of the *New Zealand First Party* took the post of deputy prime minister and treasurer. The creation of the coalition with its strong anti–immigration, anti–Asian tone is likely to have an impact on New Zealand's relationship with its neighbors. Certainly within the country the likelihood is that a purely Asian–based political party may form as well.

While the shifting political landscape attracted most the most attention, there were other issues of importance in 1997.

Race relations between the indigenous Maoris and the British–descended New Zealanders have not been good in recent years. The problem dates back to the 1840 *Treaty of Waitangi* which first saw the British officially establish themselves in New Zealand and proved to be the beginning of the loss of Maori land to the new Anglo immigrants.

The Maori, which constitute about 15% of the population today, have shared little in the development of modern New Zealand. After public demonstrations in early 1995, both sides agreed to a multi–million dollar settlement involving both money and the return of Maori lands. The May 1995 deal also includes an official apology for land which was confiscated as a result of conflict in the 1860s. By 1997 the government had agreed to the return of an equivalent of $450 million, and some expected the eventual total to reach $750 million. Most New Zealanders hoped the settlement would mark the beginning of improved relations.

Foreign Policy

A significant step was taken in 1995 to put New Zealand-U.S. relations back on track when Prime Minister Bolger headed for Washington for a meeting with President Bill Clinton. The last meeting between heads of state of the two countries had occurred in 1984 during the Reagan administration. Soon after the 1984 meeting, then Prime Minister David Lange, banned a U.S. ship from entering a New Zealand port because it was suspected of carrying nuclear weapons. Anti–nuclear legislation was then passed which in turn led to a break in military ties and an end of top level contact between the two countries. New Zealand has indicated that it is willing to undertake joint operations with the U.S. but that it is up to Washington to decide what it wishes to do. The rift between the two countries resulted in New Zealand's exclusion from the *ANZUS* defense pact following the rift. The commander of U.S. forces in the Pacific visited the country in April 1994. This may have provided the opening for the Prime Minister's trip to Washington.

The Bolger visit did not end the standoff in military relations, but overall relations appear to have been mended. The Prime Minister had the opportunity to meet with the Clinton administration officials, including the Vice President and Secretaries of State and Defense. Mr. Bolger also met with key Republican figures.

New Zealand was outraged at French nuclear tests in the Pacific in 1995. The government sent a ship with two members of parliament to Mururoa Atoll to observe. Military cooperation with France

New Zealand

Polo tournament at Cambridge, New Zealand

was suspended and the ambassador to France was briefly recalled.

The issue of establishing a common aviation market with Australia was continued from the previous year with little progress. In May, Auckland hosted the annual meeting of the Asian Development Bank. New Zealand, like Australia, is attempting to turn toward Asia, with its tremendous potential as an export market. However, it was reported that the New Zealand media does not have a permanent representative stationed in the area. The old European–dominated world has a strong pull in Wellington.

Culture

Apart from the Maori community, life in New Zealand is predominantly British—moreso than in any other nation of the British Commonwealth except for the British Isles. Isolated and relatively small, it has a reputation for being provincial and conservative, whereas British cultural values have rapidly changed since World War II. Thus, the old saying that New Zealanders are more British than the British has some validity today.

The accent of the great majority of the people is similar to that of the middle and upper class gentry of England, and in the southern highlands around Dunedin and Invercargill, English is spoken with the ac-cent of the Scottish speech of ancestors of the people.

Economy

Agriculture, livestock raising and dairy-ing predominate in the New Zealand economy. Mining and other industries have been added in the post World War II era which will continue gradual expansion. The economy is very dependent on foreign trade and this has caused some difficulty for the unskilled worker. The government has taken the position, however, that this is the best course for the country in the long term. The current government has undertaken significant privatization. The past years have seen a restructuring of the economy which make it one of the least regulated in the world. Significant cuts in welfare have also been undertaken and there were significant losses in jobs.

This situation, however, now appears to have improved.

The economy grew by 5.5% for the year ending June 1995, compared to 6.2% for the previous year. More recent growth though has been closer to 3%. Inflation for calendar 1996 was a bit over 2%. Exports grew by about 4% in 1995 to $21 billion but were done again for 1996 to around $13.6 billion.

The average citizen received an early Christmas present on December 13, 1995 when the government announced a tax cut valued at $710 million to take effect in July 1996. This is to be followed by a $1 billion cut. The middle class tax rate of 28% will decrease and the threshold for the higher bracket will be raised from 33%. The government also intends to spend more over the next several years. It can well afford to do so. The budget went from a $1 billion deficit in 1992, to a $2.9 billion surplus in 1995, and is expected to increase to almost $6 billion by 1998. Government debt stood at $38 billion in June 1995, but is predicted to fall to $19 billion (18% of GDP) by 1999. New Zealand's small economy remains healthy if not robust.

The Future

With the continuing success of the East Asia region, New Zealand should work hard to develop existing links with its neighbors. It would be wise to emulate Australia's tilt toward East Asia for economic and political reasons. But to do so it may have to moderate the influence of some of the more racist elements in the society which have attracted so much attention in recent years.

Christchurch: Anglican Cathedral at night

Courtesy: New Zealand Information Service

The Republic of PALAU

President Kuniwo Nakamura

Area: 364 sq. mi. of land on approximately 200 (mostly tiny) islands.
Population: 16,952 (estimated).
Capital City: Koror (Pop. 10,501, estimated).
Language: Palauan (official), but English is widely used in government and commerce.
Principal Religion: Predominantly Roman Catholic and Protestant Christianity.
Currency: U.S. dollar.
Annual GDP per capita: U.S. $5,000 (estimated).
Former Political Status: The last remaining entity in the UN Trust Territory of the Pacific, it was largely responsible for its domestic affairs. The U.S. remained the UN–designated trustee for Palau, responsible for its international relations, until the country declared its independence.
Independence date: October 2, 1994.
Chief of State: Kuniwo Nakamura, President.

The background of the Palauans is a mixed heritage made up of peoples from Micronesia, Malaya, Polynesia and the Philippines. Japan administered them and made Palau the center of its South Pacific activities during World War II. After the war, the United States assumed their administration which was formally terminated in 1994.

The main source of income is working for the government. Palau still receives 90% of its government revenue from the United States. People also support themselves through a combination of subsistence agriculture and fishing.

SOLOMON ISLANDS

Prime Minister Solomon Mamaloni

Area: 10,640 sq. mi.
Population: 412,902 (estimated).
Capital City: Honiara (Pop. 25,000, estimated) on the island of Guadalcanal.
Languages: Over 100 indigenous tongues, with a Melanesian pidgin used for simplified communication. English is used in government and commerce.
Principal Religion: Nominally Christian, with many denominations and indigenous beliefs.
Main Exports: Fish, timber, copra, palm oil.
Currency: Solomon Islands dollar.
Annual GDP per capita: U.S. $2,590 (estimated).
Former Political Status: British protectorate.
Independence Date: July 7, 1978.
Chief of State: Queen Elizabeth II.
Head of Government: Solomon Mamaloni, Prime Minister (since November 7, 1994).

The Solomons were named after an early Spanish explorer's belief that they were the source of the biblical King Solomon's gold mines. But despite that early European contact, the inhabitants' resistance to Western encroachment kept the islands outside of the colonial system until the late nineteenth century. The British established a protectorate.

Today, the vast majority of the population is involved in subsistence agriculture though there is considerable commercial economic activity as well ranging from a large lumbering establishment to fish processing.

On November 7, 1994, Solomon Mamaloni was elected Prime Minister. He defeated Sir Beddeley Devesi, 29 votes to 18 in a secret ballot election in the national Parliament. This is his third term of office.

The government faced a minor political crisis in March 1994 when Michael Miana, Minister of Tourism and Culture, was charged with 28 counts of misconduct. He is the first cabinet officer to face such charges.

Prime Minister Solomon Mamaloni announced that a newly reorganized national reconnaissance and surveillance force will be in operation by 1998. Recent border incursions by the Bougainville Revolutionary Army (BRA) from Papua New Guinea (PNG) over the last years may have prompted the announcement. In March 1994, the PNG government paid the Solomon Islands $500,000 for damages incurred from an illegal border violation in 1992, which took the lives of three people.

The new force will be separated from the Ministry of Police and National Security, and will be used to monitor exports by sea and for other national security matters including border patrol. Under an agreement signed at the end of 1994, the force is trained in Port Moresby, PNG. In peace time, it will be used for civil work projects and disaster relief.

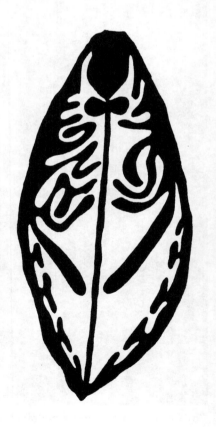

His Majesty the King of Tonga

Sir Tulaga Manuella

Area: 283 sq. mi. (171 islands).
Population: 106,466 (estimated).
Capital City: Nuku'alofa (Pop. 32,000, estimated). Languages: Tongan, English.
Principal Religion: Christianity.
Main Exports: Coconut oil, copra, bananas, other fruits and vegetables.
Currency: Pa'anga.
Annual GDP per capita: U.S. $2,160 (estimated).
Former Political Status: British Protectorate.
Independence Date: June 4, 1970.
Chief of State: His Majesty King Taufa'ahau Tupou IV.
Head of Government: His Royal Highness Prince Farafehi Tu'ipelehake, Prime Minister (since December 1965).

Tonga's monarchy, which today operates as a constitutionally ordained one, has existed since the 10th century. The current royal family, however, has only held the throne since the nineteenth century. The government includes a one house legislature that represents both commoners and nobles.

Most of its people, who speak a language derived from Samoan, live in villages and work in the production of cash crops ranging from coconuts, and bananas to vanilla beans. Some manufacturing goes on mostly associated with food processing. Although tourism has begun to grow, unemployment is high and many people have left the country. Education and health care is free and Tonga has a high literacy rate.

Area: 10 sq. mi. (nine islands).
Population: 10,146 (estimated).
Capital City: Funafuti (Pop. 3,000, estimated).
Languages: Tuvaluan, English.
Principal Religion: Christianity, mostly Protestant.
Main Export: Copra.
Currency: Tuvaluan and/or Australian dollar.
Annual Per Capita GDP Income: U.S. $800.
Former Political Status: British Protectorate as the Ellice Islands.
Independence Date: October 1, 1978.
Chief of State: Queen Elizabeth II, represented by Governor General Sir Tulaga Manuella.
Head of Government: Bikenibeu Paeniu, Prime Minister (since December 23, 1996).

Part of the British Commonwealth, Tuvalu has few natural resources. The originally coral base of the islands makes them a poor site for agriculture. Even finding enough fresh water is at times difficult. Nevertheless, its people live largely on a subsistence farming and fishing economy. The sale of the country's postage stamps are an important source of outside revenue.

The vast majority of the population is of Polynesian origin. Formally known as the Ellice Islands, the small island community is economically poorer than many of its neighbors. The prime minister is

The Republic of VANUATU

President Jean–Marie Leye

chosen from a 12 person parliament. Councils also operate on the outer islands.

Area: 4,750 sq. mi. (82 islands).

Population: 177,504 (estimated).

Capital City: Port Vila (Pop. 21,000 estimated).

Languages: English and French.

Principal Religion: Christianity, (Presbyterian, Anglican, Catholic) with local influences.

Main Exports: Copra, cocoa.

Annual GDP per capita: U.S. $1,220 (estimated).

Currency: Vatu.

Former Political Status: British Protectorate as the New Hebrides.

Independence Date: July 30, 1980.

Chief of State: Jean–Marie Leye, President (since March 1994).

Head of Government: Serge Vohor, Prime Minister (since September 1996).

Vanuatu's people are primarily Melanesian but there are also small minorities of Europeans, Chinese and Polynesians. Economically the islands are doing relatively well compared to many others in the region. Although many of the inhabitants practice subsistence agriculture the economy also includes large scale plantation farming of cocoa to coffee for the export market. Tourism offers additional revenue as does a developing banking industry.

Following an inconclusive election and a vote of no confidence by the legislature, Maxime Carlot Korman, the country's prime minister, was succeeded in that office in December 1995 by Serge Vohor, leader of another faction in his *Union of Moderate Parties* coalition. However, he, too, suffered the fate of his predecessor and was forced from office the following February when Vanuatu's legislators passed a vote of no confidence *in him.* Car-

lot Korman was restored to his old job.

By August 1996 there was continued bickering within the ranks of the *UMP,* and in this odd game of "musical chairs," a new vote of no confidence once again resulted in the ouster of Carlot Korman; Serge Vohor took the helm of office for a second time in less than eight months in September 1996.

Another element in the confused state of affairs in the country occurred a month later when the 300–strong Vanuatu Mobile Force (VMF), which constitutes the nation's army, briefly abducted President Jean–Marie Leye as part of an ongoing dispute about back pay. Vohor's new justice minister (himself, a former prime minister), Fr. Walter Lini, immediately ordered the arrest of 138 members of the VMF, although he made it clear that those not involved in the kidnapping would be allowed to return to their duties upon taking an oath of allegiance to that very volatile government.

Earlier, in December 1993 the People's Republic of China signed an agreement with the government to finance up to 75% of a $3.6 million dollar hydroelectric dam on the northern island of Mallicolo. China will also provide some forty technicians for the project. It also helped Vanuatu build its new parliament buildings and maintains an ambassador to the country. Japan is helping to build a second hydro-

WESTERN SAMOA

**His Highness
Sasuga Malietoa Tanumafili II**

electric dam on the Sarakata River on Santo Island.

Area: 1,097 sq. mi. (Two large islands—Savai'i and Upolu—and seven smaller ones).

Population: 217,000 (estimated).

Capital City: Apia (Pop. 30,000 estimated) on Upolu.

Languages: Somoan, English.

Principal Religion: Christianity.

Main Exports: Coconut oil and cream, taro.

Currency: Tala.

Annual GDP per capita: U.S. $2,000 (estimated).

Former Political Status: UN trusteeship administered by New Zealand.

Independence Date: January 1, 1962.

Head of State: His Highness Sasuga Malietoa Tanumafili II.

Head of Government: Tofilau Eti Alesana, Prime Minister (since April 1988).

A constitutional monarchy like Tonga, Western Samoa has been a German colony and later a New Zealand League of Nations Mandate. The vast majority of its people are farmers who produce a wide variety of crops ranging from coconuts and bananas to tropical fruits, nuts and yams. There have been efforts to expand the islands industrial base with foreign aid. Tourism is also an important part of the local economy.

Most inhabitants are descended from Polynesians who arrived thousands of years ago. There are as well small communities of Europeans and Chinese.

The Samoan coast

THE DEPENDENCIES

The active interest of the United States and European nations in ruling colonies in the countries of Asia was dramatically lessened by two elements of World War II: Japanese military conquest, and the economic drain of the war against Germany and Japan. Shortly after the end of the war two colonial wars erupted, the first against the French in Indochina and the second against the Dutch in Indonesia. The necessity for the West to yield to nationalistic pressures made it clear that the age of colonialism in Asia was over. Nevertheless, a few communities still remain under the control of the Western powers.

French Dependencies

New Caledonia

Area: 8,550 square miles.
Population: 187,784 (estimated).
Annual GDP per capita: U.S. $8,000 (estimated).

This island group is located east of Australia. Its economic importance is as a major exporter of nickel. It has a limited degree of self–government, but it was not scheduled to become independent before 1989 at the earliest.

The indigenous Kanakas (or Kanaks) who are Melanesians, are outnumbered by the combined European, Asian and Polynesian settlers. The majority wants a continuation of French rule, but a militant group of the Kanakas demands independence—which Paris fears might destabilize French Polynesia to the east—and has resorted to violence. President Mitterrand visited the island in early 1985 in an atmosphere of crisis, and offered it limited independence in association with France. This proposal seemed to please neither side.

In elections held in September 1985, the Kanaks won majorities in three of the four regions, although pro–French elements (Europeans and Asians) won an overall majority in the territorial assembly.

The French government of then Premier Jacques Chirac in 1986 canceled the previous political concessions pending the outcome of elections. A referendum held in September 1987 was boycotted by most of the Kanaks, and accordingly the vote was 98% in favor of continued existence as a French territory (rather than as an independent state). Pro–independence demonstrations by Kanaks were then suppressed by French police.

In June 1988, a new French government worked out an agreement with both sides; following a year (1989) of direct French rule, there would be a period of limited self–government and accelerated economic development, followed by a referendum on independence in 1998. Although highly controversial, this agreement was approved in a referendum held in both France and New Caledonia.

French Polynesia

Area: 1,545 square miles.
Population: 224,911 (estimated).
Annual GDP per capita: U.S. $8,000 (estimated).

Scattered over a wide area in the South Pacific, this group of islands includes the famous tourist attraction of Tahiti. The islands have limited self–government. The most controversial issue in recent years has been French nuclear tests which were a cause of grave concern and charges of serious environmental contamination.

In the generation since the French established a military facility there many of the inhabitants have moved from work in a subsistence agricultural setting to jobs working for the military and of course for the famous tourist trade.

New Zealand Dependency

Cook Islands

Sir Geoffrey Henry

Area: 90 square miles.
Population: 19,561 (estimated).
Annual GDP per capita: $3,000 (estimated).
Prime Minister: Sir Geoffrey Henry (since 1989).

These islands, located about 1,700 miles northeast of New Zealand, have a predominantly Polynesian population. They have had internal self–government since 1965, but New Zealand continues to control their defense and foreign relations.

The northern islands are relatively poor; the southern islands are rather prosperous.

The Cook Islands is one of the world's smallest land areas, with 18,500 people, spread over one of the largest sea areas in the world. It is known as a tax haven and has a reputation for rough and tumble politics. Unfortunately, the country also has a foreign debt of approximately NZ$100 million.

United States Dependencies

Guam

Area: 212 square miles.
Population: 156,974 (estimated).
Annual GDP per capita: $14,000 (estimated).

The United States acquired Guam, which is the southernmost of the Marianas, from Spain in 1898 as a result of the Spanish American War. The population is predominantly Micronesian and Catholic.

Guam has self–government but is not yet a Territory or Commonwealth like Puerto Rico. Its residents are U.S. citizens but do not vote in American national elections. Guam has been the site of a major U.S. air base since it was recaptured from the Japanese during World War II. Now that the U.S. has lost its naval base in the Philippines, it is considered as a possible alternative site.

American Samoa

Area: 76 square miles.
Population: 59,566 (estimated).
Annual GDP per capita: $2,600 (1991 est.)

The inhabitants of these seven islands, located just east of Western Samoa, are mostly Polynesian. They enjoy limited self–government under the jurisdiction of the Department of the Interior. The main occupations are farming and fishing.

The U.S. has recently launched a major effort to improve the economic well–being of the territory by stimulating private enterprise to take over government–administered enterprises ("privatization").

The lush jungle on Guam cannot erase the traces of World War II

Photo by Cdr. Thornton W. Wilt

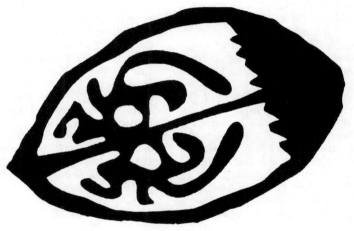

199

Selected Bibliography of Key English Language Sources

For those with computer resources, we have added some internet (World Wide Web) resources which will help in maintaining current understanding of the areas covered by this book. Sources containing ".com" may involve a charge for use.

General

Borrego, John et al., eds. *Capital, the State, and Late Industrialization; Comparative Perspectives on the Pacific Rim*. Boulder, CO: Westview Press, 1996.

Bundy, Barbara K. et al., eds. *The Future of the Pacific Rim: Scenarios for Regional Cooperation*. New York: Praeger, 1994.

Cotterell, Arthur. *East Asia: from Chinese Predominance to the Rise of the Pacific Rim*. New York: Oxford University Press, 1994.

Gibney, Frank. *The Pacific Century: America and Asia in a Changing World*. New York: Scribner's Sons, 1992.

Indorf, Hans H. and Patrick M. Mayerchak. *Linkage or Bondage: U.S. Economic Relations with the ASEAN Region*. Westport, CT: Greenwood Press, 1989.

Jones, Eric L. *Coming Full Circle: an Economic History of the Pacific Rim*. Boulder, CO: Westview Press, 1993.

Kapur, Ashok, ed. *Diplomatic Ideas and Practices of Asian States*. New York: Brill, 1990.

Mayerchak, Patrick M. *Scholars' Guide to Washington, D.C. for Southeast Asian Studies: Brunei, Burma, Cambodia, Indonesia, Laos, Malaysia, Philippines, Singapore, Thailand, Vietnam*. Washington, D.C.: Smithsonian Institution Press, 1983.

Moore, Larry F. and P. Devereaux Jennings, eds. *Human Resource Management on the Pacific Rim: Institutions, Practices, and Attitudes*. Hawthorne, NY: Walter De Gruyter, 1995.

Muhlhausler, Peter. *Linguistic Ecology: Language Change and Linguistic Imperialism in the Pacific Rim*. New York: Routledge, 1996.

Seagrave, Sterling. *Lords of the Rim: the Invisible Empire of the Overseas Chinese*. New York: Putnam, 1995.

Simon, Denis F., ed. *Techno–Security in an Age of Globalization: Perspectives from the Pacific Rim*. Armonk, NY: M.E. Sharpe, 1997.

Taylor, Robert H. *Asia and the Pacific*. 2 v. New York: Facts on File, 1991.

Thompson, Roger C. *The Pacific Basin since 1945: a History of the Foreign Relations of the Asian, Australasian, and American Rim States and the Pacific Islands*. White Plains, NY: Longman Publishing, 1994.

Vogel, Ezra F. *The Four Little Dragons: the Spread of Industrialization in East Asia*. Cambridge, MA: Harvard University Press, 1991.

Weinbaum, Marvin G. and Chetan Kumar, eds. *South Asia Approaches the Millennium: Reexamining National Security*. Boulder, CO: Westview Press.

Asiaweek Magazine —http://www.pathfinder.com/@@eQYLkAQAKcL3YXSV/@Asiaweek/

The Asia Pacific Network http://h-net2.msu.edu/~asia/

Asian Studies Virtual Library —http://coombs.anu.edu.au/WWWVL-AsianStudies.html

East and Southeast Asia

Alagappa, Muthiah, ed. *Political Legitimacy in Southeast Asia: the Quest for Moral Authority*. Stanford, CA: Stanford University Press, 1995.

Balassa, Bela. *Economic Policies in the Pacific Area Developing Countries*. New York: New York University Press, 1991.

Ball, Desmond, ed. *The Transformation of Security of the Asia–Pacific Region*. London: Frank Cass & Company, 1996.

Borno, Silvio et al. *Political Credibility and Economic Development*. New York: St. Martin's Press, 1995.

Chowdhury, Anis. *Asia Pacific Economies: an Analytical Survey*. New York: Routledge, 1997.

Christie, Clive J. *A Modern History of Southeast Asia: Decolonization, Nationalism, and Separatism*. New York: Tauris Academic Studies, 1996.

Leifer, Michael, ed. *Dictionary of the Modern Politics of South–East Asia*. New York: Routledge, 1995.

Levine, Alan J. *The United States and the Struggle for Southeast Asia, 1945–1975*. New York: Praeger, 1995.

MacIntyre, Andrew, ed. *Business and Government in Industrialising Asia*. Ithaca, NY: Cornell University Press, 1994.

McCloud, Donald G. *Southeast Asia: Tradition and Modernity in the Contemporary World*. Boulder, CO: Westview Press, 1995.

Neher, Clark D. *Southeast Asia in the New International Era*. Boulder, CO: Westview Press, 2nd ed. 1994.

Reid, Anthony. *Southeast Asia in the Age of Commerce, 1450–1680, Volume 1: the Lands below the Winds*. New Haven, CT: Yale University Press, 1990.

Reid, Anthony. *Southeast Asia in the Age of Commerce, 1450–1680, Volume 2: Expansion and Crisis*. New Haven, CT: Yale University Press, 1993.

Rigg, Jonathan. *Southeast Asia: a Region in Transition*. Boston, MA: Unwin Hyman, 1991.

Shaffer, Lynda N. *Maritime Southeast Asia to 1500*. Armonk, NY: M.E. Sharpe, 1996.

Tartling, Nicholas, ed. *The Cambridge History of Southeast Asia, Volume 1: from Ear-*

ly Times to c. 1800. New York: Cambridge University Press, 1992.

Tartling, Nicholas, ed. *The Cambridge History of Southeast Asia, Volume 2: the Nineteenth and Twentieth Centuries*. New York: Cambridge University Press, 1992.

Viviano, Frank. *Dispatches from the Pacific Century*. Reading, MA: Addison–Wesley, 1993.

World Bank Staff. The East Asia Miracle: Economic Growth and Public Policy. New York: Oxford University Press, 1993.

Yamamoto, Tadashi, ed. *Emerging Civil Society in the Asia Pacific Community; Nongovernmental Underpinnings of the Emerging Asia Regional Community*. Seattle, WA: University of Washington Press, 1995.

South China Morning Post Coundown to History —http://www.scmp.com/1997/ —(dedicated to Hong Kong handover)

The Japan Times —http://www.japantimes.co.jp/home.html

Korean Herald —http://www.koreaherald.co.kr/

China News Digest —http://www.cnd.org:8001/

China News Service —http://www.chinanews.com/

The Straits Times —http://straitstimes.asia1.com/

—Bangkok Post Internet Edition —http://www.bangkokpost.net/

Thailand Information Site—http://www.thaiindex.com/

The Philipino Express —http://www.filipinoexpress.com/

Laos Virtual Library Site —http://www.lao.net/laoVL.html

Malaysian Homepage —http://www.jaring.my/

Australia

Adelman, Howard et al., eds. *Immigration and Refugee Policy; Australia and Canada Compared*. Toronto: University of Toronto Press, 1994.

Andrews, E.M. *The Anzac Illusion: Anglo–Australian Relations during World War I*. New York: Cambridge University Press, 1993.

The Australian Reference Dictionary. New York: Oxford University Press, 1992.

Baker, Richard W., ed. *The ANZUS States and Their Region: Regional Policies of Australia, New Zealand, and the United States*. New York: Praeger, 1994.

Bassett, Jan. *The Oxford Illustrated Dictionary of Australian History*. New York: Oxford University Press, 1993.

Beilharz, Peter. *Transforming Labor: Labour Tradition and the Labor Decade in Australia*. New York: Cambridge University Press, 1994.

Bottomley, Gillian. *From Another Place: Migration and the Politics of Culture.* New York: Cambridge University Press, 1992.

Brawley, Sean. *The White Peril; Foreign Relations and Asian Immigration to Australasia and North America, 1919–1978.* Sydney: University of New South Wales Press, 1995.

Brett, Judith et al. eds. *Developments in Australian Politics.* South Melbourne: Macmillan Education Australia, 1994.

Broeze, Frank. *Mr. Brooks and the Australian Trade: Imperial Business in the Nineteenth Century.* Melbourne: Carlton University Press, 1993.

Butlin, N.G. *Forming a Colonial Economy, Australia 1810–1850.* New York: Cambridge University Press, 1994.

Campbell, Colin and John Halligan. *Political Leadership in an Age of Constraint: the Australian Experience.* Pittsburgh, PA: University of Pittsburgh Press, 1992.

Davidson, Alastair. *The Invisible State: the Formation of the Australian State, 1788–1901.* New York: Cambridge University Press, 1991.

Docherty, James C. *Historical Dictionary of Australia.* Lanham, MD: Scarecrow Press, 1992.

Edwards, Peter and Gregory Pemberton. *Crises and Commitments: the Politics and Diplomacy of Australia's Involvement in Southeast Asian Conflicts, 1948–1965.* North Sydney: Allen & Unwin/Australian War Memorial, 1992.

Emy, Hugh V. *Remaking Australia: the State, the Market and Australia's Future.* St. Leonards, NSW: Allen & Unwin, 1993.

Gray, Ian. *Politics in Place; Social Power Relations in an Australian Country Town.* New York: Cambridge University Press, 1991.

Hassam, Andrew. *Sailing to Australia: Shipboard Diaries by Nineteenth–Century British Emigrants.* New York: Manchester University Press, 1994.

Heathcote, R.L. *Australia.* London: Longman Scientific & Technical, 2nd ed. 1994.

Inglis, K.S. *Australian Colonists: an Exploration of Social History 1788–1870.* Carlton, Victoria: Melbourne University Press, 1993.

Jamrozik, Adam et al. *Social Change and Cultural Transformation in Australia.* New York: Cambridge University Press, 1995.

Kenny, John. *Before the First Fleet; Europeans in Australia, 1606–1777.* Kenthurst, NSW: Kangaroo Press, 1995.

Lane, P.H. *An Introduction to the Australian Constitution.* Holmes Beach, FL: Gaunt, Inc., 1990.

Lines, William J. *Taming the Great South Land: a History of the Conquest of Nature in Australia.* Berkeley, CA: University of California Press, 1991.

McIntyre, W. David. *Background into the ANZUS Pact: Strategy and Diplomacy, 1945–55.* New York: St. Martin's Press, 1995.

McMinn, W.G. *Nationalism and Federalism in Australia.* New York: Oxford University Press, 1994.

Murphy, Brian. *The Other Australia: Experiences of Migration.* New York: Cambridge University Press, 1993.

Pettman, Jan. *Living in the Margins: Racism, Sexism and Feminism in Australia.* North Sydney: Allen & Unwin, 1992.

Trainor, Luke. *British Imperialism and Australian Nationalism: Manipulation, Conflict and Compromise in the Late Nineteenth Century.* New York: Cambridge University Press, 1994.

Asia Pacific Magazine Page —http://coombs.anu.edu.au/asia-pacific-magazine

Australian Broadcasting Corportion — http://www.abc.net.au/

Koori News (Aboriginal News) —http://www.nrg.com.au/koorimail/

Brunei *Darussalam*

Ranjit Singh, D.S. *Historical Dictionary of Brunei Darussalam.* Lanham, MD: Scarecrow Press, 1997.

Burma (*Myanmar*)

Aung San Suu Kyi, ed. by Michael Aris, foreward by Vaclav Havel. *Freedom from Fear and Other Writings.* New York: Penguin, 1991.

Becka, Jan. *Historical Dictionary of Myanmar.* Lanham, MD: Scarecrow Press, 1995.

Herbert, Patricia M. *Burma.* Santa Barbara, CA: ABC–CLIO, 1991.

Lintner, Bertil. *Burma in Revolt; Opium and Insurgency since 1948.* Boulder, CO: Westview Press, 1994.

Maung, Mya. *The Burma Road to Poverty.* New York: Praeger, 1991.

Smith, Martin. *Burma: Insurgency and the Politics of Ethnicity.* Atlantic Highlands, NJ: Zed Books, 1991.

Cambodia

Chandler, David P. *A History of Cambodia.* Boulder, CO: Westview Press, 2nd ed. 1992.

Dith, Pran and Kim DePaul, eds. *Children of Cambodia's Killing Fields: Memoirs of Survivors.* New Haven, CT: Yale University Press, 1997.

Ebihara, May M. et al., eds. *Cambodian Culture since 1975: Homeland and Exile.* Ithaca, NY: Cornell University Press, 1994.

Haas, Michael. *Genocide by Proxy: Cambodian Pawn on a Superpower Chessboard.* New York: Praeger, 1991.

Kiernan, Ben, ed. *Genocide and Democracy in Cambodia: the Khmer Rouge, the United Nations and the International Community.* New Haven, CT: Yale University Southeast Asia Studies, 1993.

Kiernan, Ben. *The Pol Pot Regime: Race, Power, and Genocide in Cambodia under the Khmer Rouge, 1975–79.* New Haven, CT: Yale University Press, 1996.

Mabbett, Ian and David Chandler. *The Khmers.* Malden, MA: Blackwell Publishers, 1995.

Marin, Marie Alexandrine. *Cambodia: a Shattered Society.* Berkeley, CA: University of California Press, 1994.

Nguyen–vo, Thu–houng. *Khmer–Viet Relations and the Third Indochina Conflict.* Jefferson, NC: McFarland & Company, 1992.

Ross, Russell R., ed. *Cambodia, a Country Study.* Washington, DC: U.S. GPO, 3rd ed. 1990.

Welaratna, Usha. *Beyond the Killing Fields: Voices of the Cambodian Survivors in America.* Stanford, CA: Stanford University Press, 1993.

China

Brook, Timothy. *Quelling the People: the Military Suppression of the Beijing Democracy Movement.* New York: Oxford University Press, 1992.

Cheng, Chu–Yuan. *Behind the Tiananmen Massacre.* Boulder, CO: Westview Press, 1990.

Dernberger, Robert F. et al., eds. *The Chinese; Adapting the Past, Facing the Future.* Ann Arbor, MI: Center for Chinese Studies, University of Michigan, 2nd ed. 1991.

Dryer, Edward L. *China at War, 1901–1949.* White Plains, NY: Longman Publishing, 1995.

Fairbank, John King. *China: a New History.* Cambridge, MA: Harvard University Press, 1992.

Faust, John R. and Judith F. Kornberg. *China in World Politics.* Boulder, CO: Lynne Rienner, 1995.

Fewsmith, Joseph. *Dilemmas of Reform in China; Political Conflict and Economic Debate.* Armonk, NY: M.E. Sharpe, 1994.

Finkelstein, David Michael. *Washington's Taiwan Dilemma, 1949–1950; from Abandonment to Salvation.* Fairfax, VA: George Mason University Press, 1993.

Fitzgerald, John. *Awakening China: Politics, Culture, and Class in the Nationalist Revolution.* Stanford, CA: Stanford University Press, 1996.

Foot, Rosemary. *The Practice of Power: US Relations with China since 1949.* New York: Oxford University Press, 1995.

Giquel, Prosper. Edited and translated by Steven A. Leibo. *A Journal of the Chinese Civil War, 1864.* Honolulu, HI: University of Hawaii Press, 1985.

Goldstein, Alice and Wang Feng, eds. *China; the Many Facets of Demographic Change.* Boulder, CO: Westview Press, 1996.

Goodman, David S.G. and Gerald Segal, eds. *China in the Nineties: Crisis Manage-*

ment and Beyond. New York: Oxford University Press, 1991.

Grasso, June et al. *Modernization and Revolution in China.* Armonk, NY: M.E. Sharpe, 1991.

Hook, Brian and Dennis Twitchett. *The Cambridge Encyclopedia of China.* New York: Cambridge University Press, 2nd ed. 1991.

Hsu, Immanuel C. *China without Mao: the Search for a New Order.* New York: Oxford University Press, 1990.

Hsu, Immanuel C. *The Rise of Modern China.* New York: Oxford University Press, 1990.

Jiaqi, Yan and Gao Gao. Translated by D.W.K. Kwok. *Turbulent Decade: a History of the Cultural Revolution.* Honolulu, HI: University of Hawaii Press, 1996.

Joseph, William A. et al., eds. *New Perspectives on the Cultural Revolution.* Cambridge, MA: Harvard University Press, 1991.

Ju, Yanan. *Understanding China; Center Stage of the Fourth Power.* Albany, NY: State University of New York Press, 1996.

Kennedy, Thomas L. *The Arms of Kiangnan: Modernization in the Chinese Ordnance Industry, 1860–1895.* Boulder, CO: Westview Press, 1978.

Kluver, Alan R. *Legitimating the Chinese Economic Reforms; a Rhetoric of Myth and Orthodoxy.* Albany, NY: State University of New York Press, 1996.

Lampton, David M. et al., eds. *United States and China Relations at a Crossroads.* Lanham, MD: University Press of America, 1995.

Lardy, Nicholas R. *Foreign Trade and Economic Reform in China, 1978–1990.* New York: Cambridge University Press, 1992.

Leibo, Steven A. *Transferring Technology to China: Prosper Giquel and the Self–Strengthening Movement.* Berkeley, CA: University of California Press, Institute of East Asian Studies, 1985.

Leung, Edwin Pak–Wah, ed. *Historical Dictionary of Revolutionary China, 1839–1976.* Westport, CT: Greenwood Press, 1992.

Levine, Marilyn Avra. *The Found Generation: Chinese Communists in Europe during the Twenties.* Seattle, WA: University of Washington Press, 1993.

Lieberthal, Kenneth. *Governing China.* New York: W.W. Norton, 1995.

Lin, Bih–Jaw and James T. Myers. *Contemporary China and the Changing International Community.* Columbia, SC: University of South Carolina Press, 1994.

Mathias, Jim, ed. *Computers, Language Reform, and Lexicography in China: a Report.* Pullman, WA: Washington State University Press, 1980.

Meisner, Maurice. *The Deng Xiaoping Era: an Inquiry into the Fate of Chinese Socialism, 1978–1994.* New York: Hill & Wang, 1996.

Miles, James A. *The Legacy of Tiananmen: China in Disarray.* Ann Arbor, MI: University of Michigan, 1995.

Murowchick, Robert E., ed. *China: Ancient Culture, Modern Land.* Norman, OK: University of Oklahoma Press, 1994.

Nie Zeng Jifen. Translated and annotated by Thomas L. Kennedy; edited by Thomas L. Kennedy and Micki Kennedy. *Testimony of a Confucian Woman: the Autobiography of Mrs. Nie Zeng Jifen, 1852–1942.* Athens, GA: University of Georgia Press, 1993.

Ogden, Suzanne. *China's Unresolved Issues; Politics, Development, and Culture.* Englewood Cliffs, NJ: Prentice–Hall, 3rd ed. 1995.

Overholt, William H. *The Rise of China: How Economic Reform is Creating a New Superpower.* New York: W.W. Norton, 1993.

Rawski, Thomas G. and Lilliam M. Li, eds. *Chinese History in Economic Perspective.* Berkeley, CA: University of California Press, 1992.

Schell, Orville. *Mandate of Heaven: a New Generation of Entrepreneurs, Dissidents, Bohemians, and Technocrats Lays Claim to China's Future.* New York: Simon & Schuster, 1994.

Segal, Gerald and Richard H. Yang, eds. *Chinese Economic Reform; the Impact on Security.* New York: Routledge, 1996.

Selden, Mark. *The Political Economy of Chinese Development.* Armonk, NY: M.E. Sharpe, 2nd ed. 1992.

Shambaugh, David. *Beautiful Imperialist: China Perceives America, 1972–1990.* Princeton, NJ: Princeton University Press, 1991.

Shanor, Donald and Constance Shanor. *China Today.* New York: St. Martin's Press, 1995.

Shih, Chih–yu. *China's Just World: the Morality of Chinese Foreign Policy.* Boulder, CO: Lynne Rienner Publishers, 1993.

Sullivan, Lawrence R., ed. *China since Tiananmen; Political, Economic, and Social Conflicts.* Armonk, NY: M.E. Sharpe, 1995.

Sun, Yan. *The Chinese Reassessment of Socialism, 1976–1992.* Princeton, NJ: Princeton University Press, 1995.

Sutter, Robert G. *Shaping China's Future in World Affairs: the Role of the United States.* Boulder, CO: Westview Press, 1996.

Tan, Qingshan. *The Making of China Policy: from Normalization to the Post–Cold War Era.* Boulder, CO: Lynne Rienner, 1992.

Wang, Hui. *The Gradual Revolution: China's Economic Reform Movement.* New Brunswick, NJ: Transaction Publishers, 1994.

Wasserstrom, Jeffrey N. and Elizabeth J. Perry, eds. *Popular Protest and Political Culture in Modern China.* Boulder, CO: Westview Press, 1994.

Wei–ming, Tu, ed. *China in Transformation.* Cambridge, MA: Harvard University Press, 1994.

White, Gordon. *Riding the Tiger: the Politics of Economic Reform in Post–Mao China.* Stanford, CA: Stanford University Press, 1993.

Worden, Robert L. et al., eds. *China, a Country Study.* Washington, DC: U.S. GPO, 4th ed. 1988.

Young, Susan. *Private Business and Economic Reform in China.* Armonk, NY: M.E. Sharpe, 1995.

Zhai, Qiang. *The Dragon, the Lion, and the Eagle; Chinese–British–American Relations, 1949–1958.* Kent, OH: Kent State University Press, 1994.

Zhang, Shu Guang. *Deterrence and Strategic Culture: Chinese–American Confrontations, 1949–1958.* Ithaca, NY: Cornell University Press, 1992.

Hong Kong

Cameron, Nigel. *An Illustrated History of Hong Kong.* New York: Oxford University Press, 1991.

Chan, Ming K., ed. *Precarious Balance: Hong Kong between China and Britain.* Armonk, NY: M.E. Sharpe, 1994.

Roberti, Mark. *The Fall of Hong Kong: Britain's Betrayal and China's Triumph.* New York: John Wiley & Sons, 1994.

Roberts, Elfed Vaughan et al. *Historical Dictionary of Hong Kong and Macau.* Lanham, MD: Scarecrow Press, 1992.

Segal, Gerald. *The Fate of Hong Kong: the Coming of 1997 and What Lies Beyond.* New York: St. Martin's Press, 1993.

Shipp, Steve. *Hong Kong, China: a Political History of the British Crown Colony's Transfer to Chinese Rule.* Jefferson, NC: McFarland & Company, 1995.

Indonesia

Anwar, Dewi Fortuna. *Indonesia in ASEAN: Foreign Policy and Regionalism.* New York: St. Martin's Press, 1994.

Booth, Anne, ed. *The Oil Boom and After: Indonesian Economic Policy and Performance in the Suharto Era.* New York: Oxford University Press, 1992.

Bresnan, John. *Managing Indonesia: the Modern Political Economy.* New York: Columbia University Press, 1993.

Cribb, Robert. *Historical Dictionary of Indonesia.* Lanham, MD: Scarecrow Press, 1992.

Frederick, William H. and Robert L. Worden, eds. *Indonesia, a Country Study.* Washington, DC: U.S. GPO, 5th ed. 1993.

Hill, Hal, ed. *Indonesia's New Order: the Dynamics of Socio–Economic Transformation.* Honolulu, HI: University of Hawaii Press, 1994.

Kipp, Rita Smith. *Dissociated Identities: Ethnicity, Religion, and Class in an Indonesian Society.* Ann Arbor, MI: University of Michigan Press, 1993.

Krausse, Gerald H. and Sylvia C. Engelen Krausse. *Indonesia*. Santa Barbara, CA: ABC–CLIO, 1994.

Lubis, Mochtar. Indonesia: *Land under the Rainbow*. New York: Oxford University Press, 1990.

MacIntyre, Andrew. *Business and Politics in Indonesia*. North Sydney, NSW: Allen & Unwin, 1991.

Ramage, Douglas E. *Politics in Indonesia: Democracy, Islam, and the Ideology of Tolerance*. New York: Routledge, 1995.

Ricklefs, Merle Calvin. *A History of Modern Indonesia: c. 1300 to the Present*. Stanford, CA: Stanford University Press, 1993.

Roff, Sue Rabbitt. *Timor's Anschluss: Indonesian and Australian Policy in East Timor, 1974–1976*. Lewiston, NY: Edwin Mellen Press, 1992.

Schwartz, Adam. *A Nation in Waiting: Indonesia in the 1990s*. Boulder, CO: Westview Press, 1994.

Williams, Walter L. *Javanese Lives: Women and Men in Modern Indonesian Society*. New Brunswick, NJ: Rutgers University Press, 1991.

Japan

Abe, Etsuo and Robert Fitzgerald, eds. *The Origins of Japanese Industrial Power: Strategy, Institutions and the Development of Organisational Capability*. London: Frank Cass & Company, 1995.

Abe, Hitoshi et al. Translated by James W. White. *The Government and Politics of Japan*. Tokyo: University of Tokyo Press, 1994.

Alinson, Gary D. and Yasunori Sone, eds. *Political Dynamics in Contemporary Japan*. Ithaca, NY: Cornell University Press, 1993.

Banno, Junji. *The Establishment of the Japanese Constitutional System*. New York: Routledge, 1995.

Browring, Richard and Peter Kornicki, eds. *The Cambridge Encyclopedia of Japan*. New York: Cambridge University Press, 1993.

Buckley, Roger. *US–Japan Alliance Diplomacy, 1945–1990*. New York: Cambridge University Press, 1992.

Curtis, Gerald L., ed. *Japan's Foreign Policy after the Cold War: Coping with Change*. Armonk, NY: M.E. Sharpe, 1993.

Dolan, Ronald E. and Robert L. Worden. *Japan, a Country Study*. Washington, DC: U.S. GPO, 5th ed. 1992.

Flanagan, Scott C. et al. *The Japanese Voter*. New Haven, CT: Yale University Press, 1991.

Funabashi, Yoichi, ed. *Japan's International Agenda*. New York: New York University Press, 1994.

Garby, Craig and Mary Brown Bullock, eds. *Japan: a New Kind of Superpower?* Baltimore, MD: Johns Hopkins University Press, 1994.

Giffard, Sydney. *Japan among the Powers, 1880–1990*. New Haven, CT: Yale University Press, 1994.

Gordon, Andrew, ed. *Postwar Japan as History*. Berkeley, CA: University of California Press, 1993.

Green, Michael J. *Arming Japan: Defense Production, Alliance Politics, and the Postwar Search for Autonomy*. New York: Columbia University Press, 1995.

Hane, Mikiso. *Modern Japan: a Historical Survey*. Boulder, CO: Westview Press, 2nd ed. 1992.

Hayao, Kenji. *The Japanese Prime Minister and Public Policy*. Pittsburgh, PA: University of Pittsburgh Press, 1993.

Herbig, Paul A. *Innovation Japanese Style: a Cultural and Historical Perspective*. Westport, CT: Quorum Books, 1995.

Herzog, Peter J. *Japan's Pseudo–Democracy*. New York: New York University Press, 1993.

Hsu, Robert C. *The MIT Encyclopedia of the Japanese Economy*. Cambridge, MA: MIT Press, 1994.

Huber, Thomas M. *Strategic Economy in Japan*. Boulder, CO: Westview Press, 1994.

Inoguchi, Takashi. *Japan's Foreign Policy in an Era of Global Change*. New York: St. Martin's Press, 1993.

Irokawa, Daikichi. Translated by John K. Urda. *The Age of Hirohito: in Search of Modern Japan*. New York: Free Press, 1995.

Ito, Takatoshi. *The Japanese Economy*. Cambridge, MA: MIT Press, 1992.

Japan: an Illustrated Encyclopedia. 2 vols. New York: Kodansha America, 1994.

Johnson, Chalmers. *Japan: Who Governs?* New York: W.W. Norton, 1995.

Johnson–Freese, Joan. *Over the Pacific: Japanese Space Policy into the Twenty–First Century*. Dubuque, IA: Kendall/Hunt Publishing, 1993.

Kataoka, Tetsuya, ed. *Creating Single–Party Democracy: Japan's Postwar Political System*. Stanford, CA: Hoover Institution Press, 1992.

Kataoka, Tetsuya. *The Price of a Constitution: the Origin of Japan's Postwar Politics*. New York: Crane Russak & Company, 1991.

Kishima, Takako. *Political Life in Japan: Democracy in a Reversible World*. Princeton, NJ: Princeton University Press, 1991.

Koppel, Bruce M., ed. *Japan's Foreign Aid: Power and Policy in a New Era*. Boulder, CO: Westview Press, 1993.

Krugman, Paul R., ed. *Trade with Japan: Has the Door Opened Wider?* Chicago: University of Chicago Press, 1991.

Lincoln, Edward J. *Japan's New Global Role*. Washington, DC: Brookings Institution Press, 1993.

Luney, Percy R., Jr. and Kazuyuki Takahashi, eds. *Japanese Constitutional Law*. Tokyo: University of Tokyo Press, 1993.

Maher, John C. and Gaynor Macdonald, eds. *Diversity in Japanese Culture and Language*. New York: Kegan Paul International, 1995.

McNeil, Frank. *Democracy in Japan: the Emerging Global Concern*. New York: Crown Publishing, 1994.

Miyoshi, Masao. *Off Center: Power and Culture Relations between Japan and the United States*. Cambridge, MA: Harvard University Press, 1991.

Murphy, R. Taggart. *The Weight of the Yen*. New York: W.W. Norton, 1996.

Nester, William R. *American Power, the New World Order and the Japanese Challenge*. New York: St. Martin's Press, 1993.

Oppenheim, Phillip. *Japan without Blinders: Coming to Terms with Japan's Economic Success*. New York: Kodansha America, 1992.

Ozaki, Robert S. *Human Capitalism: the Japanese Enterprise System as World Model*. New York: Kodansha America, 1991.

Ozawa, Ichiro. *Blueprint for a New Japan: the Rethinking of a Nation*. New York: Kodansha America, 1994.

Ramseyer, J. Mark and Frances McCall Rosenbluth. *Japan's Political Marketplace*. Cambridge, MA: Harvard University Press, 1993.

Reischauer, Edwin O. and Marius Jansen. *The Japanese Today*. Cambridge, MA: Harvard University Press, rev. ed. 1995.

Sato, Ryuzo. *The Chrysanthemum and the Eagle: the Future of U.S.–Japan Relations*. New York: New York University Press, 1994.

Smith, Dennis B. *Japan since 1945: the Rise of an Economic Superpower*. New York: St. Martin's Press, 1995.

Smith, Patrick. *Japan: a Reinterpretation*. New York: Pantheon, 1997.

Tachi, Ryuichiro. *The Contemporary Japanese Economy: an Overview*. Tokyo: University of Tokyo Press, 1993.

Unger, Daniel and Paul Blackburn, eds. *Japan's Emerging Global Role*. Boulder, CO: Lynne Rienner, 1993.

Uriu, Robert M. *Troubled Industries: Confronting Economic Change in Japan*. Ithaca, NY: Cornell University Press, 1996.

Van Wolferen, Karel. *The Enigma of Japanese Power*. New York: Vintage Books, 1990.

Vestal, James E. *Planning for Change: Industrial Policy and Japanese Economic Development, 1945–1990*. New York: Oxford University Press, 1993.

Woronoff, Jon. *The Japanese Economic Crisis*. New York: St. Martin's Press, 1993.

Yasutomo, Dennis T. *The New Multilateralism in Japan's Foreign Policy*. New York: St. Martin's Press, 1995.

Korea

Bandow, Doug, ed. *The U.S.–South Korea Alliance: Time for a Change*. New Brunswick, NJ: Transaction Publishers, 1992.

Bedeski, Robert E. *The Transformation of South Korea: Reform and Reconstruction in the Sixth Republic under Roh Tae Woo, 1987–1992.* New York: Routledge, 1994.

Cho, Sun. *The Dynamics of Korean Economic Development.* Washington, DC: Institute for International Economics, 1994.

Cumings, Bruce. *Korea's Place in the Sun: a Modern History.* New York: W.W. Norton, 1997.

Das, Dilip K. *Korean Economic Dynamism.* New York: St. Martin's Press, 1992.

Eberstadt, Nicholas. *Korea Approaches Reunification.* Armonk, NY: M.E. Sharpe, 1995.

Hwang, Eui–Gak. *The Korean Economies: a Comparison of North and South.* New York: Oxford University Press, 1993.

Kihl, Young Whan. *Korea and the World: beyond the Cold War.* Boulder, CO: Westview Press, 1994.

Kim, Byonung–Lo Philo. *Two Koreas in Development: a Comparative Study of Principles and Strategies of Capitalist and Communist Third World Development.* New Brunswick, NJ: Transaction Publishers, 1992.

Kim, Dae Jung. *Mass Participatory Economy: Korea's Road to World Economic Power.* Lanham, MD: University Press of America, 1996.

Kim, Gye–Dong. *Foreign Intervention in Korea.* Brookfield, VT: Dartmouth Publishing Company, 1993.

Kim, Hakjoon. *Korea's Relations with Her Neighbors in a Changing World.* Elizabeth, NJ: Hollym International, 1993.

Koo, Hagen, ed. *State and Society in Contemporary Korea.* Ithaca, NY: Cornell University Press, 1993.

Kuznets, Paul W. *Korean Economic Development: an Interpretive Model.* New York: Praeger, 1994.

Kwack, Sung Yeung, ed. *The Korean Economy at a Crossroad: the Development Prospects, Liberalization, and South–North Economic Integration.* New York: Praeger, 1994.

Lee, Chae–Jin. *China and Korea: Dynamic Relations.* Stanford, CA: Hoover Institution Press, 1996.

Lee, Hyung–Koo. *The Korean Economy: Perspectives for the Twenty–First Century.* Albany, NY: State University of New York Press, 1996.

Lee, Peter H., ed. *Sourcebook of Korean Civilization, vol. 1: from Early Times to the Sixteenth Century.* New York; Columbia University Press, 1993.

Lee, Peter H., ed. *Sourcebook of Korean Civilization, vol. 2: from the Seventeenth Century to the Modern Period.* New York: Columbia University Press, 1996.

Macdonald, Donald Stone. *The Koreans; Contemporary Politics and Society.* Boulder, CO: Westview Press, 3rd ed. 1996.

McNamara, Dennis L. *Trade and Transformation in Korea, 1876–1945.* Boulder, CO: Westview Press, 1996.

Mazarr, Michael J. *North Korea and the*

Bomb: a Case Study in Nonproliferation. New York: St. Martin's Press, 1995.

Nahm, Andrew C. *Historical Dictionary of the Republic of Korea.* Lanham, MD: Scarecrow Press, 1993.

Oliver, Robert T. *A History of the Korean People in Modern Times: 1800 to the Present.* Cranbury, NJ: University of Delaware Press, 1993.

Pae, Sung Moon. *Korea Leading Developing Nations: Economy, Democracy, and Welfare.* Lanham, MD: University Press of America, 1992.

SaKong, Il. *Korea in the World Economy.* Washington, D.C.: Institute for International Economics, 1993.

Savada, Andrea Matles, ed. *North Korea, a Country Study.* Washington, DC: U.S. GPO, 4th ed. 1994.

Savada, Andrea Matles and William R. Shaw, eds. *South Korea, a Country Study.* Washington, DC: U.S. GPO, 4th ed. 1992.

Simons, Geoff. *Korea: the Search for Sovereignty.* New York: St. Martin's Press, 1995.

Laos

Castle, Timothy N. *At War in the Shadow of Vietnam: U.S. Military Aid to the Royal Lao Government, 1955–1975.* New York: Columbia University Press, 1993.

Cordell, Helen. *Laos.* Santa Barbara, CA: ABC–CLIO, 1991.

Savada, Andrea Matles. *Laos, a Country Study.* Washington, DC: U.S. GPO, 3rd ed. 1995.

Stuart–Fox, Martin. *Historical Dictionary of Laos.* Lanham, MD: Scarecrow Press, 1992.

Macau

Cremer, R.D., ed. *Industrial Economy of Macau in the 1990s.* Hong Kong: UEA Press, 1990.

Porter, Jonathan. *Macau, the Imaginary City: Culture and Society, 1557 to the Present.* Boulder, CO: Westview Press, 1996.

Roberts, Elfed Vaughn et al. *Historical Dictionary of Hong Kong and Macau.* Lanham, MD: Scarecrow Press, 1992.

Malaysia

Bowie, Alisdair. *Crossing the Industrial Divide: State, Society, and the Politics of Economic Transformation in Malaysia.* New York: Columbia University Press, 1991.

Bruton, Henry J. *Sri Lanka and Malaysia.* New York: Oxford University Press, 1992.

Gullick, John M. *Rulers and Residents: Influence and Power in the Malay States, 1870–1920.* New York: Oxford University Press, 1992.

Jomo, K.S. *Industrialising Malaysia: Policy,*

Performance, Prospects. New York: Routledge, 1993.

Kaur, Amarjit. *Historical Dictionary of Malaysia.* Lanham, MD: Scarecrow Press, 1993.

Means, Gordon P. *Malaysian Politics: the Second Generation.* New York: Oxford University Press, 1991.

Munro–Kua, Anne. *Authoritarian Populism in Malaysia.* New York: St. Martin's Press, 1997.

Mongolia

Akiner, Shirin, ed. *Mongolia Today.* New York: Kegan Paul International, 1991.

Nordby, Judith. *Mongolia.* Santa Barbara, CA: ABC–CLIO, 1993.

Sanders, Alan J.K. *Historical Dictionary of Mongolia.* Lanham, MD: Scarecrow Press, 1996.

Worden, Robert L. and Andrea Matles Savada, eds. *Mongolia, a Country Study.* Washington, DC: U.S. GPO, 2nd ed. 1991.

New Zealand

Baker, Richard W., ed. *The ANZUS States and Their Region: Regional Policies of Australia, New Zealand, and the United States.* New York: Praeger, 1994.

Barretta–Herman, Angela. *Welfare State to Welfare Society: Restructuring New Zealand Social Services.* New York: Garland Publishing, 1994.

Harris, Paul et al., eds. *New Zealand Politics Source Book.* Palmerston North, NZ: Dunsmore Press, 1992.

Jackson, William K. and Alan McRobie. *Historical Dictionary of New Zealand.* Lanham, MD: Scarecrow Press, 1996.

McClymont, W.G. *The Exploration of New Zealand.* Westport, CT: Greenwood Press, 1986.

McKinnon, Malcolm. *Independence and Foreign Policy: New Zealand in the World since 1935.* Auckland: Auckland University Press, 1993.

McLaughlin, Gordon, ed. *New Zealand Encyclopedia.* New York: Macmillan Publishing, 1988.

McLeay, Elizabeth. *The Cabinet and Political Power in New Zealand.* New York: Oxford University Press, 1995.

Rice, Geoffrey W., ed. *The Oxford History of New Zealand.* New York: Oxford University Press, 2nd ed. 1992.

Sharp, Andrew, ed. *Leap into the Dark: the Changing Role of the State in New Zealand since 1984.* Auckland: Auckland University Press, 1994.

Sinclair, Keith, ed. *The Oxford Illustrated History of New Zealand.* New York: Oxford University Press, 1990.

New Zealand News —http://www.press.co.nz/

Mauri Organizations Web Page —http://www.maori.org.nz/index.html

Papua New Guinea

Rannells, Jackson. *PNG: a Fact Book on Modern Papua New Guinea*. New York: Oxford University Press, 2nd ed. 1995.

Turner, Ann. *Historical Dictionary of Papua New Guinea*. Lanham, MD: Scarecrow Press, 1994.

The Philippines

Brands, H.W. *Bound to Empire: the United States and the Philippines*. New York: Oxford University Press, 1992.

Broad, Robin. *Plundering Paradise: the Struggle for the Environment in the Philippines*. Berkeley, CA: University of California Press, 1993.

Cullather, Nick. *Illusions of Influence: the Political Economy of United States–Philippines Relations, 1942–1960*. Stanford, CA: Stanford University Press, 1994.

Dolan, Ronald E., ed. *Philippines, a Country Study*. Washington, DC: U.S. GPO, 4th ed. 1993.

Doronilla, Amando. *The State, Economic Transformation, and Political Change in the Philippines, 1946–1972*. New York: Oxford University Press, 1992.

Guillermo, Artemio R. *Historical Dictionary of the Philippines*. Lanham, MD: Scarecrow Press, 1997.

Kerkvliet, Benedict J. *Everyday Politics in the Philippines*. Berkeley, CA: University of California Press, 1990.

Reid, Robert H. and Eileen Guerrero. *Corazon Aquino and the Brushfire Revolution*. Baton Rouge, LA: Louisiana State University Press, 1995.

Steinberg, David Joel. *The Philippines: a Singular and a Plural Place*. Boulder, CO: Westview Press, 2nd ed. 1990.

Thompson, W. Scott. *The Philippines in Crisis: Development and Security in the Aquino Era, 1986–1992*. New York: St. Martin's Press, 1992.

Timberman, David G. *A Changeless Land: Continuity and Change in Philippine Politics*. Armonk, NY: M.E. Sharpe, 1991.

Singapore

Hill, Michael and Lian Kwen Fee. *The Politics of Nation Building and Citizenship in Singapore*. New York: Routledge, 1995.

Huff, W.G. *The Economic Growth of Singapore: Trade and Development in the Twentieth Century*. New York: Cambridge University Press, 1994.

LePoer, Barbara Leitch, ed. *Singapore, a Country Study*. Washington, DC: U.S. GPO, 2nd ed. 1991.

Mulliner, K. and Lian The–Mulliner. *Historical Dictionary of Singapore*. Lanham, MD: Scarecrow Press, 1991.

Regnier, Philippe. Translated by Christopher Hurst. *Singapore: City–State in South–East Asia*. Honolulu, HI: University of Hawaii Press, 1991.

Rodan, Garry, ed. *Singapore Changes Guard: Social, Political and Economic Directions in the 1990s*. New York: St. Martin's Press, 1993.

Von Alten, Florian. *The Role of Government in the Singapore Economy*. New York: Peter Lang Publishing, 1995.

Taiwan

Copper, John F. *Historical Dictionary of Taiwan*. Lanham, MD: Scarecrow Press, 1993.

Copper, John F. *Words across the Taiwan Strait: a Critique of Beijing's "White Paper" on China's Reunification*. Lanham, MD: University Press of America, 1995.

Finkelstein, David Michael. *Washington's Dilemma, 1949–1950: from Abandonment to Salvation*. Fairfax, VA: George Mason University Press, 1993.

Hickey, Dennis Van Vranken. *United States–Taiwan Security Ties: from Cold War to Beyond Containment*. New York: Praeger, 1994.

Hood, Steven J. *The Kuomintang and the Democratization of Taiwan*. Boulder, CO: Westview Press, 1997.

Hwang, Y. Dolly. *The Rise of a New World Economic Power: Postwar Taiwan*. Westport, CT: Greenwood Press, 1991.

Lasater, Martin L. *U.S. Interests in the New Taiwan*. Boulder, CO: Westview Press, 1993.

Lee, Lai To. *The Reunification of China: PRC–Taiwan Relations in Flux*. New York: Praeger, 1991.

Moody, Peter R., Jr. *Political Change on Taiwan: a Study of Ruling Party Adaptability*. New York: Praeger, 1992.

Schive, Chi. *Taiwan's Economic Role in East Asia*. Washington, DC: Center for Strategic and International Studies, 1995.

Skoggard, Ian A. *The Indigenous Dynamic in Taiwan's Postwar Development: the Religious and Historical Roots of Entrepreneurship*. Armonk, NY: M.E. Sharpe, 1996.

Sutter, Robert G. and William R. Johnson, eds. *Taiwan in World Affairs*. Boulder, CO: Westview Press, 1994.

Tsang, Steve, ed. *In the Shadow of China: Political Developments in Taiwan since 1949*. Honolulu, HI: University of Hawaii Press, 1993.

Wachman, Alan M. *Taiwan: National Identity and Democratization*. Armonk, NY: M.E. Sharpe, 1994.

Wang, N.T., ed. *Taiwan's Enterprises in Global Perspective*. Armonk, NY: M.E. Sharpe, 1992.

Wu, Hsin–Hsing. *Bridging the Strait: Taiwan, China, and the Prospects for Reunification*. New York: Oxford University Press, 1994.

Wu, Jaushieh Joseph. *Taiwan's Democratization: Forces behind the New Momentum*. New York: Oxford University Press, 1995.

Zhao, Suisheng. *Power by Design: Constitution–Making in Nationalist China*. Honolulu, HI: University of Hawaii Press, 1996.

Thailand

Campbell, Burnham O. et al., eds. *The Economic Impact of Demographic Change in Thailand, 1980–2015*. Honolulu, HI: University of Hawaii Press, 1993.

Krongkaew, Medhi, ed. *Thailand's Industrialization and Its Consequences*. New York: St. Martin's Press, 1995.

LePoer, Barbara Leitch, ed. *Thailand, a Country Study*. Washington, DC: U.S. GPO, 6th ed. 1989.

Muscat, Robert J. *The Fifth Tiger: a Study of Thai Development Policy*. Armonk, NY: M.E. Sharpe, 1994.

Stowe, Judith A. *Siam Becomes Thailand: a Story of Intrigue*. Honolulu, HI: University of Hawaii Press, 1991.

Warr, Peter G., ed. *The Thai Economy in Transition*. New York: Cambridge University Press, 1993.

Vietnam

Chapuis, Oscar M. *A History of Vietnam: from Hong Bang to Tu Duc*. Westport, CT: Greenwood Press, 1995.

Cima, Ronald J., ed. *Vietnam, a Country Study*. Washington, DC: U.S. GPO, 1989.

Clodfelter, Michael. *Vietnam in Military Statistics: a History of the Indochina Wars, 1772–1991*. Jefferson, NC: McFarland & Company, 1995.

Davidson, Phillip B. *Vietnam at War: the History, 1946–1975*. New York: Oxford University Press, 1991.

Hunt, Michael H. *Lyndon Johnson's War: America's Cold War Crusade in Vietnam, 1945–1968*. New York: Hill & Wang, 1996.

Jamieson, Neil L. *Understanding Vietnam*. Berkeley, CA: University of California Press, 1993.

Kamm, Henry. *Dragon Ascending: Vietnam and the Vietnamese*. New York: Arcade Publishing, 1996.

Kerkvliet, Benedict J. Tria and Doug J. Porter, eds. *Vietnam's Rural Transformation*. Boulder, CO: Westview Press, 1995.

Lomperis, Timothy J. *From People's War to People's Rule: Insurgency, Intervention, and the Lessons of Vietnam*. Chapel Hill, NC: University of North Carolina Press, 1996.

Moses, George D. *Vietnam, an American Ordeal*. Englewood Cliffs, NJ: Prentice–Hall, 1994.

The Pentagon Papers. New York: Bantam Books, 1971.

SarDesai, D.R. *Vietnam: the Struggle for National Identity*. Boulder, CO: Westview Press, 2nd ed. 1992.

Stern, Lewis M. *Imprisoned or Missing in Vietnam: Policies of the Vietnamese Government Concerning Captured and Unac-*

counted for United States Soldiers, 1969–1994. Jefferson, NC: McFarland & Company, 1995.

Tonnesson, Stein. *The Vietnamese Revolution of 1945: Roosevelt, Ho Chi Minh and de Gaulle in a World at War*. Newbury Park, CA: Sage Publications, 1991.

Vandemark, Brian. *Into the Quagmire: Lyndon Johnson and the Escalation of the Vietnam War*. New York: Oxford University Press, 1991.

Pacific Islands

Craig, Robert D., ed. *Historical Dictionary of Oceania*. Westport, CT: Greenwood Press, 1981.

Gorman, G.E. and J.J. Mills. *Fiji*. Santa Barbara, CA: ABC–CLIO, 1994.

Lal, Brij V. *Broken Waves: a History of the Fiji Islands in the Twentieth Century*. Honolulu, HI: University of Hawaii Press, 1992.

Leibowitz, Arnold H. *Embattled Island: Palau's Struggle for Independence*. New York: Praeger, 1996.

Levy, Neil M. *Micronesia Handbook*. Chico, CA: Moon Publications, 4th ed. 1997.

Sahlins, Marshall D. *Islands of History*. Chicago: University of Chicago Press, 1987.

Stanley, David. *South Pacific Handbook*. Chico, CA: Moon Publications, 6th ed. 1996.

Wuerch, William L. and Dirk Anthony Ballendorf. *Historical Dictionary of Guam and Micronesia*. Lanham, MD: Scarecrow Press, 1994.

Guide to the Marshal Islands —http://www.clark.net/pub/rmiemb/

Papua New Guinea Information —http://coombs.anu.edu.au/SpecialProj/PNG/WWWVL-PNG.html

Guide to American Samoa —http://www.ipacific.com/samoa/samoa.html

Author's Home Page —http://www.sage.edu/html/RSC/programs/globcomm/world/esawp.html

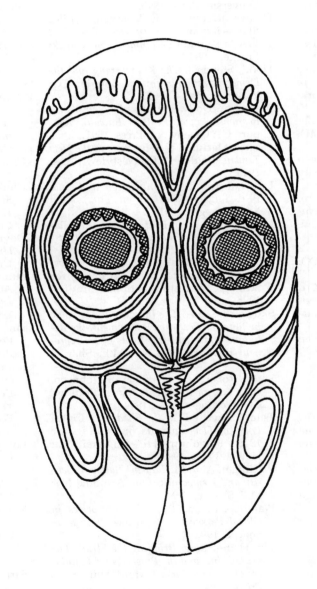